Parametric Solid Modeling Projects

Sham Tickoo
Professor
Purdue University Northwest
Hammond, Indiana, USA

Contributing Authors
Tickoo Institute of Emerging Technologies (TIET)
Gurgaon, India

CADCIM Technologies
Indiana, USA

BPB PUBLICATIONS

ISBN: 978-93-88176-48-4

(For distribution in SAARC countries only)

Distributors

COMPUTER BOOK CENTRE
12, Shrungar Shopping Centre
M.G. Road
BENGALURU–560001
Ph: 25587923/25584641

BPB BOOK CENTRE
376 Old Lajpat Rai Market
DELHI-110006
Ph: 23861747

DECCAN AGENCIES
4-3-329, Bank Street
HYDERABAD-500195
Ph: 24756967/24756400

INFOTECH
G-2, Sidhartha Building, 96 Nehru Place
NEW DELHI-110019
Ph: 26438245

MICRO MEDIA
Shop No. 5, Mahendra Chambers
150 DN Rd. Next to Capital Cinema
V.T (C.S.T.) Station
MUMBAI-400001

BPB PUBLICATIONS
20, Ansari Road, Darya Ganj
New Delhi-110002
Ph: 23254990/23254991

Published by Manish Jain for BPB Publications, 20 Ansari Road, Darya Ganj
New Delhi-110002 and Printed Repro India Pvt. Ltd, Mumbai

DEDICATION

To teachers, who make it possible to disseminate knowledge to enlighten the young and curious minds of our future generations

To students, who are dedicated to learning new technologies and making the world a better place to live in

THANKS

To the faculty and students of the MET department of Purdue University Northwest for their cooperation

To employees of CADCIM Technologies for their valuable help

Note

If you are a faculty member, you can register by clicking on the following link to access the teaching resources: ***http://www.cadcim.com/Registration.aspx***. The student resources are available at ***http://www.cadcim.com***. We also provide **Live Virtual Online Training** on various software packages. For more information, write us at ***sales@cadcim.com***.

Table of Contents

Dedication iii

Preface vii

Project 1
Wheel Assembly 1-1

Project 2
Metal Shear Assembly 2-1

Project 3
Angle Clamp Assembly 3-1

Project 4
Hand Punch Press Assembly........ 4-1

Project 5
Ball Valve Assembly 5-1

Project 6
Pneumatic Gripper Assembly........ 6-1

Project 7
Car Jack Assembly........ 7-1

Project 8
Wrench Assembly 8-1

Project 9
Hand Drill Assembly........ 9-1

Project 10
Sheet Bending Machine Assembly 10-1

Project 11
Reduction Gear Box Assembly 11-1

Project 12
Single Stage Centrifugal Pump Assembly........ 12-1

Project 13
Single Plate Clutch Assembly 13-1

Project 14
Vertical Twin Steam Engine Assembly 14-1

This page is intentionally left blank

Preface

The **Parameter Solid Modeling Projects** is a parametric modeling book written to help users learn and design real-world models. Structured in pedagogical sequence, the book contains real-world engineering projects that begin with simple part assemblies and gradually progress toward complex industrial models.

After completing this book, the students will be able to design real-world/industrial projects with ease. Additionally, they will be able to design all components, develop assemblies, and generate the 2D drawings of the parts and assemblies along with Bill of material.

The main features of the book are as follows:

- **Project Based Approach**
  The author has adopted a project-based approach to explain various real-world Mechanical Engineering Drawings. Moreover, each project contains drawings of its parts created as per the industrial standards. This enables the users to understand the concepts of drafting and modeling of the industrial components.

- **Real-world Mechanical Engineering Projects**
  The author has used 14 different project assemblies as real-world projects. The projects have been divided into more than 250 parts, 14 assemblies and 200 drawings to help the users understand the concepts of real-world engineering projects. After reading this book, users will be able to create different projects using drafting standards with ease.

- **Technical Support**
  You can get online technical support by contacting techsupport@cadcim.com.

The following points need to be taken care of while creating different projects:

a) ANSI standard should be followed as the drafting standard.
b) Standard parts like Nuts, Bolts, Gears, Bearing etc can also be taken from the toolbox available in any CAD software.

Accessing Electronic Files
If you want to order the electronic files of the projects contained in this book, please contact us at sales@cadcim.com

- **Online Tutoring Service for the Projects**

The team at CADCIM Technologies utilizes the latest enhancements in technology and Internet to offer online tutoring services, thus turning the concept of virtual teaching into reality. We provide effective and affordable online step by step tutoring on various projects in the **Parametric Solid Modeling Projects** book. The time and cost for tutoring services will depend upon the size of the project.

Hardware/Software Requirements for Online Tutoring Services
- Dual core processor, 4 GB RAM, 250GB hard drive
- High speed internet connection
- Mike and speakers
- The software package on which you want the online tutoring must be installed on your computer
- Remote computer access software such as NetMeeting

This page is intentionally left blank

Project 1

Wheel Assembly

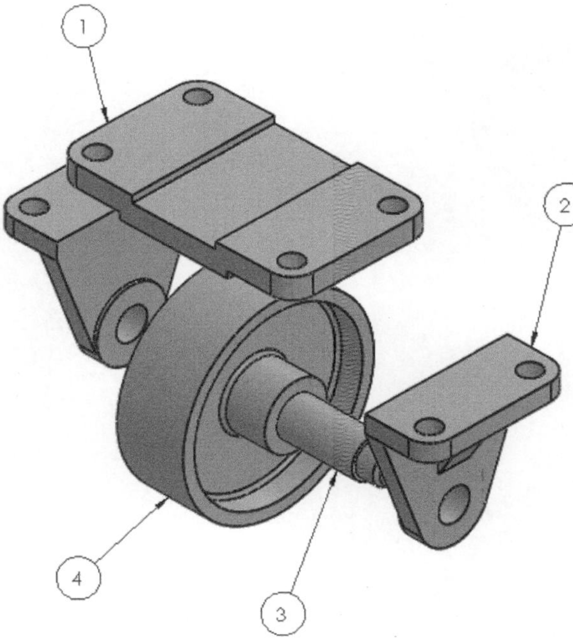

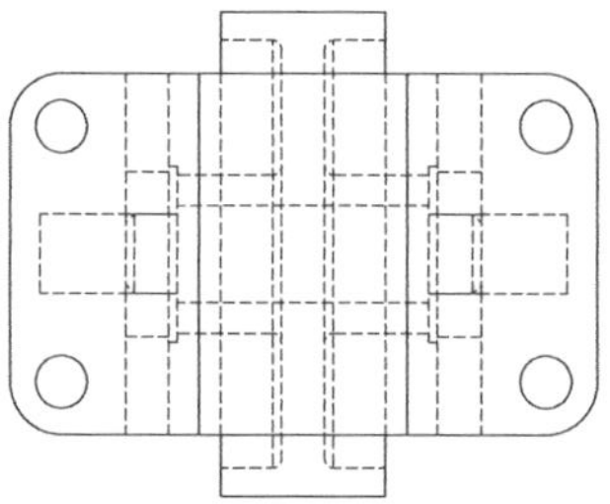

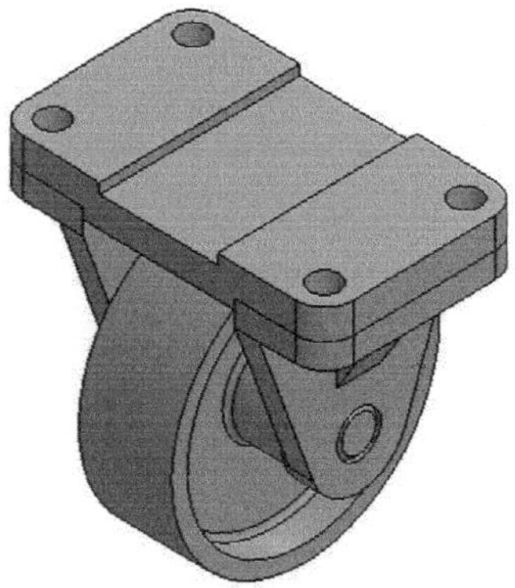

ITEM NO.	PART NUMBER	QTY.
1	Top Plate	1
2	Axle Support	2
3	Axle	1
4	Wheel	1

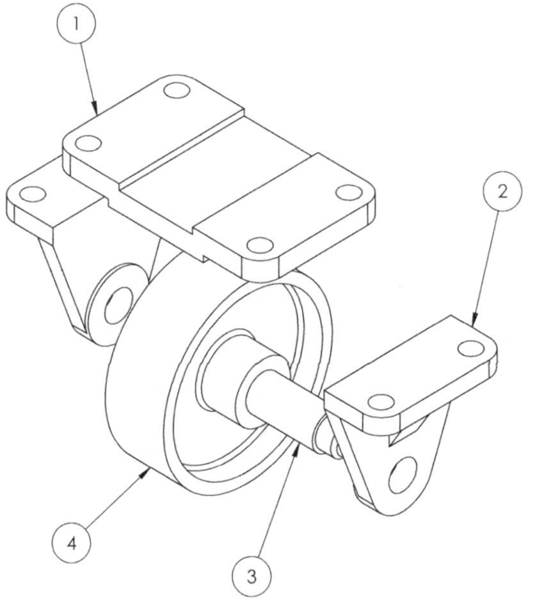

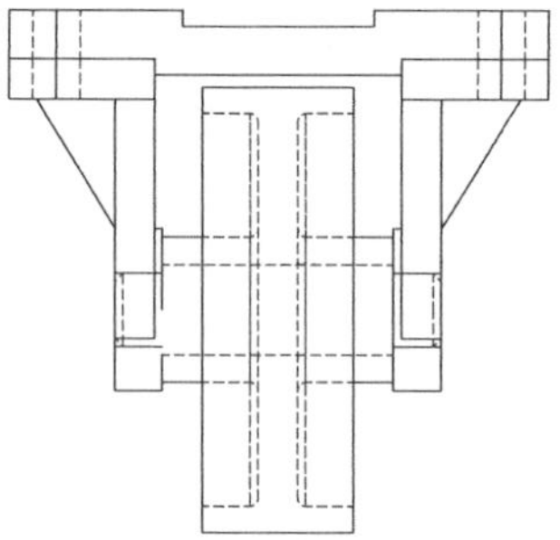

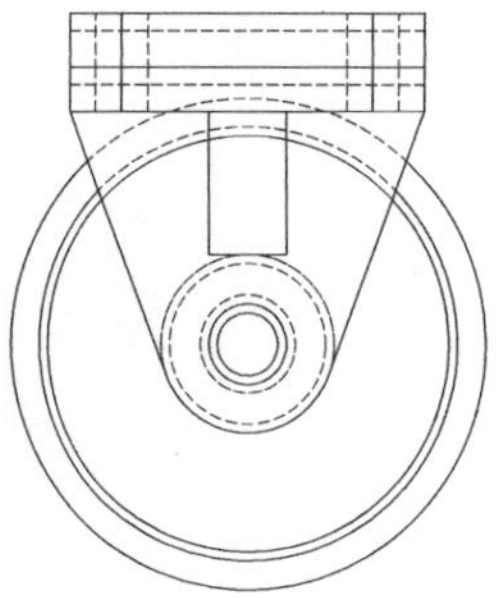

TOLERANCES UNLESS OTHERWISE SPECIFIED

X---------------- +/- 0.5
X.X-------------- +/- 0.2
X.XX------------- +/- 0.1
ANGLE----------- +/- 0.5°

ALL DIMENSIONS IN MM

FIRST ISSUED	
DRAWN BY	
CHECKED BY	
APPROVED BY	

CADCIM TECHNOLOGIES

Axle Support

SIZE	DRG NO.	SHEET REV
A3	1-000	A
SCALE 1:2		SHEET 1 OF 5

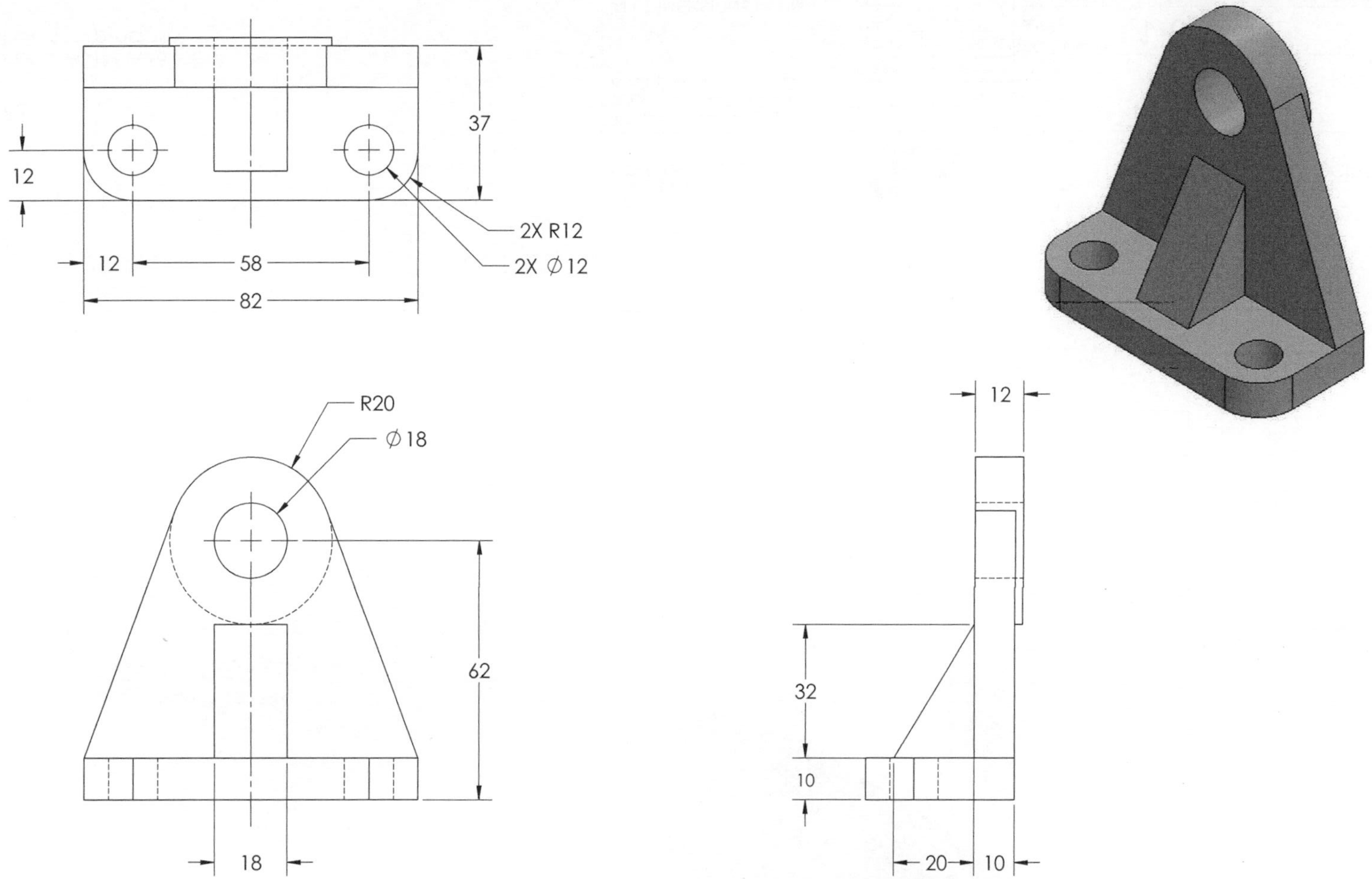

NOTES

1- Material ASTM A36 Steel
2- Deburr sharp edges

TOLERANCES UNLESS OTHERWISE SPECIFIED

X ---------- +/- 0.5
X.X ---------- +/- 0.2
X.XX ---------- +/- 0.1
ANGLE ---------- +/- 0.5°

ALL DIMENSIONS IN MM

FIRST ISSUED
DRAWN BY
CHECKED BY
APPROVED BY

CADCIM TECHNOLOGIES

Axle Support

SIZE: A3 | DRG NO.: 1-001 | SHEET REV: A

SCALE 1:1 | SHEET 2 OF 5

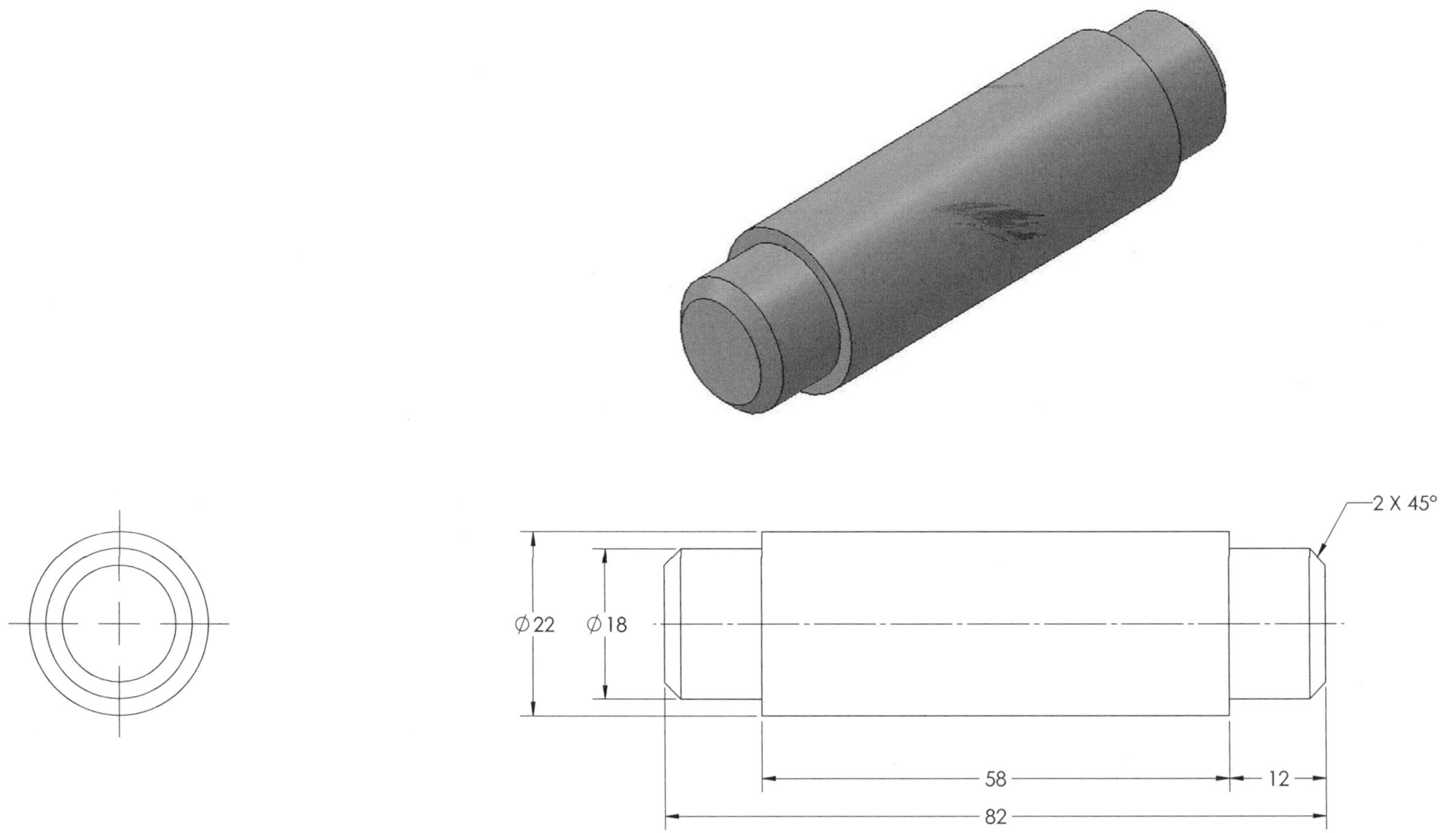

NOTES

1- Material ASTM A36 Steel
2- Deburr sharp edges

TOLERANCES UNLESS OTHERWISE SPECIFIED			CADCIM TECHNOLOGIES		
X---------- +/- 0.5	FIRST ISSUED		Axle		
X.X---------- +/- 0.2	DRAWN BY				
X.XX---------- +/- 0.1	CHECKED BY				
ANGLE---------- +/- 0.5°	APPROVED BY		SIZE A3	DRG NO. 1-002	SHEET REV A
ALL DIMENSIONS IN MM			SCALE 2:1		SHEET 3 OF 5

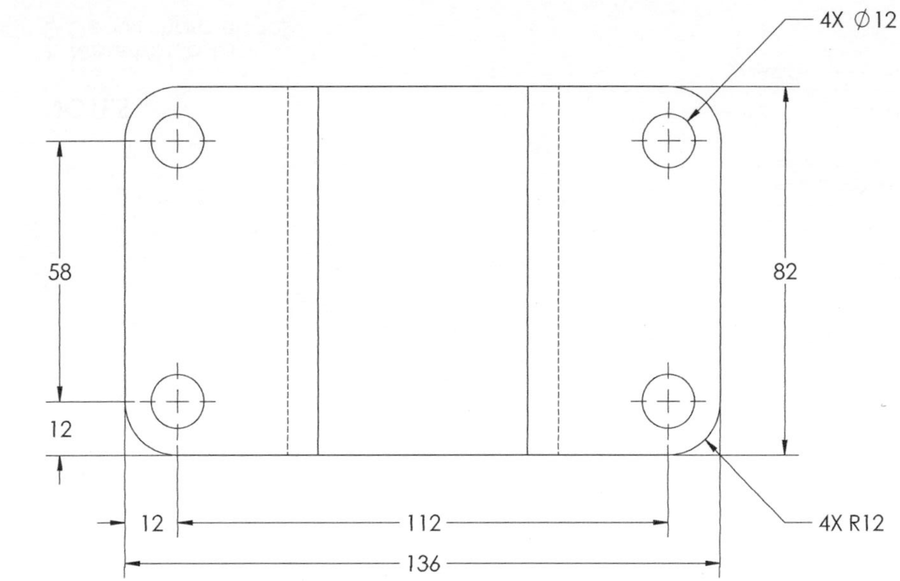

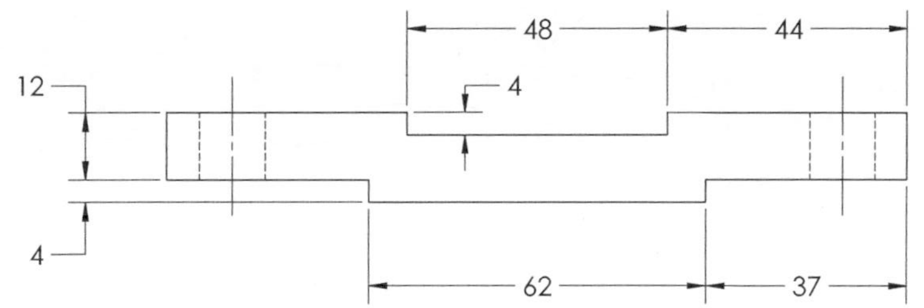

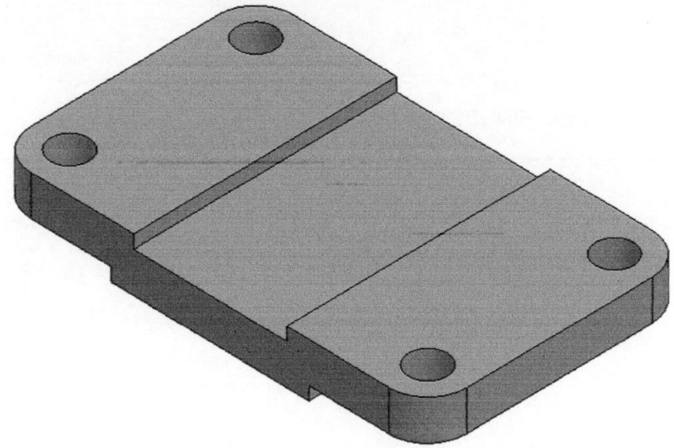

NOTES

1- Material ASTM A36 Steel
2- Deburr sharp edges

TOLERANCES UNLESS OTHERWISE SPECIFIED

X------------------- +/- 0.5
X.X----------------- +/- 0.2
X.XX---------------- +/- 0.1
ANGLE-------------- +/- 0.5°

ALL DIMENSIONS IN MM

FIRST ISSUED	
DRAWN BY	
CHECKED BY	
APPROVED BY	

CADCIM TECHNOLOGIES

Top Plate

SIZE	DRG NO.	SHEET REV
A3	1-003	A
SCALE 1:1		SHEET 4 OF 5

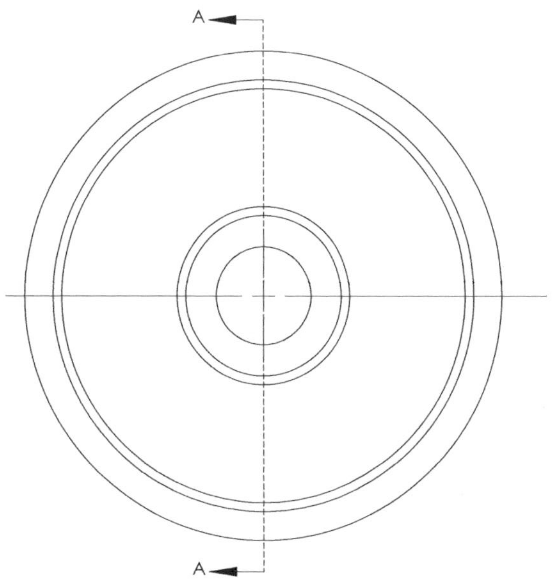

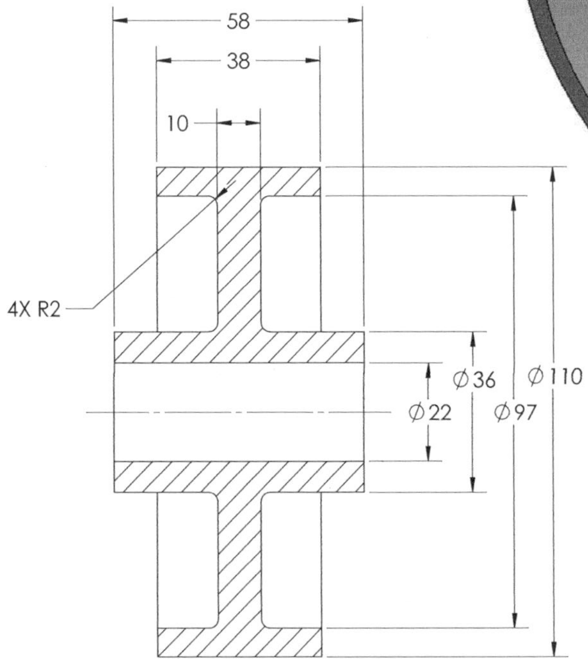

SECTION A-A

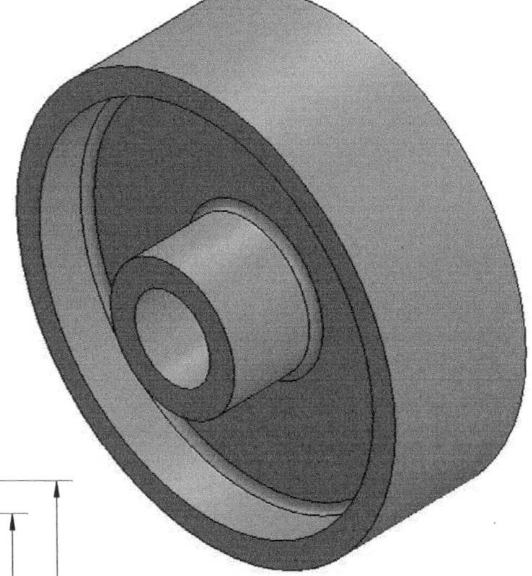

NOTES

1- Material Cast Iron
2- Deburr sharp edges

TOLERANCES UNLESS OTHERWISE SPECIFIED		CADCIM TECHNOLOGIES
X---------- +/- 0.5 X.X---------- +/- 0.2 X.XX---------- +/- 0.1 ANGLE---------- +/- 0.5°	FIRST ISSUED DRAWN BY CHECKED BY APPROVED BY	Wheel
ALL DIMENSIONS IN MM		SIZE A3 · DRG NO. 1-004 · SHEET REV A
		SCALE 1:1 · SHEET 5 OF 5

Project 2

Metal Shear Assembly

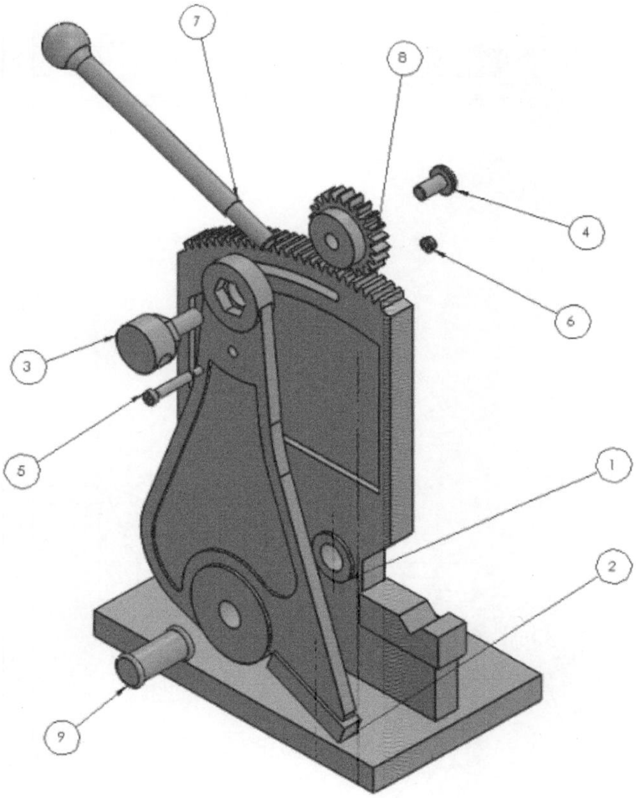

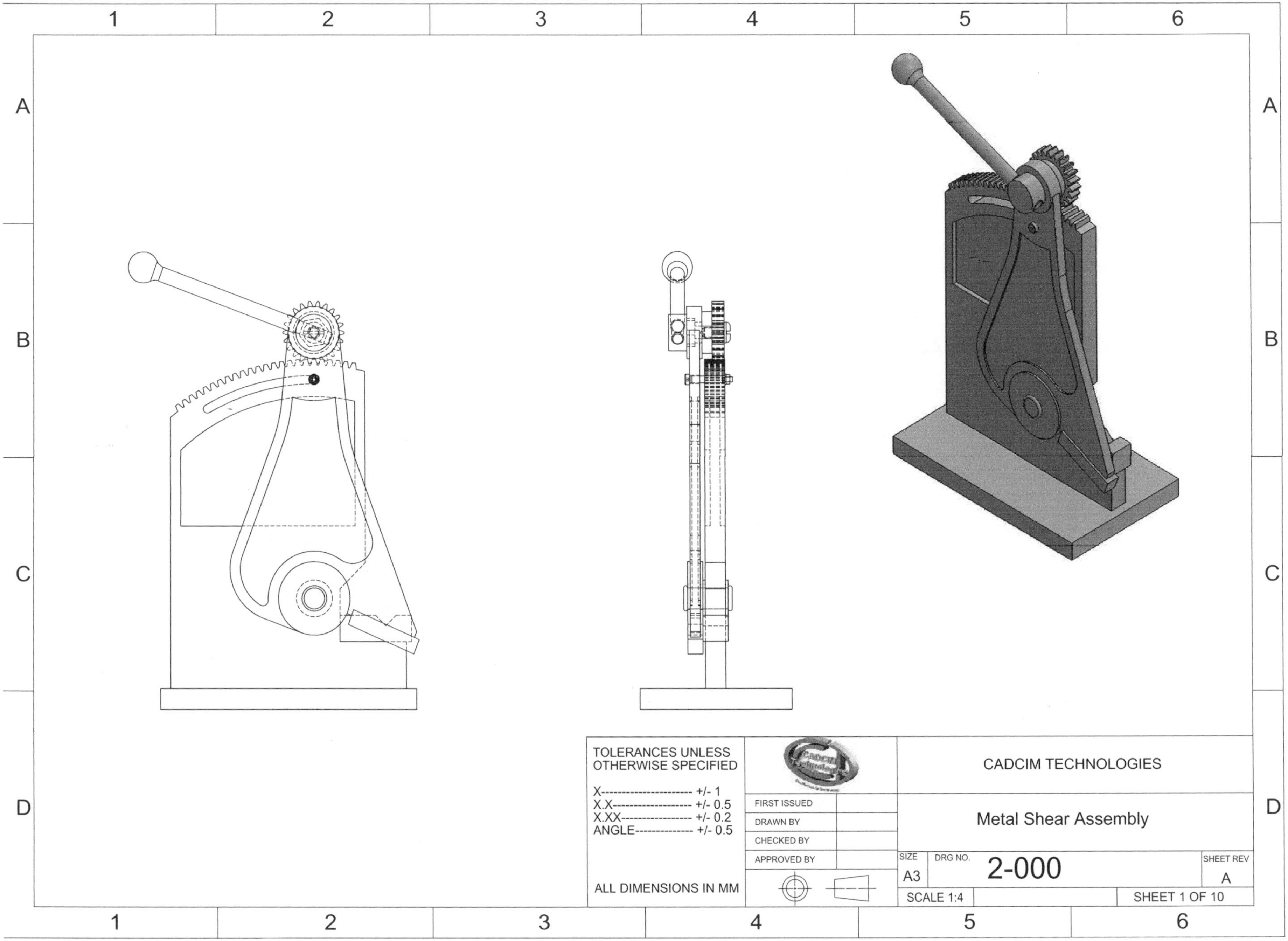
1
2
3
4
5
6
A
B
C
D
TOLERANCES UNLESS OTHERWISE SPECIFIED
X---------------------- +/- 1
X.X------------------- +/- 0.5
X.XX----------------- +/- 0.2
ANGLE-------------- +/- 0.5
ALL DIMENSIONS IN MM
FIRST ISSUED
DRAWN BY
CHECKED BY
APPROVED BY
CADCIM TECHNOLOGIES
Metal Shear Assembly
SIZE
A3
DRG NO.
2-000
SHEET REV
A
SCALE 1:4
SHEET 1 OF 10

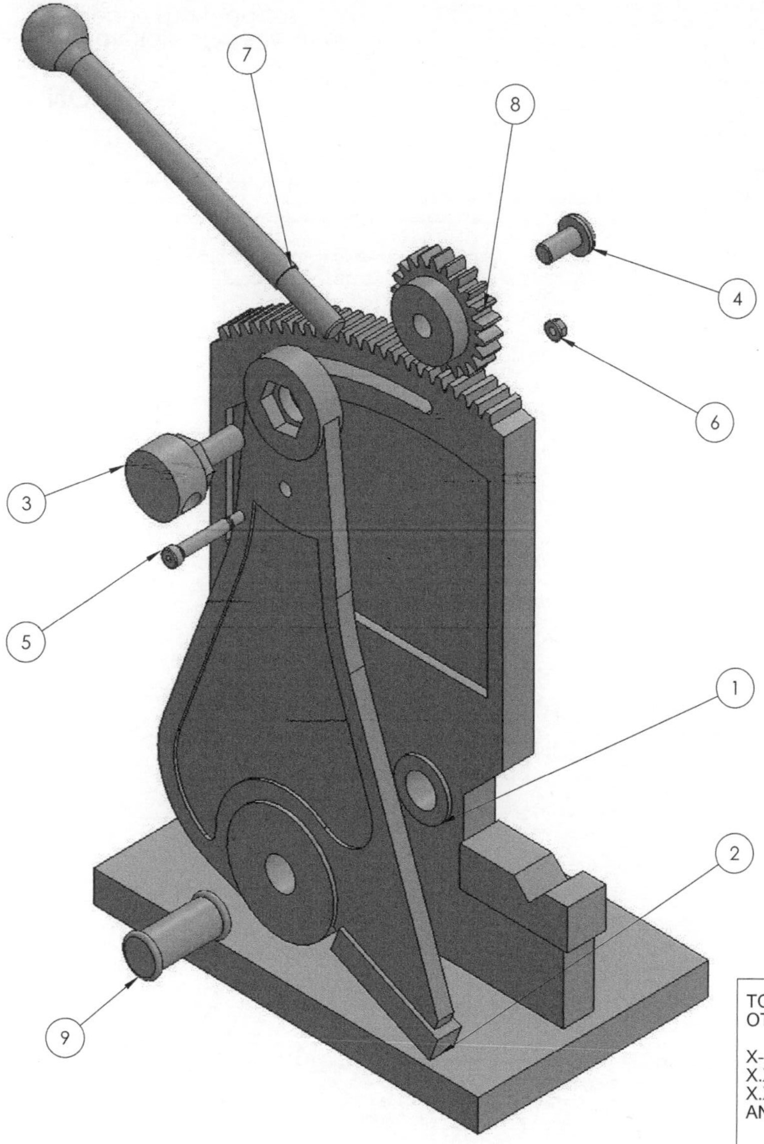

ITEM NO.	PART NUMBER	QTY.
1	Body	1
2	Shears	1
3	Lock Pin	1
4	M10X1.5 Pan Head Screw-ANSI B18.6.7M	1
5	M6.5 Hexagon Socket Head Shoulder Screw-ANSI B18.3.3M	1
6	M5X0.8 Hex flange nut-ANSI B18.2.2.4	1
7	cotter pin	1
8	ANSI Metric-Spur gear 2.5M 22T-20PA-12FW	1
9	Joint Pin	1

TOLERANCES UNLESS OTHERWISE SPECIFIED

X---------------------- +/- 1
X.X------------------- +/- 0.5
X.XX----------------- +/- 0.2
ANGLE-------------- +/- 0.5

ALL DIMENSIONS IN MM

FIRST ISSUED
DRAWN BY
CHECKED BY
APPROVED BY

CADCIM TECHNOLOGIES

Metal Shear Exploded

SIZE A3 | DRG NO. 2-000 | SHEET REV A

SCALE 2:1 | SHEET 2 OF 10

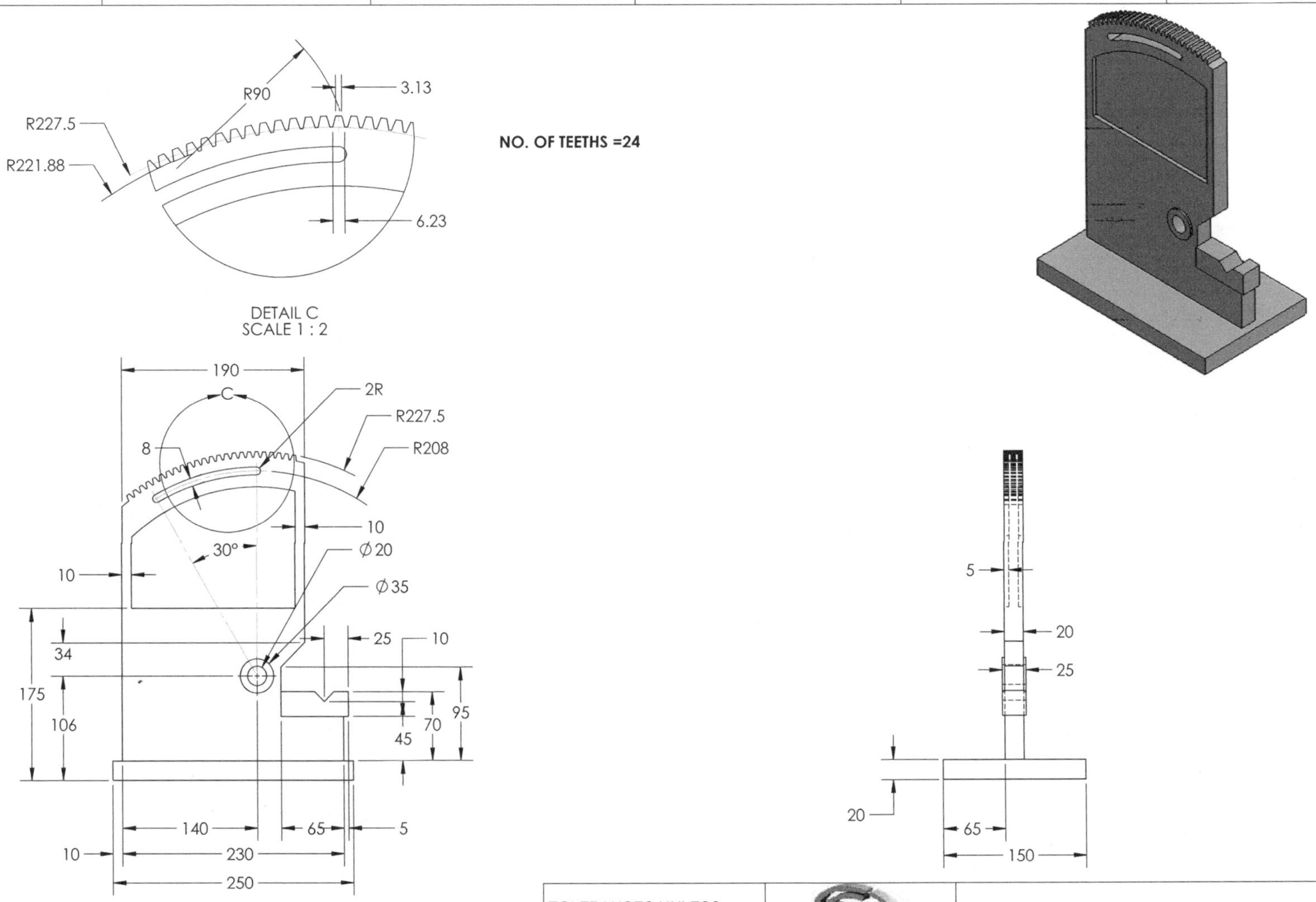

NOTES

1- Material ASTM A36 Steel
2- Deburr sharp edges

TOLERANCES UNLESS OTHERWISE SPECIFIED

X---------------------- +/- 1
X.X-------------------- +/- 0.5
X.XX------------------- +/- 0.2
ANGLE-------------- +/- 0.5

ALL DIMENSIONS IN MM

FIRST ISSUED
DRAWN BY
CHECKED BY
APPROVED BY

CADCIM TECHNOLOGIES

Body

SIZE	DRG NO.	SHEET REV
A3	2-001	A
SCALE 1:4		SHEET 3 OF 10

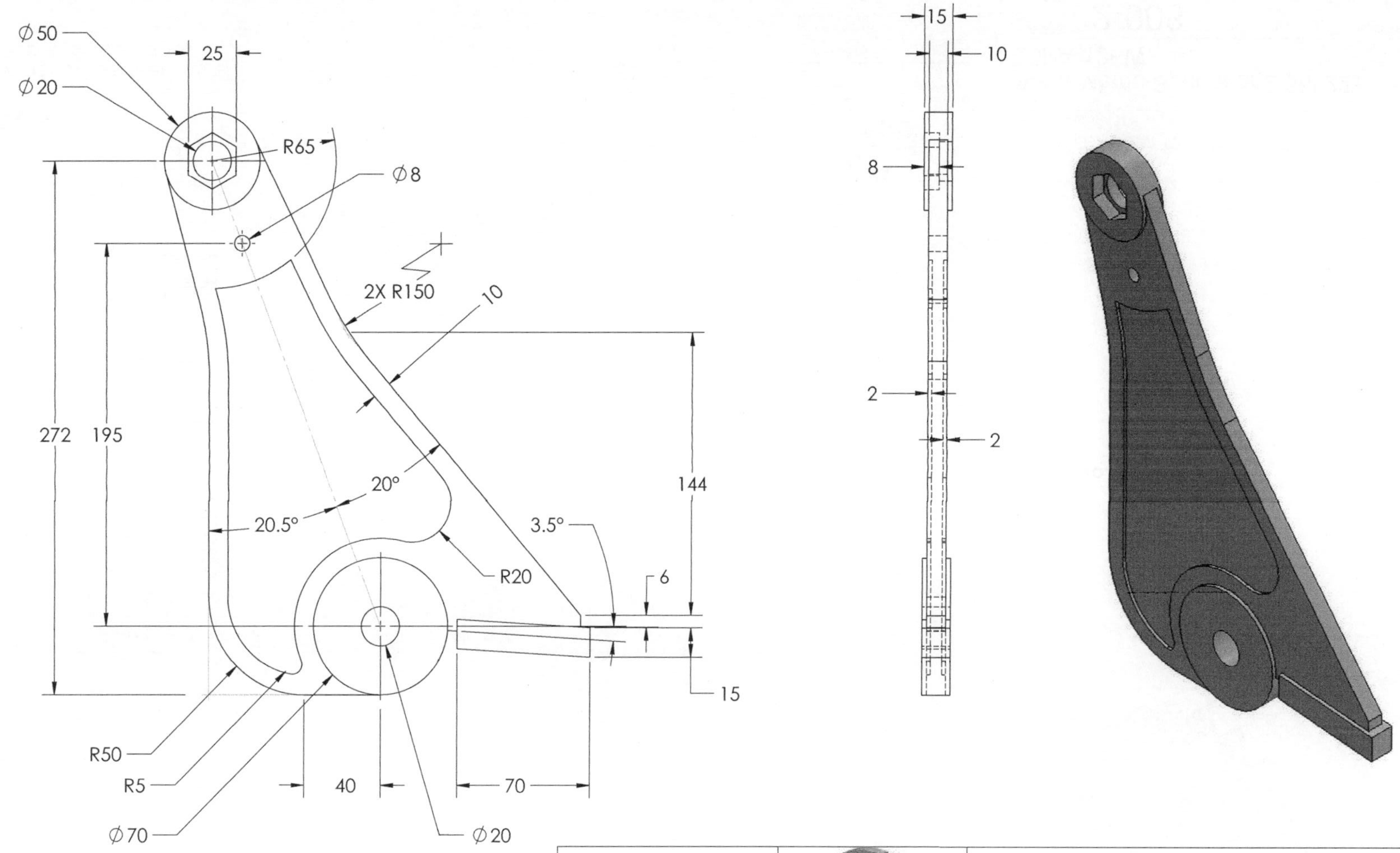

NOTES

1- Material ASTM A36 Steel
2- Deburr sharp edges

TOLERANCES UNLESS OTHERWISE SPECIFIED

X------------------- +/- 1
X.X----------------- +/- 0.5
X.XX---------------- +/- 0.2
ANGLE--------------- +/- 0.5

ALL DIMENSIONS IN MM

FIRST ISSUED	
DRAWN BY	
CHECKED BY	
APPROVED BY	

CADCIM TECHNOLOGIES

Shears

SIZE	DRG NO.	SHEET REV
A3	2-002	A
SCALE 1:2		SHEET 4 OF 10

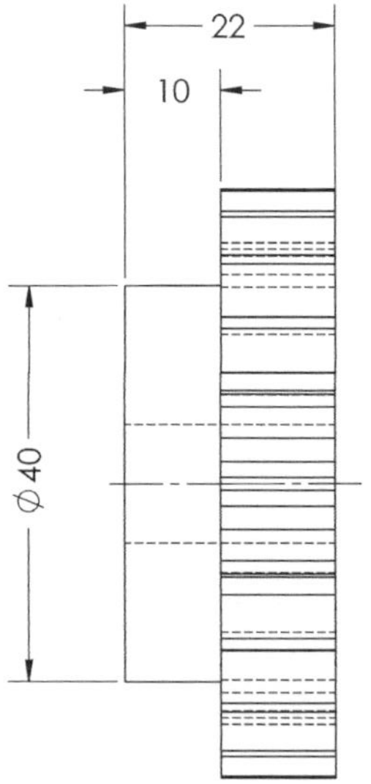

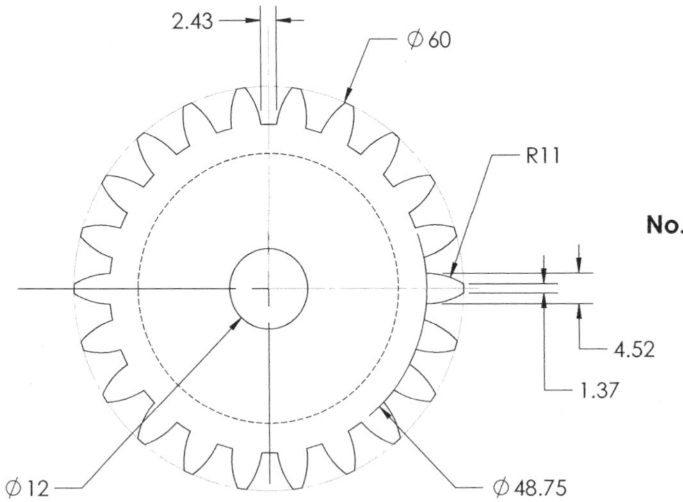

No. of teeths 22

NOTES

1- Material Tool Steel
2- Deburr sharp edges

TOLERANCES UNLESS OTHERWISE SPECIFIED

X---------------------- +/- 1
X.X-------------------- +/- 0.5
X.XX------------------ +/- 0.2
ANGLE---------------- +/- 0.5

ALL DIMENSIONS IN MM

FIRST ISSUED	
DRAWN BY	
CHECKED BY	
APPROVED BY	

CADCIM TECHNOLOGIES

ANSI Metric-Spur gear 2.5M 22T-20PA-12FW

SIZE	DRG NO.	SHEET REV
A3	2-003	A
SCALE 3:2		SHEET 5 OF 10

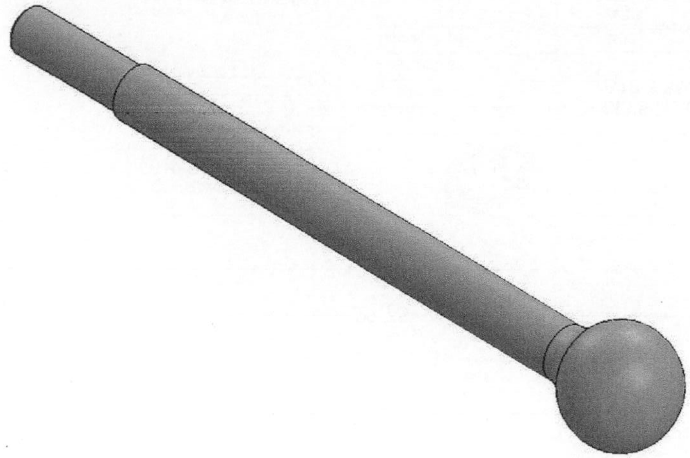

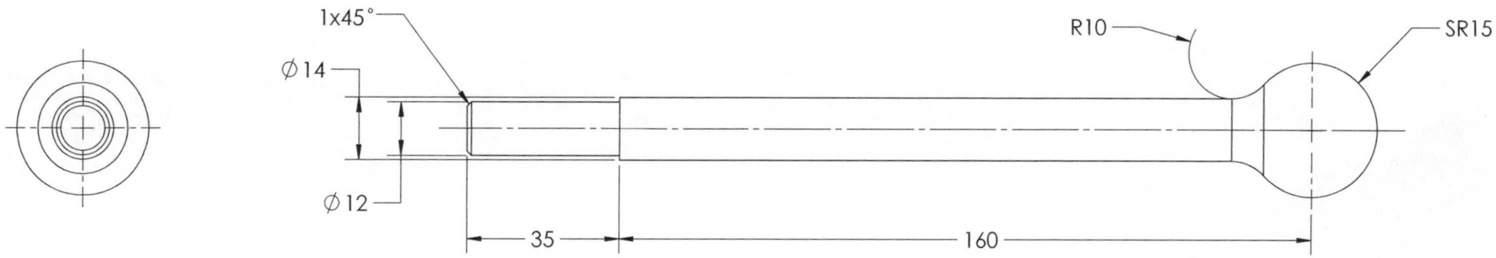

NOTES

1- Material ASTM A36 Steel
2- Deburr sharp edges

TOLERANCES UNLESS OTHERWISE SPECIFIED		CADCIM TECHNOLOGIES
X---------- +/- 1 X.X---------- +/- 0.5 X.XX---------- +/- 0.2 ANGLE---------- +/- 0.5	FIRST ISSUED DRAWN BY CHECKED BY APPROVED BY	Cotter Pin
ALL DIMENSIONS IN MM		SIZE A3 DRG NO. 2-004 SHEET REV A
		SCALE 1:1 SHEET 6 OF 10

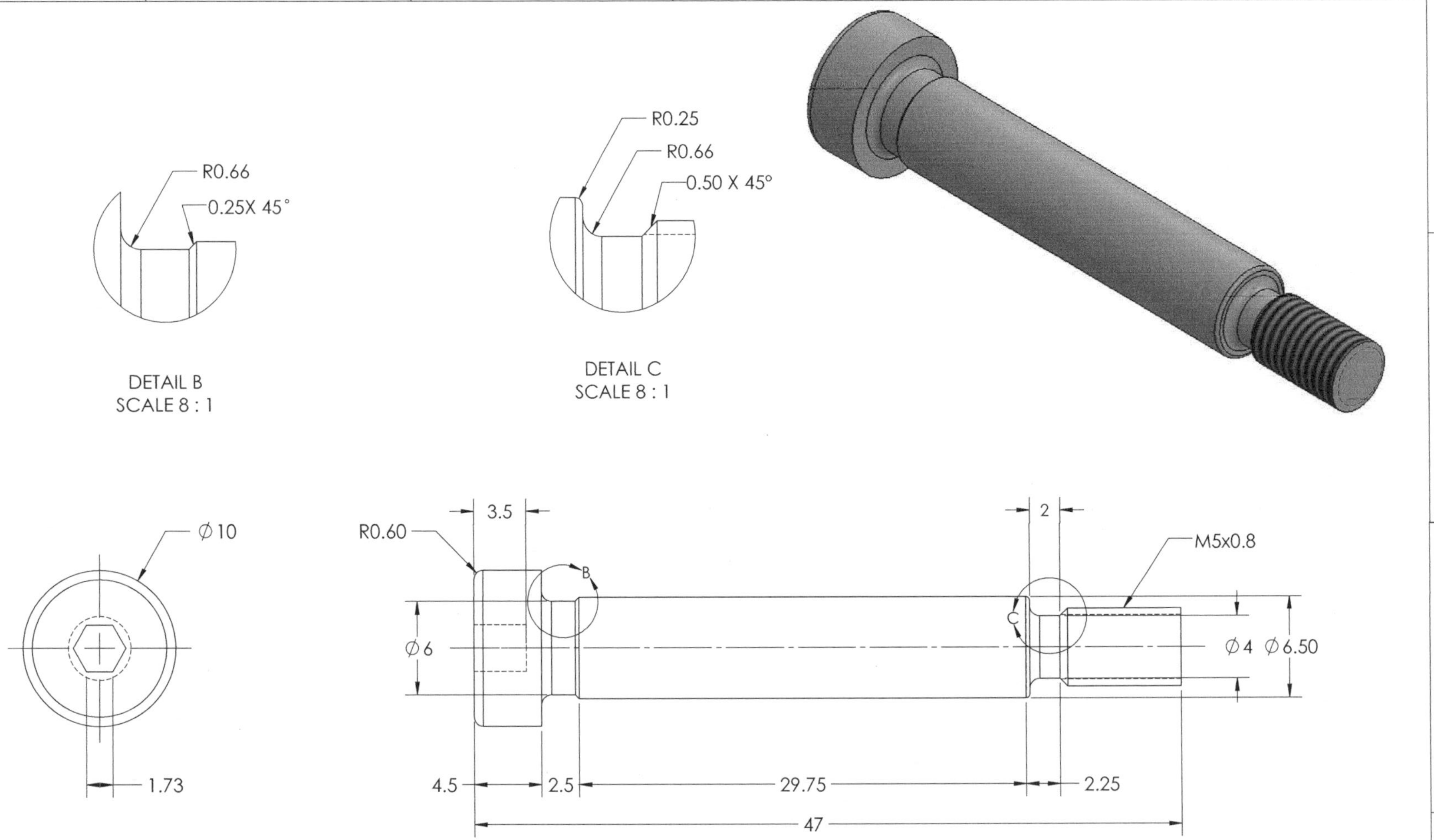

NOTES

1- Material Stainless steel
2- Deburr sharp edges

TOLERANCES UNLESS OTHERWISE SPECIFIED

X	+/- 1
X.X	+/- 0.5
X.XX	+/- 0.2
ANGLE	+/- 0.5

ALL DIMENSIONS IN MM

CADCIM TECHNOLOGIES

FIRST ISSUED	
DRAWN BY	
CHECKED BY	
APPROVED BY	

M6.5 Hexagon Socket Head Shoulder Screw- ANSI B18.3.3M

SIZE A3 | DRG NO. 2-005 | SHEET REV A

SCALE 4:1 | SHEET 7 OF 10

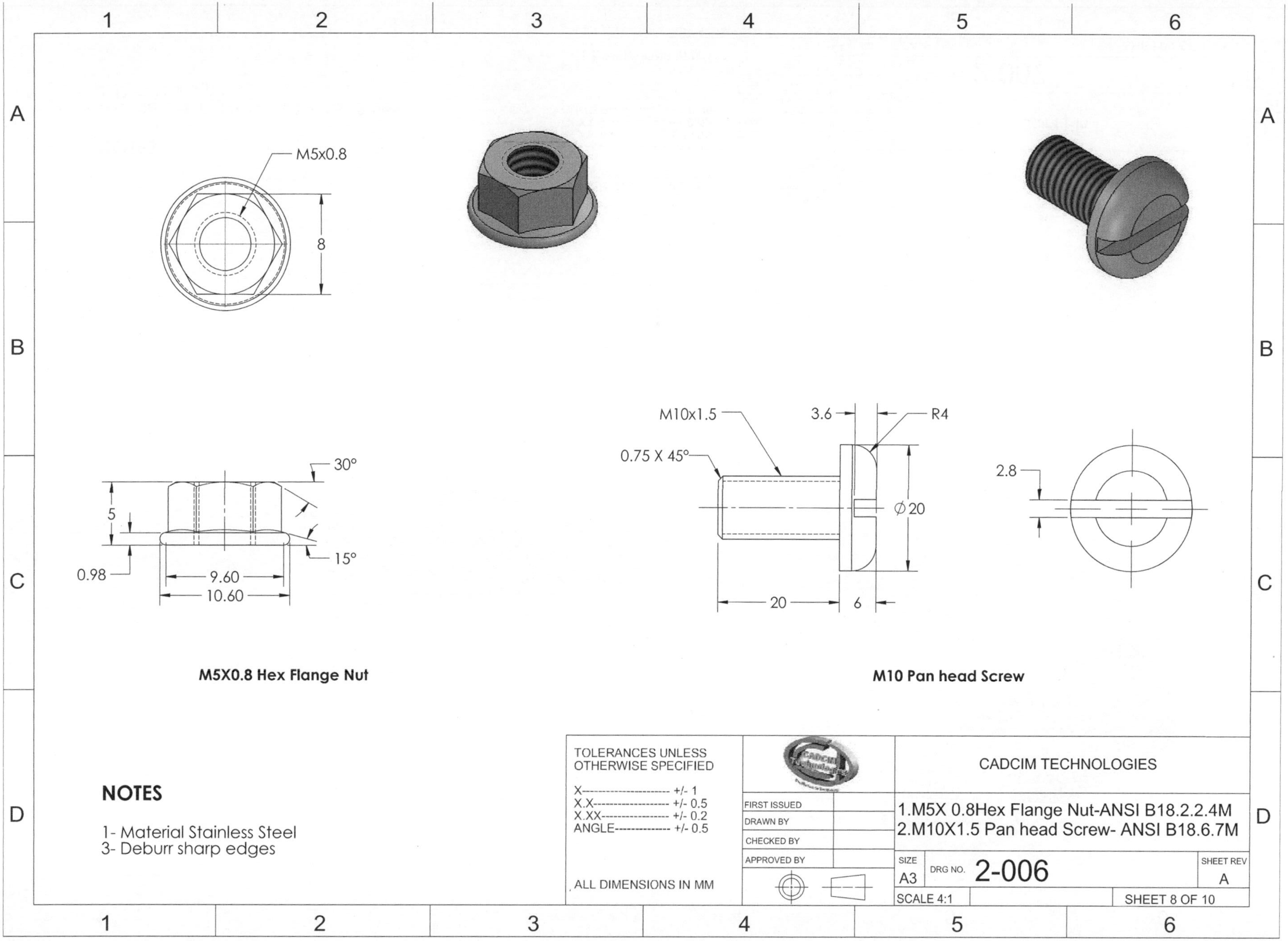
M5x0.8
8
30°
5
15°
0.98
9.60
10.60
M5X0.8 Hex Flange Nut
M10x1.5
3.6
R4
0.75 X 45°
Ø20
20
6
2.8
M10 Pan head Screw
NOTES
1- Material Stainless Steel
3- Deburr sharp edges
TOLERANCES UNLESS OTHERWISE SPECIFIED
X +/- 1
X.X +/- 0.5
X.XX +/- 0.2
ANGLE +/- 0.5
ALL DIMENSIONS IN MM
FIRST ISSUED
DRAWN BY
CHECKED BY
APPROVED BY
CADCIM TECHNOLOGIES
1.M5X 0.8Hex Flange Nut-ANSI B18.2.2.4M
2.M10X1.5 Pan head Screw- ANSI B18.6.7M
SIZE A3
DRG NO. 2-006
SHEET REV A
SCALE 4:1
SHEET 8 OF 10

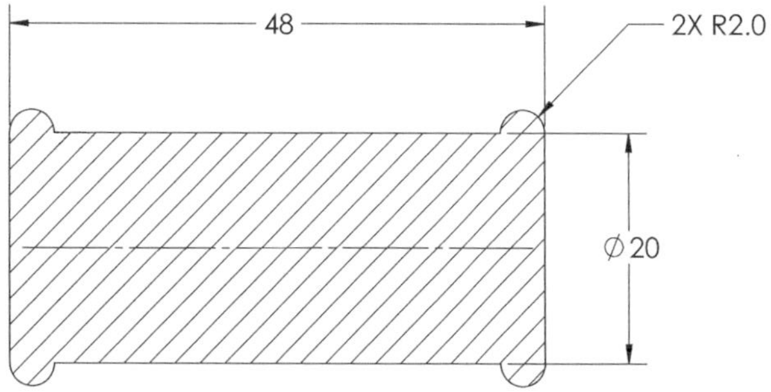

SECTION C-C

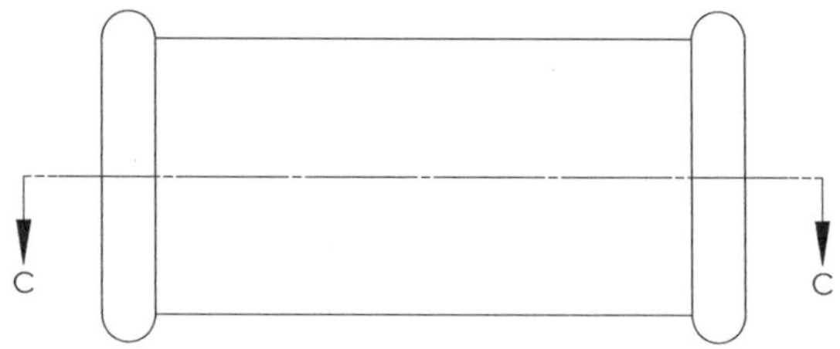

NOTES

1- Material Mild Steel (ASTM A36 Steel)
2- Deburr sharp edges

TOLERANCES UNLESS OTHERWISE SPECIFIED

X---------------------- +/- 0.1
X.X-------------------- +/- 0.05
X.XX------------------ +/- 0.02
ANGLE--------------- +/- 0.05

ALL DIMENSIONS IN MM

FIRST ISSUED
DRAWN BY
CHECKED BY
APPROVED BY

CADCIM TECHNOLOGIES

Joint Pin

SIZE	DRG NO.	SHEET REV
A3	2-007	A
SCALE 2:1		SHEET 9 OF 10

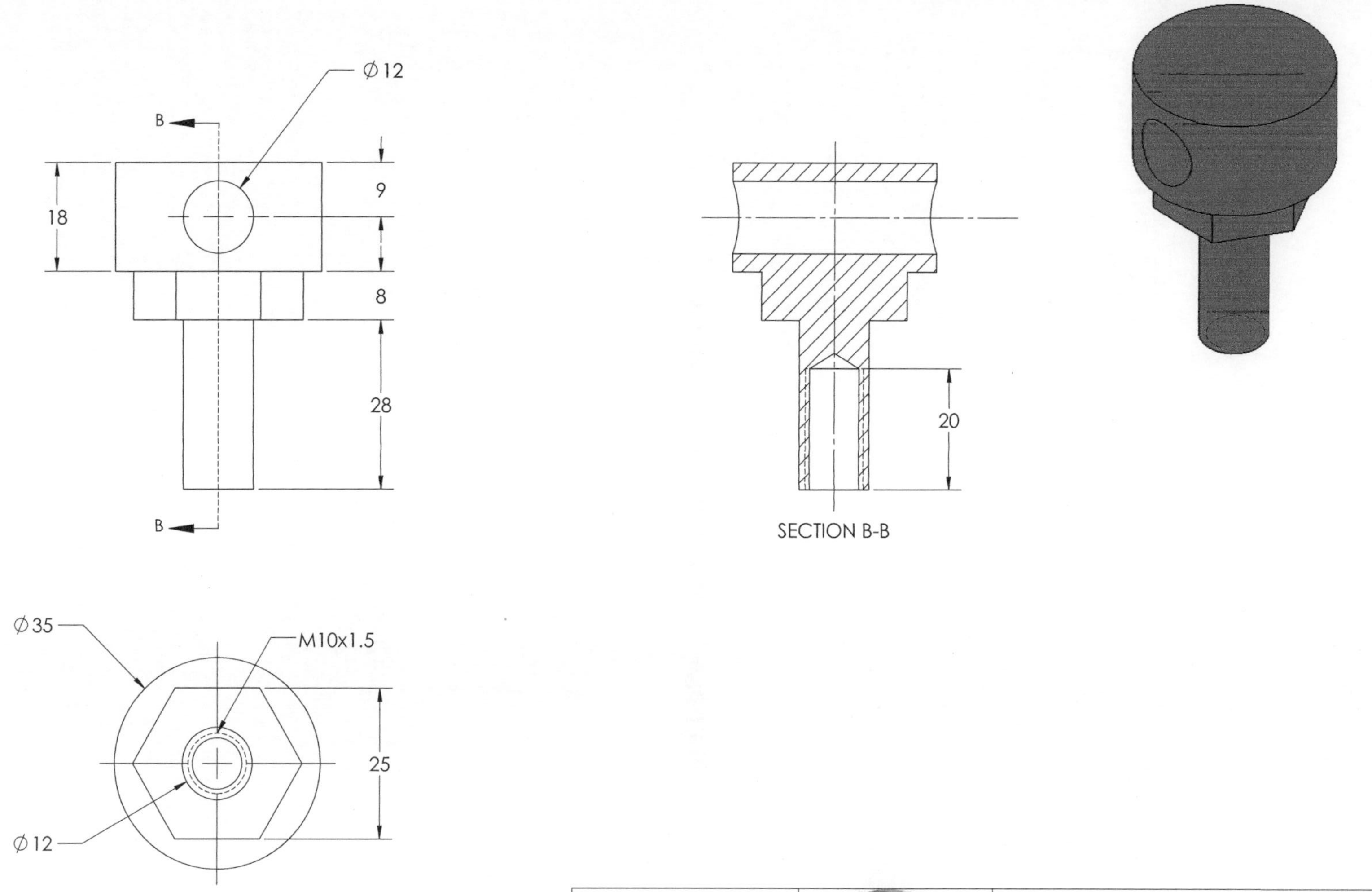

NOTES

1- Material ASTM A36 Steel
2- Deburr sharp edges

TOLERANCES UNLESS OTHERWISE SPECIFIED		CADCIM TECHNOLOGIES
X---------- +/- 1	FIRST ISSUED	Lock Pin
X.X---------- +/- 0.5	DRAWN BY	
X.XX---------- +/- 0.2	CHECKED BY	
ANGLE---------- +/- 0.5	APPROVED BY	SIZE A3 · DRG NO. 2-008 · SHEET REV A
ALL DIMENSIONS IN MM		SCALE 1:1 · SHEET 10 OF 10

This page is intentionally left blank

Project 3

Angle Clamp Assembly

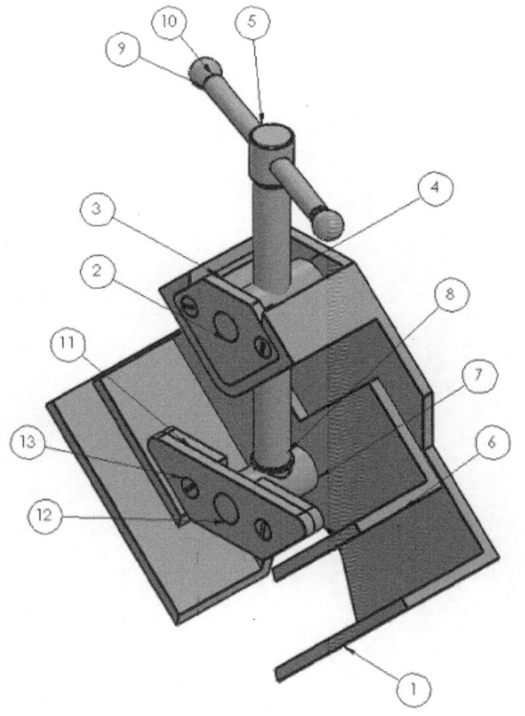

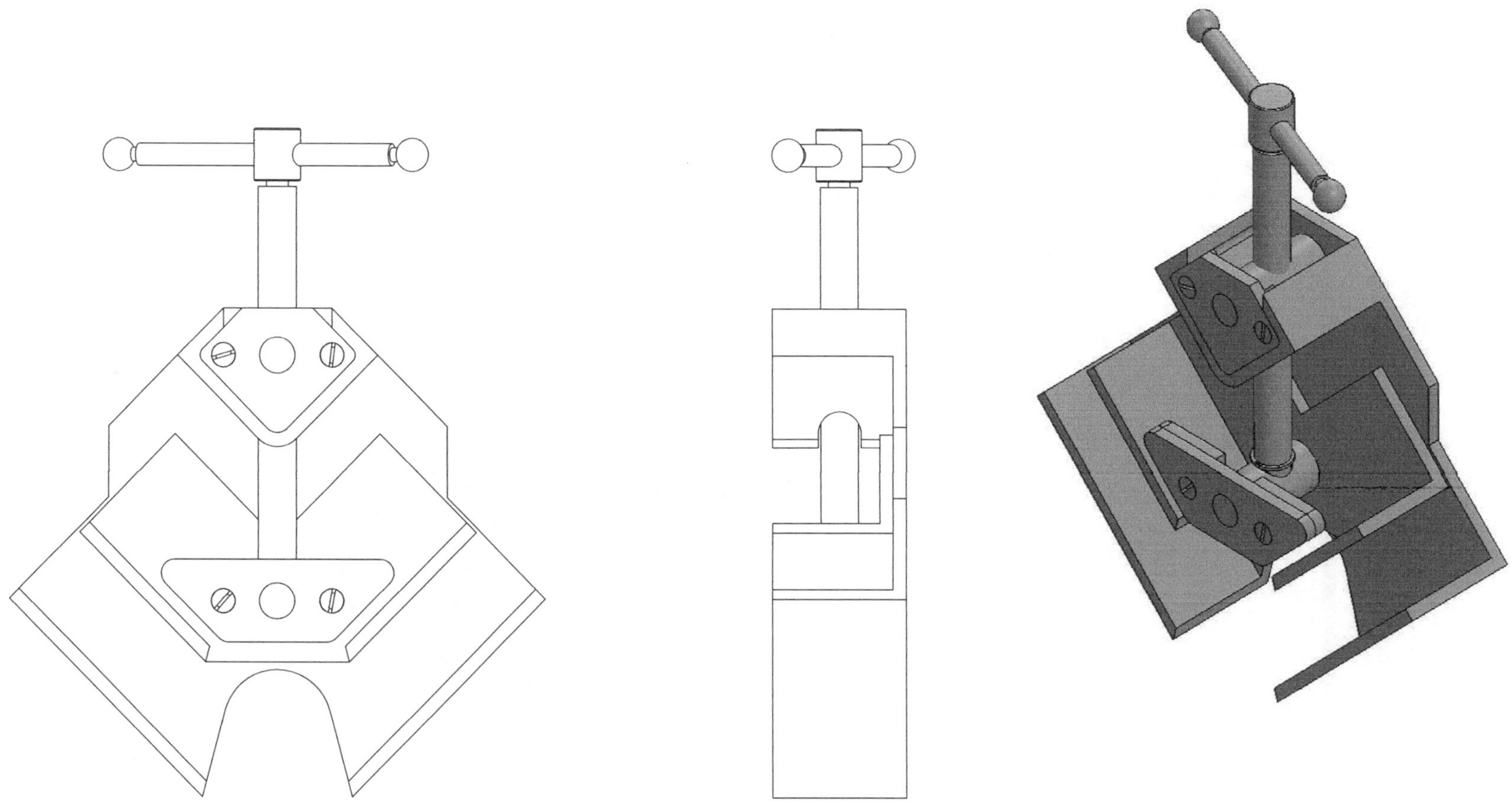

TOLERANCES UNLESS OTHERWISE SPECIFIED		CADCIM TECHNOLOGIES
X---------------------- +/- 1 X.X------------------- +/- 0.5 X.XX----------------- +/- 0.2 ANGLE-------------- +/- 0.5	FIRST ISSUED DRAWN BY CHECKED BY APPROVED BY	Angle Cramp Assembly
ALL DIMENSIONS IN MM		SIZE A3 · DRG NO. 3-000 · SHEET REV A
		SCALE 2:1 · SHEET 1 OF 13

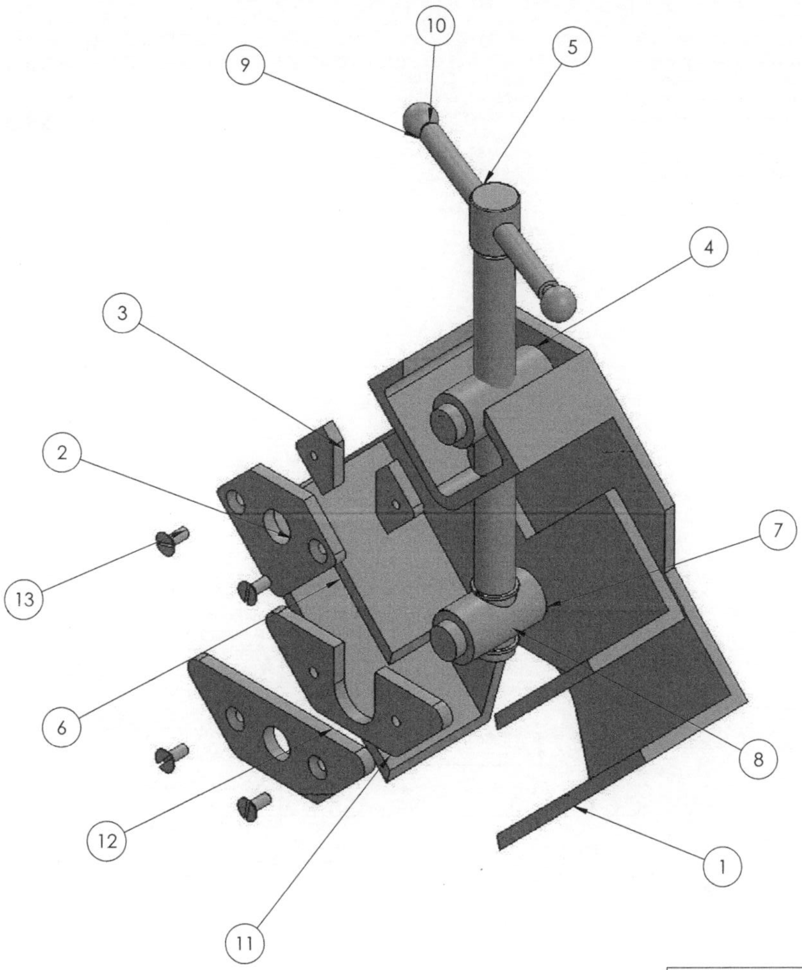

ITEM NO.	PART NUMBER	QTY.
1	Angle clamp Body	1
2	Clamp Cover	1
3	Clamp Insert	2
4	Rear Pin	1
5	Clamp Screw	1
6	Clamp	1
7	Front Pin	1
8	Snap ring	2
9	Clamp Rod	1
10	Clamp rod globes	2
11	Plate 1	1
12	Plate 2	1
13	M4x 0.7 Flat head slotted screw- ANSI B18.6.7M	4

TOLERANCES UNLESS OTHERWISE SPECIFIED

X---------------------- +/- 1
X.X------------------ +/- 0.5
X.XX---------------- +/- 0.2
ANGLE-------------- +/- 0.5

ALL DIMENSIONS IN MM

FIRST ISSUED	
DRAWN BY	
CHECKED BY	
APPROVED BY	

CADCIM TECHNOLOGIES

Angle Clamp Exploded

SIZE	DRG NO.	SHEET REV
A3	3-000	A
SCALE 2:3	SHEET 2 OF 13	

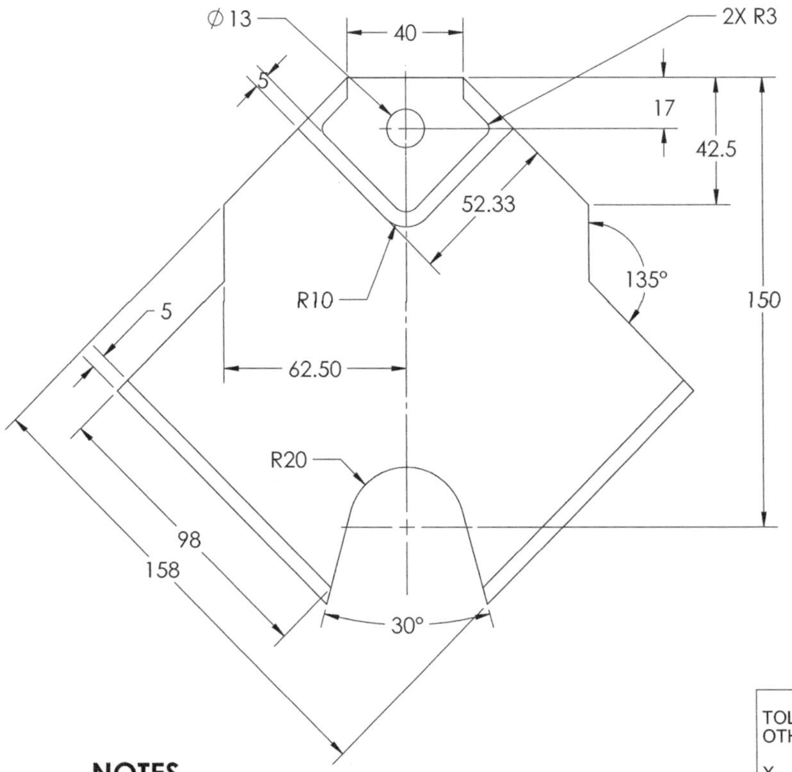

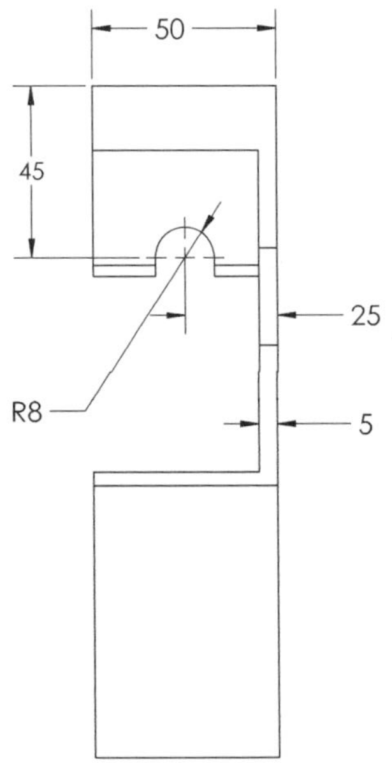

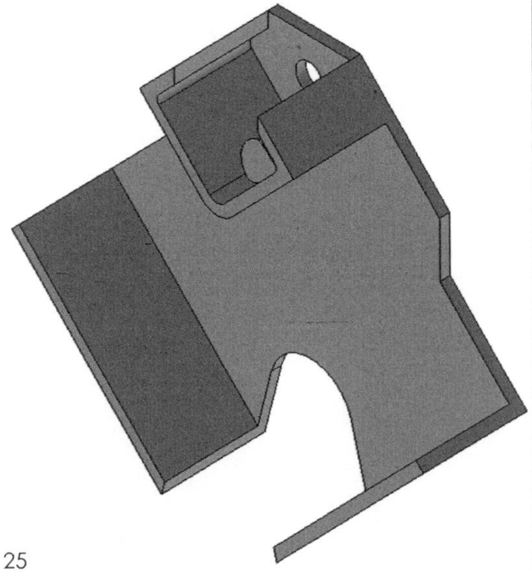

NOTES

1- Material Mild Steel (ASTM A36 Steel)
2- Deburr sharp edges

TOLERANCES UNLESS OTHERWISE SPECIFIED		CADCIM TECHNOLOGIES
X---------- +/- 1 X.X---------- +/- 0.5 X.XX---------- +/- 0.2 ANGLE---------- +/- 0.5	FIRST ISSUED DRAWN BY CHECKED BY APPROVED BY	Angle clamp body
ALL DIMENSIONS IN MM		SIZE A3 · DRG NO. 3-001 · SHEET REV A
		SCALE 2:3 · SHEET 3 OF 13

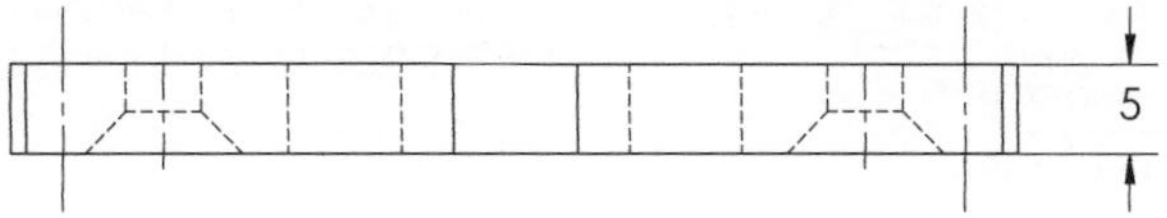

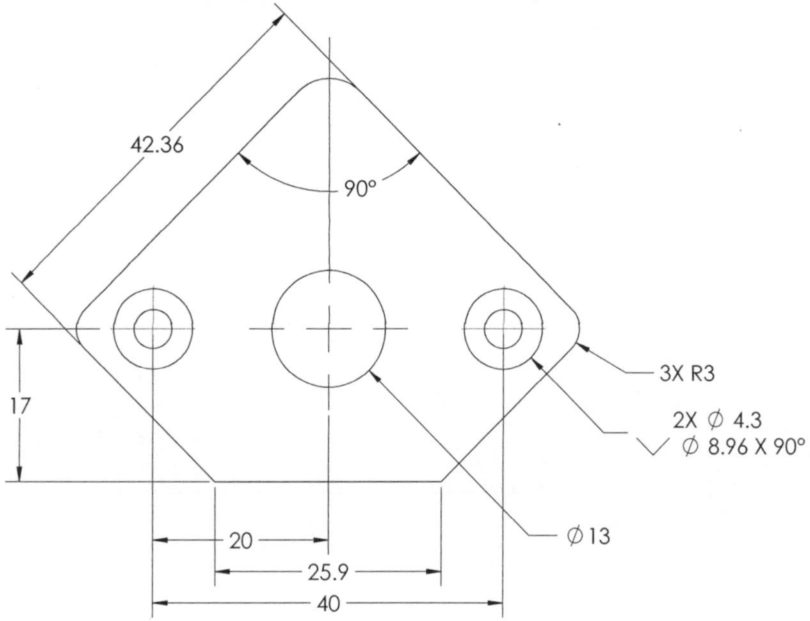

NOTES

1- Material Gray Cast Iron
2- Deburr sharp edges

TOLERANCES UNLESS OTHERWISE SPECIFIED		CADCIM TECHNOLOGIES
X---------- +/- 1 X.X---------- +/- 0.5 X.XX---------- +/- 0.2 ANGLE---------- +/- 0.5	FIRST ISSUED DRAWN BY CHECKED BY APPROVED BY	Clamp Cover
ALL DIMENSIONS IN MM		SIZE A3 · DRG NO. 3-002 · SHEET REV A SCALE 2:1 · SHEET 4 OF 13

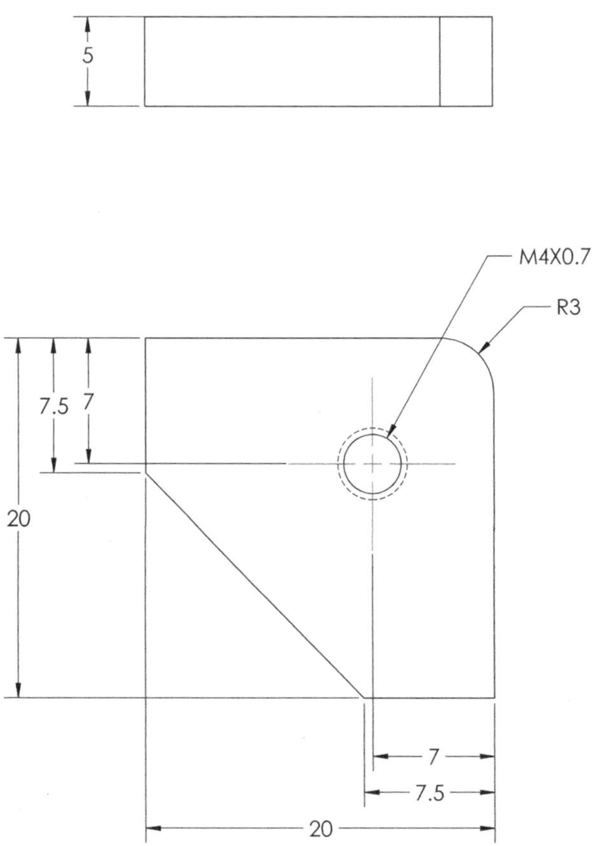

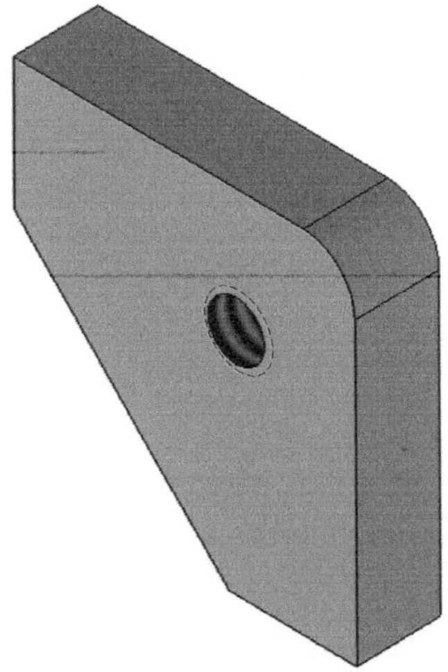

NOTES

1- Material Mild Steel (ASTM A36 Steel)
2- Deburr sharp edges

TOLERANCES UNLESS OTHERWISE SPECIFIED		CADCIM TECHNOLOGIES
X---------- +/- 1 X.X---------- +/- 0.5 X.XX---------- +/- 0.2 ANGLE---------- +/- 0.5	FIRST ISSUED DRAWN BY CHECKED BY APPROVED BY	Clamp Insert
ALL DIMENSIONS IN MM		SIZE A3 · DRG NO. 3-003 · SHEET REV A
		SCALE 4:1 · SHEET 5 OF 13

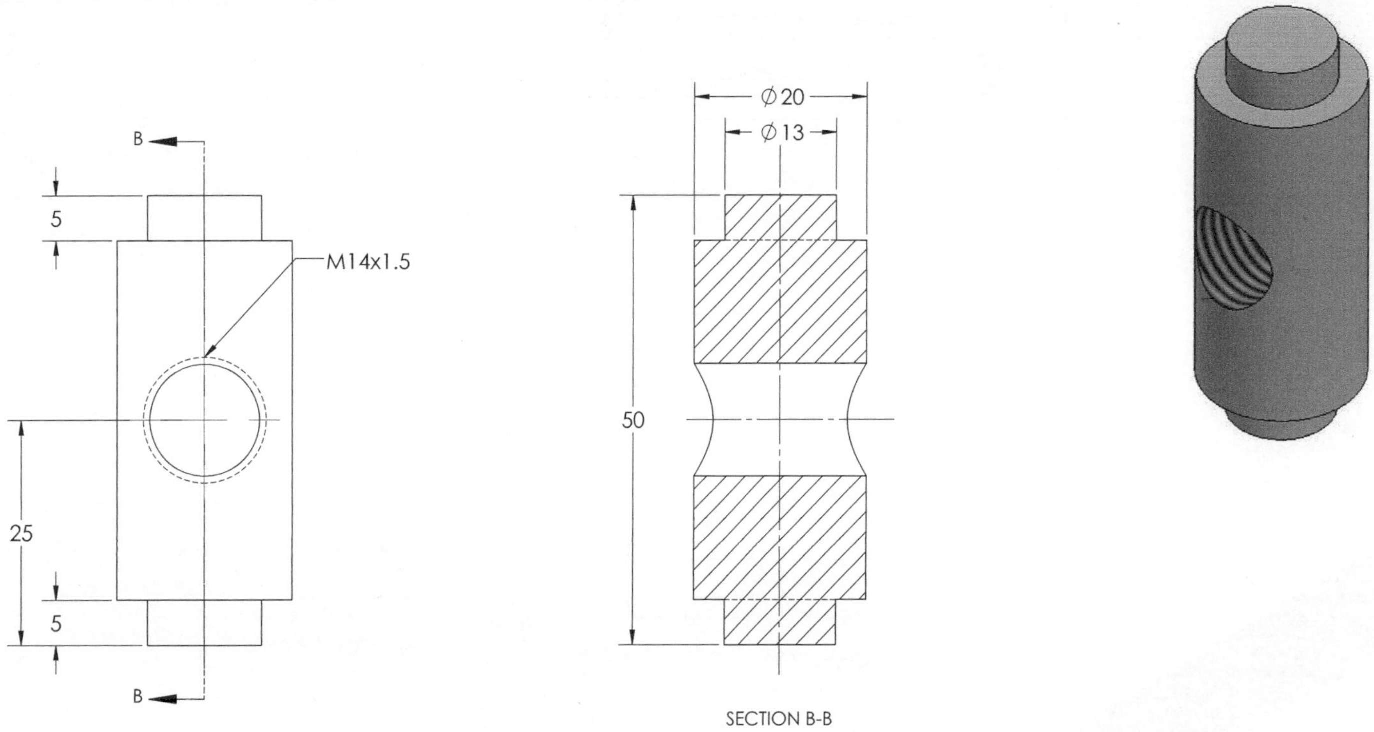

NOTES

1- Material Mild Steel (ASTM A36 Steel)
2- Deburr sharp edges

TOLERANCES UNLESS OTHERWISE SPECIFIED		CADCIM TECHNOLOGIES		
X---------- +/- 1 X.X---------- +/- 0.5 X.XX---------- +/- 0.2 ANGLE---------- +/- 0.5	FIRST ISSUED DRAWN BY CHECKED BY APPROVED BY	Rear Pin		
ALL DIMENSIONS IN MM		SIZE A3	DRG NO. 3-004	SHEET REV A
		SCALE 2:1		SHEET 6 OF 13

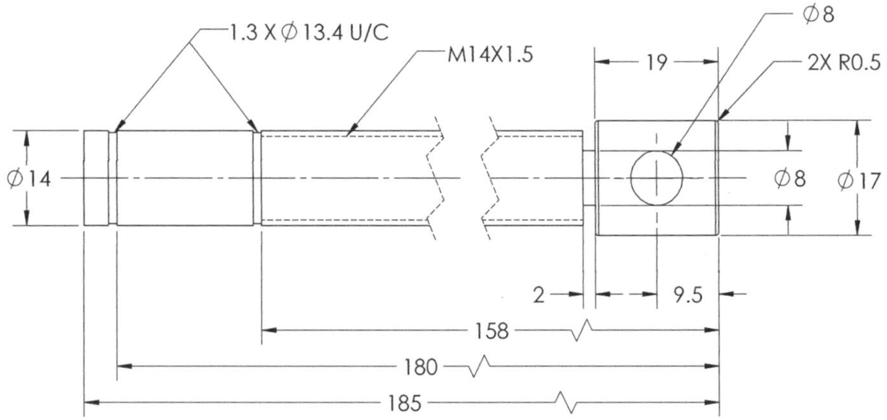

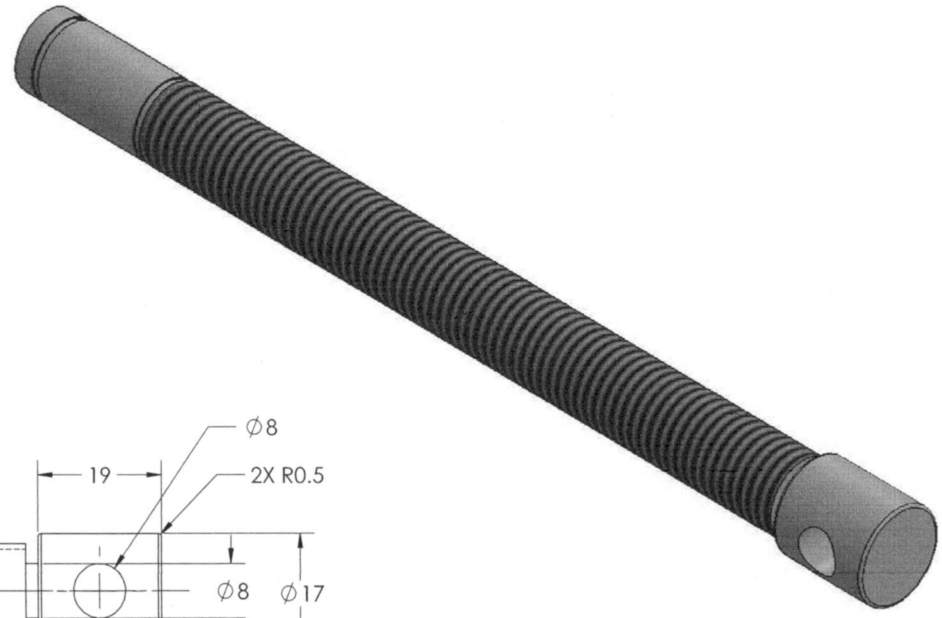

NOTES

1- Material Mild Steel (ASTM A36 Steel)
2- Deburr sharp edges

TOLERANCES UNLESS OTHERWISE SPECIFIED		CADCIM TECHNOLOGIES
X---------- +/- 0.1	FIRST ISSUED	Clamp Screw
X.X---------- +/- 0.05	DRAWN BY	
X.XX---------- +/- 0.02	CHECKED BY	
ANGLE---------- +/- 0.05	APPROVED BY	SIZE A3 · DRG NO. 3-005 · SHEET REV A
ALL DIMENSIONS IN MM		SCALE 3:2 · SHEET 7 OF 13

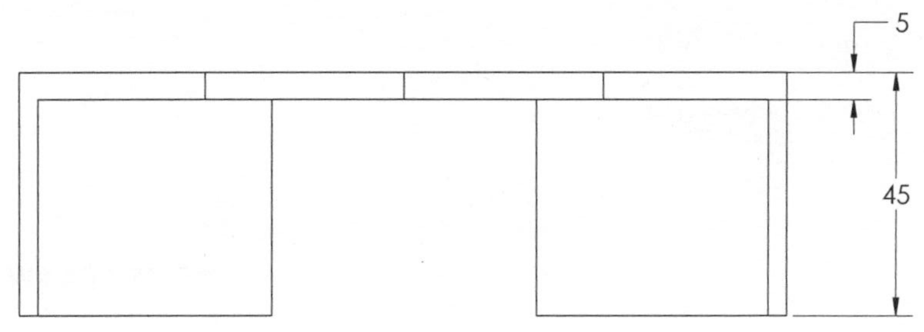

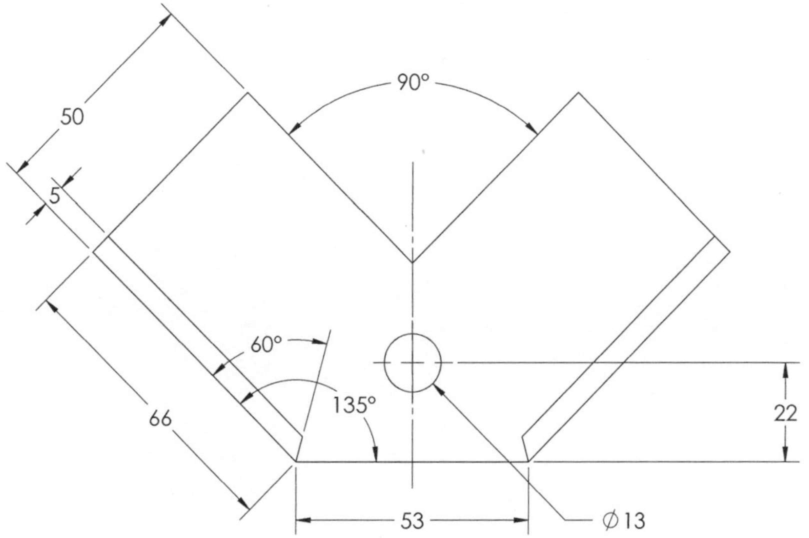

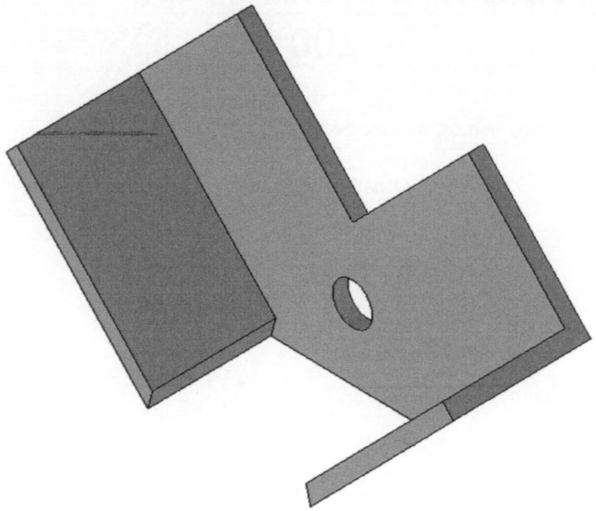

NOTES

1- Material Mild Steel (ASTM A36 Steel)
2- Deburr sharp edges

TOLERANCES UNLESS OTHERWISE SPECIFIED

X---------- +/- 1
X.X---------- +/- 0.5
X.XX---------- +/- 0.2
ANGLE---------- +/- 0.5

ALL DIMENSIONS IN MM

FIRST ISSUED	
DRAWN BY	
CHECKED BY	
APPROVED BY	

CADCIM TECHNOLOGIES

Clamp

SIZE	DRG NO.	SHEET REV
A3	3-006	A
SCALE 1:1		SHEET 8 OF 13

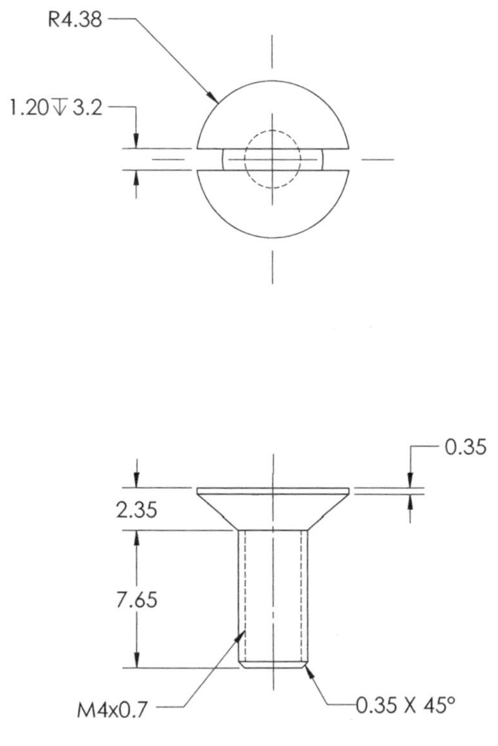

M4 X0.7 Screw

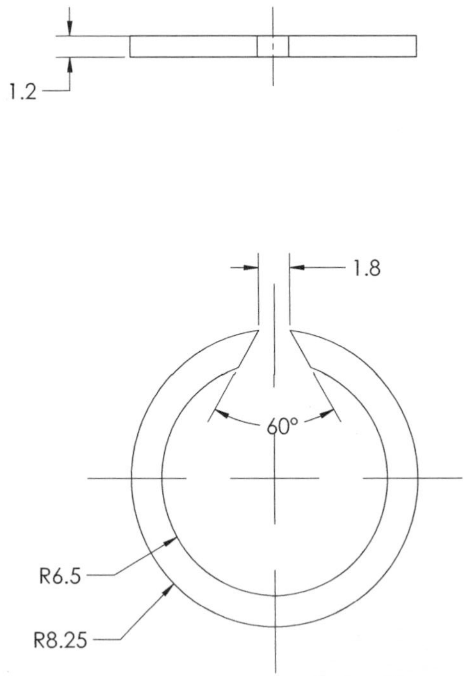

Snap rings

NOTES

1- Material Stainless Steel
2- Deburr sharp edges

TOLERANCES UNLESS OTHERWISE SPECIFIED		CADCIM TECHNOLOGIES
X---------- +/- 1	FIRST ISSUED	1. M4 X0.7 flat head Slotted Screw- ANSI B18.6.7M
X.X---------- +/- 0.5	DRAWN BY	2. Snap ring
X.XX---------- +/- 0.2	CHECKED BY	
ANGLE---------- +/- 0.5	APPROVED BY	SIZE A3 — DRG NO. 3-007 — SHEET REV A
ALL DIMENSIONS IN MM		SCALE 4:1 — SHEET 9 OF 15

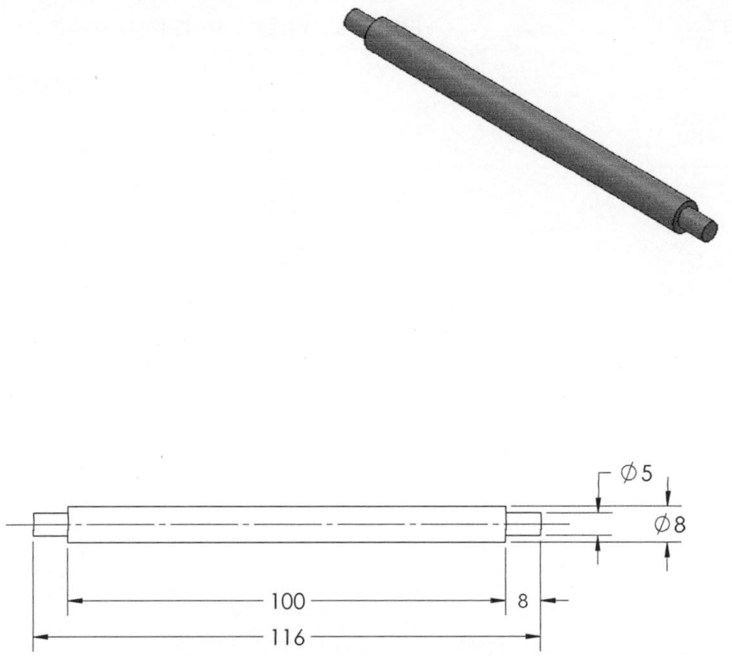

Clamp rod

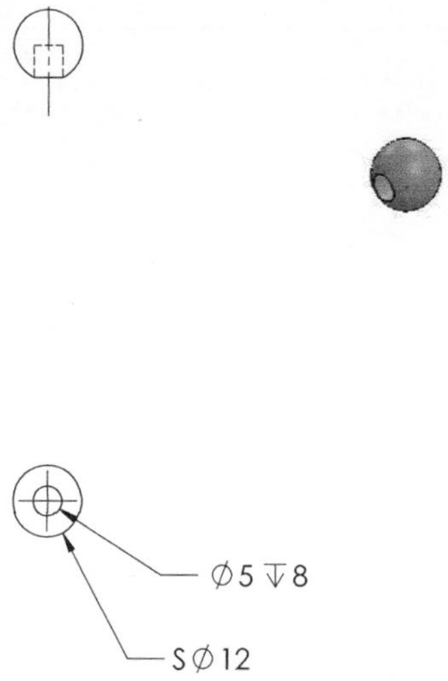

Clamp rod globes

NOTES

1- Material Gray Cast Iron
2- Deburr sharp edges

TOLERANCES UNLESS OTHERWISE SPECIFIED

X------------------- +/- 1
X.X----------------- +/- 0.5
X.XX---------------- +/- 0.2
ANGLE--------------- +/- 0.5

ALL DIMENSIONS IN MM

FIRST ISSUED
DRAWN BY
CHECKED BY
APPROVED BY

CADCIM TECHNOLOGIES

1. Clamp rod
2. Clamp rod globes

SIZE A3 | DRG NO. 3-008 | SHEET REV A

SCALE 1:1 | SHEET 10 OF 13

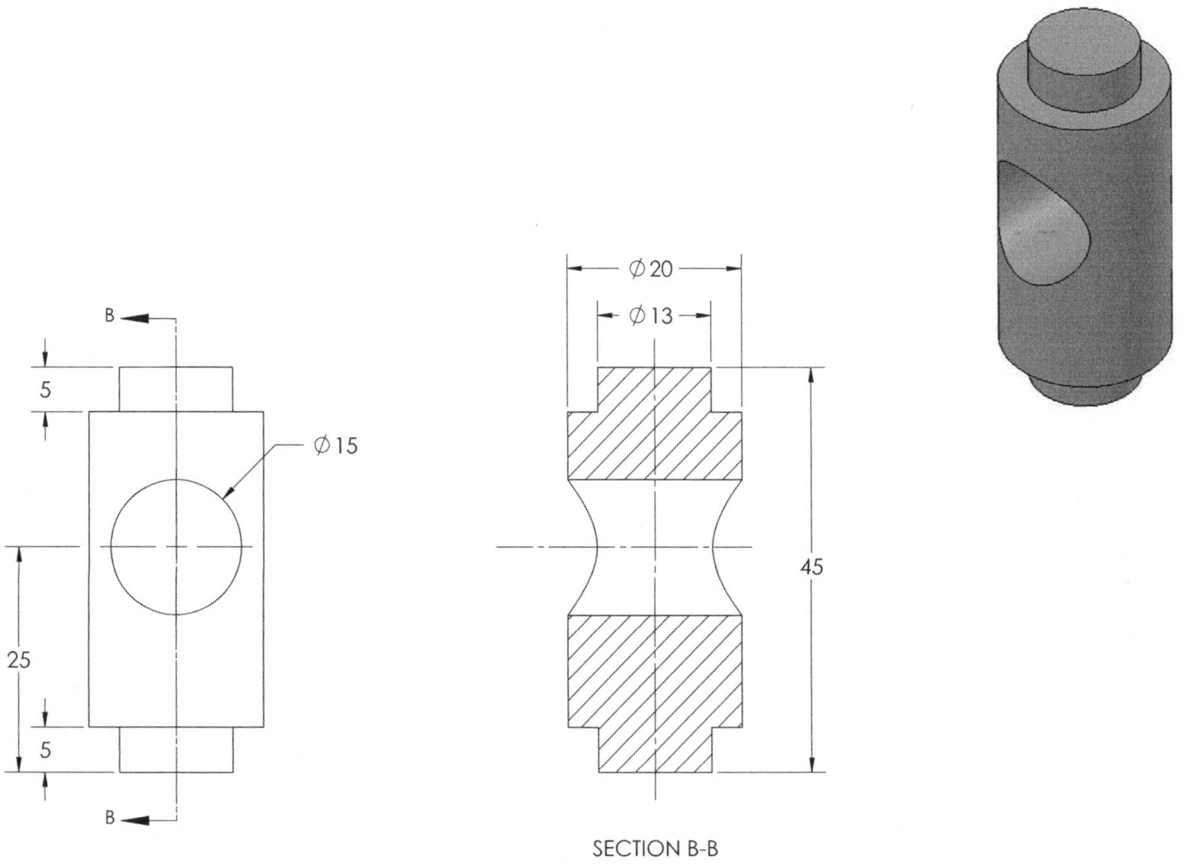

NOTES

1- Material Mild Steel (ASTM A36 Steel)
2- Deburr sharp edges

TOLERANCES UNLESS OTHERWISE SPECIFIED		CADCIM TECHNOLOGIES
X---------- +/- 1	FIRST ISSUED	Front Pin
X.X---------- +/- 0.5	DRAWN BY	
X.XX---------- +/- 0.2	CHECKED BY	
ANGLE---------- +/- 0.5	APPROVED BY	SIZE A3 · DRG NO. 3-009 · SHEET REV A
ALL DIMENSIONS IN MM		SCALE 2:1 · SHEET 11 OF 13

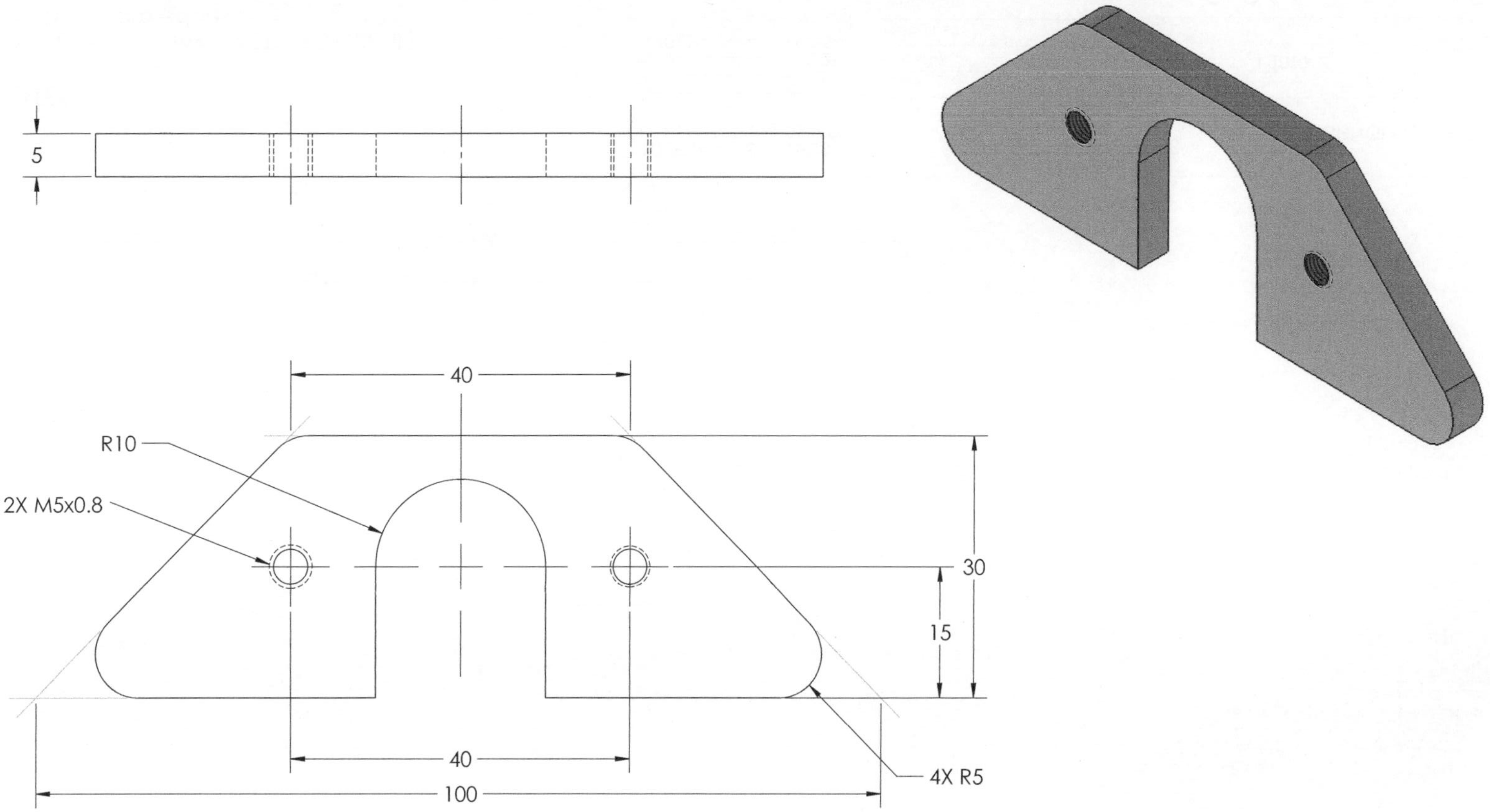

NOTES

1- Material Mild Steel (ASTM A36 Steel)
2- Deburr sharp edges

TOLERANCES UNLESS OTHERWISE SPECIFIED

X---------------------- +/- 1
X.X------------------- +/- 0.5
X.XX----------------- +/- 0.2
ANGLE-------------- +/- 0.5

ALL DIMENSIONS IN MM

FIRST ISSUED
DRAWN BY
CHECKED BY
APPROVED BY

CADCIM TECHNOLOGIES

Plate 1

SIZE	DRG NO.	SHEET REV
A3	3-010	A
SCALE 2:1		SHEET 12 OF 13

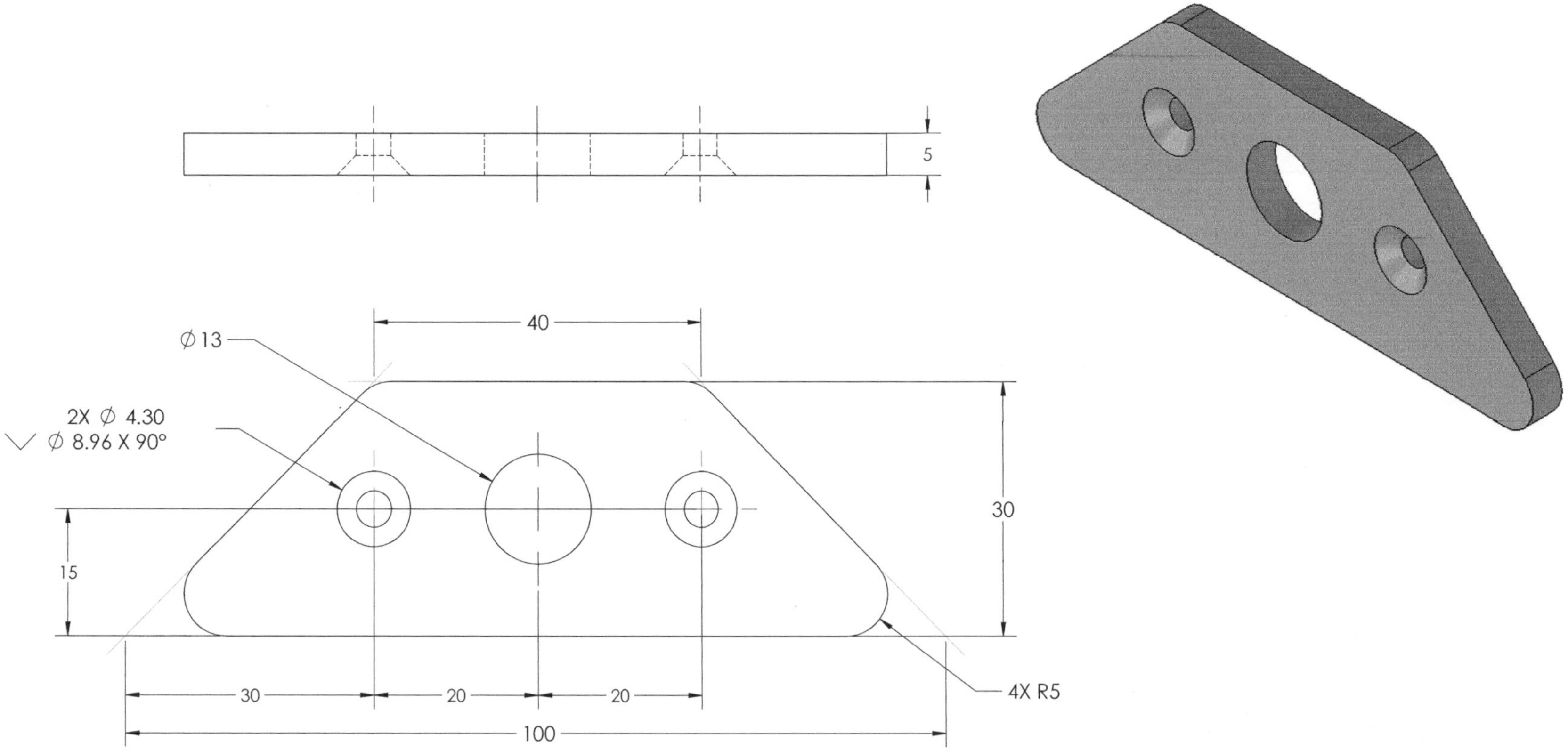

NOTES

1- Material Mild Steel (ASTM A36 Steel)
2- Deburr sharp edges

TOLERANCES UNLESS OTHERWISE SPECIFIED

X---------------------- +/- 1
X.X------------------ +/- 0.5
X.XX---------------- +/- 0.2
ANGLE-------------- +/- 0.5

ALL DIMENSIONS IN MM

FIRST ISSUED
DRAWN BY
CHECKED BY
APPROVED BY

CADCIM TECHNOLOGIES

Plate 2

SIZE A3 | DRG NO. 3-011 | SHEET REV A

SCALE 2:1 | SHEET 13 OF 13

Project 4

Hand Punch Press Assembly

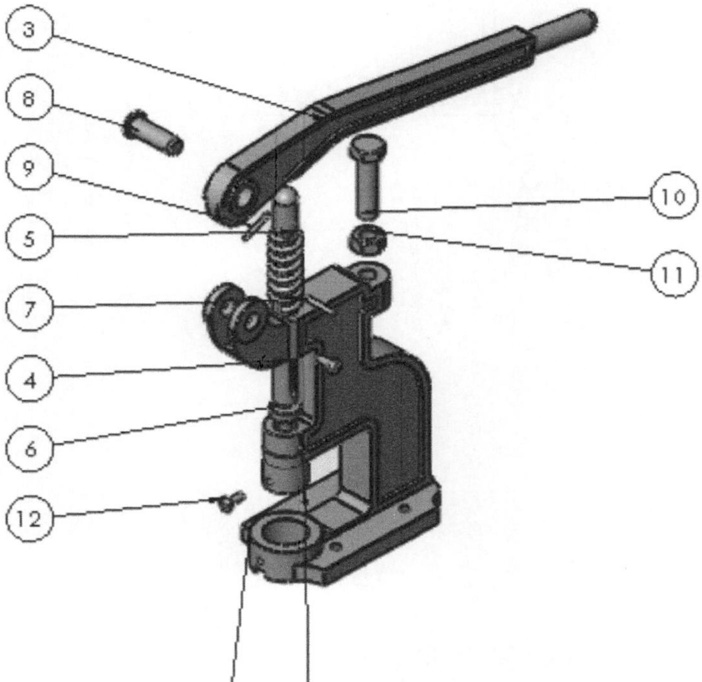

ITEM NO.	PART NUMBER	QTY.
1	Body	1
2	Mould	1
3	Lever	1
4	Punch tool Holder	1
5	Spring	1
6	Punch Tool	1
7	Taper Pin	1
8	Clevis Pin 20X60X5-ISO2341	1
9	Split Pin 5X 25- ISO1234	1
10	M20X1.5 Hex bolt-ANSI B18.2.3.5M	1
11	M20X1.5 Hex Nut-ANSI B18.2.4.1M	1
12	M8X1.25X20- Pan Slot head Screw-ANSI B18.6.7M	2

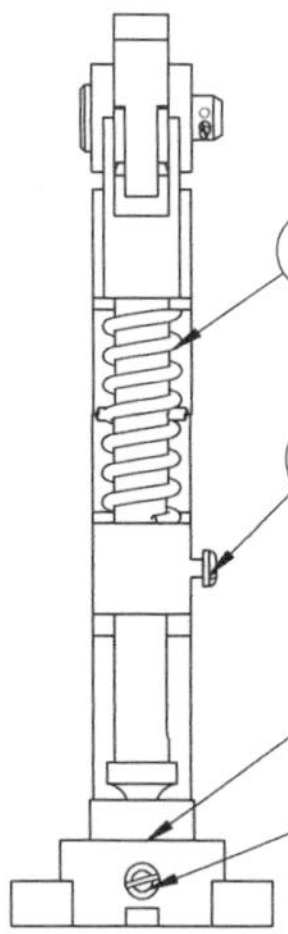

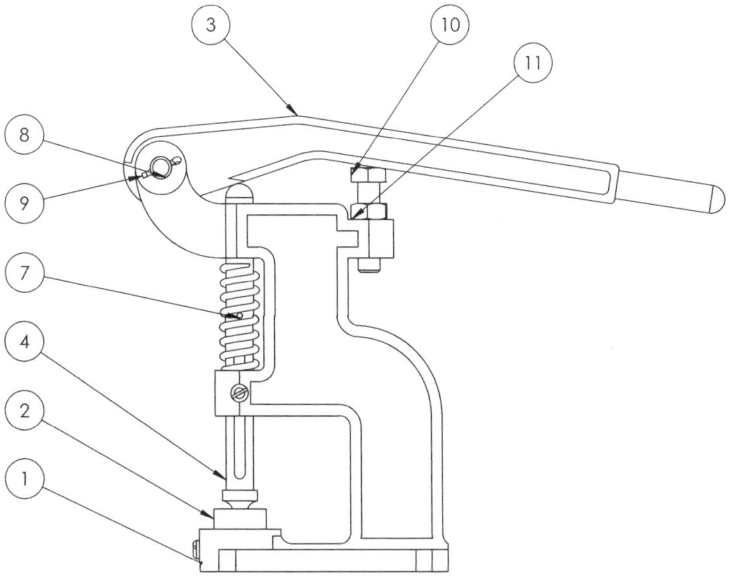

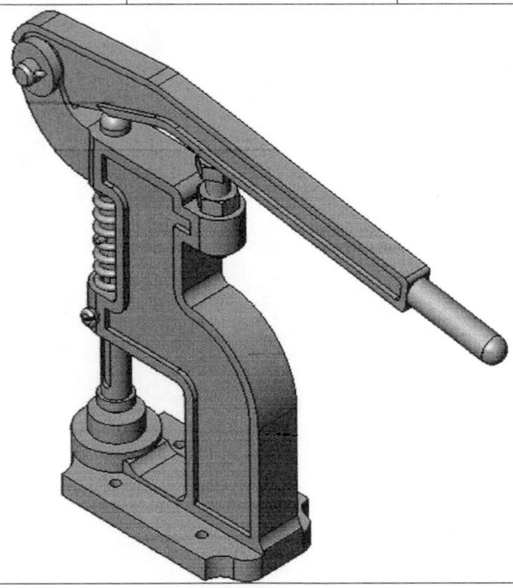

TOLERANCES UNLESS OTHERWISE SPECIFIED

X---------------------- +/- 1
X.X------------------ +/- 0.5
X.XX----------------- +/- 0.2
ANGLE-------------- +/- 0.5

ALL DIMENSIONS IN MM

FIRST ISSUED	
DRAWN BY	
CHECKED BY	
APPROVED BY	

CADCIM TECHNOLOGIES

Hand Punch Press Assembly

SIZE	DRG NO.	SHEET REV
A3	4-000	A
SCALE 1:4		SHEET 1 OF 7

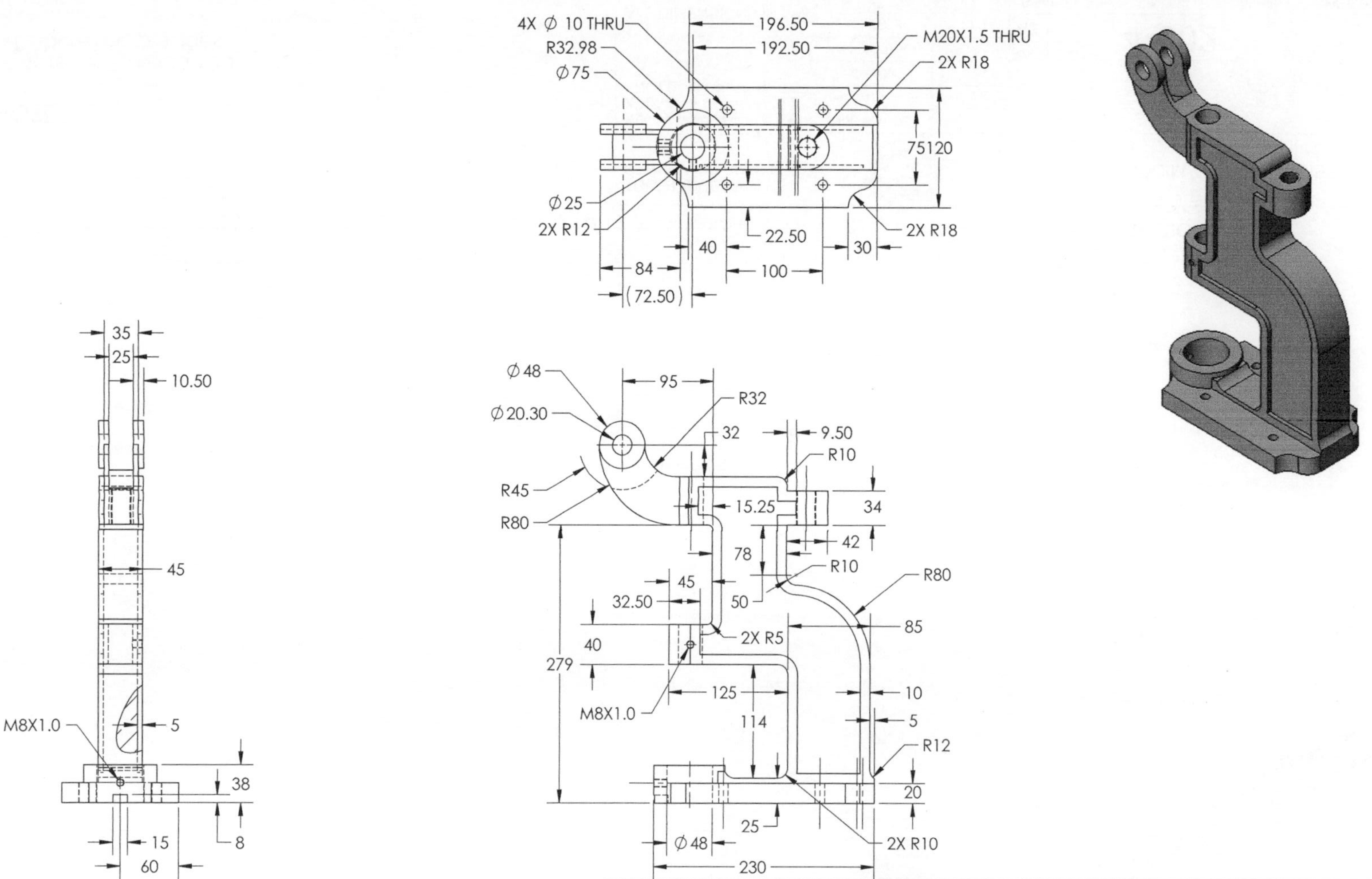

NOTES

1- Material Gray Cast Iron
2- Debure sharp edges

TOLERANCES UNLESS OTHERWISE SPECIFIED		CADCIM TECHNOLOGIES			
X---------- +/- 1	FIRST ISSUED	Body			
X.X---------- +/- 0.5	DRAWN BY				
X.XX---------- +/- 0.2	CHECKED BY				
ANGLE---------- +/- 0.5	APPROVED BY	SIZE A3	DRG NO. 4-001		SHEET REV A
ALL DIMENSIONS IN MM		SCALE 1:4		SHEET 2 OF 7	

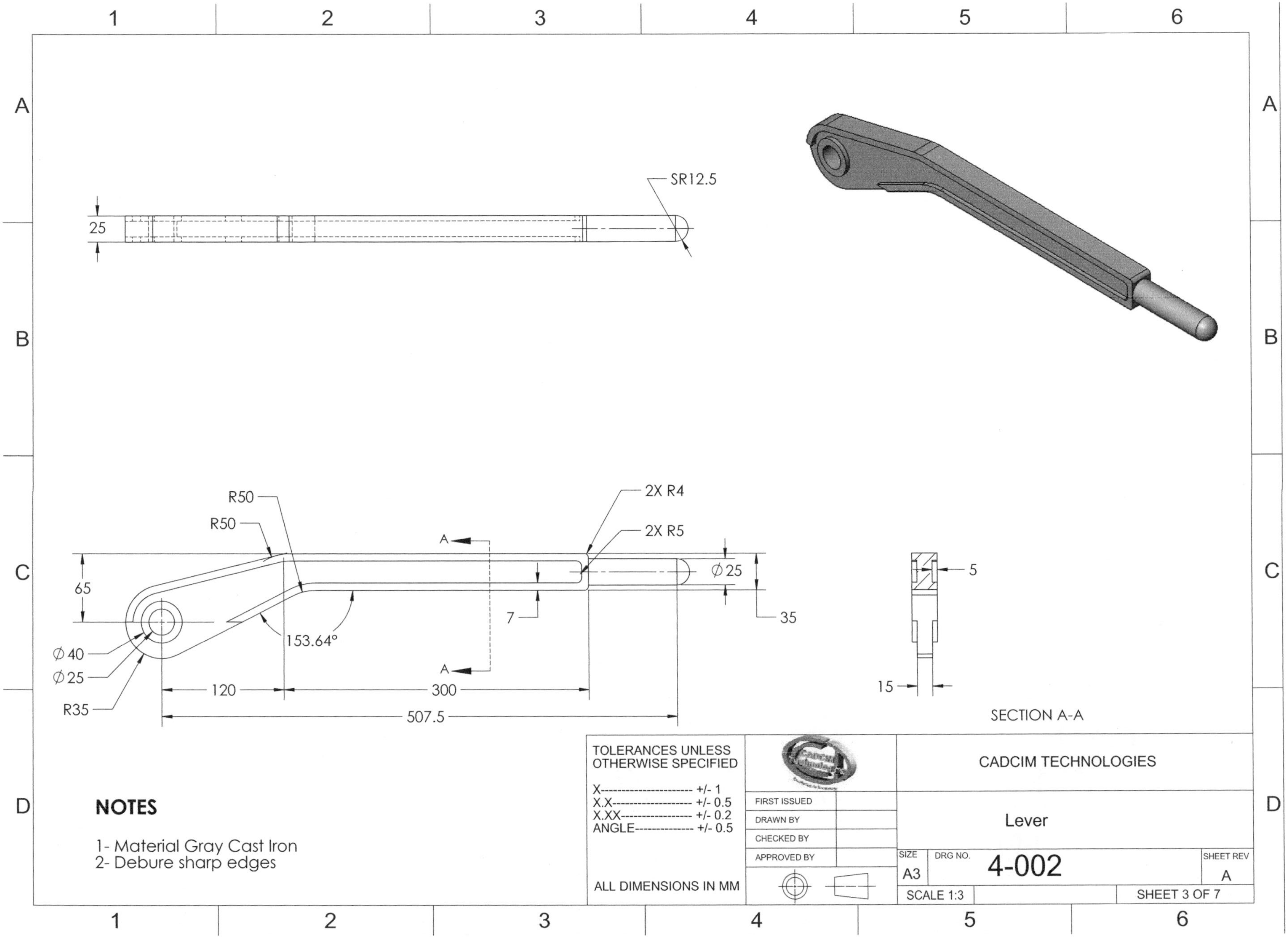
SR12.5
25
R50
R50
2X R4
2X R5
A
A
65
⌀25
35
7
153.64°
⌀40
⌀25
R35
120
300
507.5
5
15
SECTION A-A
NOTES
1- Material Gray Cast Iron
2- Debure sharp edges
TOLERANCES UNLESS OTHERWISE SPECIFIED
X---------- +/- 1
X.X---------- +/- 0.5
X.XX---------- +/- 0.2
ANGLE---------- +/- 0.5
ALL DIMENSIONS IN MM
FIRST ISSUED
DRAWN BY
CHECKED BY
APPROVED BY
CADCIM TECHNOLOGIES
Lever
SIZE A3
DRG NO. 4-002
SHEET REV A
SCALE 1:3
SHEET 3 OF 7

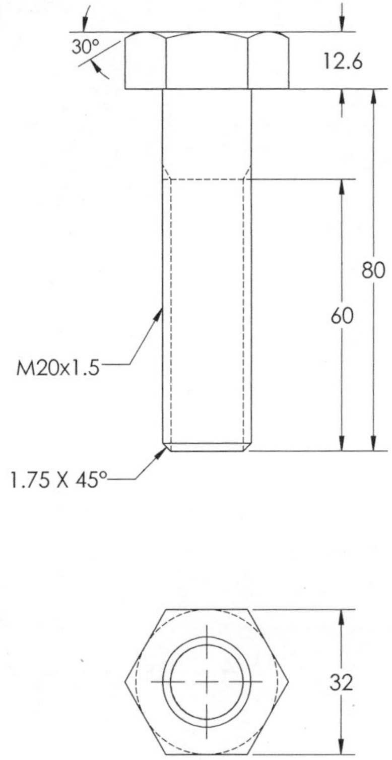

M20X1.5 Bolt

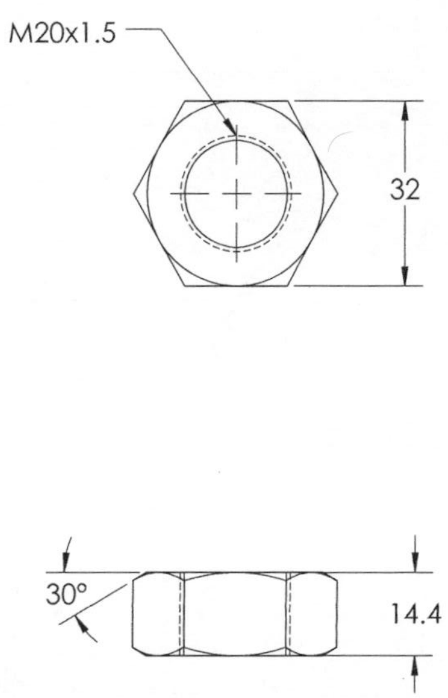

M20X1.5 Nut

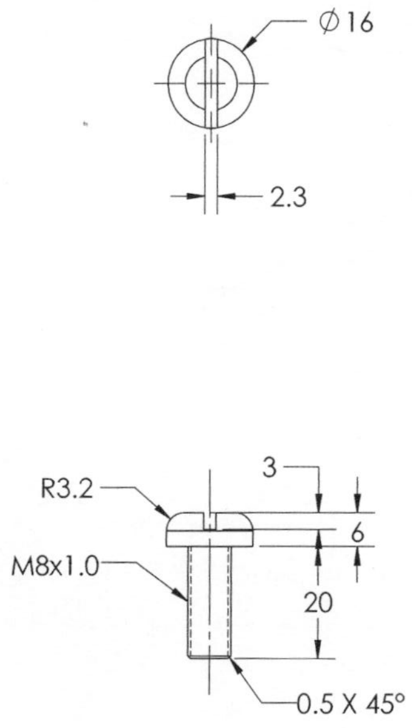

M8X1.0X20 Pan slot screw

NOTES

1- Material Stainless Steel
2- Debure sharp edges

CADCIM TECHNOLOGIES

1. M20X1.5 Hex bolt- ANSI B18.2.3.5M
2. M20X1.5 Hex Nut- ANSI B18.2.4.1M
3. M8X1.0X20 Pan slot screw- ANSI B18.6.7.1M

FIRST ISSUED		SIZE	DRG NO.	SHEET REV
DRAWN BY		A3	4-003	A
CHECKED BY		SCALE 1:1		SHEET 4 OF 7
APPROVED BY				

ALL DIMENSIONS IN MM

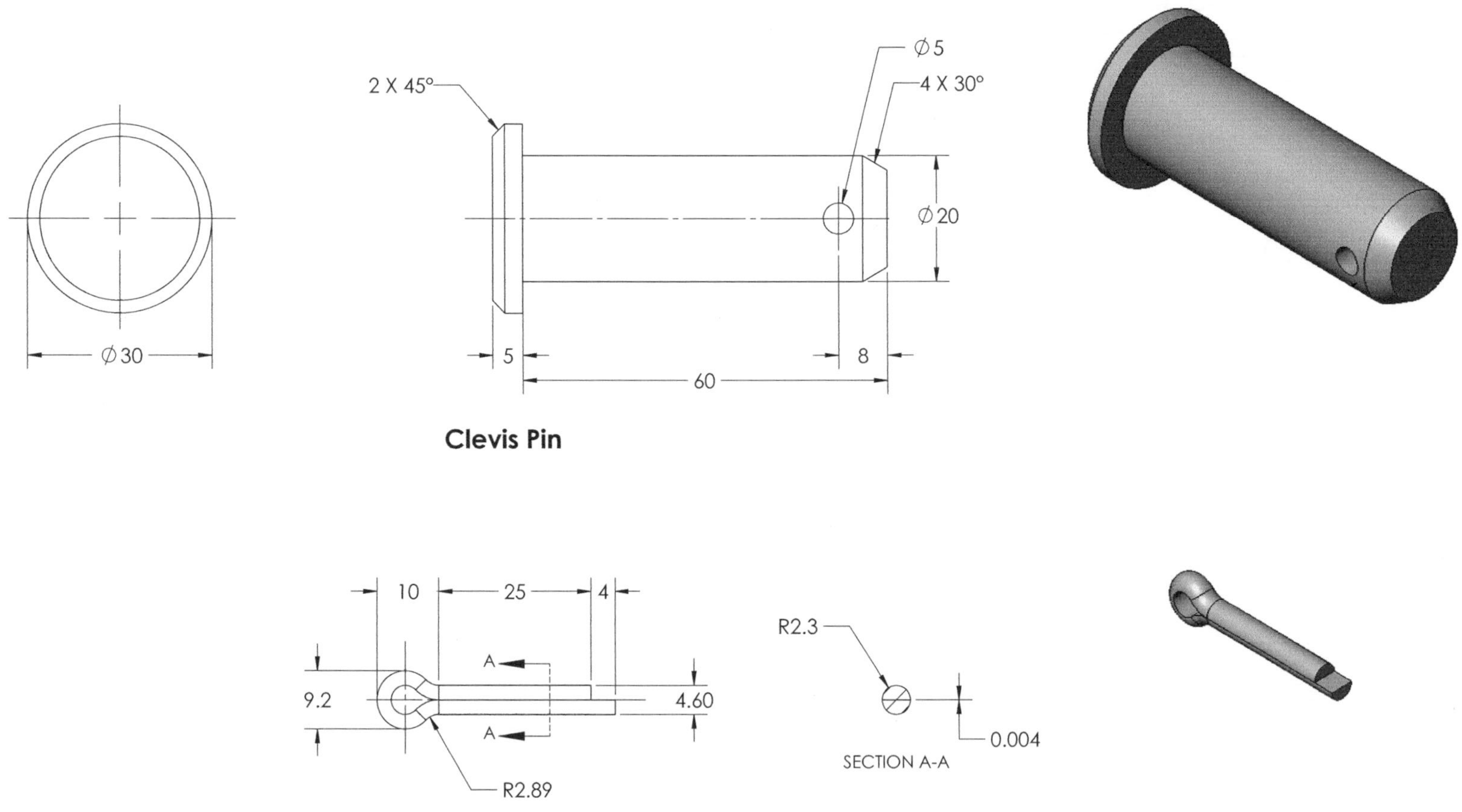

Clevis Pin

Split Pin

NOTES

1- Material Stainless Steel
2- Debure sharp edges

ALL DIMENSIONS IN MM	FIRST ISSUED / DRAWN BY / CHECKED BY / APPROVED BY	CADCIM TECHNOLOGIES
		1. Clevis Pin 20X60X5 (Headed)-ISO 2341 2. Split Pin 5X25-ISO 1234
		SIZE A3 — DRG NO. 4-004 — SHEET REV A
		SCALE 3:2 — SHEET 5 OF 7

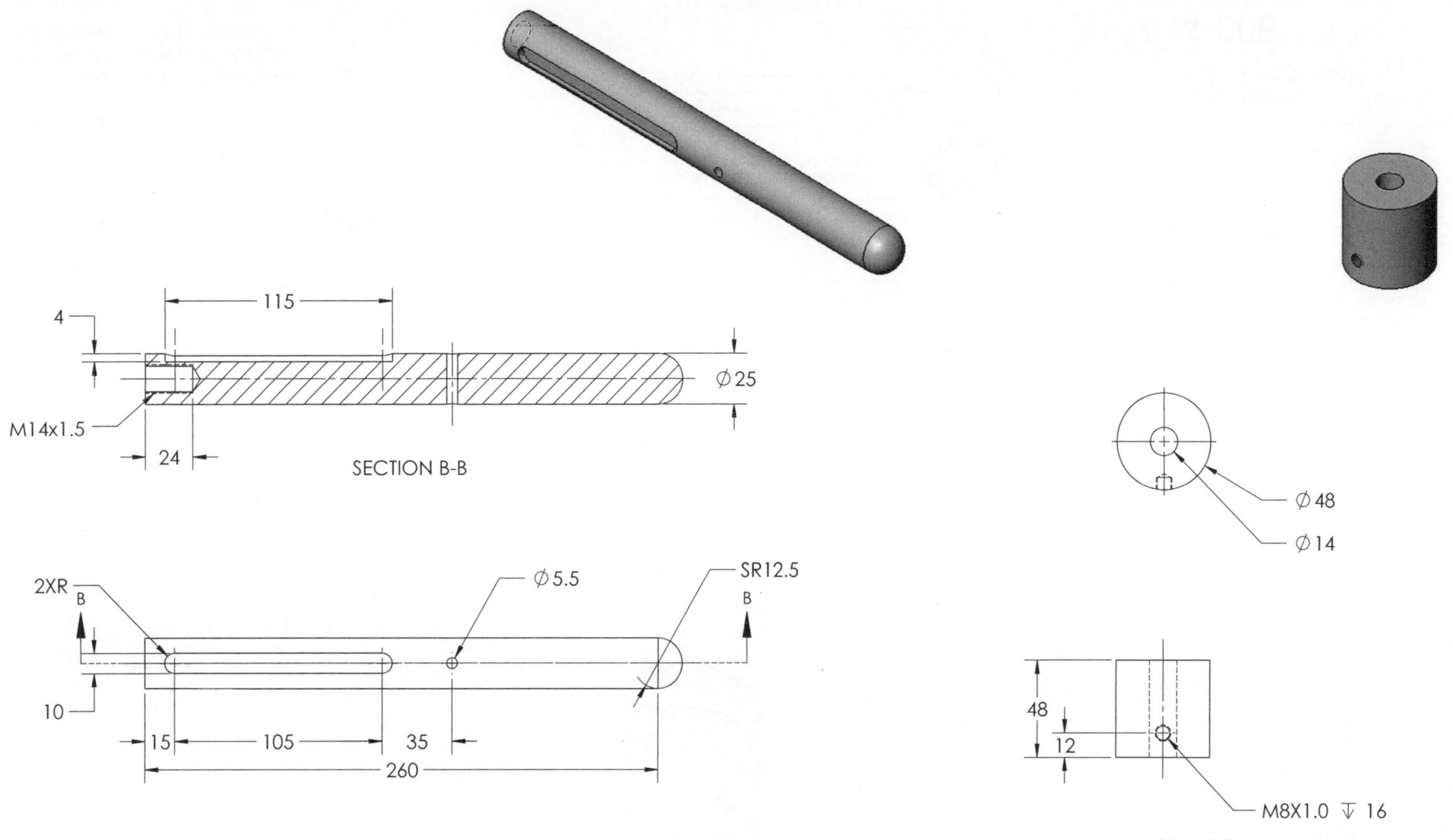

Punch Tool Holder

Mould

NOTES

1- Material Gray Cast Iron
2- Debure sharp edges

TOLERANCES UNLESS OTHERWISE SPECIFIED		CADCIM TECHNOLOGIES
X-------- +/- 1 X.X-------- +/- 0.5 X.XX-------- +/- 0.2 ANGLE-------- +/- 0.5	FIRST ISSUED DRAWN BY CHECKED BY APPROVED BY	1. Punch tool holder 2. Mould
ALL DIMENSIONS IN MM		SIZE A3 · DRG NO. 4-005 · SHEET REV A
		SCALE 1:2 · SHEET 6 OF 7

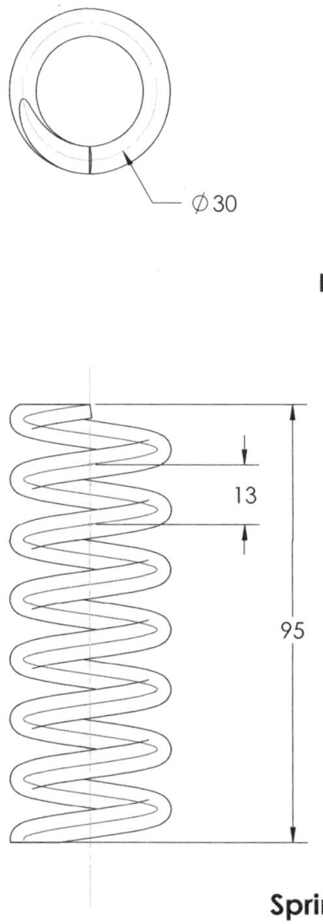

Dia of Spring 6 mm

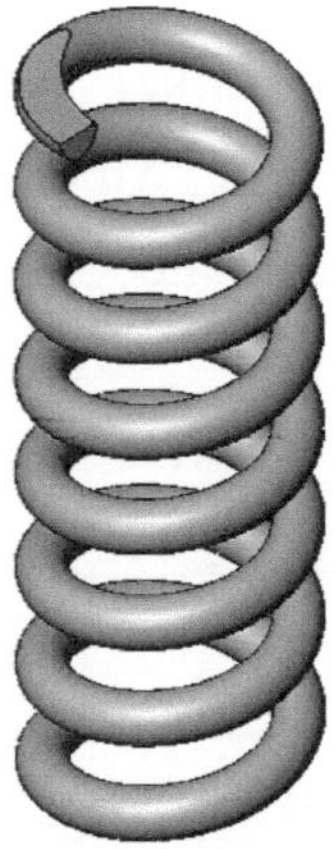

Spring

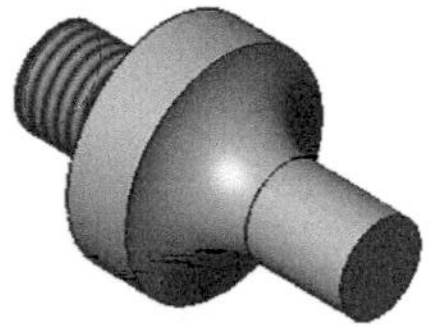

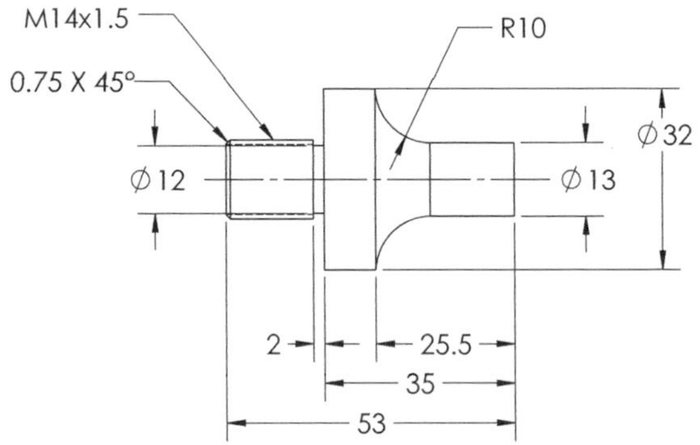

Punch Tool

NOTES

1- Material Alloy Steel wire for Spring and ASTM A36 Steel for punch tool
2- Debure sharp edges

TOLERANCES UNLESS OTHERWISE SPECIFIED		CADCIM TECHNOLOGIES
X---------- +/- 1 X.X---------- +/- 0.5 X.XX---------- +/- 0.2 ANGLE---------- +/- 0.5	FIRST ISSUED DRAWN BY CHECKED BY APPROVED BY	1. Spring 2. Punch Tool
ALL DIMENSIONS IN MM		SIZE A3 | DRG NO. 4-006 | SHEET REV A SCALE 1:1 | SHEET 7 OF 7

Project 5

Ball Valve Assembly

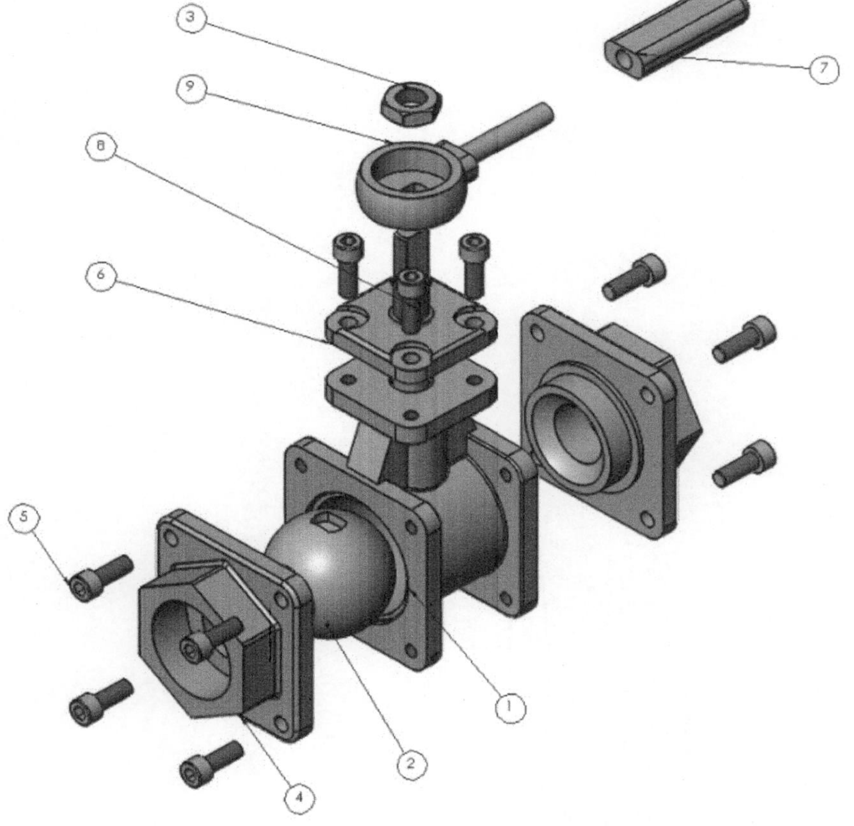

ITEM NO.	PART NUMBER	QTY.
1	Valve body	1
2	Ball	1
3	M16X2.0 Hex Jam Nut-ANSI B18.2.5M	1
4	Side Flange	2
5	M8X1.2 5Socket Head Cap Screw- ANSI B18.3.1M	12
6	Upper Flange	1
7	Handle Cover	1
8	Stem	1
9	Lever	1

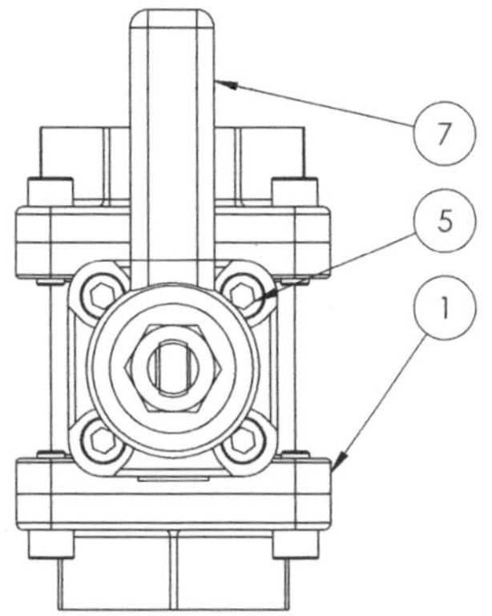

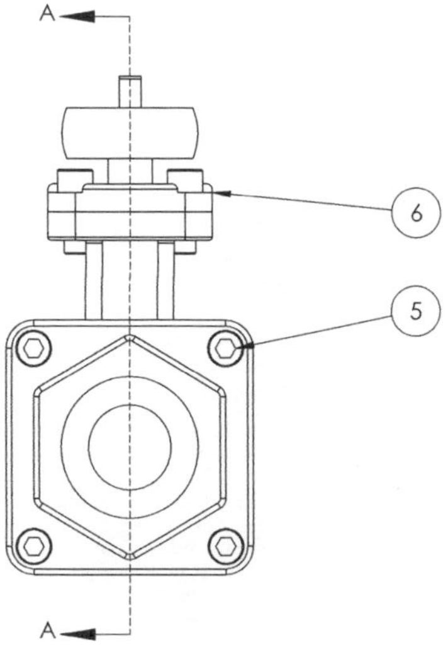

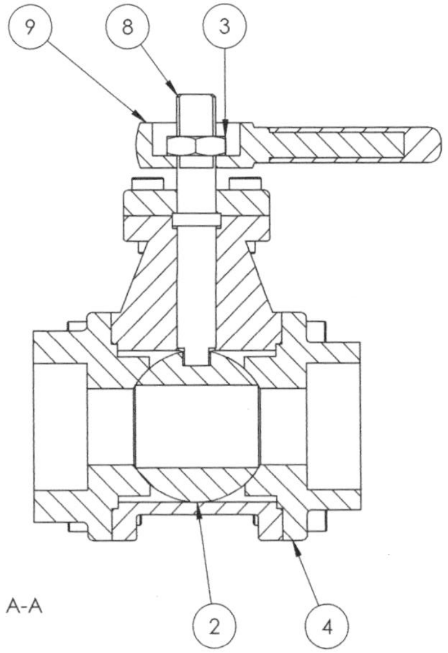

SECTION A-A

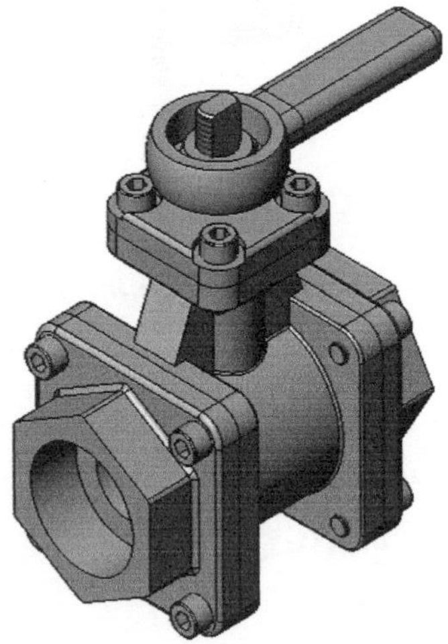

TOLERANCES UNLESS OTHERWISE SPECIFIED

X---------------------- +/- 1
X.X-------------------- +/- 0.5
X.XX------------------ +/- 0.2
ANGLE--------------- +/- 0.5

ALL DIMENSIONS IN MM

FIRST ISSUED
DRAWN BY
CHECKED BY
APPROVED BY

CADCIM TECHNOLOGIES

Ball Valve

SIZE A3 | DRG NO. 5-000 | SHEET REV A

SCALE 1:2 | SHEET 1 OF 9

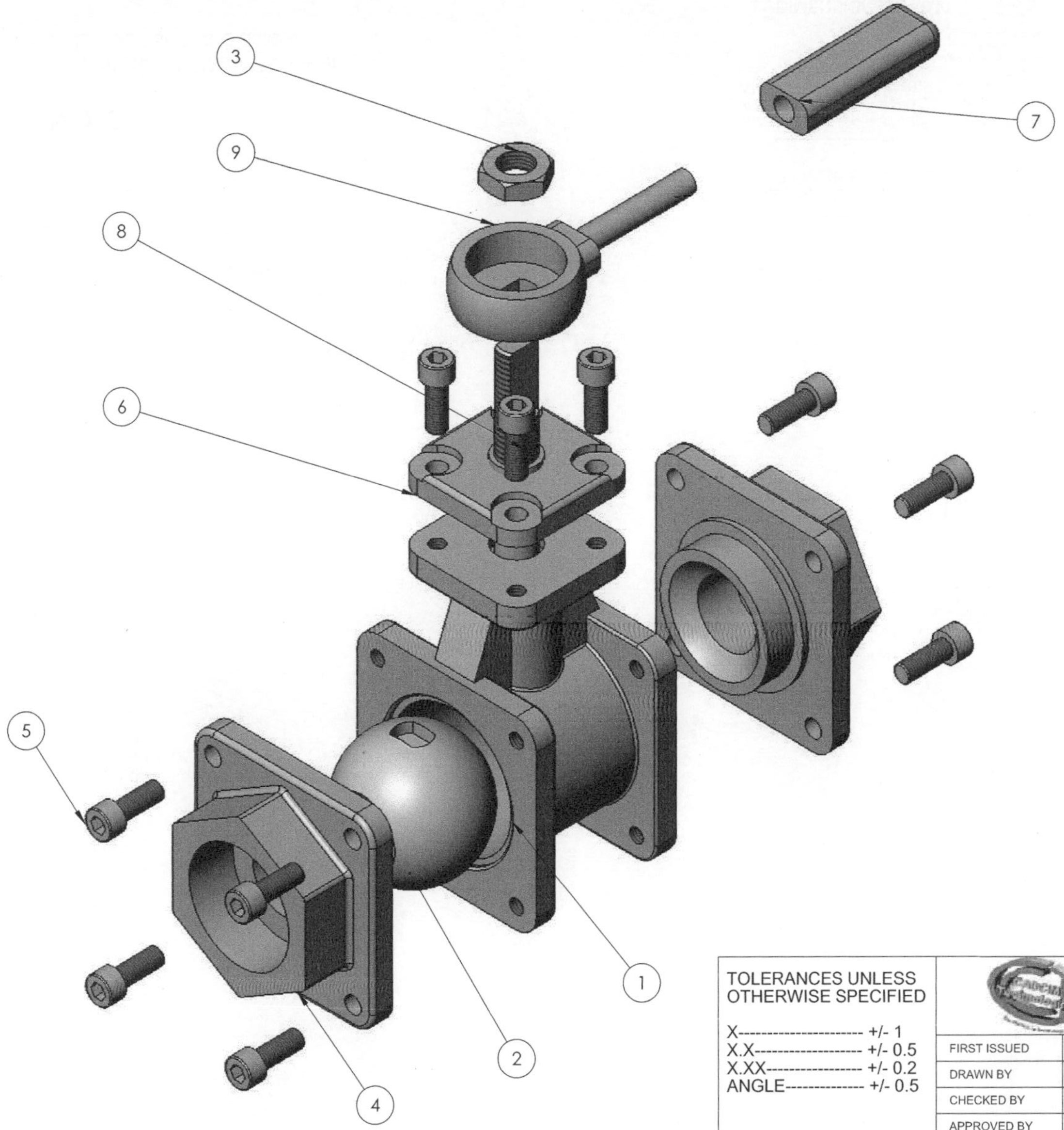

ITEM NO.	PART NUMBER	QTY.
1	Valve body	1
2	Ball	1
3	M16X2.0 Hex Jam Nut-ANSI B18.2.5M	1
4	Side Flange	2
5	M8X1.2 5Socket Head Cap Screw- ANSI B18.3.1M	12
6	Upper Flange	1
7	Handle Cover	1
8	Stem	1
9	Lever	1

TOLERANCES UNLESS OTHERWISE SPECIFIED

X---------------------- +/- 1
X.X-------------------- +/- 0.5
X.XX------------------ +/- 0.2
ANGLE--------------- +/- 0.5

ALL DIMENSIONS IN MM

FIRST ISSUED
DRAWN BY
CHECKED BY
APPROVED BY

CADCIM TECHNOLOGIES

Ball Valve Exploded

SIZE	DRG NO.	SHEET REV
A3	5-000	A
SCALE 2:3		SHEET 2 OF 9

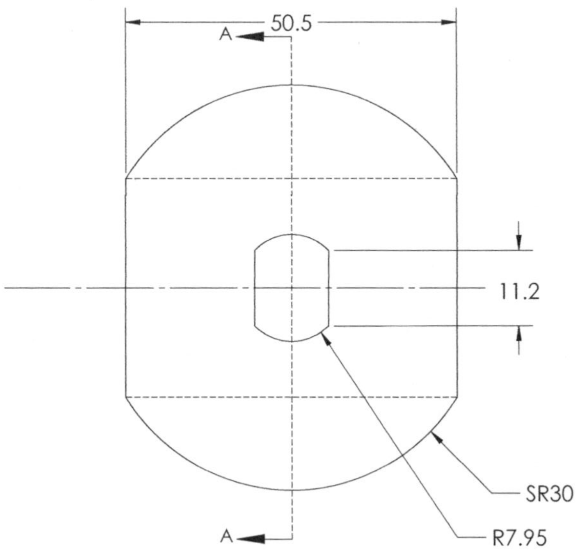

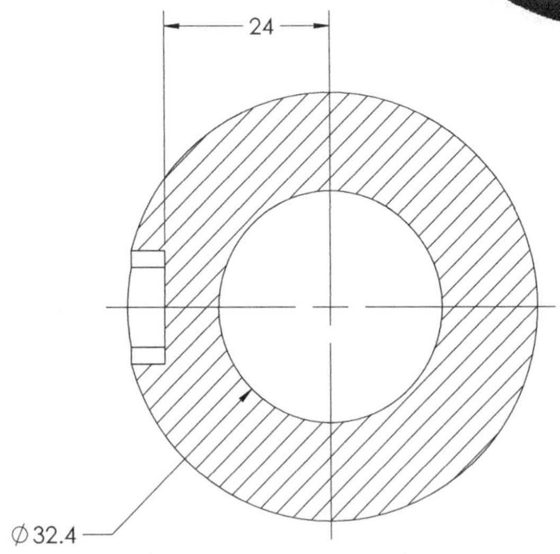

SECTION A-A

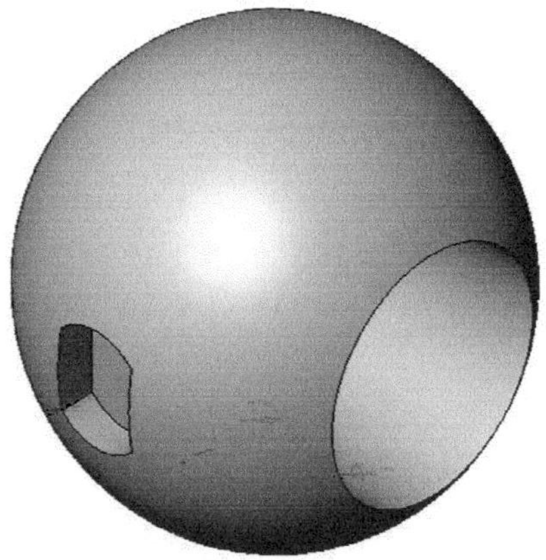

NOTES

1- Material ASTM A36 Steel
2- Deburr sharp edges

TOLERANCES UNLESS OTHERWISE SPECIFIED		CADCIM TECHNOLOGIES
X---------- +/- 1	FIRST ISSUED	Ball
X.X---------- +/- 0.5	DRAWN BY	
X.XX---------- +/- 0.2	CHECKED BY	
ANGLE---------- +/- 0.5	APPROVED BY	SIZE A3 · DRG NO. 5-001 · SHEET REV A
ALL DIMENSIONS IN MM		SCALE 3:2 · SHEET 3 OF 9

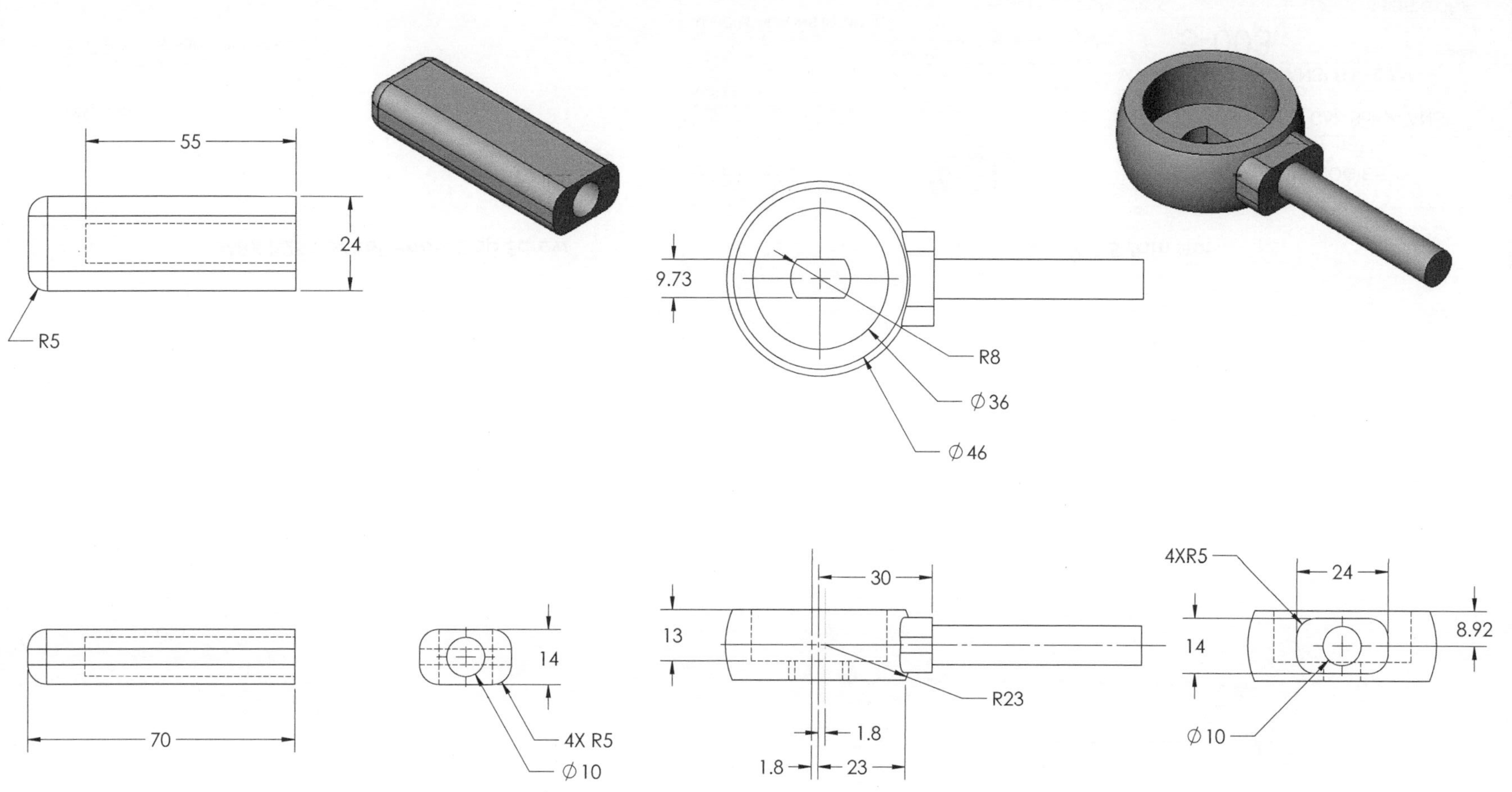

Handle Cover

Lever

NOTES

1- Material PBT for Handle Cover and ASTM A36 for handle
2- Deburr sharp edges

TOLERANCES UNLESS OTHERWISE SPECIFIED		CADCIM TECHNOLOGIES		
X---------- +/- 1	FIRST ISSUED	Handle Cover		
X.X---------- +/- 0.5	DRAWN BY			
X.XX---------- +/- 0.2	CHECKED BY			
ANGLE---------- +/- 0.5	APPROVED BY	SIZE A3	DRG NO. 5-002	SHEET REV A
ALL DIMENSIONS IN MM		SCALE 2:1		SHEET 4 OF 9

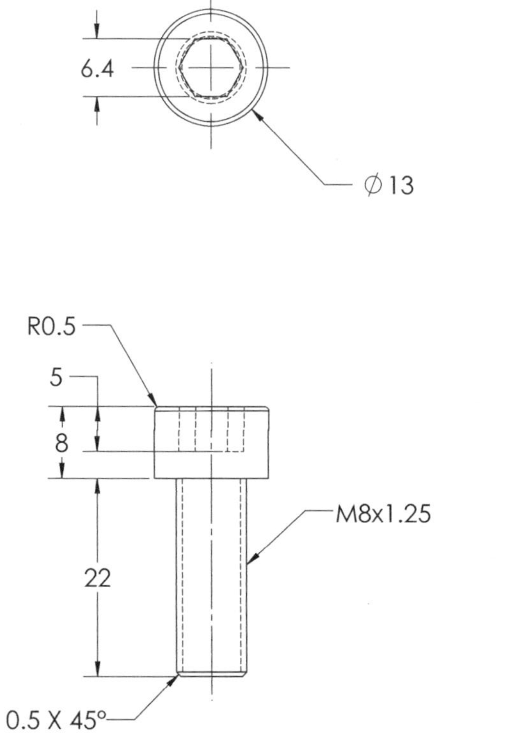

M8X1.25 Socket Head Cap Screw

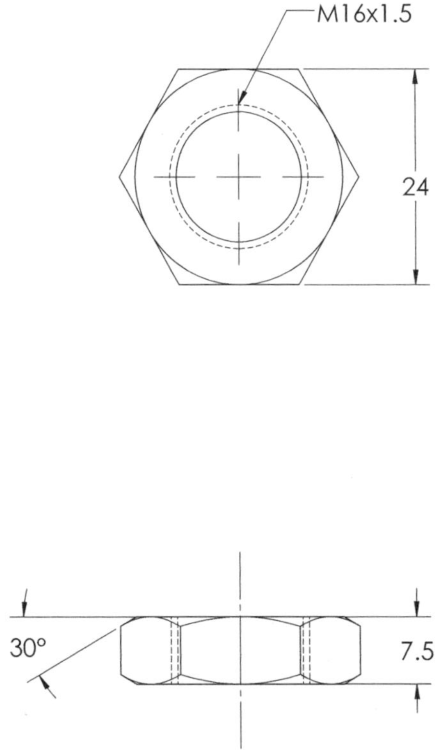

M16X 1.5 Jam Nut

NOTES

1- Material S.S
2- Deburr sharp edges

TOLERANCES UNLESS OTHERWISE SPECIFIED		CADCIM TECHNOLOGIES
X---------- +/- 1	FIRST ISSUED	1. M8X1.25 Socket Head Cap Scew- ANSI B18.3.1M
X.X---------- +/- 0.5	DRAWN BY	2. M16x 1.5 Jam Nut - ANSI B18.2.5M
X.XX---------- +/- 0.2	CHECKED BY	SIZE A3 · DRG NO. 5-003 · SHEET REV A
ANGLE---------- +/- 0.5	APPROVED BY	SCALE 2:1 · SHEET 5 OF 9
ALL DIMENSIONS IN MM		

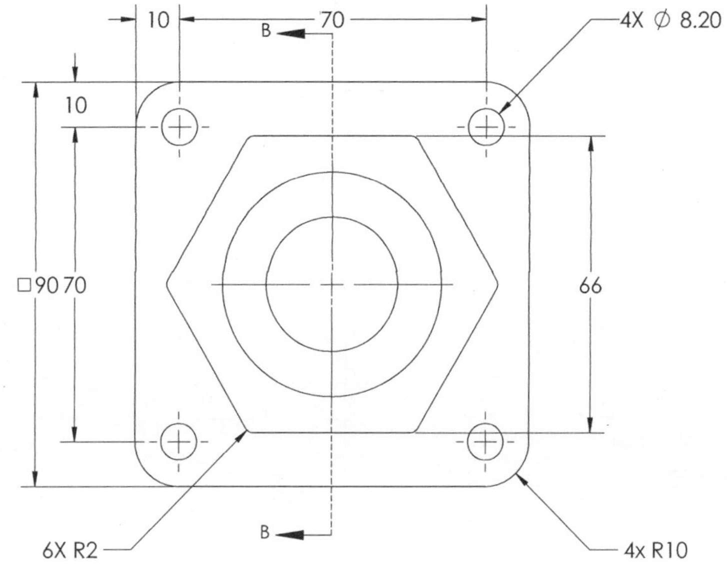

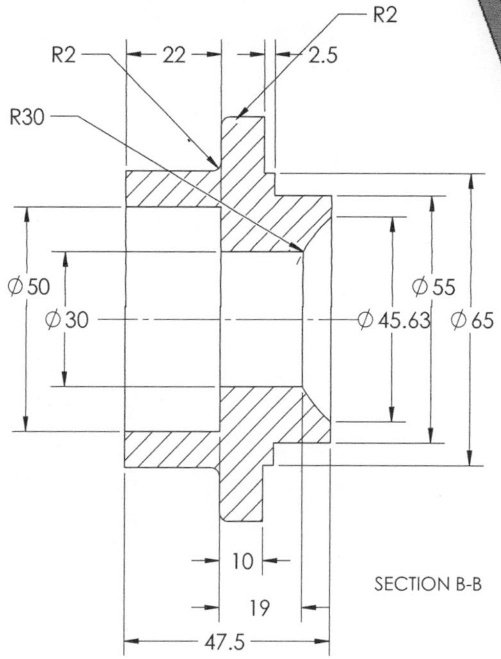

SECTION B-B

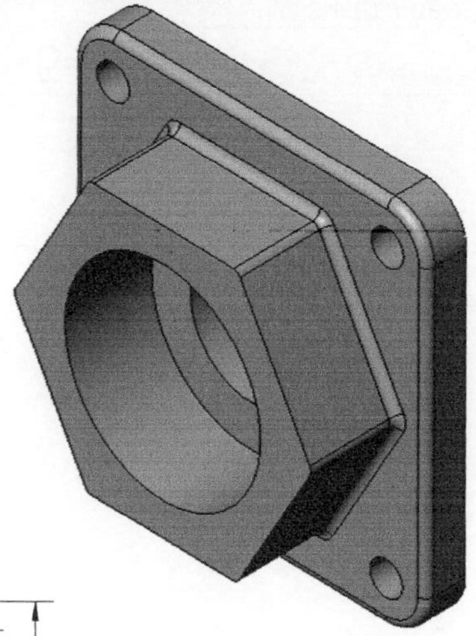

NOTES

1- Material ASTM A36 Steel
2- Deburr sharp edges

TOLERANCES UNLESS OTHERWISE SPECIFIED

X---------------------- +/- 1
X.X------------------- +/- 0.5
X.XX----------------- +/- 0.2
ANGLE-------------- +/- 0.5

ALL DIMENSIONS IN MM

FIRST ISSUED
DRAWN BY
CHECKED BY
APPROVED BY

CADCIM TECHNOLOGIES

Side Flange

SIZE	DRG NO.	SHEET REV
A3	5-004	A
SCALE 1:1		SHEET 6 OF 9

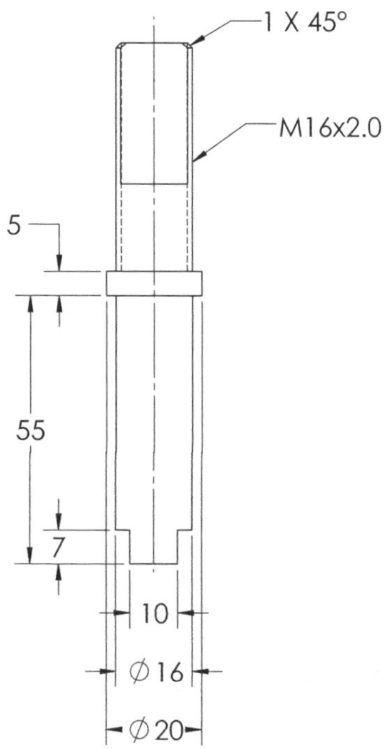

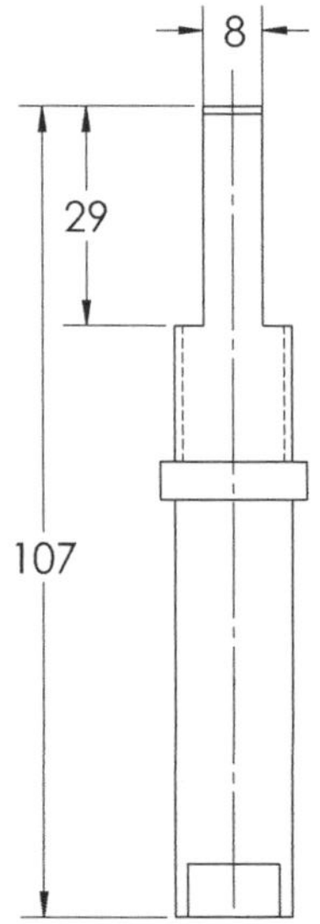

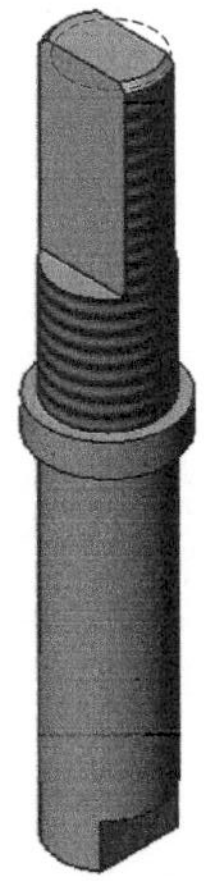

NOTES

1- Material Stainless Steel
2- Deburr sharp edges

TOLERANCES UNLESS OTHERWISE SPECIFIED		CADCIM TECHNOLOGIES
X------ +/- 1 X.X------ +/- 0.5 X.XX------ +/- 0.2 ANGLE------ +/- 0.5	FIRST ISSUED DRAWN BY CHECKED BY APPROVED BY	Stem
ALL DIMENSIONS IN MM		SIZE A3 · DRG NO. 5-005 · SHEET REV A
		SCALE 1:1 · SHEET 7 OF 9

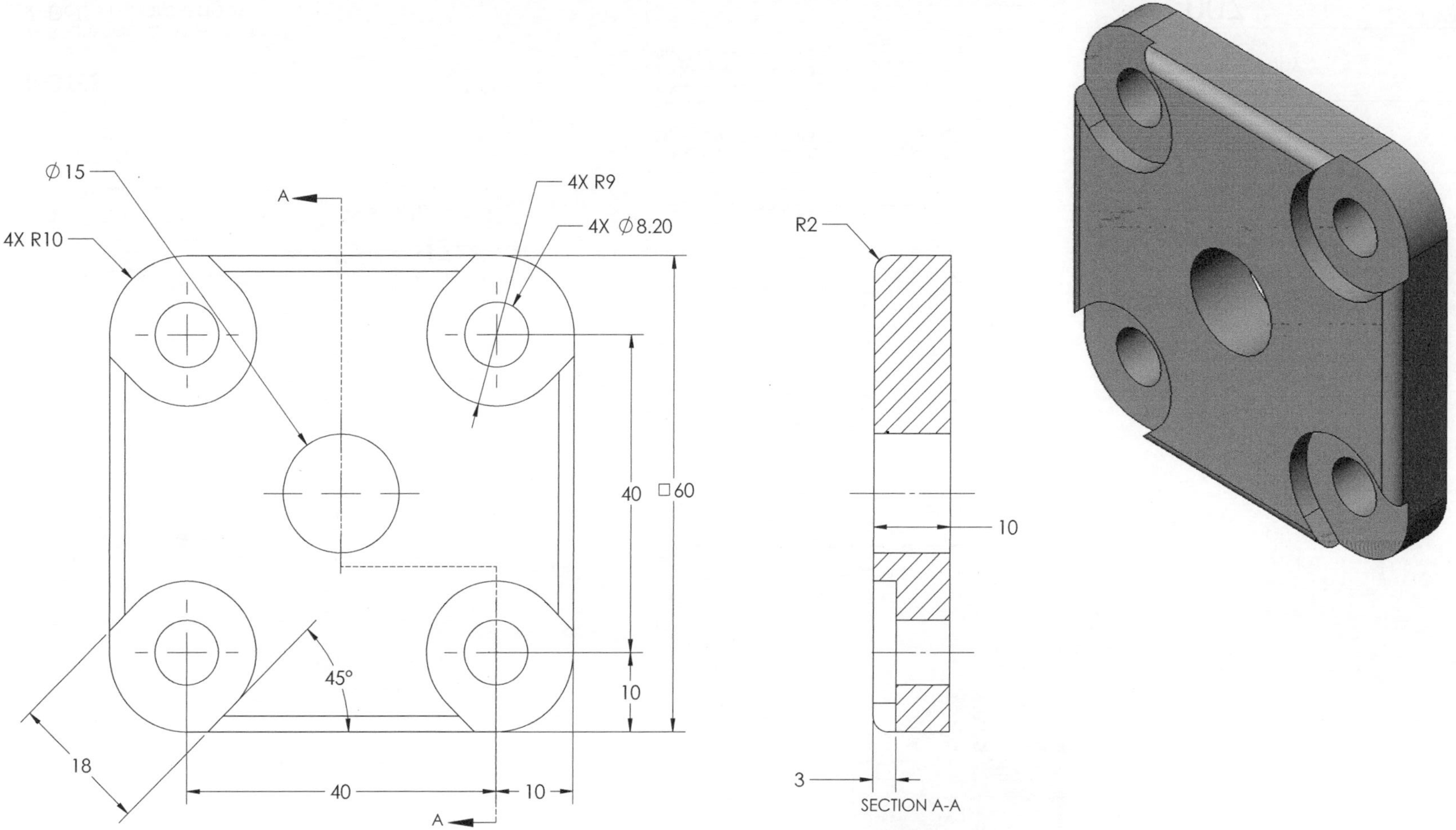

NOTES

1- Material ASTM A36 Steel
2- Deburr sharp edges

TOLERANCES UNLESS OTHERWISE SPECIFIED

X---------------------- +/- 1
X.X-------------------- +/- 0.5
X.XX------------------ +/- 0.2
ANGLE--------------- +/- 0.5

ALL DIMENSIONS IN MM

FIRST ISSUED
DRAWN BY
CHECKED BY
APPROVED BY

CADCIM TECHNOLOGIES

Upper Flange

SIZE	DRG NO.	SHEET REV
A3	5-006	A

SCALE 2:1 | SHEET 8 OF 9

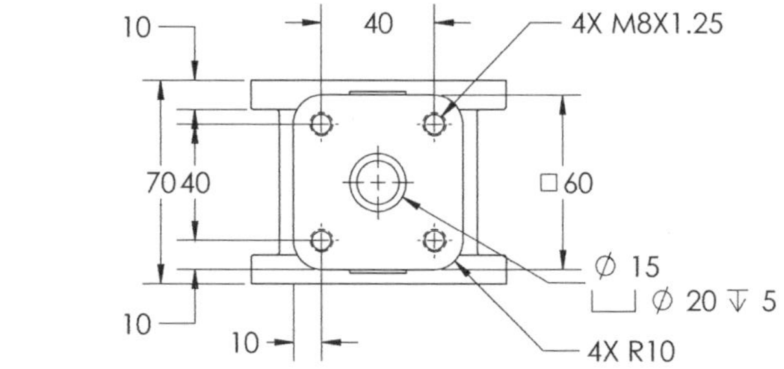

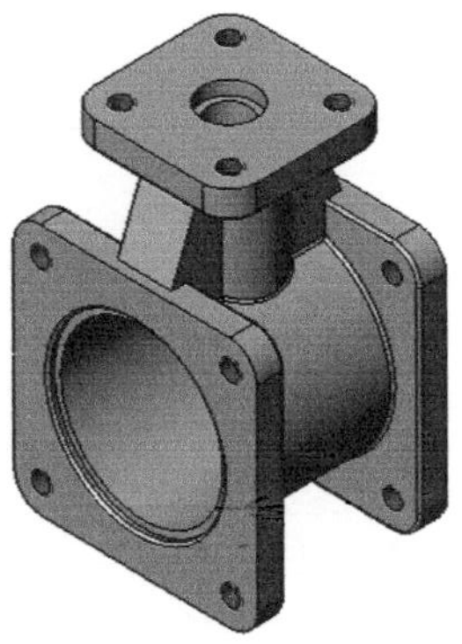

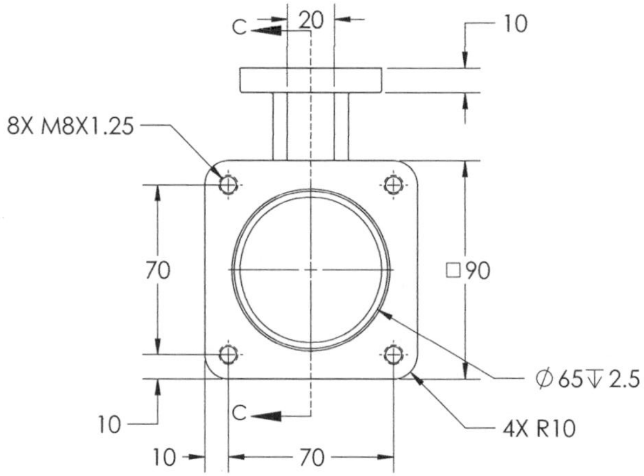

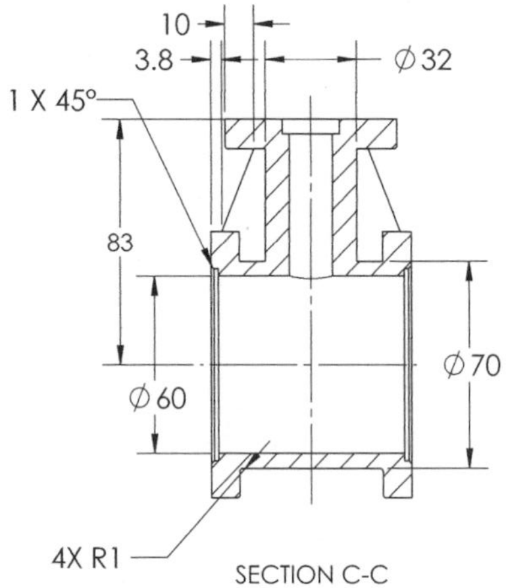

SECTION C-C

NOTES

1- Material ASTM A36 Steel
2- Deburr sharp edges

TOLERANCES UNLESS OTHERWISE SPECIFIED

X---------------------- +/- 1
X.X-------------------- +/- 0.5
X.XX------------------ +/- 0.2
ANGLE--------------- +/- 0.5

ALL DIMENSIONS IN MM

FIRST ISSUED	
DRAWN BY	
CHECKED BY	
APPROVED BY	

CADCIM TECHNOLOGIES

Valve Body

SIZE	DRG NO.	SHEET REV
A3	5-007	A
SCALE 1:2		SHEET 9 OF 9

Project 6

Pneumatic Gripper Assembly

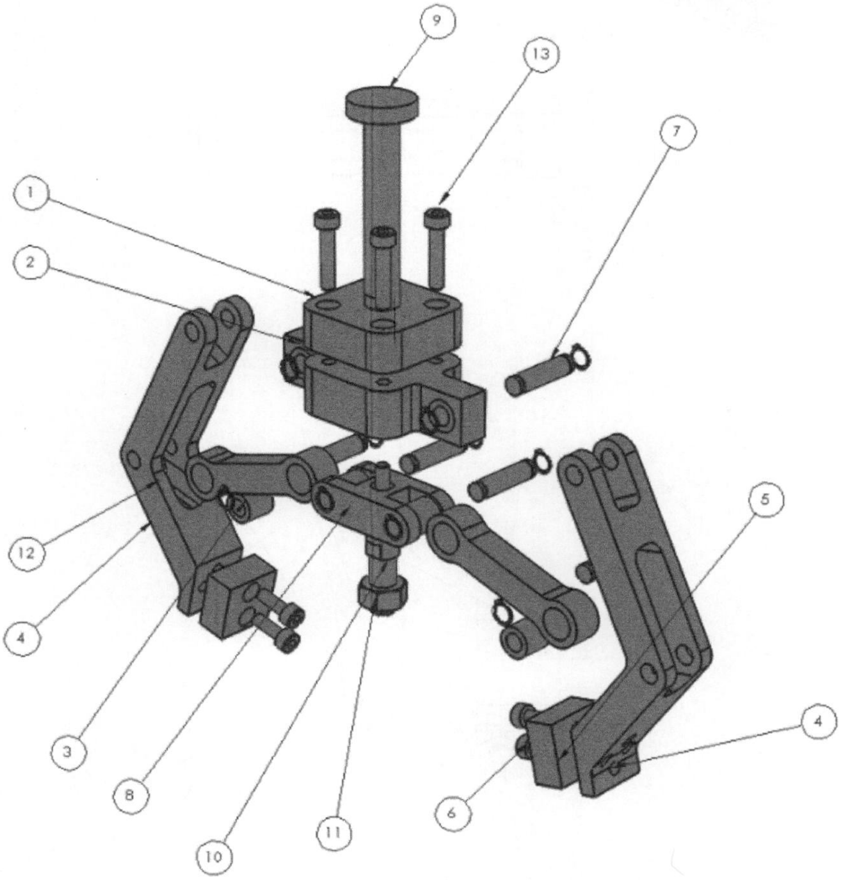

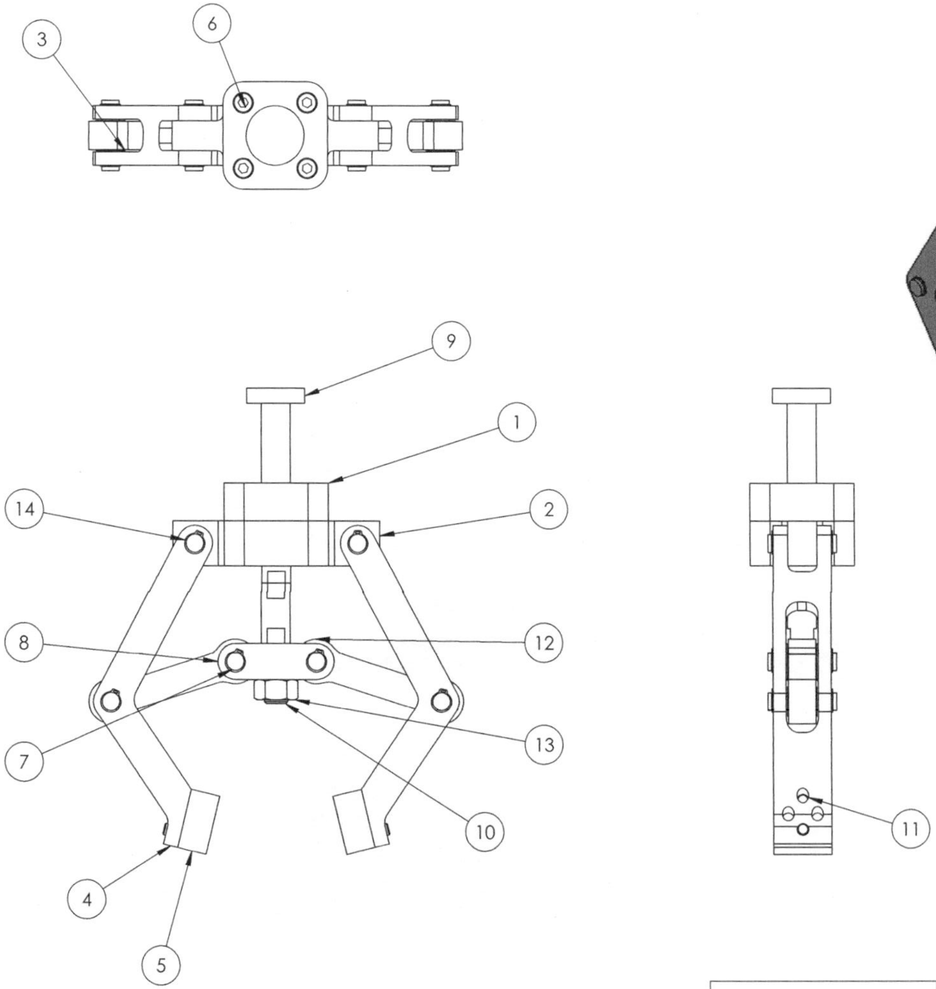

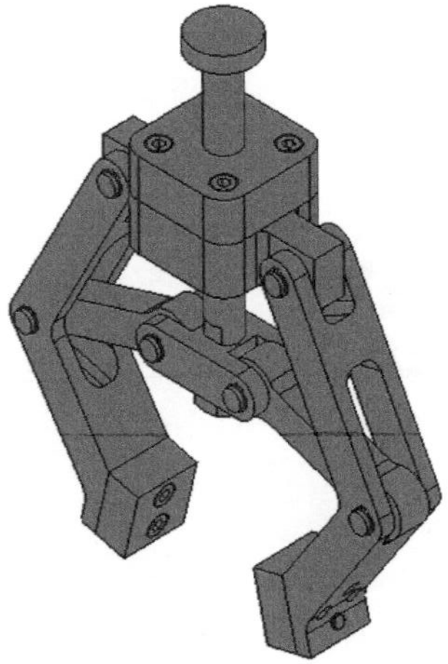

ITEM NO.	PART NUMBER	QTY.
1	Base Pad	1
2	Base	1
3	Bush	6
4	Arm	2
5	Pad	2
6	M4X0.7X20 Socket Head Cap Screw - ANSI B18.3.1M	4
7	Pin	6
8	Support Link	1
9	lever	1
10	Adjusting Rod	1
11	M4X0.7X11 Socket Head Cap Screw - ANSI B18.3.1M	4
12	link	2
13	M8X1.25 Hex Nut-ANSI B18.2.4.2M	1
14	Dia. 6 Basic External Retaining Ring- ANSI B27.7M	12

TOLERANCES UNLESS OTHERWISE SPECIFIED

X---------------------- +/- 1
X.X-------------------- +/- 0.5
X.XX------------------ +/- 0.2
ANGLE-------------- +/- 0.5

ALL DIMENSIONS IN MM

FIRST ISSUED	
DRAWN BY	
CHECKED BY	
APPROVED BY	

CADCIM TECHNOLOGIES

Pneumatic Gripper

SIZE	DRG NO.	SHEET REV
A3	6-000	A
SCALE 2:1		SHEET 1 OF 10

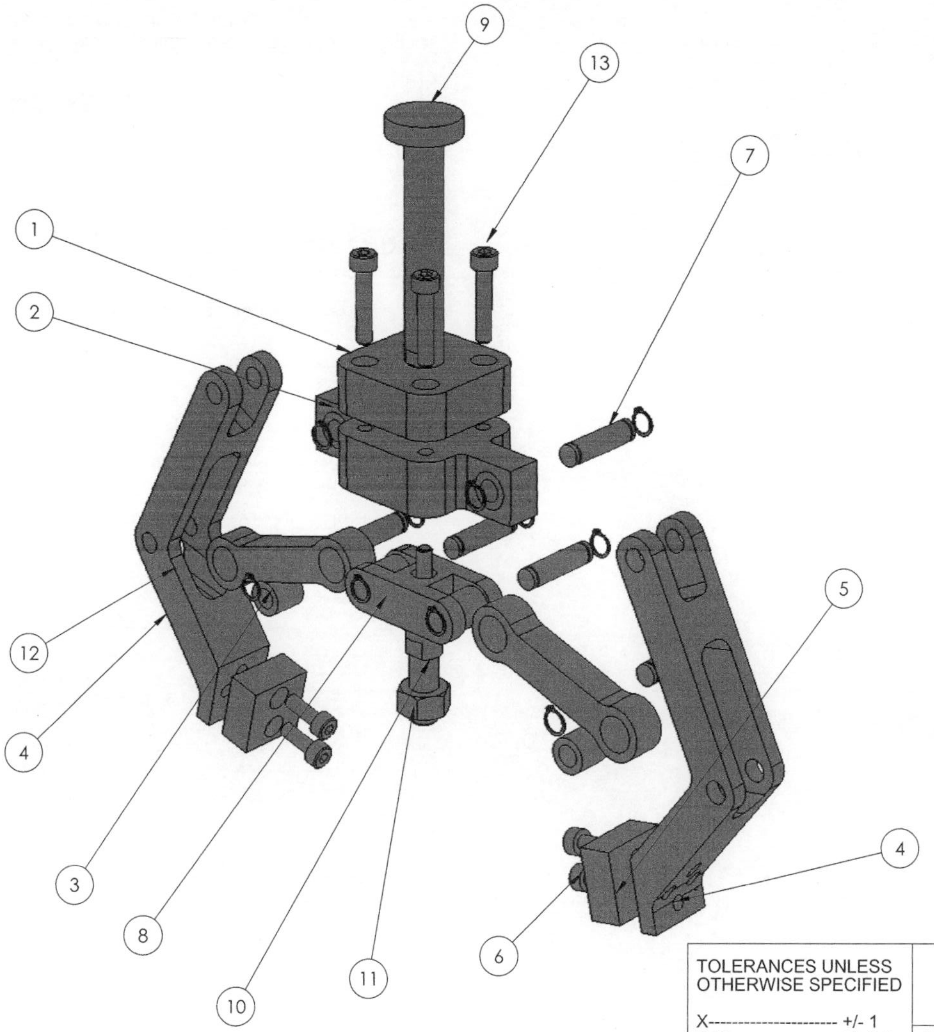

ITEM NO.	PART NUMBER	QTY.
1	Base Pad	1
2	Base	1
3	Bush	6
4	Arm	2
5	Pad	2
6	M4X0.7X11 Socket Head Cap Screw -ANSI B18.3.1M	4
7	Pin	6
8	Support Link	1
9	lever	1
10	Adjusting Rod	1
11	M8X1.25 Hex Nut-ANSI B18.2.4.2M	1
12	link	2
13	M4X0.7X20 Socket Head Cap Screw -ANSI B18.3.1M	4
14	Dia. 6 Basic External Retaining Ring- ANSI B27.7M	12

TOLERANCES UNLESS OTHERWISE SPECIFIED		CADCIM TECHNOLOGIES
X---------- +/- 1 X.X---------- +/- 0.5 X.XX---------- +/- 0.2 ANGLE---------- +/- 0.5	FIRST ISSUED DRAWN BY CHECKED BY APPROVED BY	Pneumatic Gripper Exploded
ALL DIMENSIONS IN MM		SIZE A3 · DRG NO. 6-000 · SHEET REV A
		SCALE 2:1 · SHEET 2 OF 10

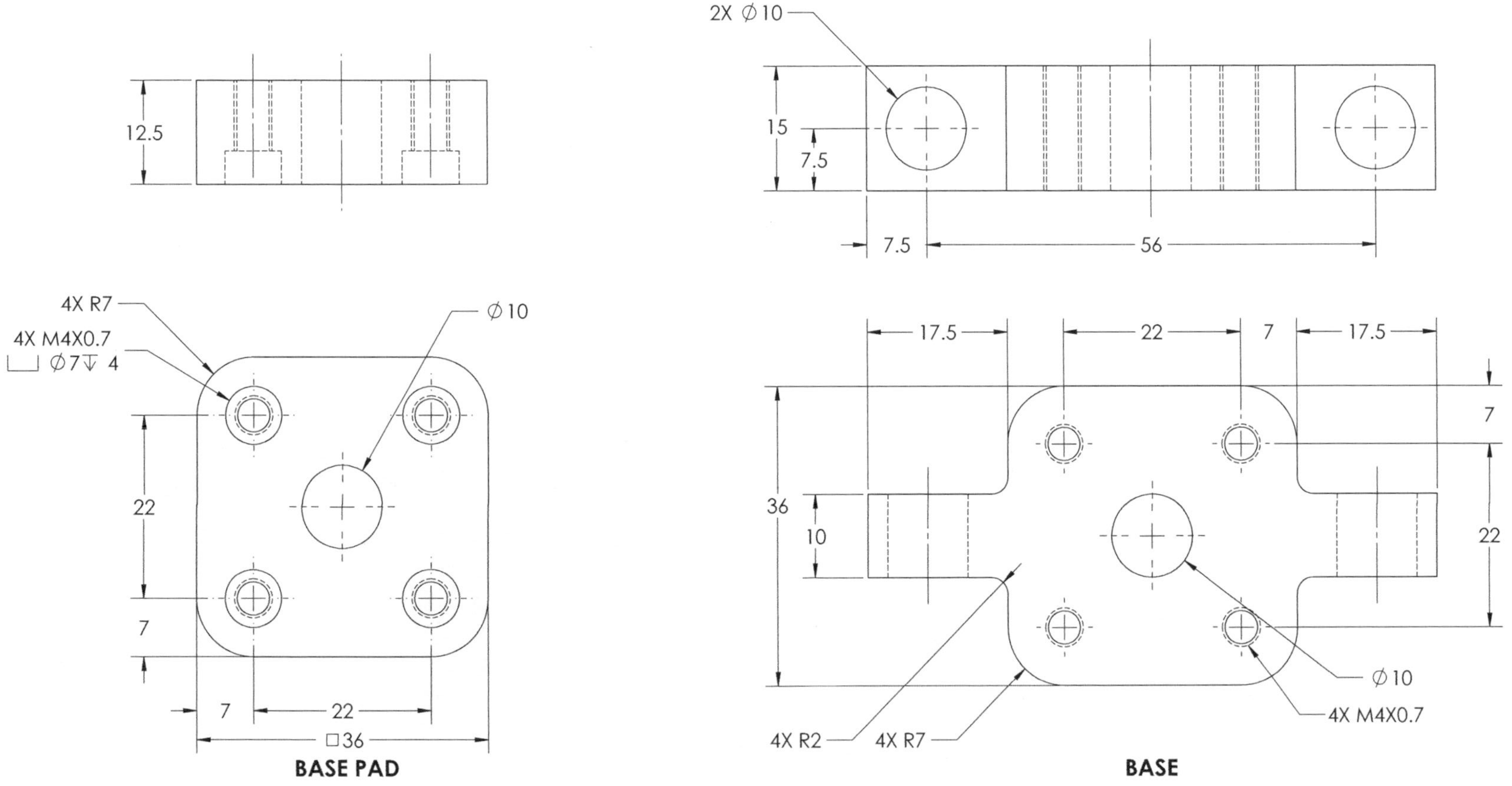

NOTES

1- Material Mild Steel (ASTM A36 Steel)
2- Deburr sharp edges

TOLERANCES UNLESS OTHERWISE SPECIFIED

X------------------ +/- 1
X.X---------------- +/- 0.5
X.XX--------------- +/- 0.2
ANGLE------------ +/- 0.5

ALL DIMENSIONS IN MM

FIRST ISSUED
DRAWN BY
CHECKED BY
APPROVED BY

CADCIM TECHNOLOGIES

Base Pad and Base

SIZE	DRG NO.	SHEET REV
A3	6-001	A
SCALE 2:1		SHEET 3 OF 10

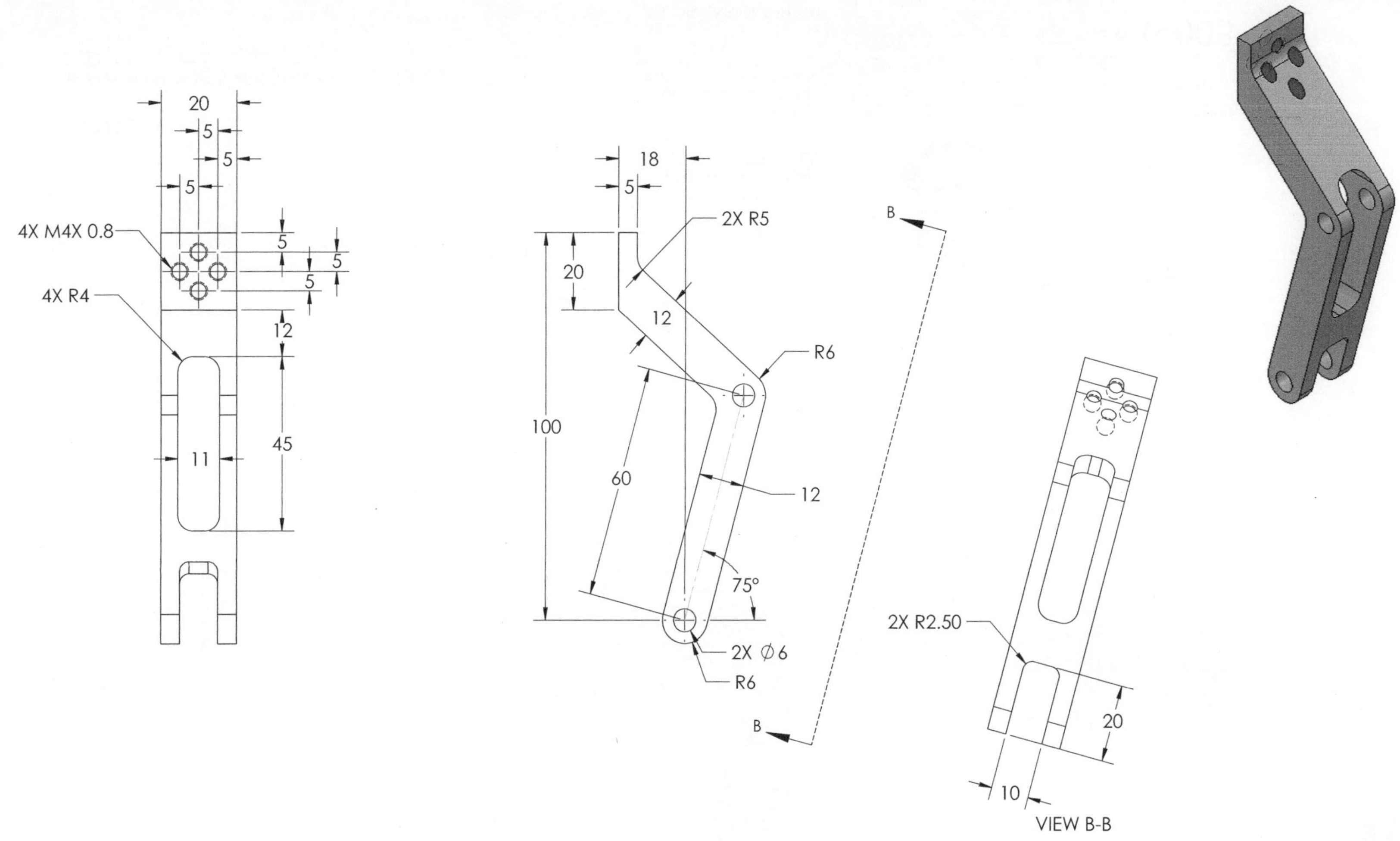

NOTES

1- Material Mild Steel (ASTM A36 Steel)
2- Deburr sharp edges

TOLERANCES UNLESS OTHERWISE SPECIFIED		CADCIM TECHNOLOGIES
X---------- +/- 1	FIRST ISSUED	Arm
X.X---------- +/- 0.5	DRAWN BY	
X.XX---------- +/- 0.2	CHECKED BY	
ANGLE---------- +/- 0.5	APPROVED BY	SIZE A3 · DRG NO. 6-002 · SHEET REV A
ALL DIMENSIONS IN MM		SCALE 1:1 · SHEET 4 OF 10

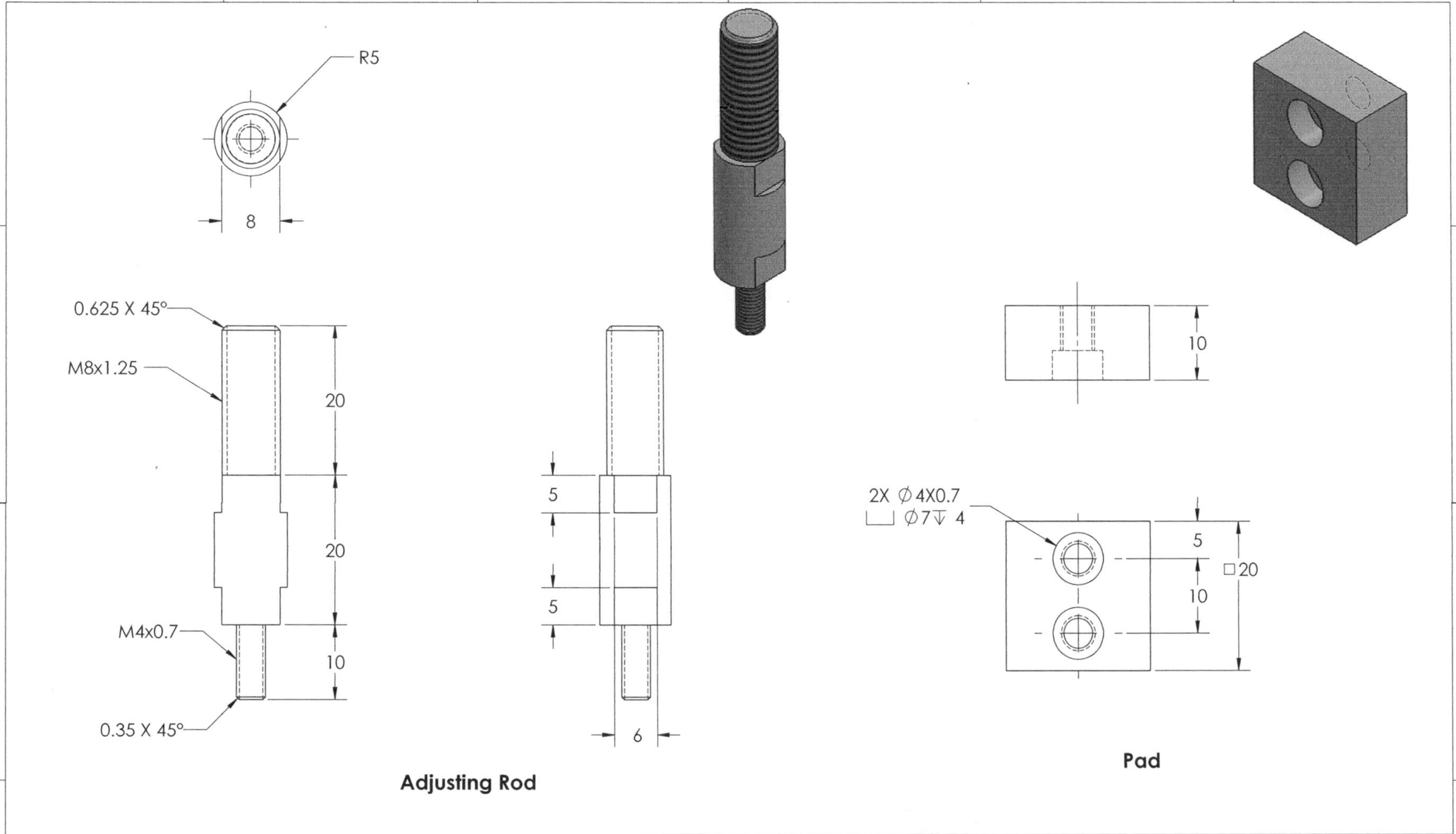

NOTES

1- Material Mild Steel (ASTM A36 Steel)
2- Deburr sharp edges

TOLERANCES UNLESS OTHERWISE SPECIFIED

X	+/- 1
X.X	+/- 0.5
X.XX	+/- 0.2
ANGLE	+/- 0.5

ALL DIMENSIONS IN MM

FIRST ISSUED
DRAWN BY
CHECKED BY
APPROVED BY

CADCIM TECHNOLOGIES

1. Adjusting Rod
2. Pad

SIZE A3 | DRG NO. 6-003 | SHEET REV A

SCALE 2:1 | SHEET 5 OF 10

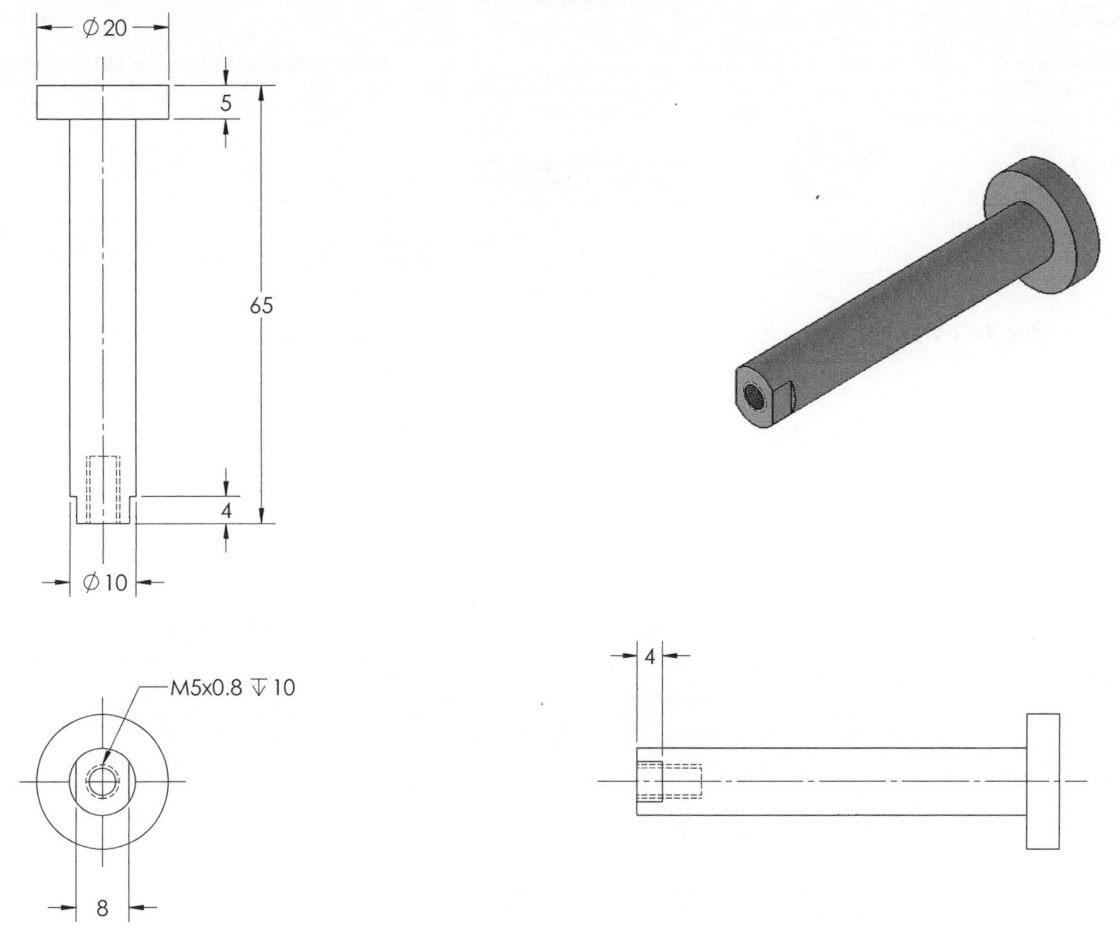

NOTES

1- Material Mild Steel (ASTM A36 Steel)
2- Deburr sharp edges

TOLERANCES UNLESS OTHERWISE SPECIFIED		CADCIM TECHNOLOGIES
X---------- +/- 1	FIRST ISSUED	Lever
X.X-------- +/- 0.5	DRAWN BY	
X.XX------- +/- 0.2	CHECKED BY	
ANGLE------ +/- 0.5	APPROVED BY	SIZE A3 DRG NO. 6-004 SHEET REV A
ALL DIMENSIONS IN MM		SCALE 3:2 SHEET 6 OF 10

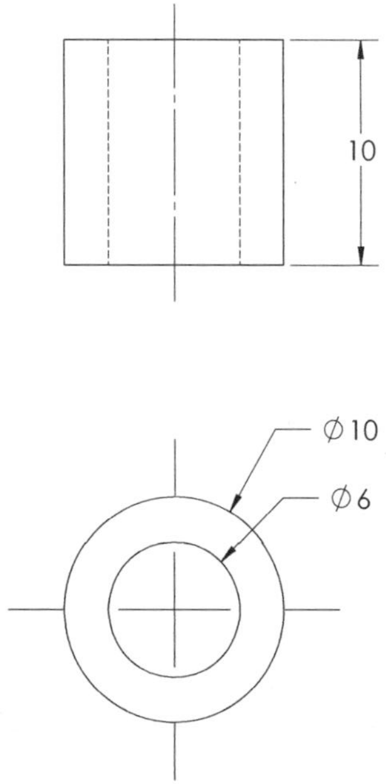

BUSH

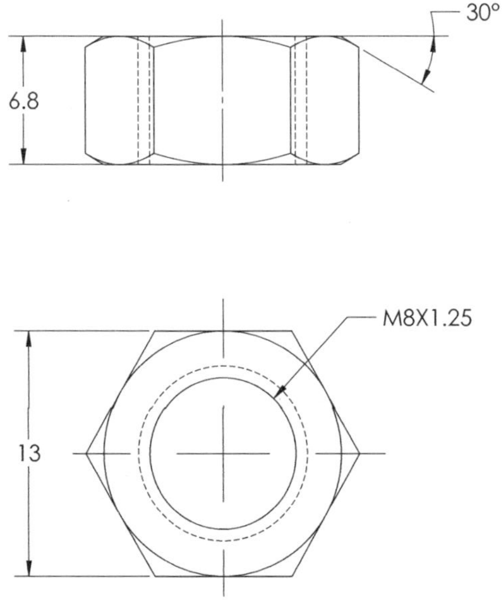

M8 X1.25 Hex Nut

NOTES

1- Material Mild Steel (ASTM A36 Steel)for Bush and S.S for Nut
2- Deburr sharp edges

TOLERANCES UNLESS OTHERWISE SPECIFIED

X---------------------- +/- 1
X.X-------------------- +/- 0.5
X.XX------------------- +/- 0.2
ANGLE------------------ +/- 0.5

ALL DIMENSIONS IN MM

FIRST ISSUED	
DRAWN BY	
CHECKED BY	
APPROVED BY	

CADCIM TECHNOLOGIES

1.Bush
2.M8X1.25 Hex Nut- ANSI B18.2.4.2M

SIZE	DRG NO.	SHEET REV
A3	6-005	A
SCALE 4:1		SHEET 7 OF 10

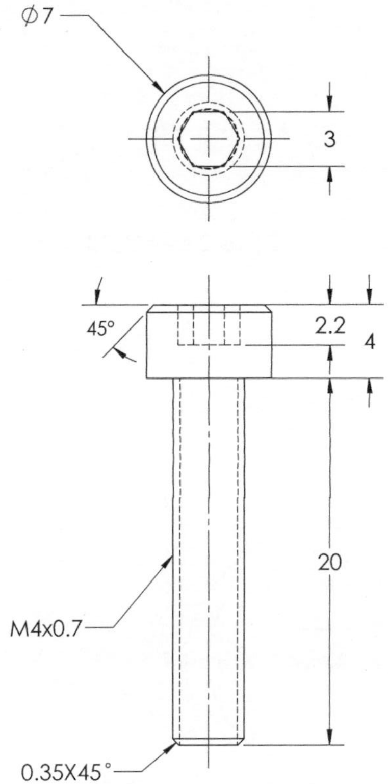

M4X0.7X 20 Cap Screw

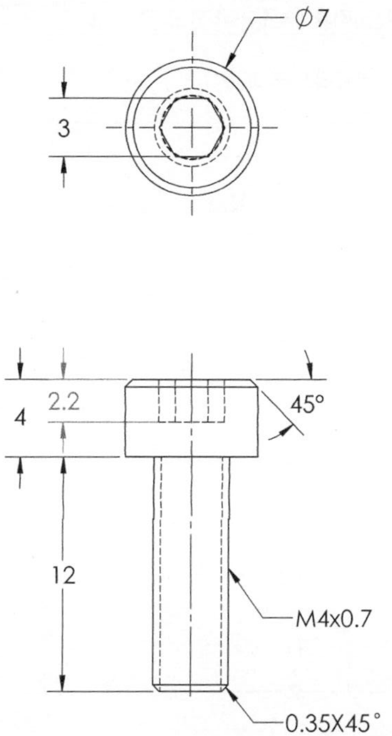

M4X0.7 X12 Cap Screw

NOTES

1- Material Stainless Steel
2- Deburr sharp edges

TOLERANCES UNLESS OTHERWISE SPECIFIED	
X	+/- 1
X.X	+/- 0.5
X.XX	+/- 0.2
ANGLE	+/- 0.5

ALL DIMENSIONS IN MM

FIRST ISSUED	
DRAWN BY	
CHECKED BY	
APPROVED BY	

CADCIM TECHNOLOGIES

1. M4X0.7 X20 Socket Head Cap Screw- ANSI B18.3.1M
2. M4X0.7 X12 Socket Head Cap Screw- ANSI B18.3.1M

SIZE	DRG NO.	SHEET REV
A3	6-006	A
SCALE 4:1		SHEET 8 OF 10

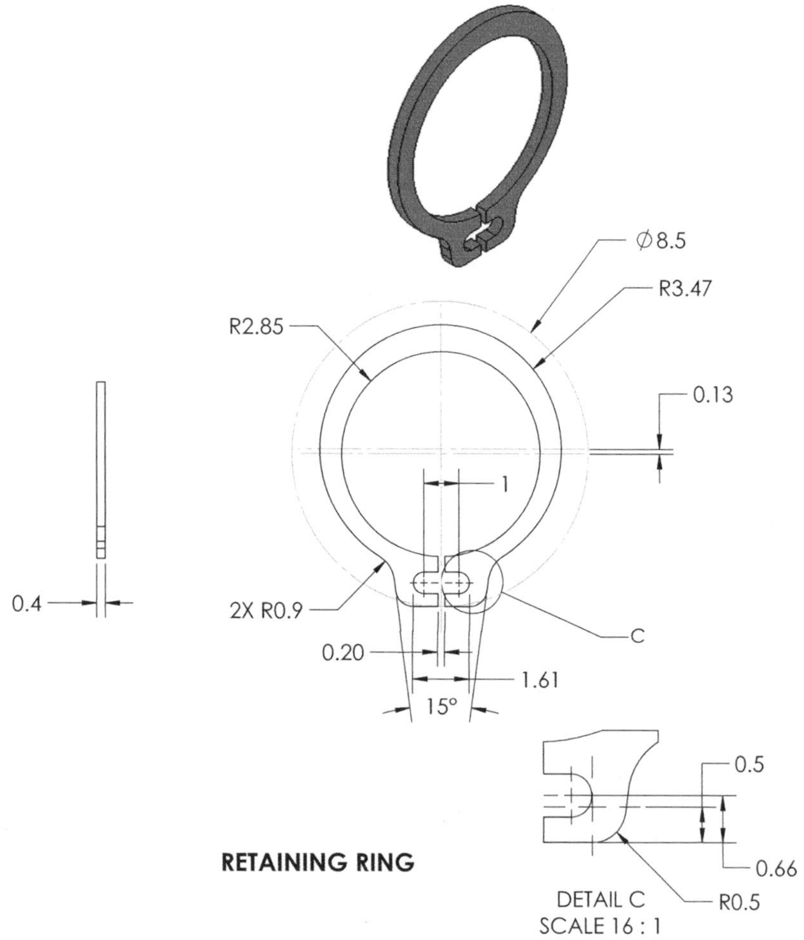

RETAINING RING

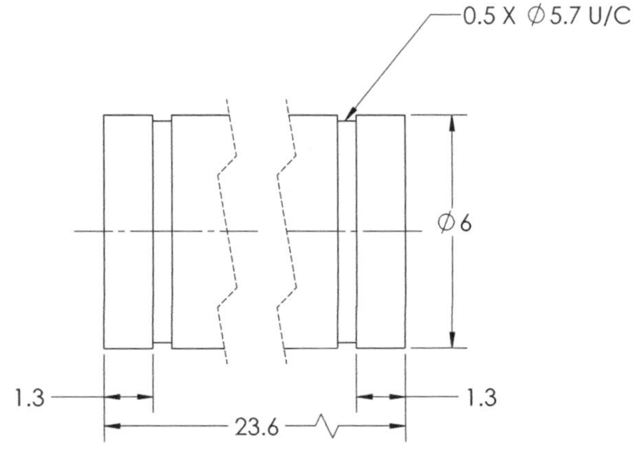

PIN

NOTES

1- Material Mild Steel (ASTM A36 Steel)
2- Deburr sharp edges

TOLERANCES UNLESS OTHERWISE SPECIFIED

X---------- +/- 1
X.X---------- +/- 0.5
X.XX---------- +/- 0.2
ANGLE---------- +/- 0.5

ALL DIMENSIONS IN MM

FIRST ISSUED
DRAWN BY
CHECKED BY
APPROVED BY

CADCIM TECHNOLOGIES

1. Ø6 Basic External Retaining Ring- ANSI B27.7M
2. Pin

SIZE	DRG NO.	SHEET REV
A3	6-007	A

SCALE 5:1 | SHEET 9 OF 10

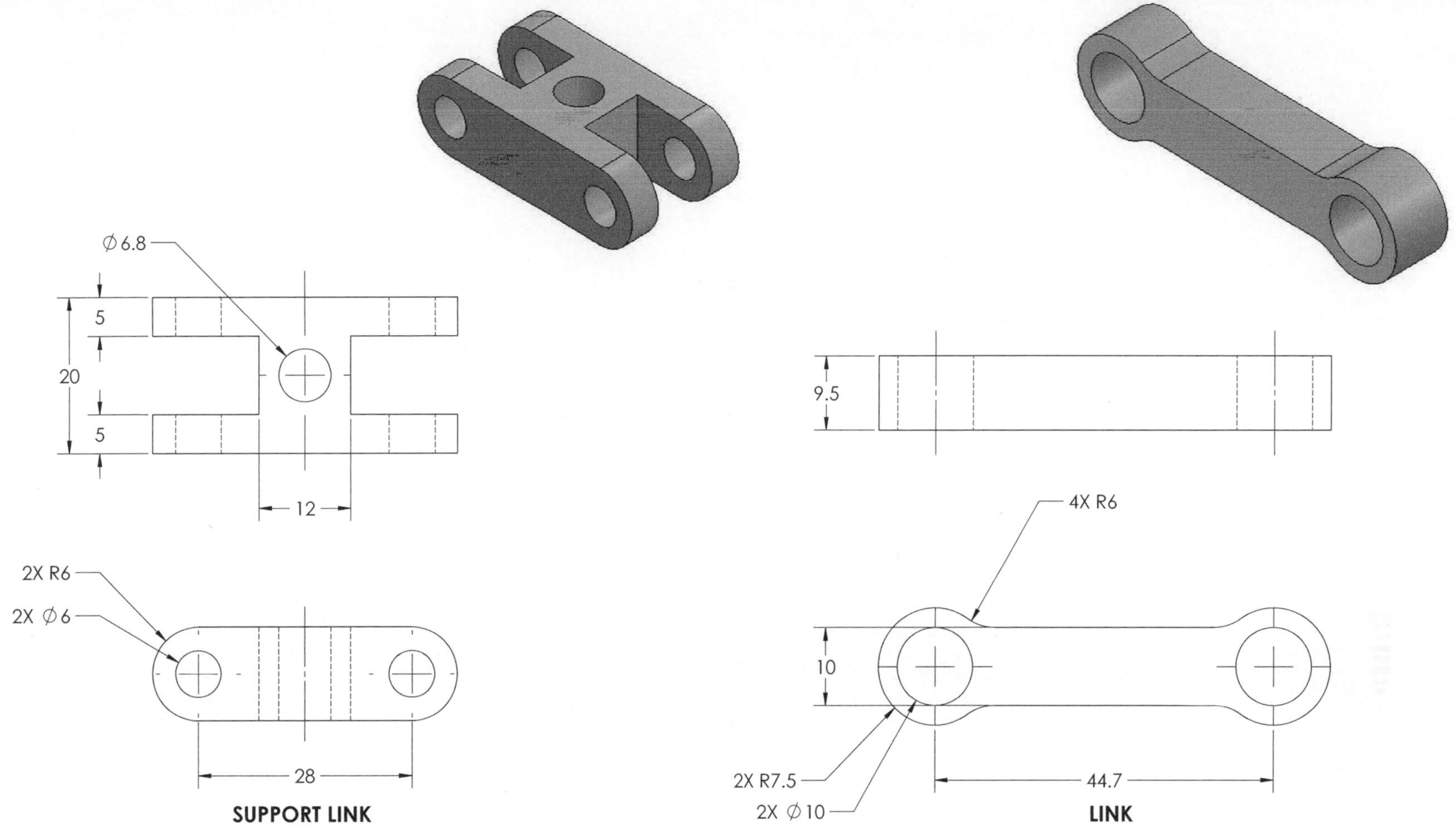

NOTES .

1- Material Mild Steel (ASTM A36 Steel)
2- Deburr sharp edges

TOLERANCES UNLESS OTHERWISE SPECIFIED		CADCIM TECHNOLOGIES
X------- +/- 1 X.X------- +/- 0.5 X.XX------- +/- 0.2 ANGLE------- +/- 0.5	FIRST ISSUED DRAWN BY CHECKED BY APPROVED BY	1. Support Link 2. Link
ALL DIMENSIONS IN MM		SIZE A3 · DRG NO. 6-008 · SHEET REV A
		SCALE 2:1 · SHEET 10 OF 10

This page is intentionally left blank

Project 7

Car Jack Assembly

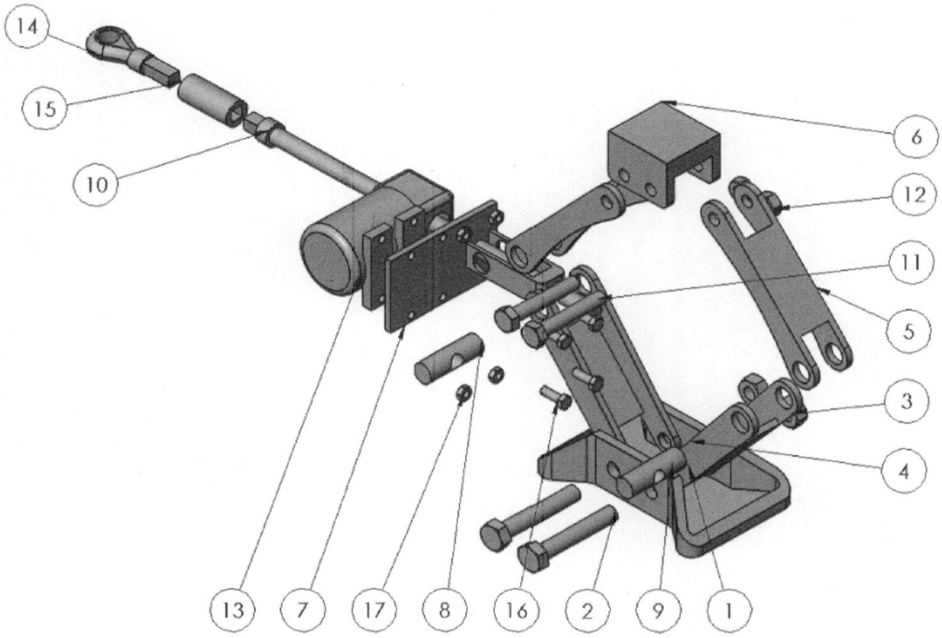

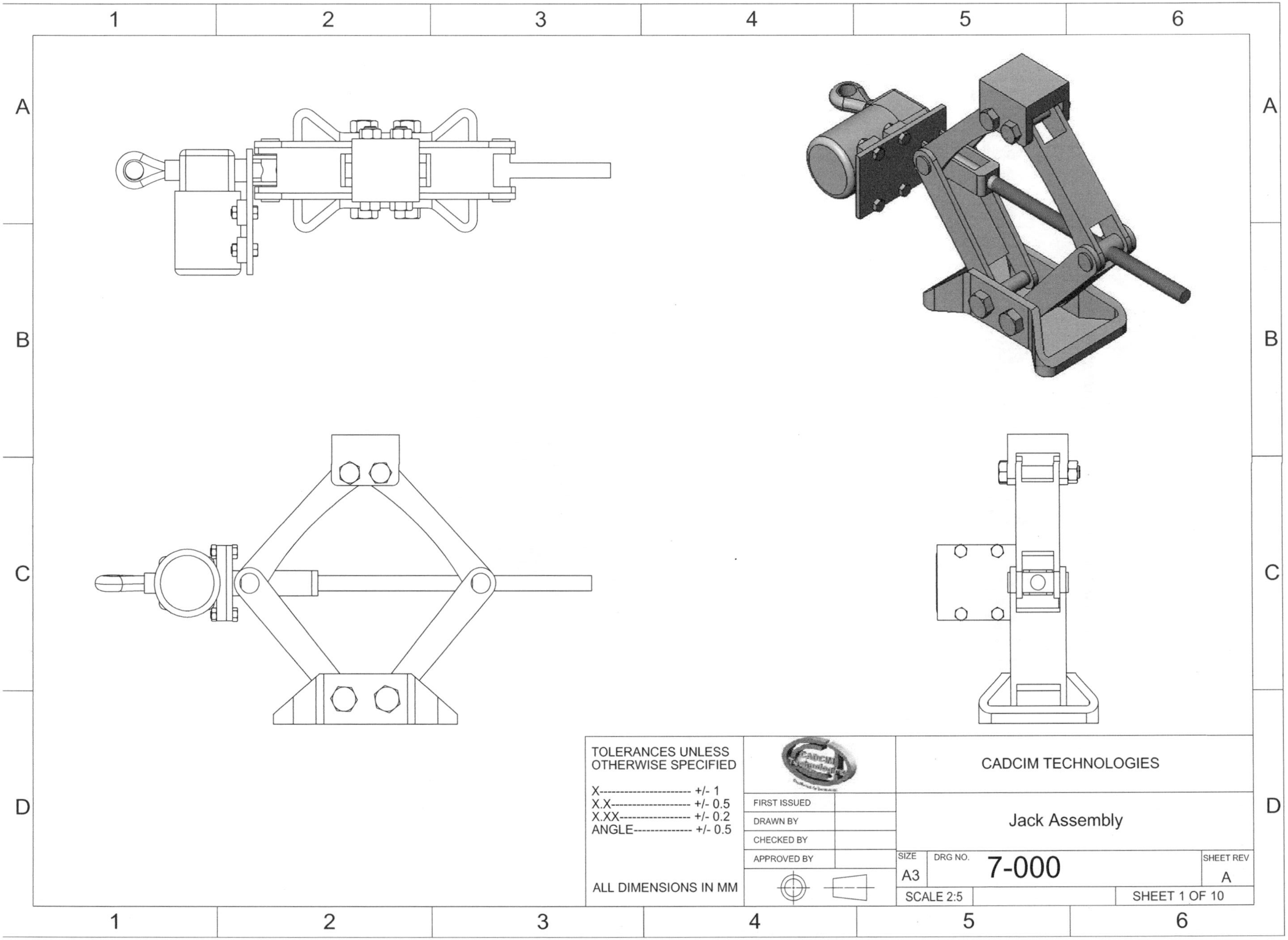

TOLERANCES UNLESS OTHERWISE SPECIFIED
X---------------------- +/- 1
X.X-------------------- +/- 0.5
X.XX------------------ +/- 0.2
ANGLE-------------- +/- 0.5
ALL DIMENSIONS IN MM
FIRST ISSUED
DRAWN BY
CHECKED BY
APPROVED BY
CADCIM TECHNOLOGIES
Jack Assembly
SIZE
A3
DRG NO.
7-000
SHEET REV
A
SCALE 2:5
SHEET 1 OF 10

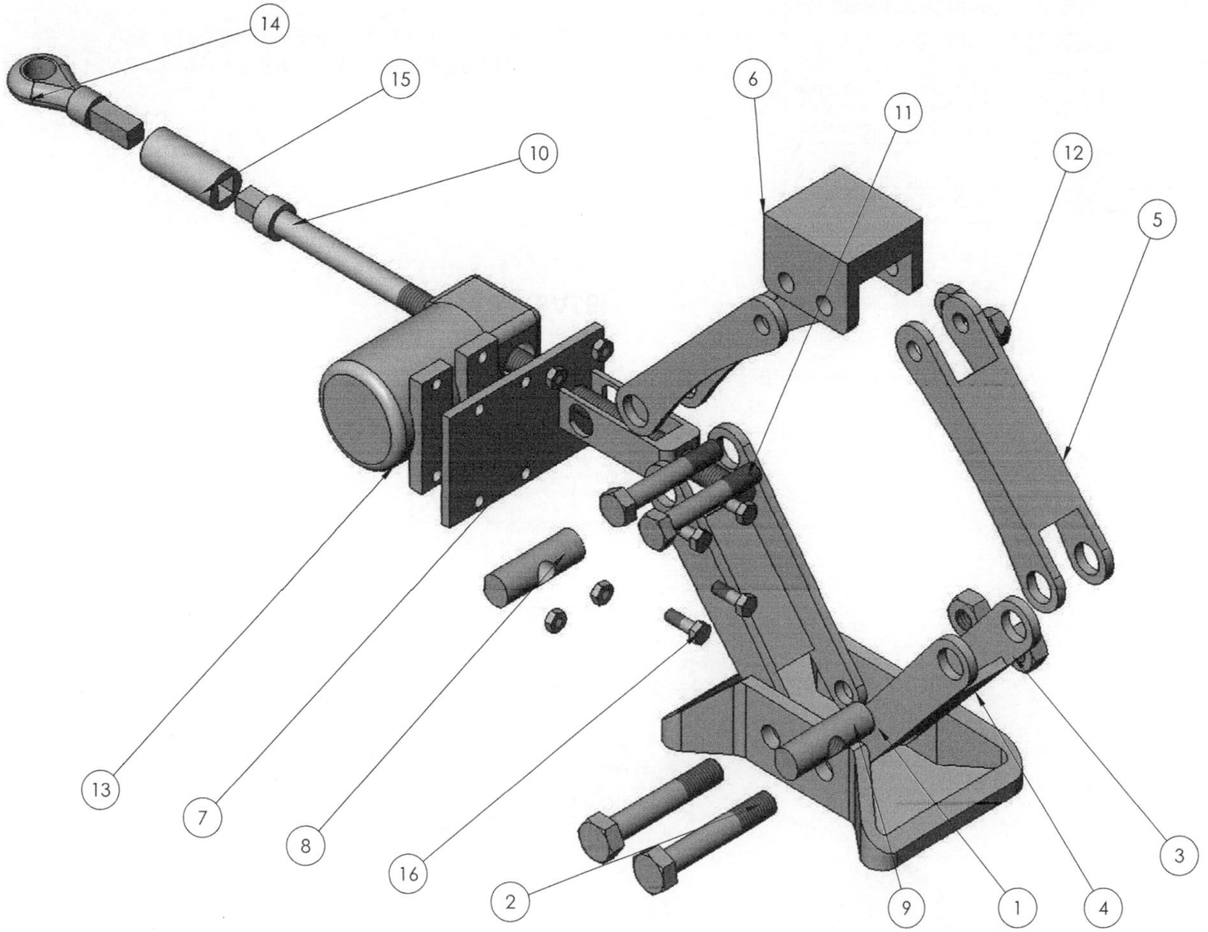

ITEM NO.	PART NUMBER	QTY.
1	JACK BASE	1
2	M12X1.75 Hex Bolt-ANSI B18.2.3.5M.SLDPRT	2
3	M12X1.75 Hex Nut-ANSI B18.2.4.2M	2
4	JACK BOTTOM LEG	2
5	JACK UPPER LEG	2
6	JACK CAP	1
7	SCREW BASE	1
8	JACK PIN WOD THREAD	1
9	JACK PIN	1
10	JACK SCREW	1
11	M10 X1.5 Hex Bolt-ANSI B18.2.3.5M	2
12	M10X1.5 Hex Nut-ANSI B18.2.4.2M	2
13	MOTOR CASE	1
14	Manual Screw	1
15	JACK ROTOR	1
16	M6X 1 X 22 Hex Bolt-ANSI B18.2.3.5M.SLDPRT	4
17	M6X1 Hex Nut- ANSI B18.2.4.2M	4

TOLERANCES UNLESS OTHERWISE SPECIFIED

X---------------------- +/- 1
X.X------------------ +/- 0.5
X.XX---------------- +/- 0.2
ANGLE-------------- +/- 0.5

ALL DIMENSIONS IN MM

FIRST ISSUED	
DRAWN BY	
CHECKED BY	
APPROVED BY	

CADCIM TECHNOLOGIES

Exploded Jack Assembly

SIZE	DRG NO.	SHEET REV
A3	7-000	A
SCALE 1:2	SHEET 2 OF 10	

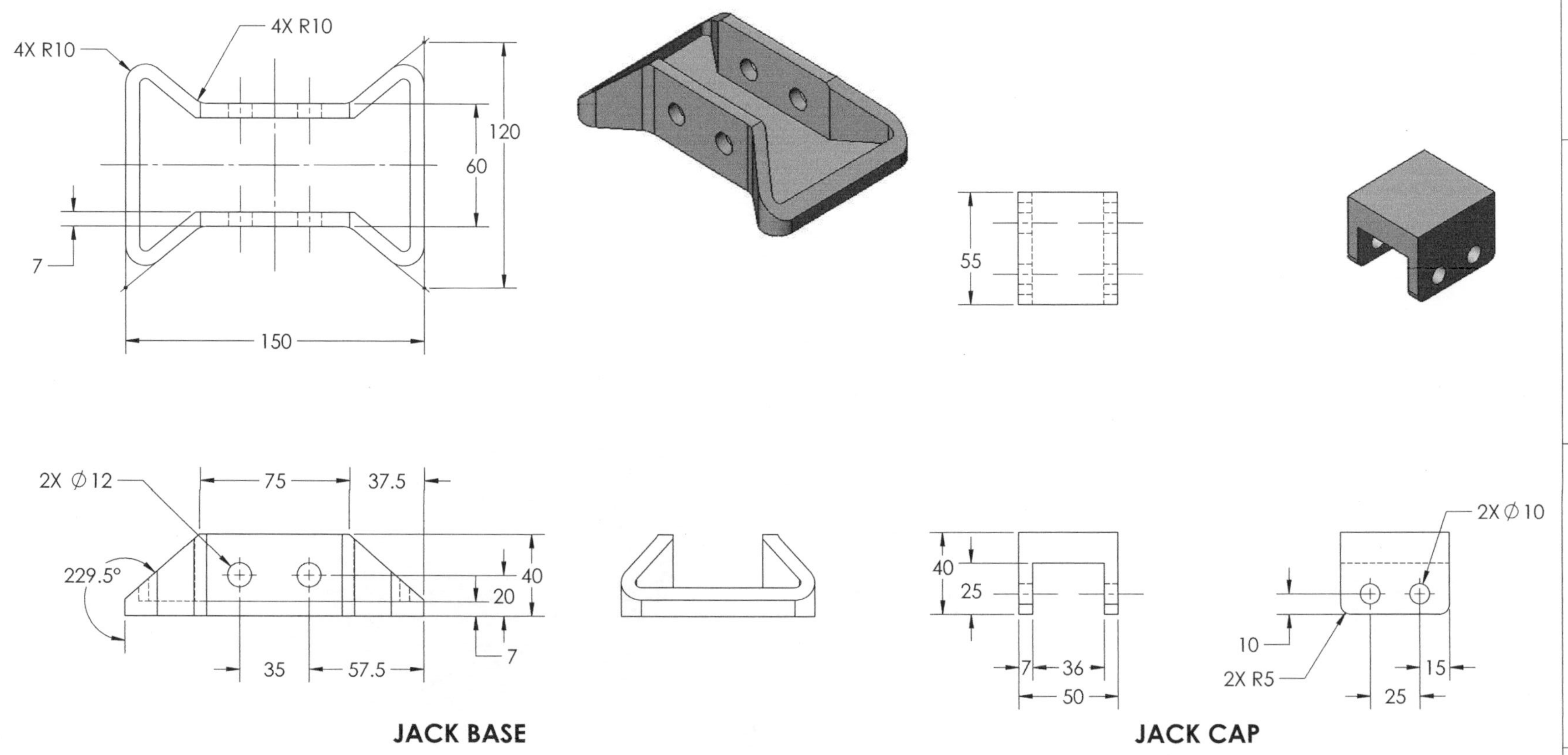

NOTES

1- Material Mild Steel(ASTM A36 STEEL)
2- Deburr sharp edges

TOLERANCES UNLESS OTHERWISE SPECIFIED		CADCIM TECHNOLOGIES
X---------- +/- 1	FIRST ISSUED	1. JACK BASE
X.X---------- +/- 0.5	DRAWN BY	2. JACK CAP
X.XX---------- +/- 0.2	CHECKED BY	
ANGLE---------- +/- 0.5	APPROVED BY	SIZE A3 · DRG NO. 7-001 · SHEET REV A
ALL DIMENSIONS IN MM		SCALE 1:2 · SHEET 3 OF 10

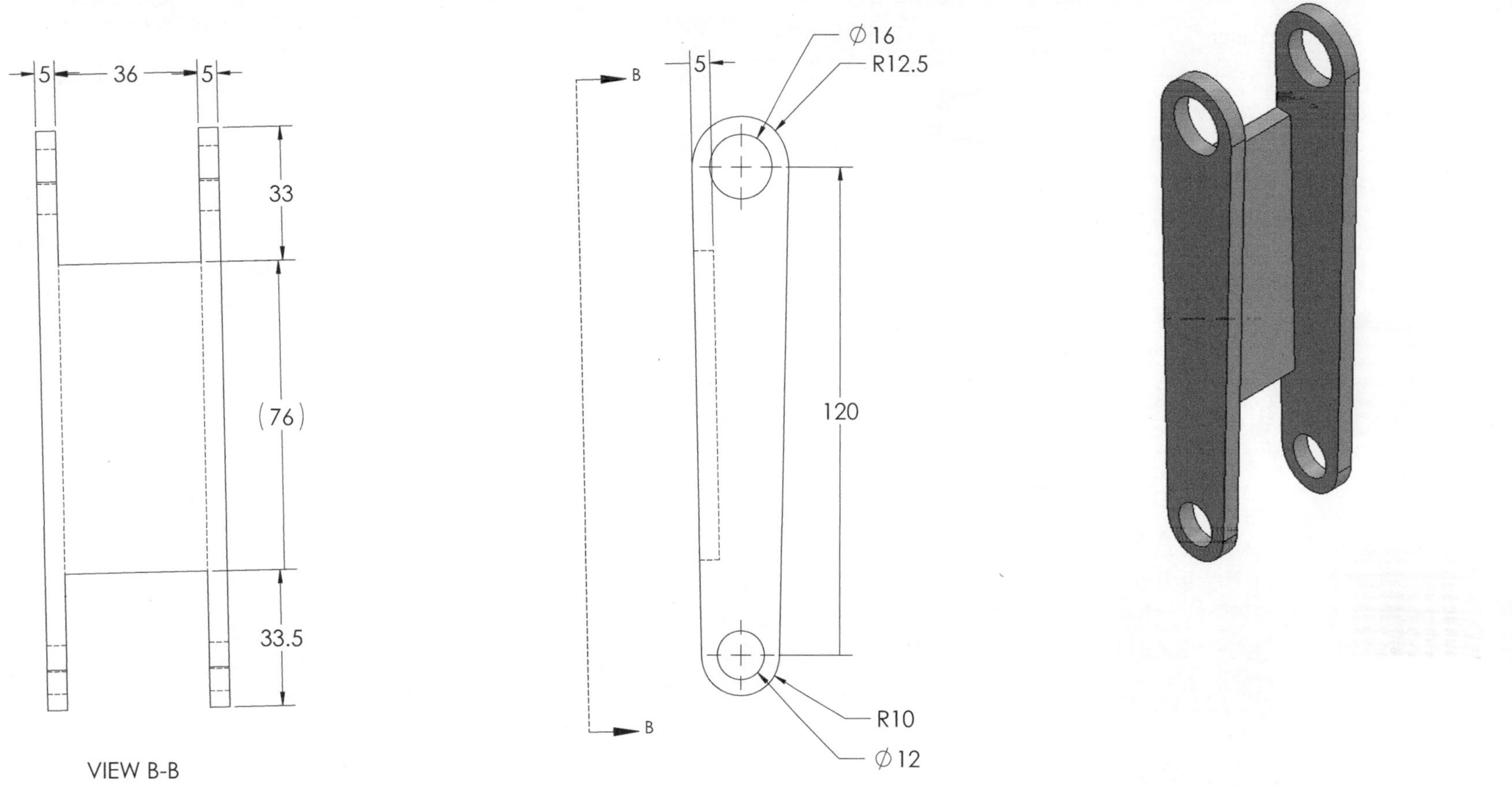

NOTES

1- Material Mild Steel(ASTM A36 Steel)
2- Deburr sharp edges

TOLERANCES UNLESS OTHERWISE SPECIFIED		CADCIM TECHNOLOGIES
X------ +/- 1	FIRST ISSUED	
X.X------ +/- 0.5	DRAWN BY	Jack Bottom Leg
X.XX------ +/- 0.2	CHECKED BY	
ANGLE------ +/- 0.5	APPROVED BY	SIZE A3 · DRG NO. 7-002 · SHEET REV A
ALL DIMENSIONS IN MM		SCALE 1:1 · SHEET 4 OF 10

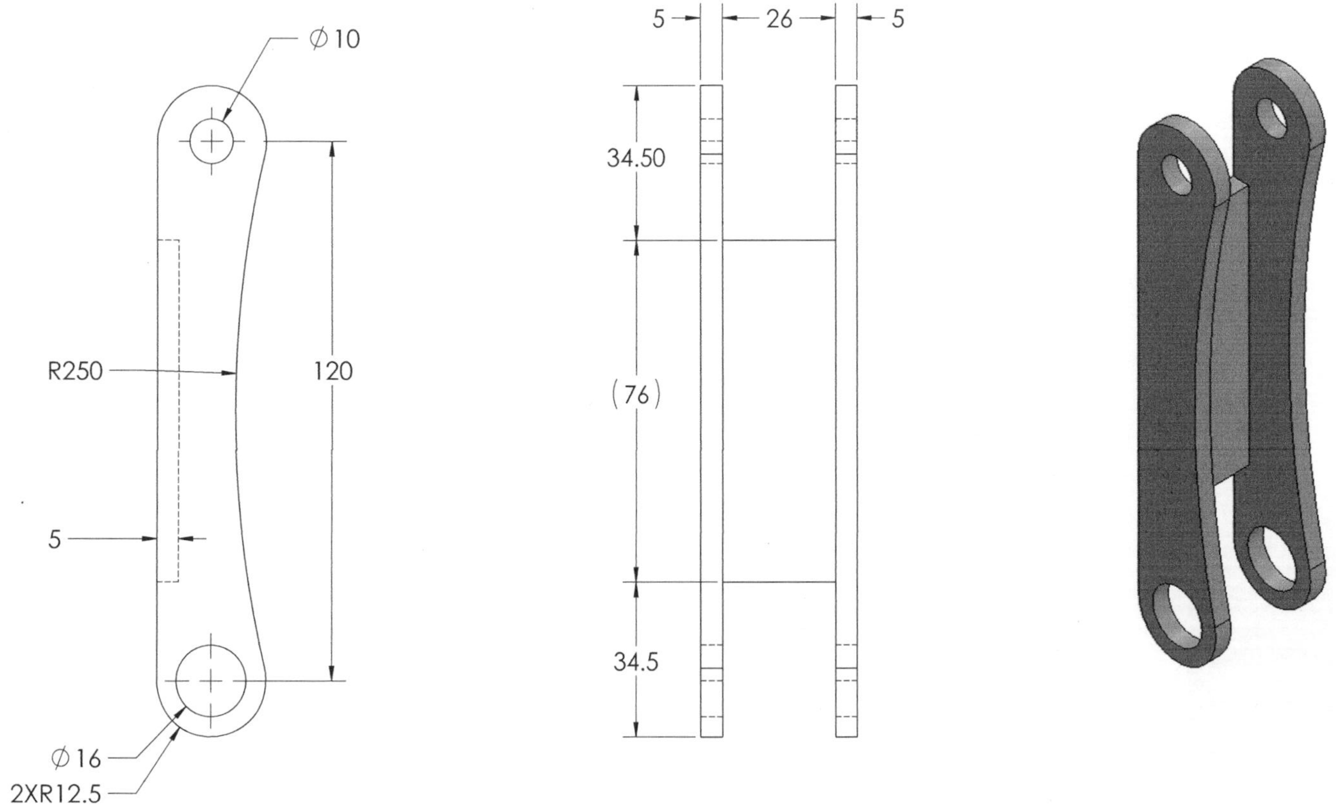

NOTES

1- Material Mild Steel (ASTM A36 Steel)
2- Deburr sharp edges

TOLERANCES UNLESS OTHERWISE SPECIFIED		CADCIM TECHNOLOGIES
X---------- +/- 1	FIRST ISSUED	Jack Upper Leg
X.X---------- +/- 0.5	DRAWN BY	
X.XX---------- +/- 0.2	CHECKED BY	
ANGLE---------- +/- 0.5	APPROVED BY	SIZE A3 · DRG NO. 7-003 · SHEET REV A
ALL DIMENSIONS IN MM		SCALE 1:1 · SHEET 5 OF 10

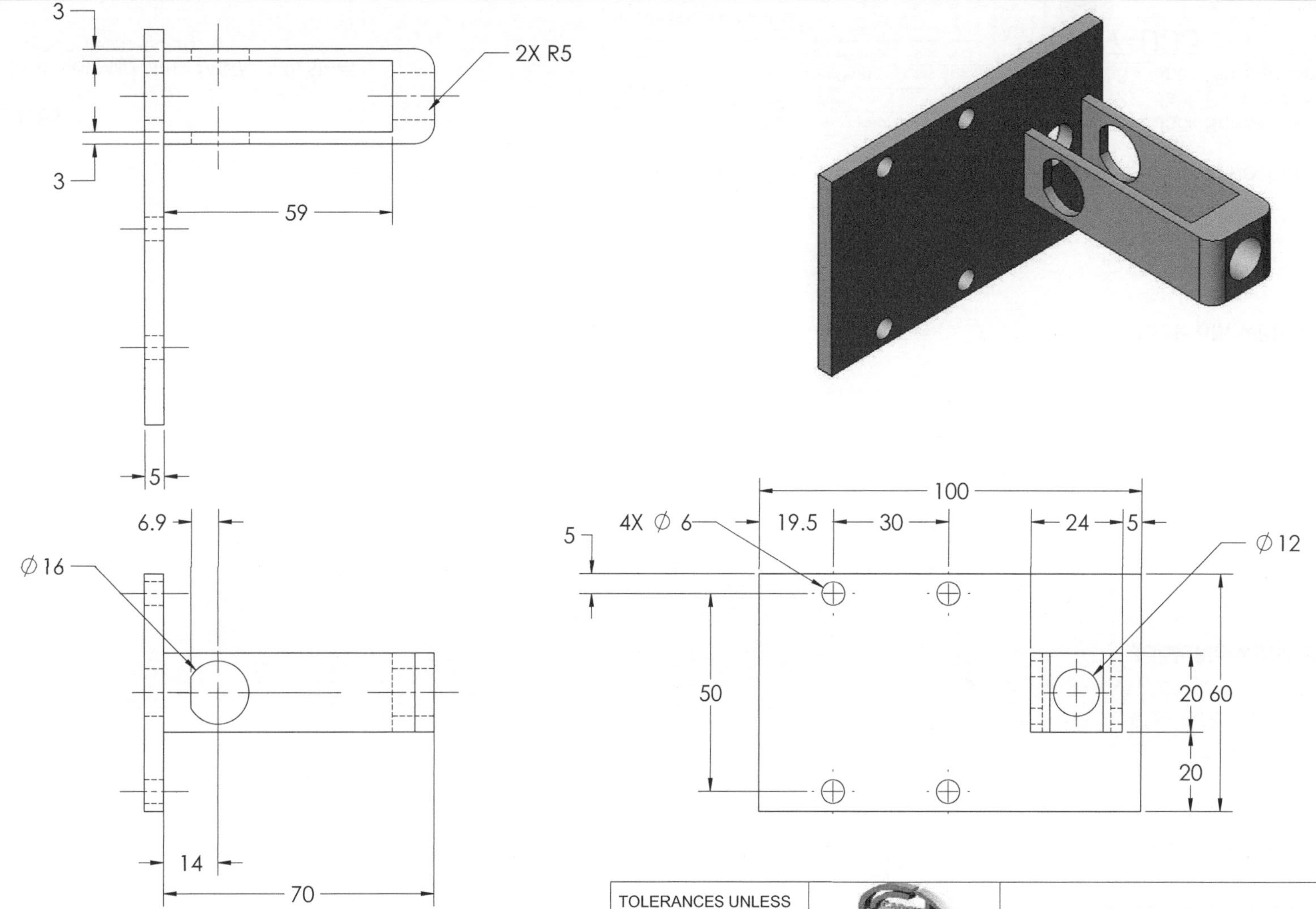

NOTES

1- Material Mild Steel (ASTM A36 Steel)
2- Deburr sharp edges

TOLERANCES UNLESS OTHERWISE SPECIFIED		CADCIM TECHNOLOGIES			
X---------- +/- 1	FIRST ISSUED	Screw Base			
X.X---------- +/- 0.5	DRAWN BY				
X.XX---------- +/- 0.2	CHECKED BY				
ANGLE---------- +/- 0.5	APPROVED BY	SIZE A3	DRG NO. 7-004		SHEET REV A
ALL DIMENSIONS IN MM		SCALE 1:1			SHEET 6 OF 10

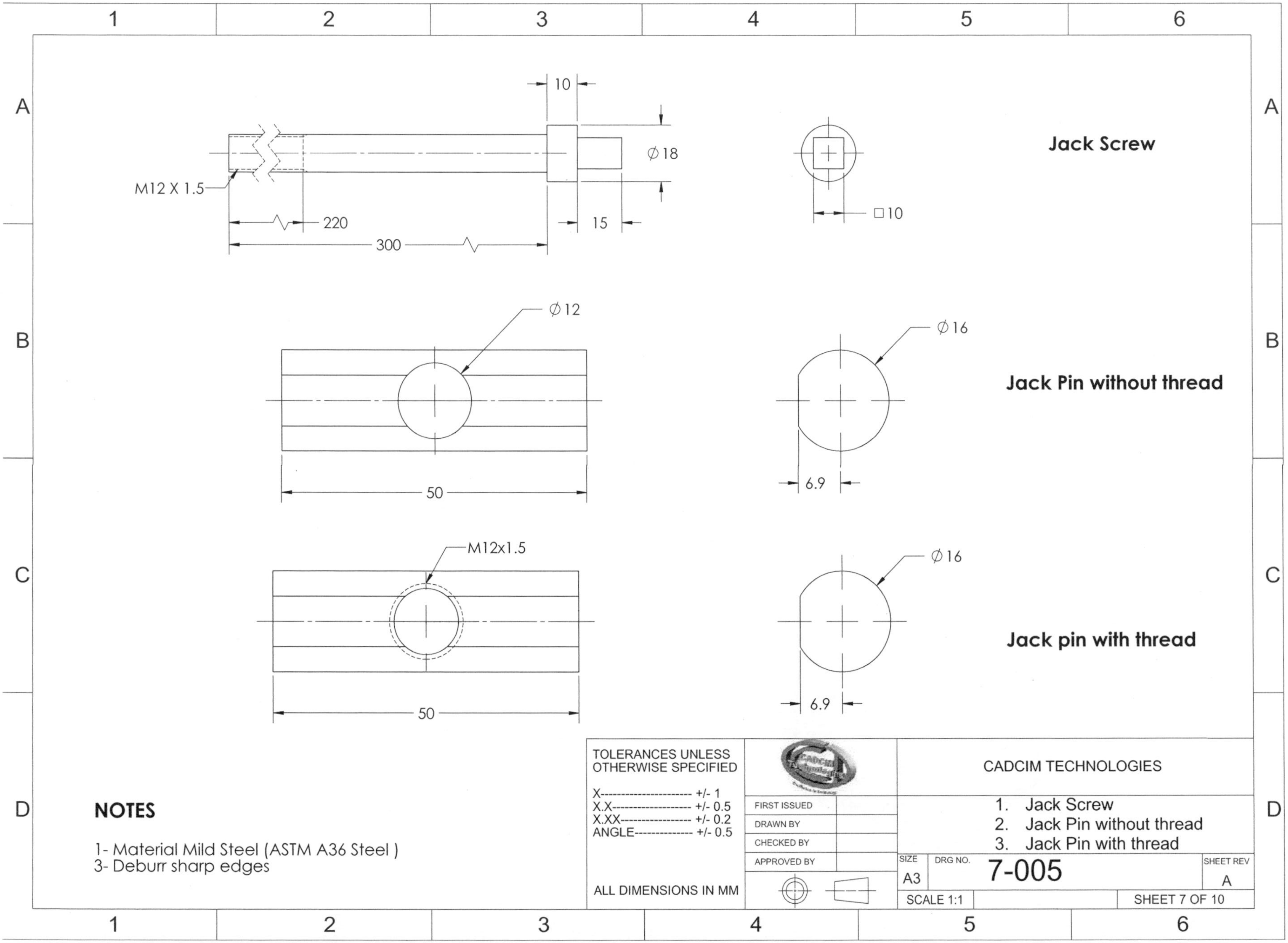
Jack Screw
10
Ø18
M12 X 1.5
220
300
15
□10
Jack Pin without thread
Ø12
Ø16
50
6.9
Jack pin with thread
M12x1.5
Ø16
50
6.9
NOTES
1- Material Mild Steel (ASTM A36 Steel)
3- Deburr sharp edges
TOLERANCES UNLESS OTHERWISE SPECIFIED
X---------------------- +/- 1
X.X------------------- +/- 0.5
X.XX----------------- +/- 0.2
ANGLE-------------- +/- 0.5
ALL DIMENSIONS IN MM
FIRST ISSUED
DRAWN BY
CHECKED BY
APPROVED BY
CADCIM TECHNOLOGIES
1. Jack Screw
2. Jack Pin without thread
3. Jack Pin with thread
SIZE
A3
DRG NO.
7-005
SHEET REV
A
SCALE 1:1
SHEET 7 OF 10

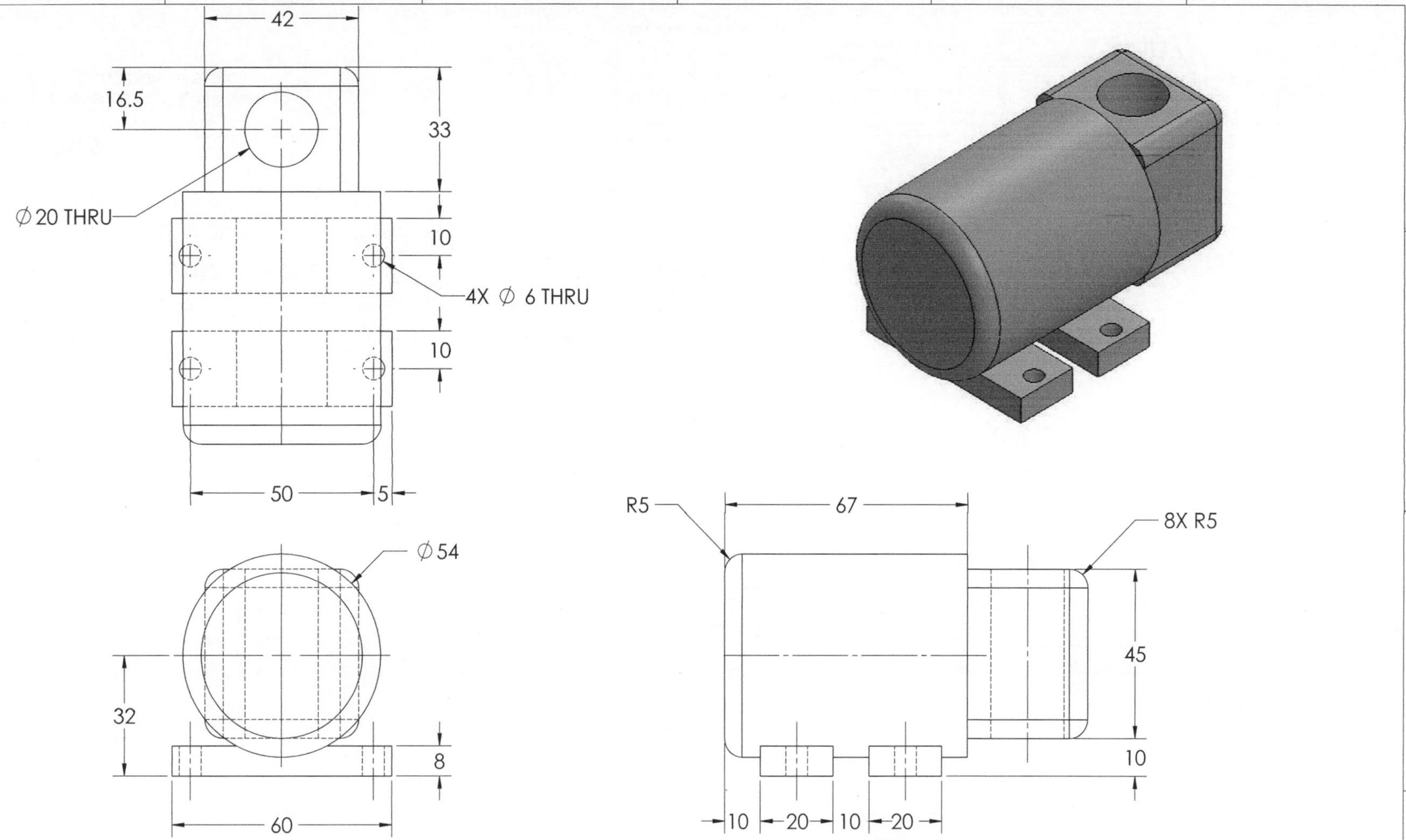

NOTES

1- Material Mild Steel(ASTM A36 STEEL)
2- Deburr sharp edges

TOLERANCES UNLESS OTHERWISE SPECIFIED		CADCIM TECHNOLOGIES
X---------- +/- 1 X.X---------- +/- 0.5 X.XX---------- +/- 0.2 ANGLE---------- +/- 0.5	FIRST ISSUED DRAWN BY CHECKED BY APPROVED BY	JACK MOTOR CASE
ALL DIMENSIONS IN MM		SIZE A3 · DRG NO. 7-006 · SHEET REV A
		SCALE 1:1 · SHEET 8 OF 10

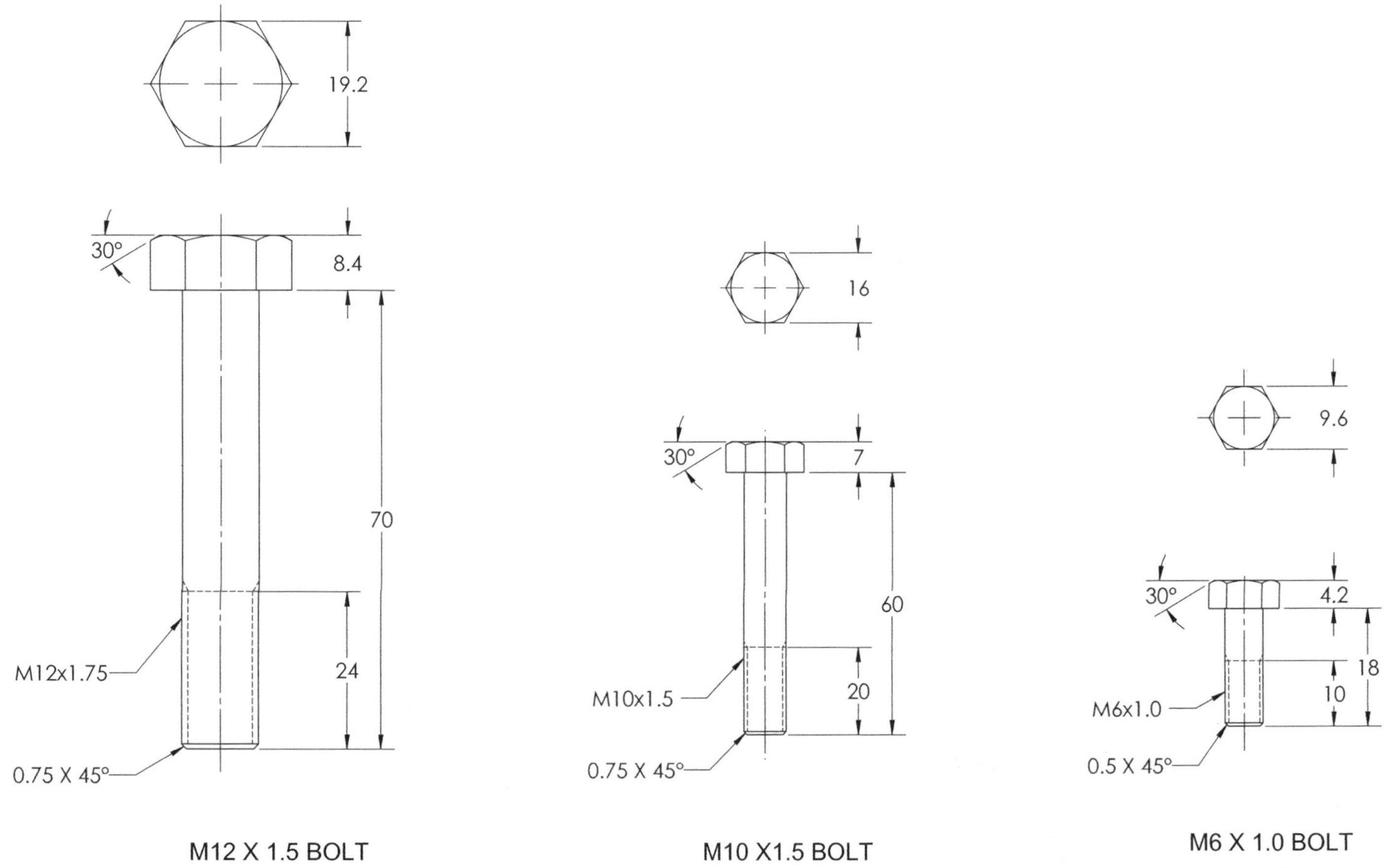

NOTES

1- Material Stainless Steel
2- Deburr sharp edges

TOLERANCES UNLESS OTHERWISE SPECIFIED

X---------- +/- 1
X.X---------- +/- 0.5
X.XX---------- +/- 0.2
ANGLE---------- +/- 0.5

ALL DIMENSIONS IN MM

FIRST ISSUED
DRAWN BY
CHECKED BY
APPROVED BY

CADCIM TECHNOLOGIES

1. M12 X 1.75 Hex Bolt -ANSI B18.2.3.5M
2. M10 X1.5 Hex Bolt -ANSI B18.2.3.5M
3. M6 X 1.0 Hex Bolt -ANSI B18.2.3.5M

SIZE	DRG NO.	SHEET REV
A3	7-007	A
SCALE 2:1		SHEET 9 OF 10

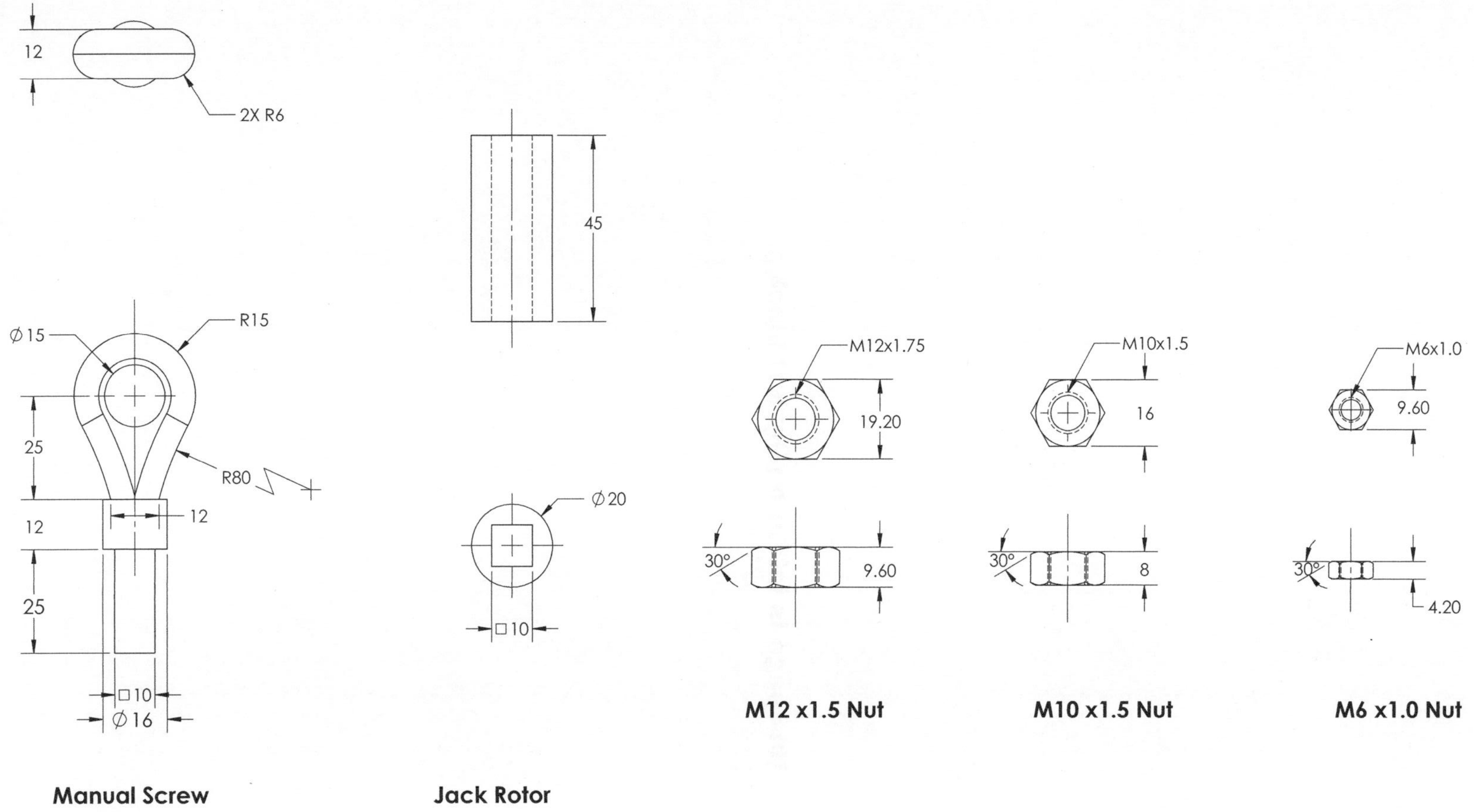

NOTES

1- Material ASTM A36 Steel (Manual Screw, jack rotor) and SS for Nuts
2- Deburr sharp edges

TOLERANCES UNLESS OTHERWISE SPECIFIED		CADCIM TECHNOLOGIES	
X---------- +/- 1 X.X---------- +/- 0.5 X.XX---------- +/- 0.2 ANGLE---------- +/- 0.5	FIRST ISSUED DRAWN BY CHECKED BY APPROVED BY	1. Manual Screw 2. Jack Rotor 3. M12 X 1.5 , M10 x 1.5 , M6X 1.0 Nut-ANSI B18.2.4.2M	
ALL DIMENSIONS IN MM		SIZE A3 DRG NO. 7-008	SHEET REV A
		SCALE 1:1	SHEET 10 OF 10

Project 8

Pipe Wrench Assembly

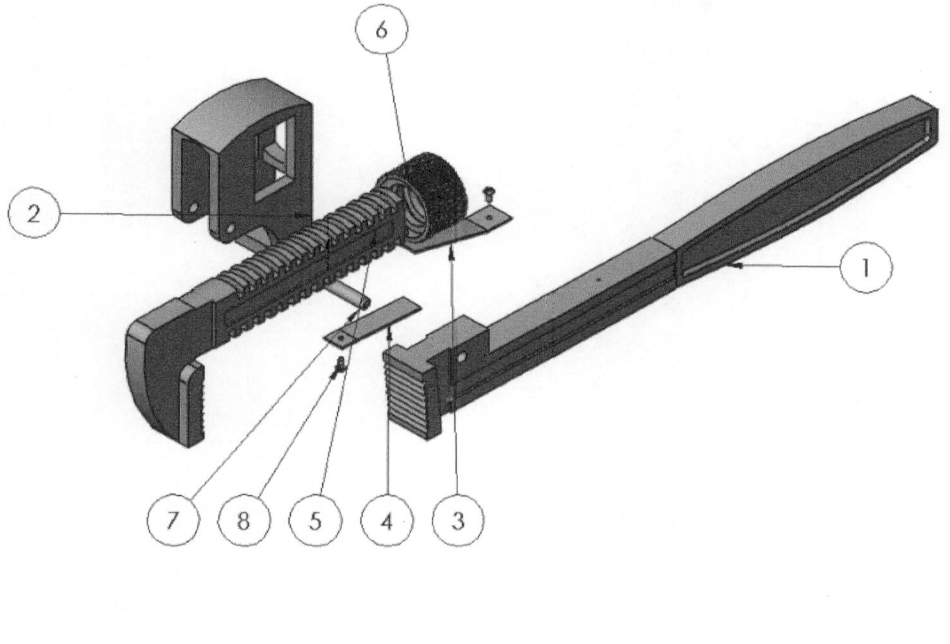

ITEM NO.	PART NUMBER	QTY.
1	Wrench Handle	1
2	Frame	1
3	Wrench plane2	1
4	Wrench plane	1
5	JAW	1
6	NUT	1
7	Wrench PIN	1
8	M2X0.4 Pan slot head screw- ANSI B18.6.7M	2

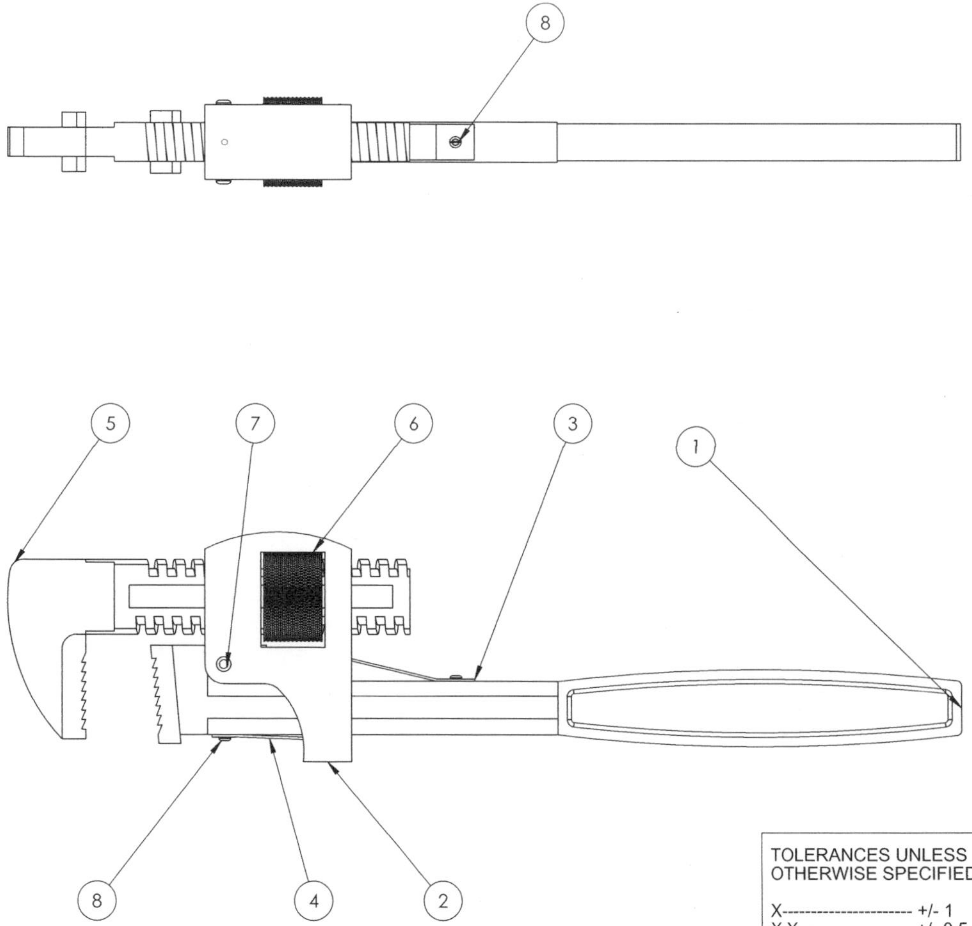

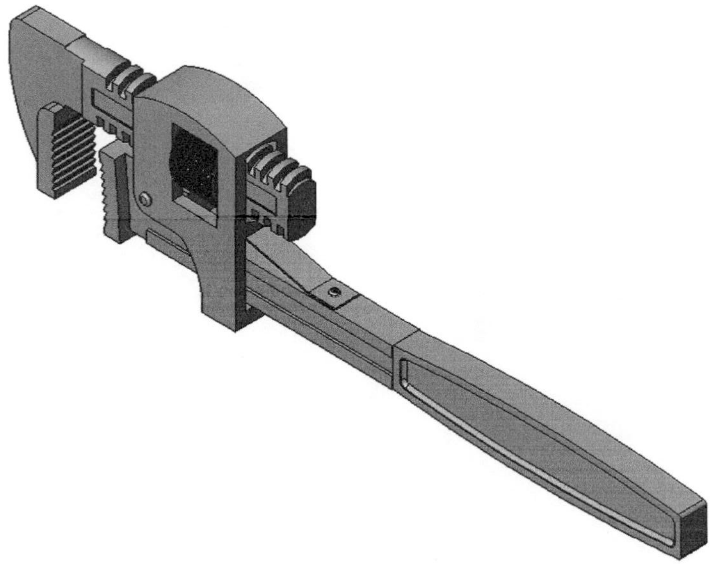

TOLERANCES UNLESS OTHERWISE SPECIFIED

X---------------------- +/- 1
X.X------------------- +/- 0.5
X.XX----------------- +/- 0.2
ANGLE-------------- +/- 0.5

ALL DIMENSIONS IN MM

FIRST ISSUED
DRAWN BY
CHECKED BY
APPROVED BY

CADCIM TECHNOLOGIES

Pipe Wrench Assembly

SIZE A3 | DRG NO. 8-000 | SHEET REV A

SCALE 2:1 | SHEET 1 OF 8

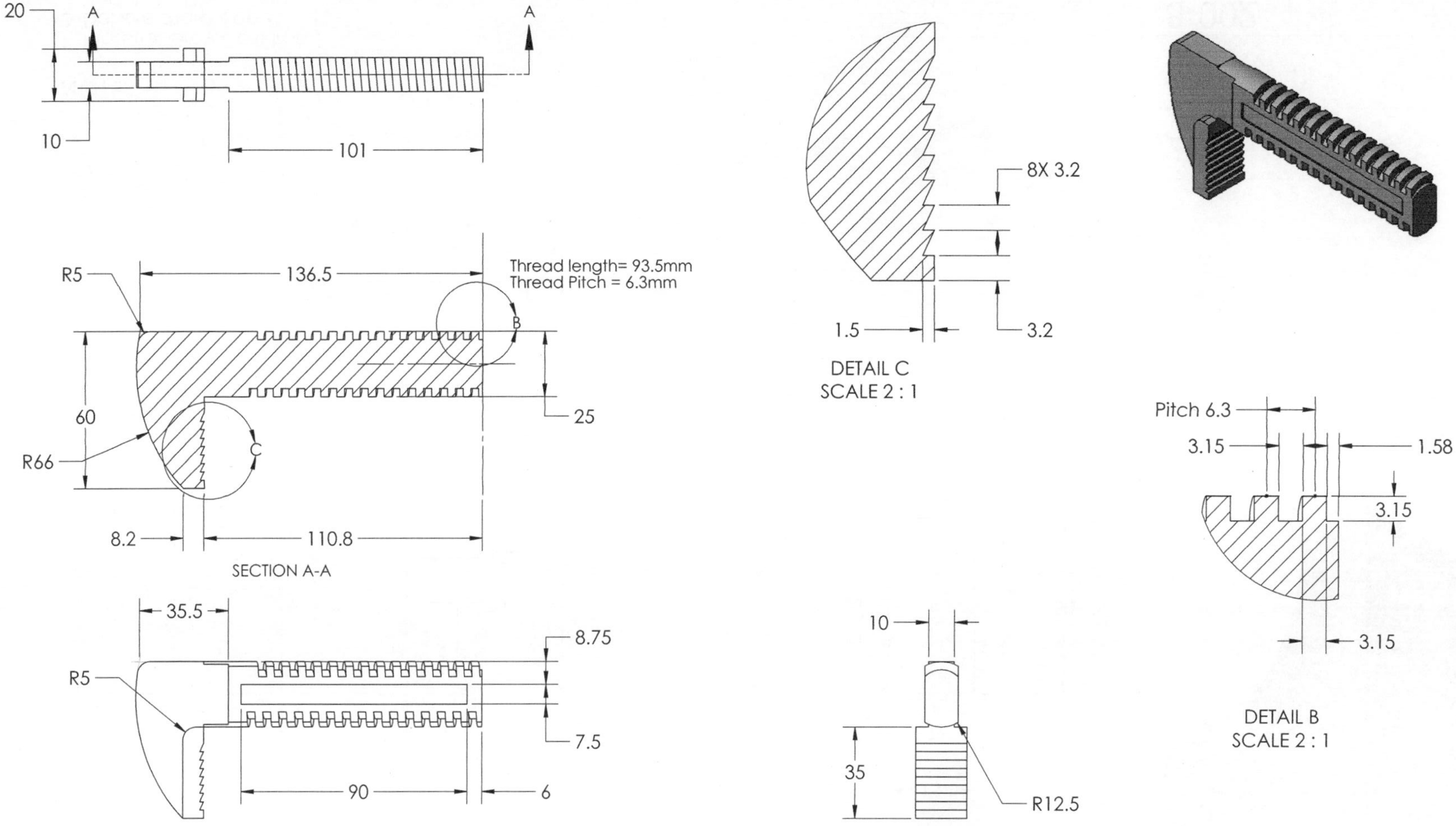

NOTES

1- Material Gray Cast Iron
2- Debure sharp edges

TOLERANCES UNLESS OTHERWISE SPECIFIED		CADCIM TECHNOLOGIES
X---------- +/- 1 X.X---------- +/- 0.5 X.XX---------- +/- 0.2 ANGLE---------- +/- 0.5	FIRST ISSUED	
	DRAWN BY	JAW
	CHECKED BY	
	APPROVED BY	SIZE A3 DRG NO. 8-001 SHEET REV A
ALL DIMENSIONS IN MM		SCALE 2:3 SHEET 2 OF 8

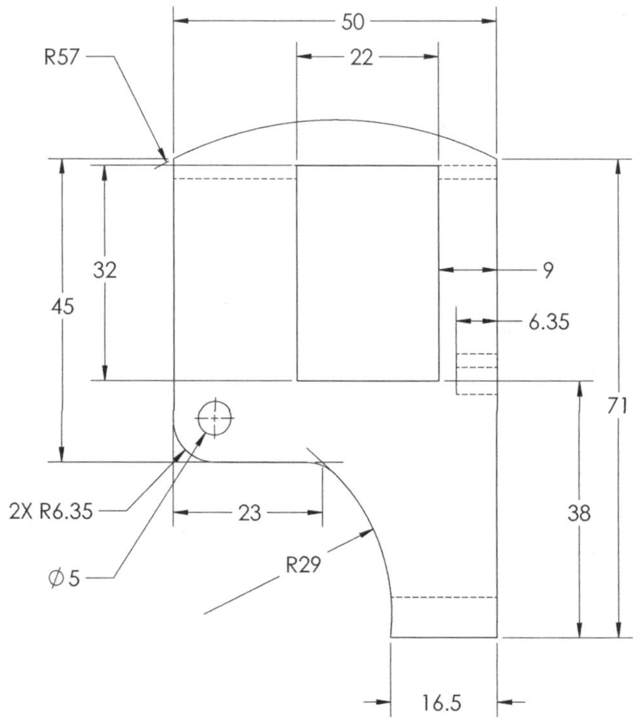

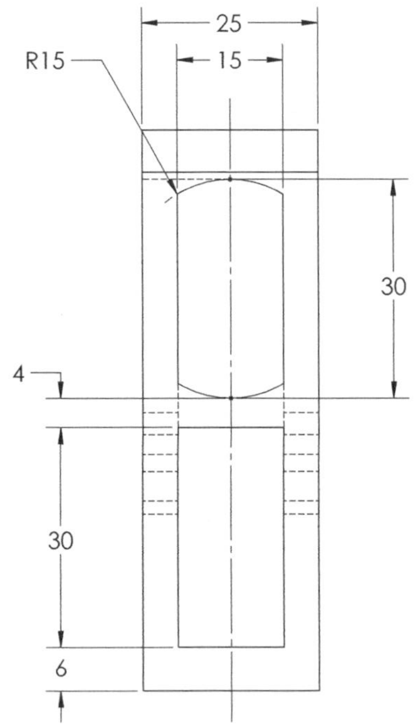

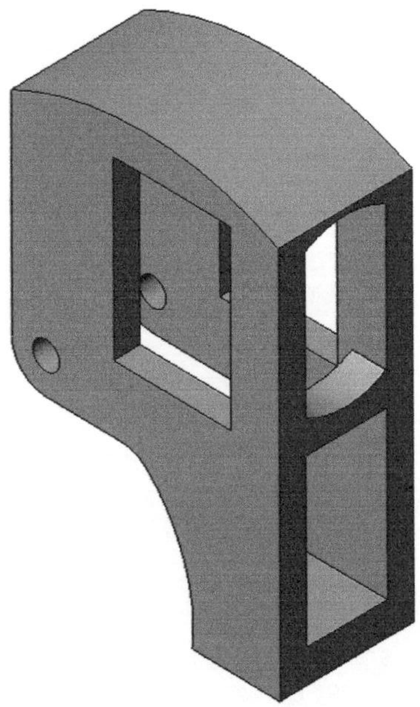

NOTES

1- Material Gray Cast Iron
2- Debure sharp edges

TOLERANCES UNLESS OTHERWISE SPECIFIED		CADCIM TECHNOLOGIES	
X---------- +/- 1	FIRST ISSUED	FRAME	
X.X---------- +/- 0.5	DRAWN BY		
X.XX---------- +/- 0.2	CHECKED BY		
ANGLE---------- +/- 0.5	APPROVED BY	SIZE A3 DRG NO. 8-002	SHEET REV A
ALL DIMENSIONS IN MM		SCALE 1:1	SHEET 3 OF 8

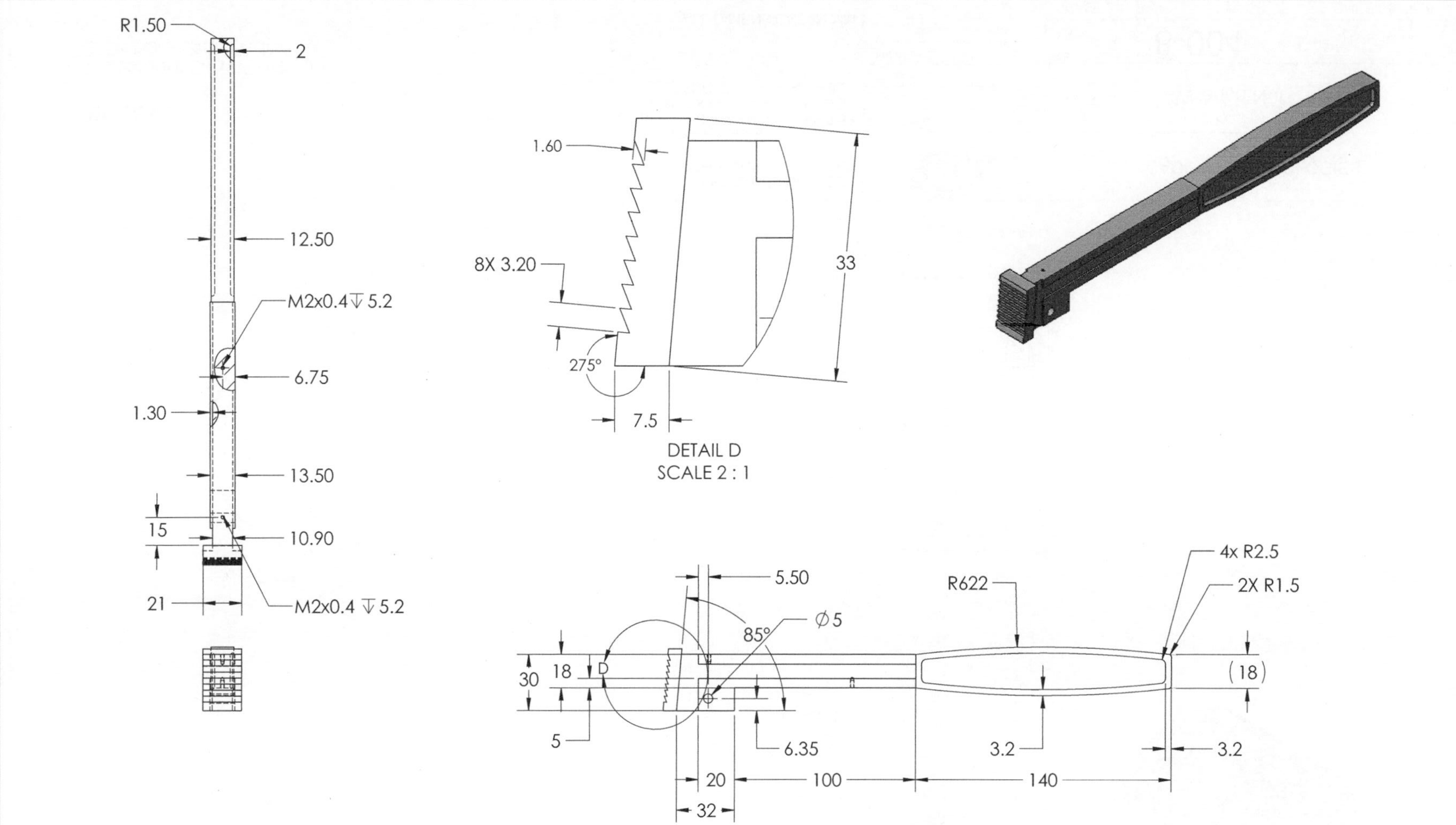

NOTES

1- Material Gray Cast Iron
2- Deburr sharp edges

TOLERANCES UNLESS OTHERWISE SPECIFIED

X---------- +/- 1
X.X---------- +/- 0.5
X.XX---------- +/- 0.2
ANGLE---------- +/- 0.5

ALL DIMENSIONS IN MM

FIRST ISSUED
DRAWN BY
CHECKED BY
APPROVED BY

CADCIM TECHNOLOGIES

WRENCH HANDLE

SIZE	DRG NO.	SHEET REV
A3	8-003	A
SCALE 1:2		SHEET 4 OF 8

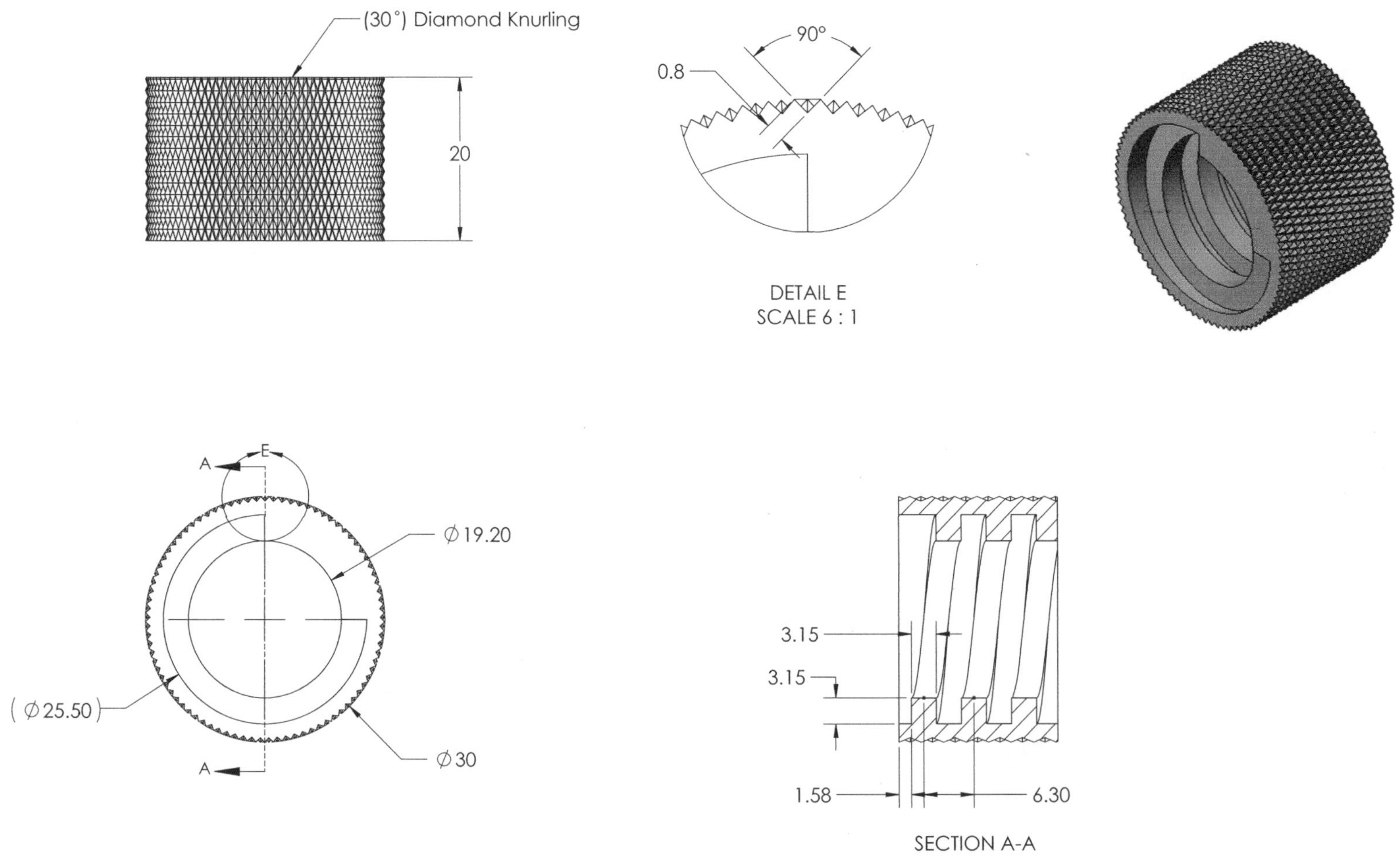

NOTES

1- Material Gray Cast Iron
2- Debure sharp edges

TOLERANCES UNLESS OTHERWISE SPECIFIED		CADCIM TECHNOLOGIES
X---------- +/- 1 X.X---------- +/- 0.5 X.XX---------- +/- 0.2 ANGLE---------- +/- 0.5	FIRST ISSUED DRAWN BY CHECKED BY APPROVED BY	Wrench Nut
ALL DIMENSIONS IN MM		SIZE A3 · DRG NO. 8-004 · SHEET REV A
		SCALE 2:1 · SHEET 5 OF 8

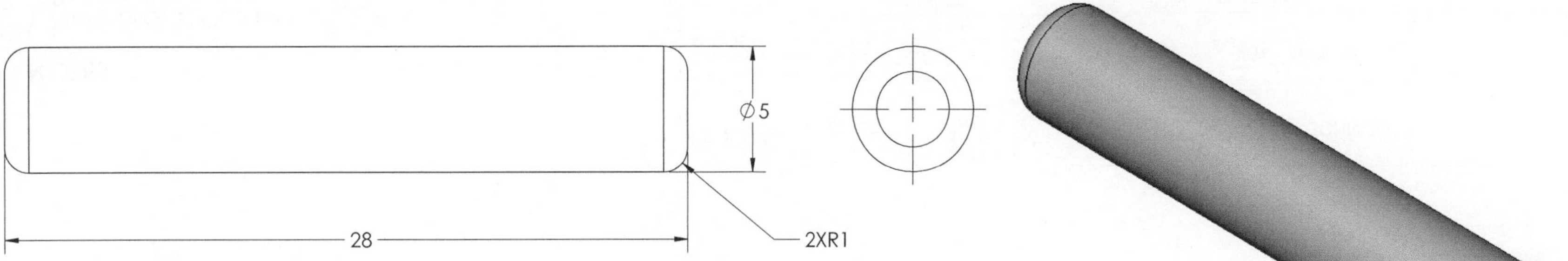

Wrench Pin

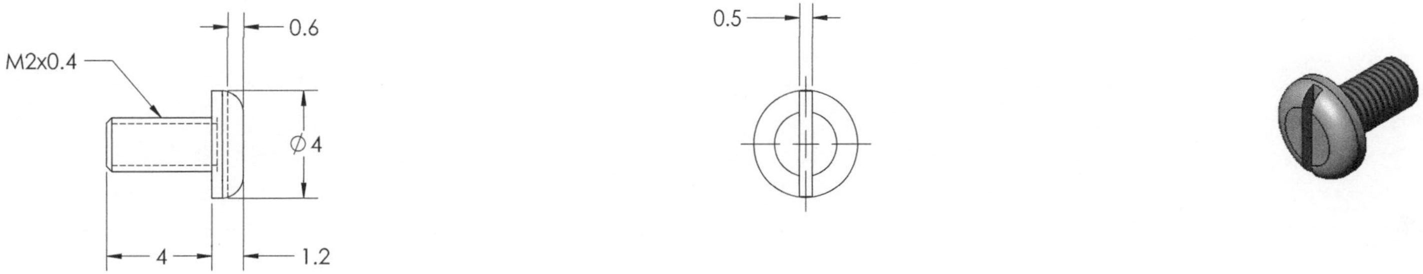

M2X0.4 Pan Slot Head Screw

NOTES

1- Material Stainless steel
2- Debure sharp edges

TOLERANCES UNLESS OTHERWISE SPECIFIED		CADCIM TECHNOLOGIES		
X---------- +/- 1 X.X---------- +/- 0.5 X.XX---------- +/- 0.2 ANGLE---------- +/- 0.5	FIRST ISSUED DRAWN BY CHECKED BY APPROVED BY	1. Wrench Pin 2. M2X0.4 Pan slot head Screw-ANSI B18.6.7M		
ALL DIMENSIONS IN MM		SIZE A3	DRG NO. 8-005	SHEET REV A
		SCALE 6:1		SHEET 6 OF 8

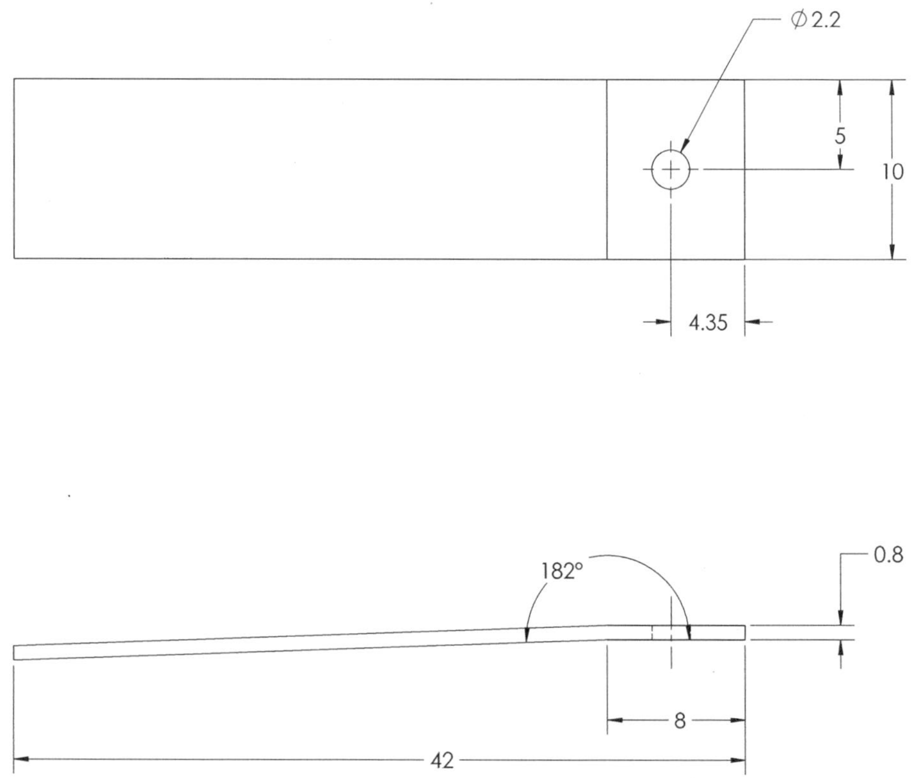

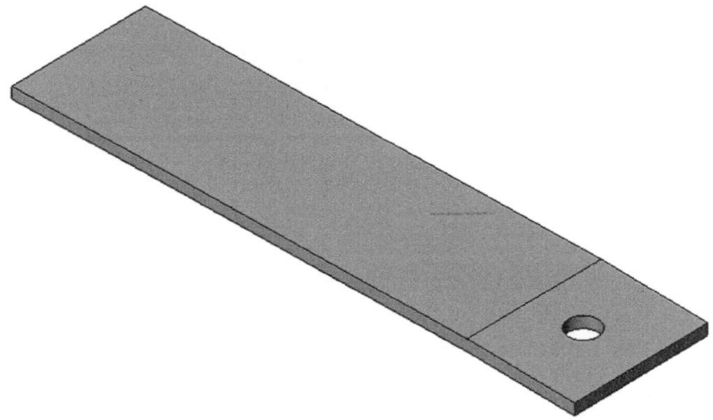

NOTES

1- Material Gray Cast Iron
2- Debure sharp edges

TOLERANCES UNLESS OTHERWISE SPECIFIED

X---------------------- +/- 1
X.X------------------- +/- 0.5
X.XX----------------- +/- 0.2
ANGLE-------------- +/- 0.5

ALL DIMENSIONS IN MM

FIRST ISSUED	
DRAWN BY	
CHECKED BY	
APPROVED BY	

CADCIM TECHNOLOGIES

Wrench Plane

SIZE	DRG NO.	SHEET REV
A3	8-006	A
SCALE 4:1		SHEET 7 OF 8

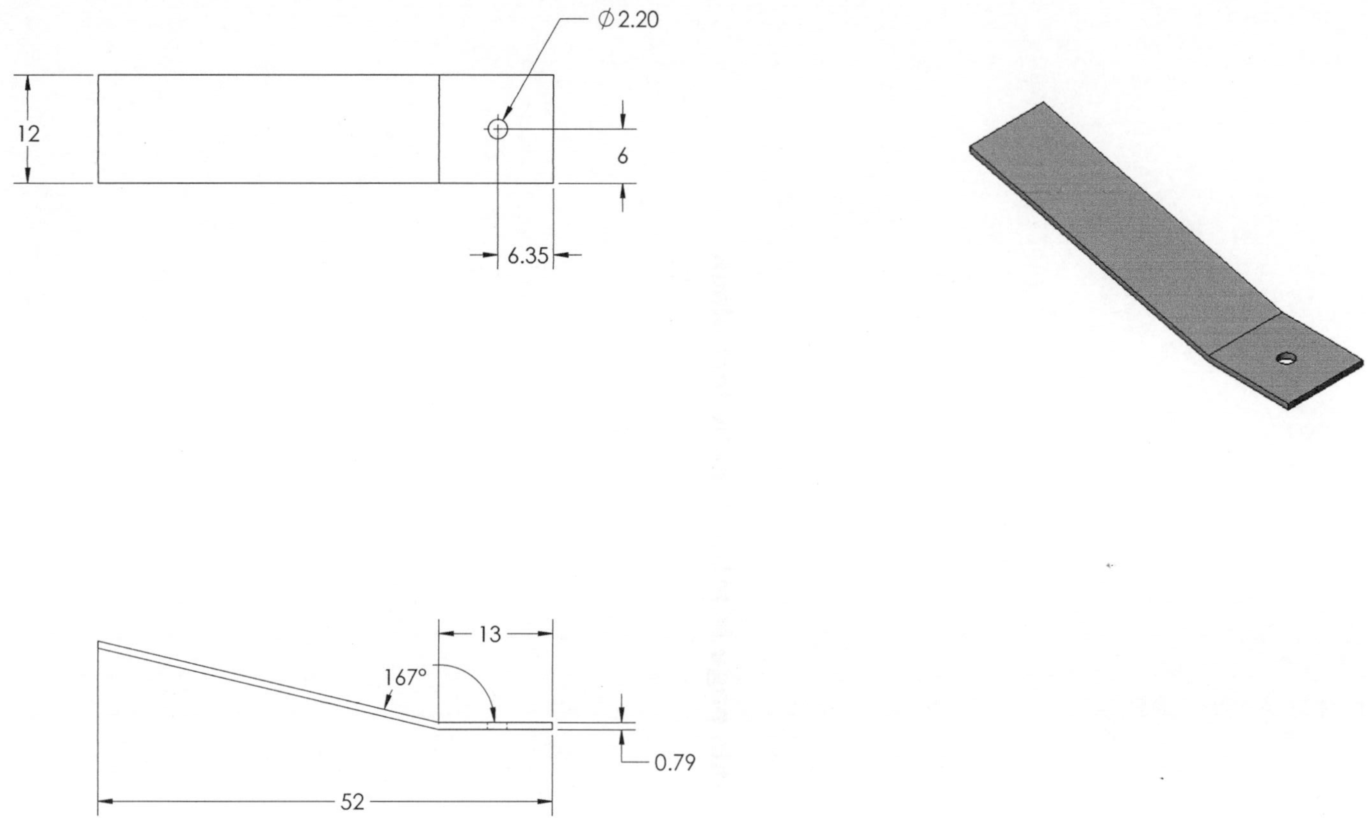

NOTES

1- Material Gray Cast Iron
2- Debure sharp edges

TOLERANCES UNLESS OTHERWISE SPECIFIED		CADCIM TECHNOLOGIES	
X---------- +/- 1 X.X---------- +/- 0.5 X.XX---------- +/- 0.2 ANGLE---------- +/- 0.5	FIRST ISSUED DRAWN BY CHECKED BY APPROVED BY	Wrench Plane 2	
ALL DIMENSIONS IN MM		SIZE A3 · DRG NO. 8-007	SHEET REV A
		SCALE 2:1	SHEET 8 OF 8

This page is intentionally left blank

Project 9

Hand Drill Assembly

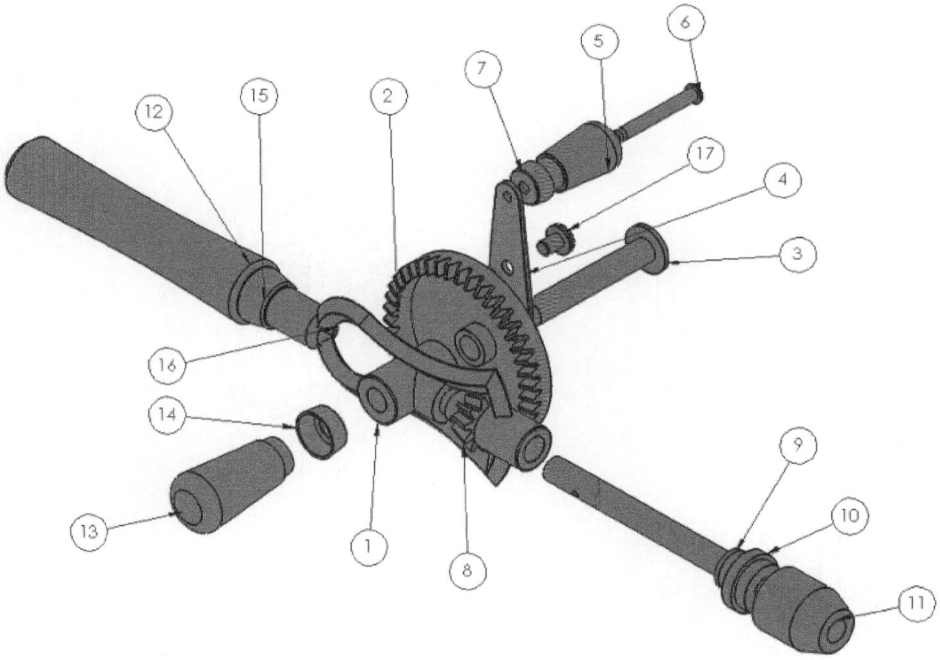

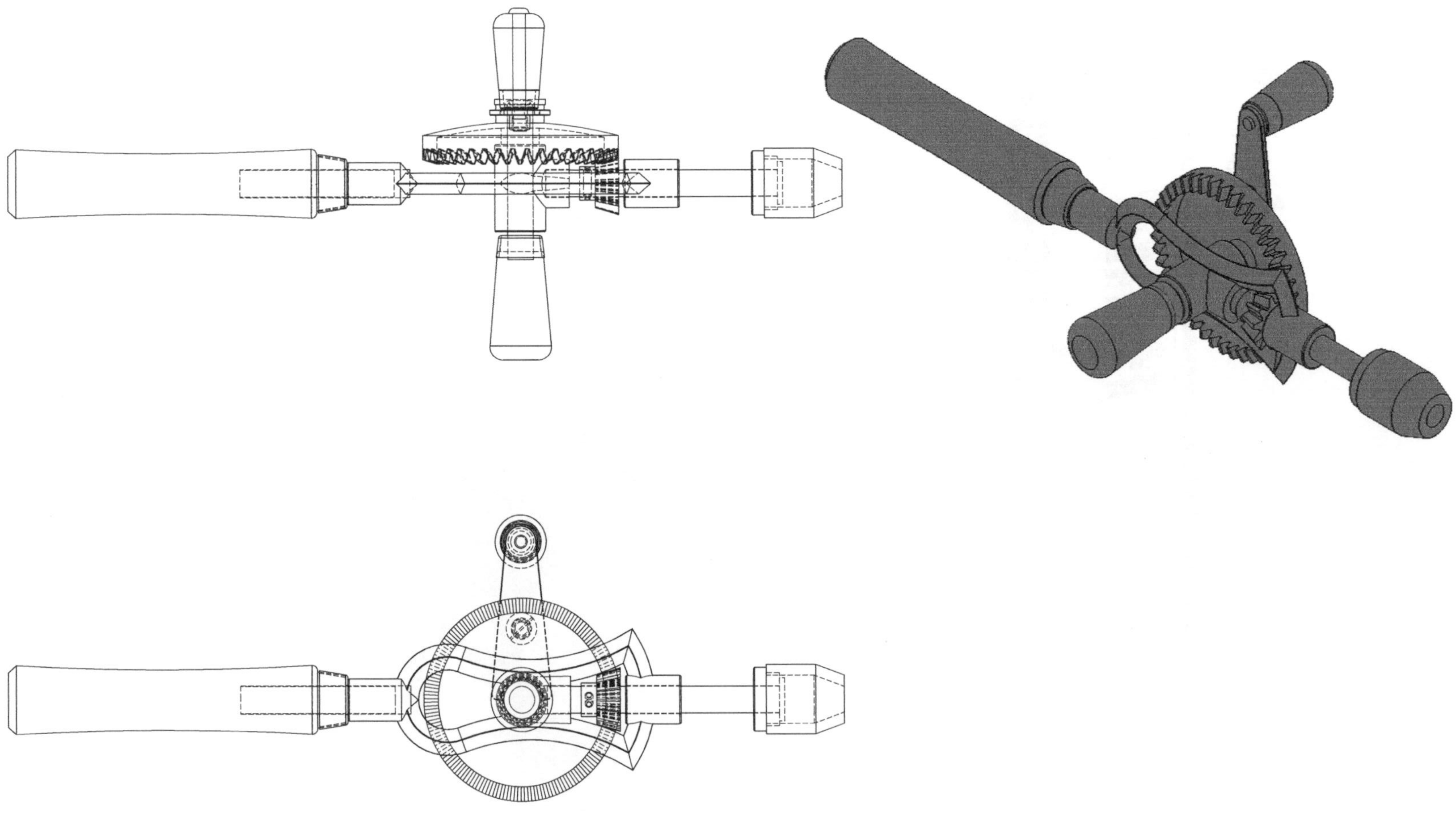

TOLERANCES UNLESS OTHERWISE SPECIFIED		CADCIM TECHNOLOGIES
X---------------------- +/- 1	FIRST ISSUED	Hand Drill Assembly
X.X------------------- +/- 0.5	DRAWN BY	
X.XX----------------- +/- 0.2	CHECKED BY	
ANGLE-------------- +/- 0.5	APPROVED BY	SIZE A3 · DRG NO. 9-000 · SHEET REV A
ALL DIMENSIONS IN MM		SCALE 1:1 · SHEET 1 OF 16

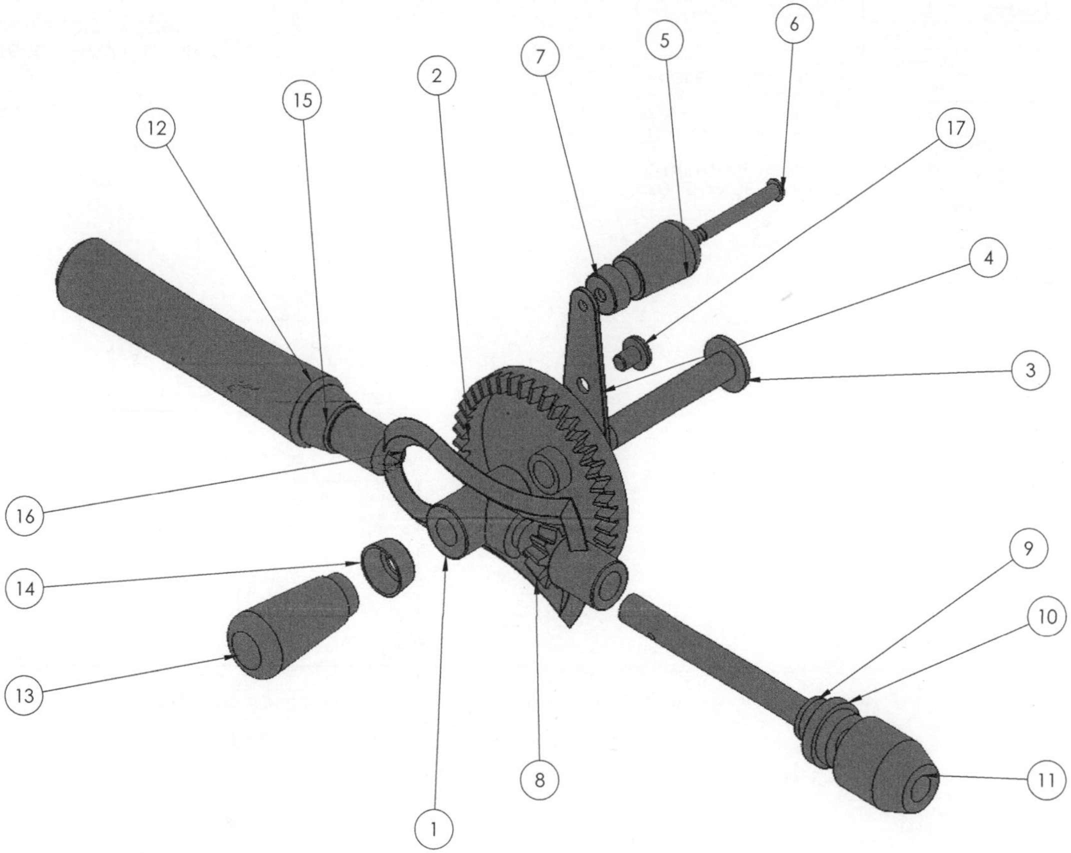

ITEM NO.	PART NUMBER	QTY.
1	housing	1
2	gear wheel	1
3	idler pinion shaft	1
4	crank	1
5	gear handle	1
6	crank knob shaft	1
7	gear handle cap	1
8	Pinion_1	1
9	driving pinion shaft	1
10	back plate chuck	1
11	chuck	1
12	main handle	1
13	side handle	1
14	cap side handle	1
15	cap main handle	1
16	main handle shaft	1
17	M6x1.0x8 Pan Slot Head Screw- ANSI B18.6.7M	1

TOLERANCES UNLESS OTHERWISE SPECIFIED

X---------------------- +/- 1
X.X-------------------- +/- 0.5
X.XX------------------ +/- 0.2
ANGLE-------------- +/- 0.5

ALL DIMENSIONS IN MM

FIRST ISSUED	
DRAWN BY	
CHECKED BY	
APPROVED BY	

CADCIM TECHNOLOGIES

Hand Drill Exploded

SIZE	DRG NO.	SHEET REV
A3	9-000	A
SCALE 2:3		SHEET 2 OF 16

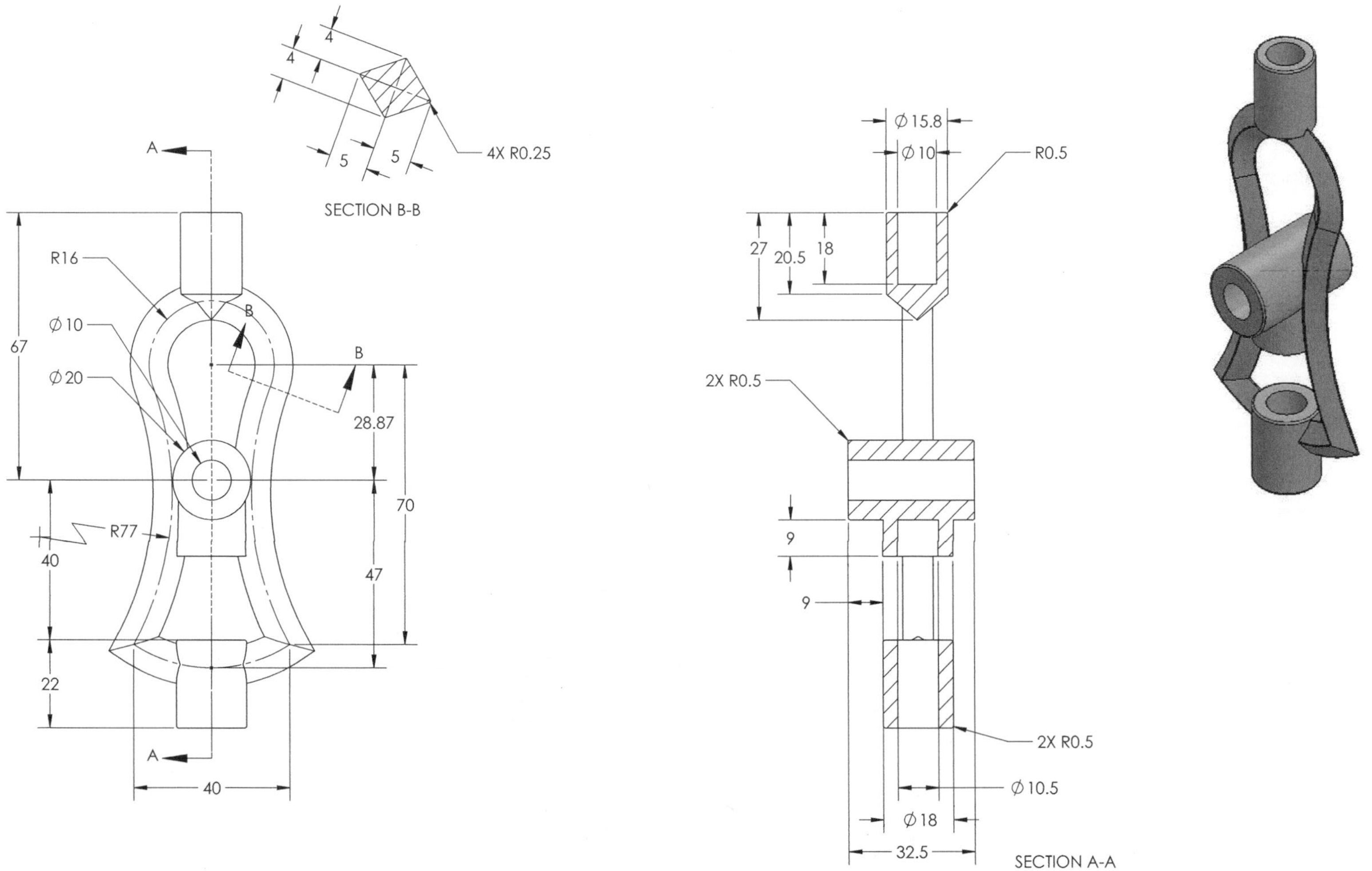

NOTES

1- Material Gray Cast Iron
2- Deburr sharp edges

TOLERANCES UNLESS OTHERWISE SPECIFIED		CADCIM TECHNOLOGIES
X---------- +/- 1	FIRST ISSUED	Housing
X.X---------- +/- 0.5	DRAWN BY	
X.XX---------- +/- 0.2	CHECKED BY	
ANGLE---------- +/- 0.5	APPROVED BY	SIZE A3 · DRG NO. 9-001 · SHEET REV A
ALL DIMENSIONS IN MM		SCALE 1:1 · SHEET 3 OF 16

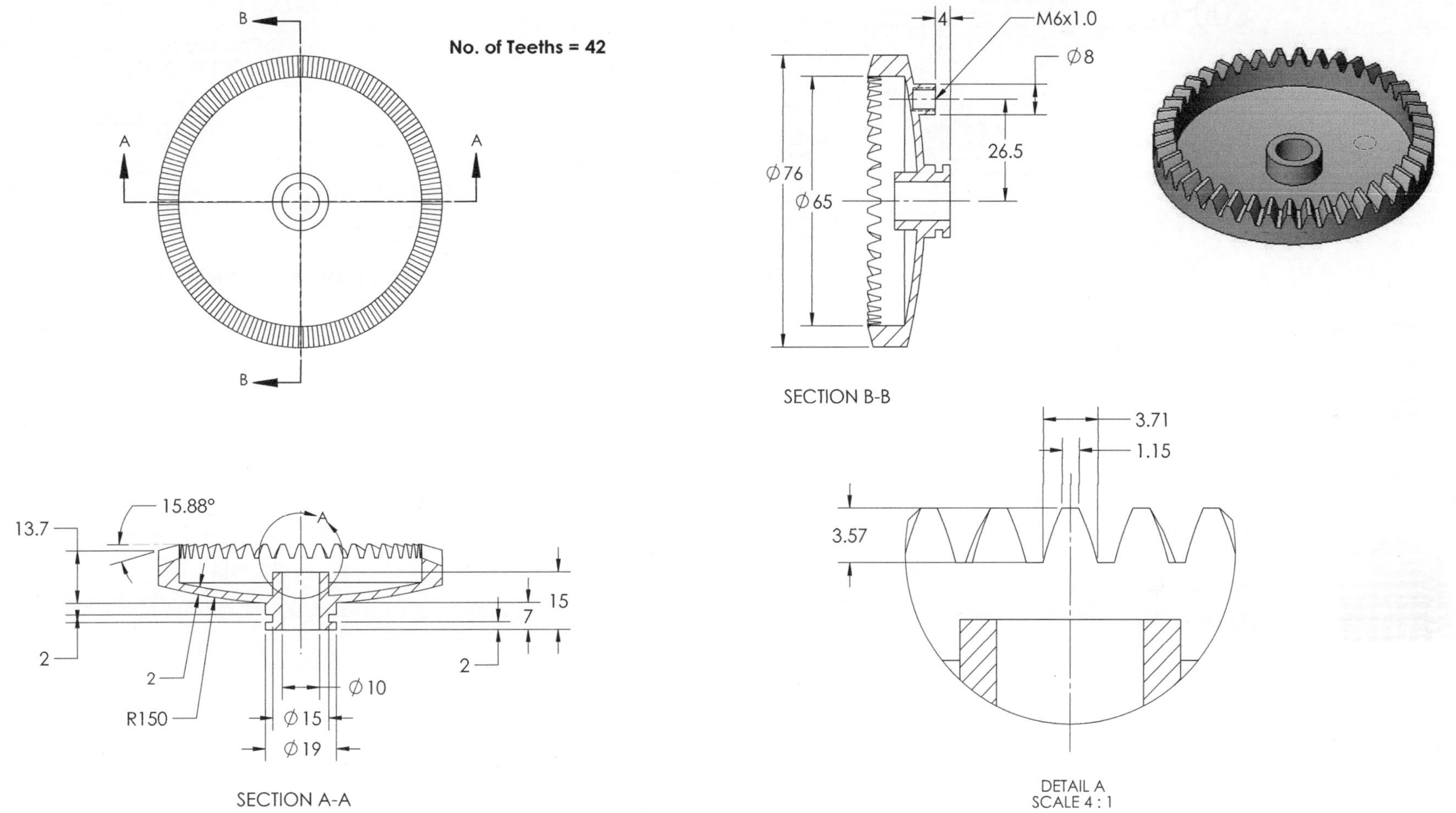

NOTES

1- Material Tool Steel
2- Deburr sharp edges

TOLERANCES UNLESS OTHERWISE SPECIFIED		CADCIM TECHNOLOGIES
X---------- +/- 1	FIRST ISSUED	Gear Wheel
X.X---------- +/- 0.5	DRAWN BY	
X.XX---------- +/- 0.2	CHECKED BY	
ANGLE---------- +/- 0.5	APPROVED BY	SIZE A3 · DRG NO. 9-002 · SHEET REV A
ALL DIMENSIONS IN MM		SCALE 1:1 · SHEET 4 OF 16

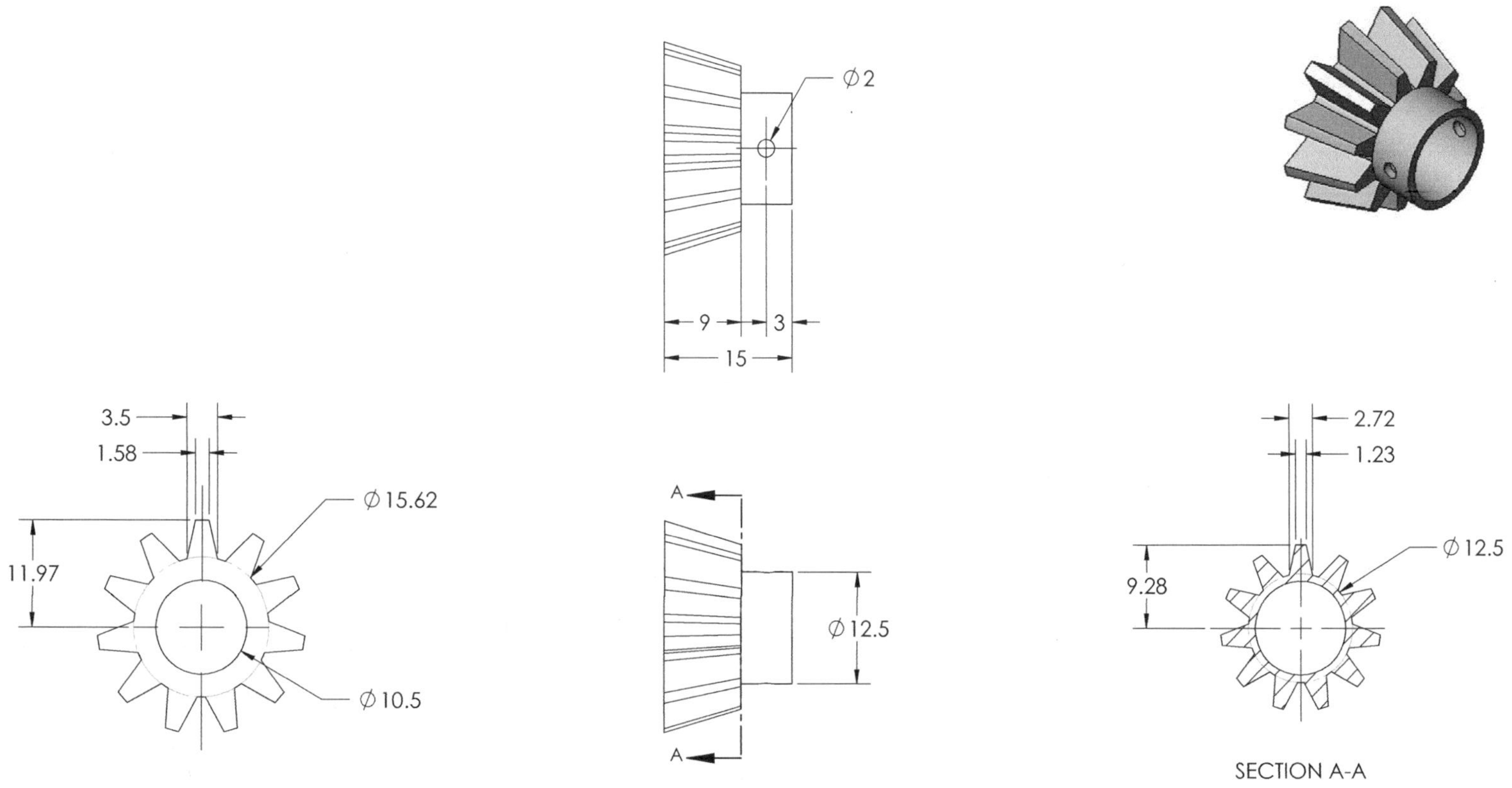

No. of teeths= 11

NOTES

1- Material Tool Steel
2- Deburr sharp edges

TOLERANCES UNLESS OTHERWISE SPECIFIED		CADCIM TECHNOLOGIES
X---------- +/- 1	FIRST ISSUED	Pinion
X.X---------- +/- 0.5	DRAWN BY	
X.XX---------- +/- 0.2	CHECKED BY	
ANGLE---------- +/- 0.5	APPROVED BY	SIZE A3 · DRG NO. 9-003 · SHEET REV A
ALL DIMENSIONS IN MM		SCALE 2:1 · SHEET 5 OF 16

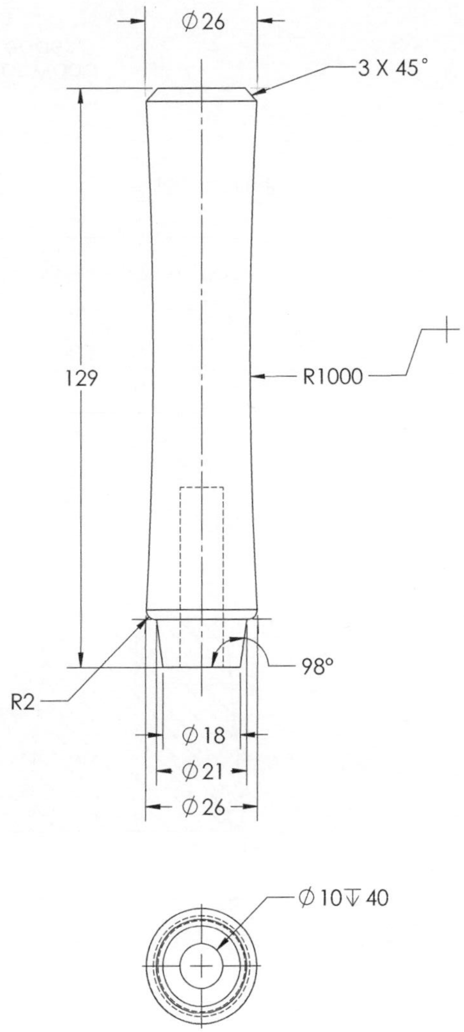

NOTES

1- Material Cedar wood
2- Deburr sharp edges

TOLERANCES UNLESS OTHERWISE SPECIFIED		CADCIM TECHNOLOGIES
X------ +/- 1	FIRST ISSUED	Main Handle
X.X------ +/- 0.5	DRAWN BY	
X.XX------ +/- 0.2	CHECKED BY	
ANGLE------ +/- 0.5	APPROVED BY	SIZE A3 — DRG NO. 9-004 — SHEET REV A
ALL DIMENSIONS IN MM		SCALE 1:1 — SHEET 6 OF 16

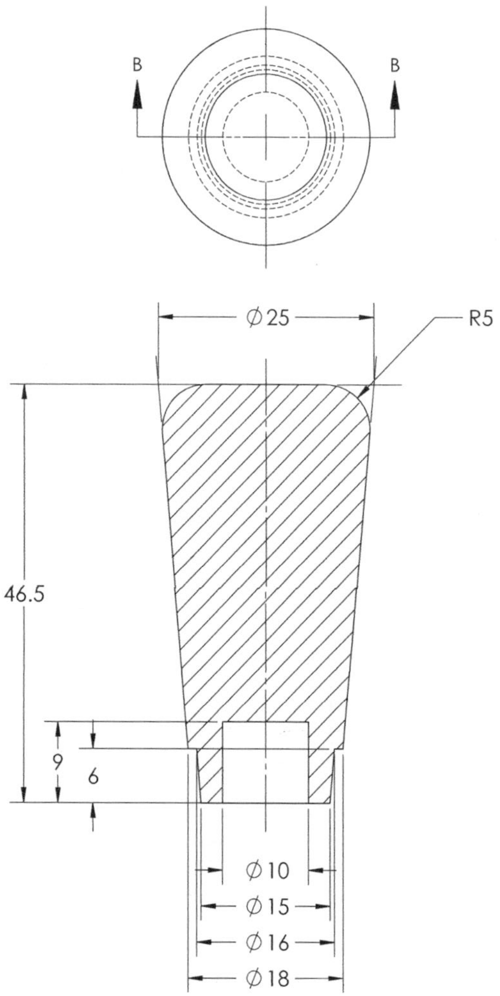

SECTION B-B

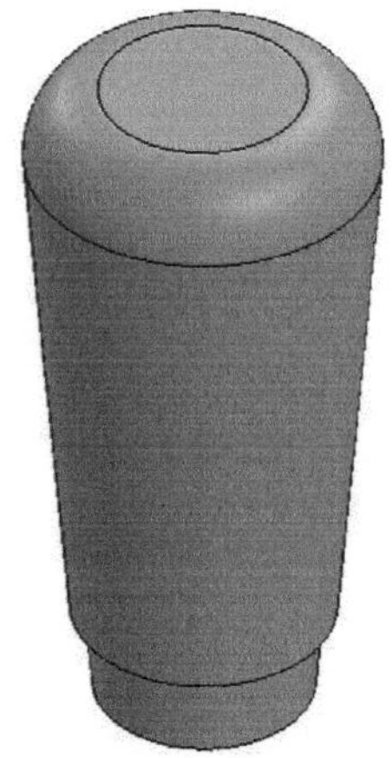

NOTES

1- Material Cedar Wood
2- Deburr sharp edges

TOLERANCES UNLESS OTHERWISE SPECIFIED		CADCIM TECHNOLOGIES
X---------- +/- 1 X.X---------- +/- 0.5 X.XX---------- +/- 0.2 ANGLE---------- +/- 0.5	FIRST ISSUED DRAWN BY CHECKED BY APPROVED BY	Side Handle
ALL DIMENSIONS IN MM		SIZE A3 · DRG NO. 9-005 · SHEET REV A
		SCALE 2:1 · SHEET 7 OF 16

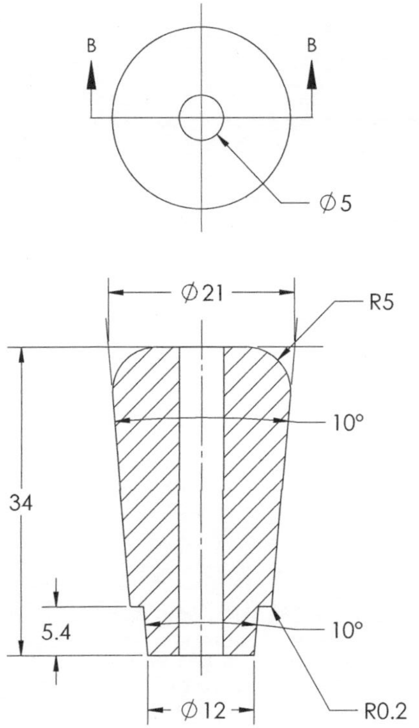

SECTION B-B

Gear Handle

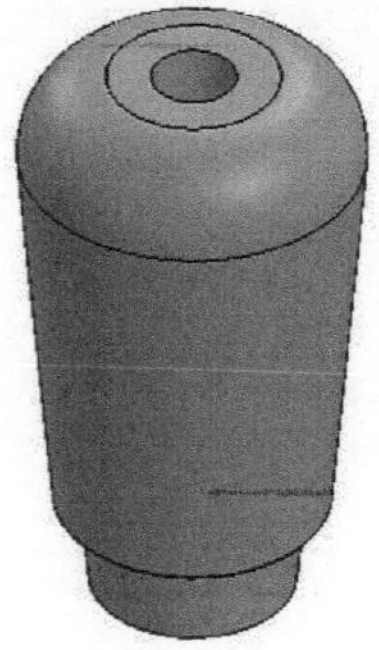

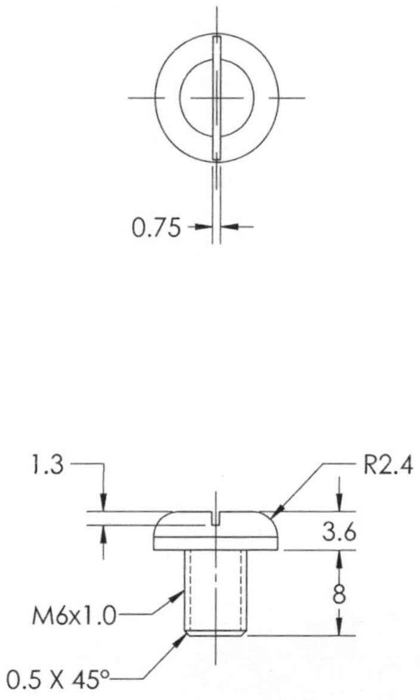

M6x1.0x8 Pan Slot Head Screw

NOTES

1- Material Cedar Wood for Gear handle and SS for Pan slot head screw
2- Deburr sharp edges

TOLERANCES UNLESS OTHERWISE SPECIFIED		CADCIM TECHNOLOGIES
X---------- +/- 1 X.X---------- +/- 0.5 X.XX---------- +/- 0.2 ANGLE---------- +/- 0.5	FIRST ISSUED DRAWN BY CHECKED BY APPROVED BY	1. Gear Handle 2. M6X1.0X8 Pan slot Head Screw- ANSI B18.6.7M
ALL DIMENSIONS IN MM		SIZE A3 · DRG NO. 9-006 · SHEET REV A
		SCALE 2:1 · SHEET 8 OF 16

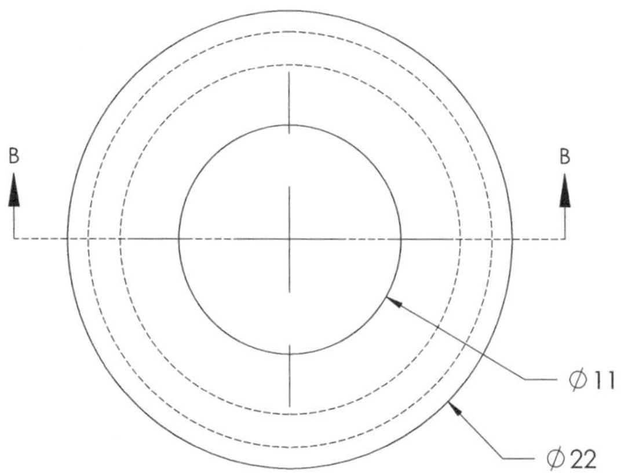

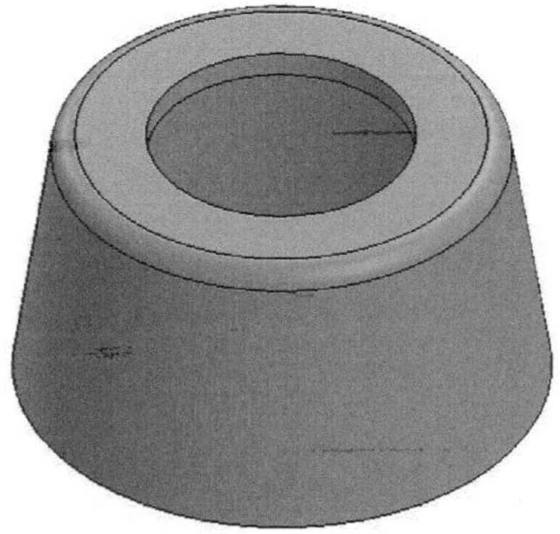

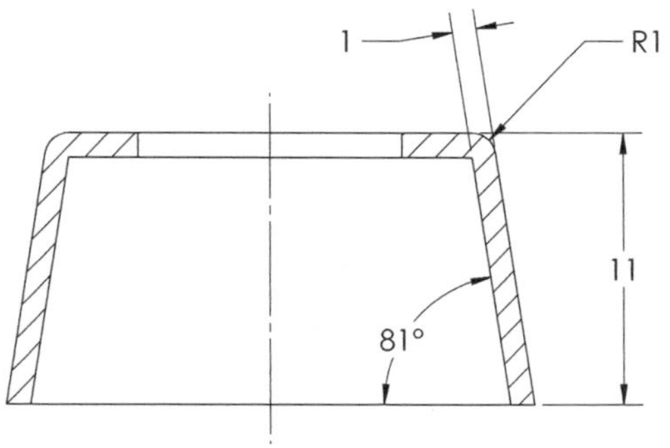

SECTION B-B

NOTES

1- Material Gray Cast Iron
2- Deburr sharp edges

TOLERANCES UNLESS OTHERWISE SPECIFIED		CADCIM TECHNOLOGIES
X---------- +/- 1 X.X---------- +/- 0.5 X.XX---------- +/- 0.2 ANGLE---------- +/- 0.5	FIRST ISSUED DRAWN BY CHECKED BY APPROVED BY	Main Handle Cap
ALL DIMENSIONS IN MM		SIZE A3 · DRG NO. 9-007 · SHEET REV A
		SCALE 4:1 · SHEET 9 OF 16

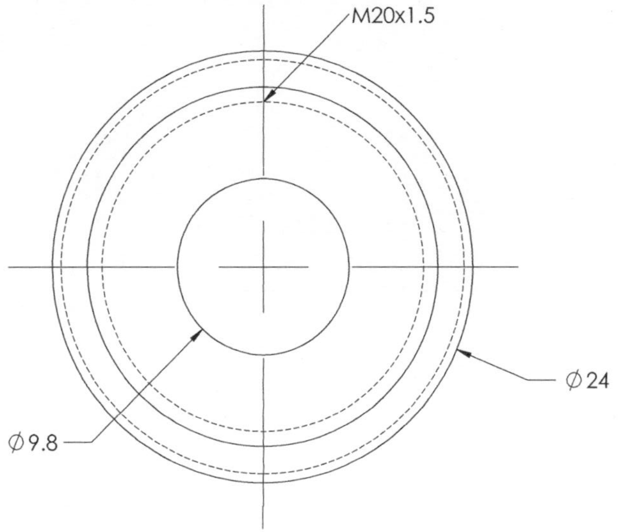

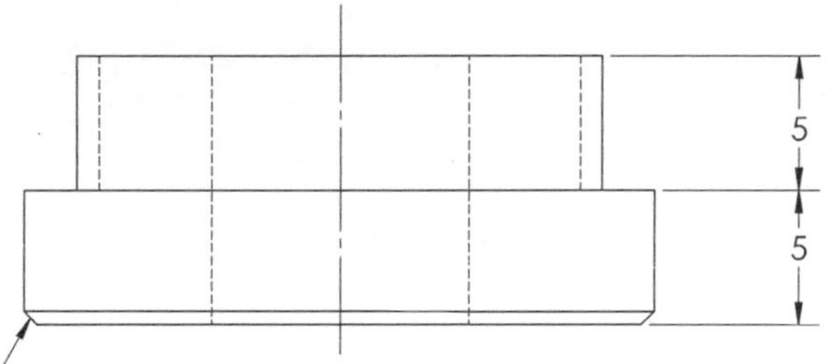

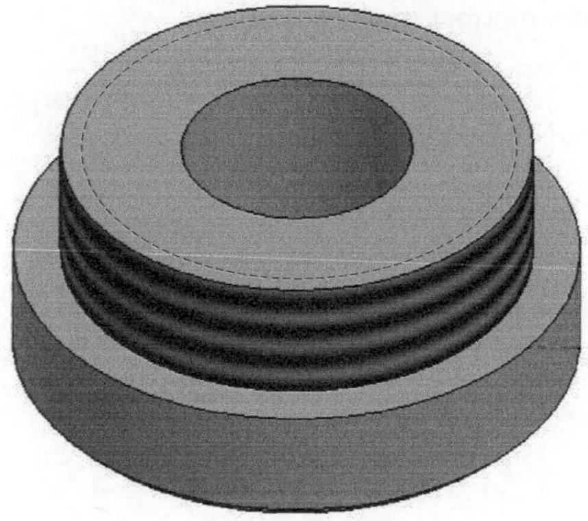

NOTES

1- Material ASTM A36 Steel
2- Deburr sharp edges

TOLERANCES UNLESS OTHERWISE SPECIFIED

X---------- +/- 1
X.X---------- +/- 0.5
X.XX---------- +/- 0.2
ANGLE---------- +/- 0.5

ALL DIMENSIONS IN MM

FIRST ISSUED	
DRAWN BY	
CHECKED BY	
APPROVED BY	

CADCIM TECHNOLOGIES

Back Plate Chuck

SIZE	DRG NO.	SHEET REV
A3	9-008	A
SCALE 4:1		SHEET 10 OF 16

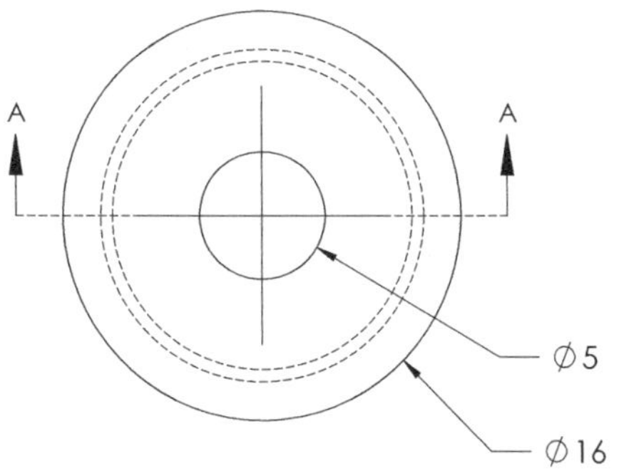

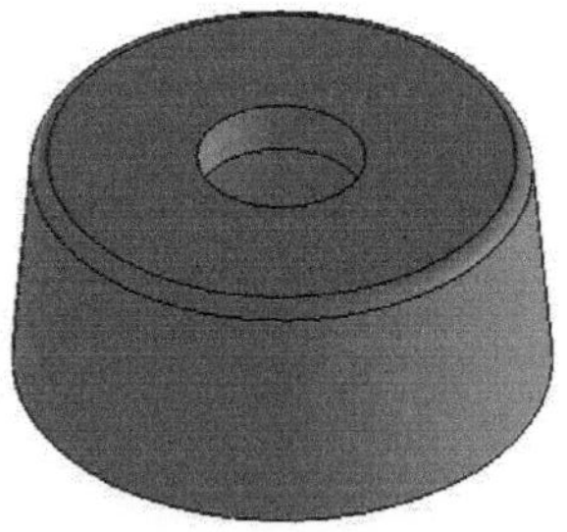

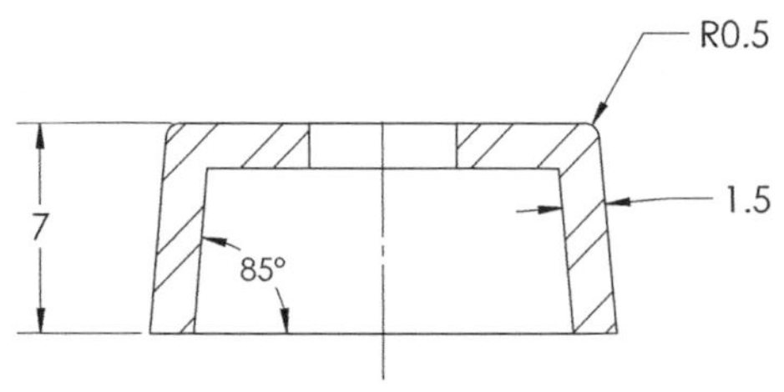

SECTION A-A

NOTES

1- Material Gray Cast Iron
2- Deburr sharp edges

TOLERANCES UNLESS OTHERWISE SPECIFIED		CADCIM TECHNOLOGIES
X------ +/- 1 X.X------ +/- 0.5 X.XX------ +/- 0.2 ANGLE------ +/- 0.5	FIRST ISSUED DRAWN BY CHECKED BY APPROVED BY	Gear Handle Cap
ALL DIMENSIONS IN MM		SIZE A3 · DRG NO. 9-009 · SHEET REV A
		SCALE 4:1 · SHEET 11 OF 16

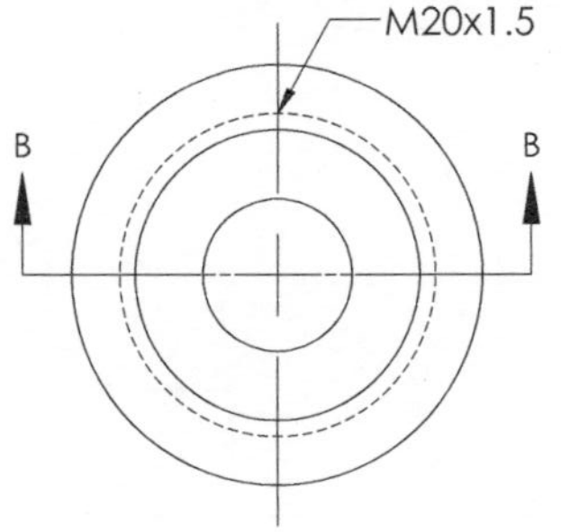

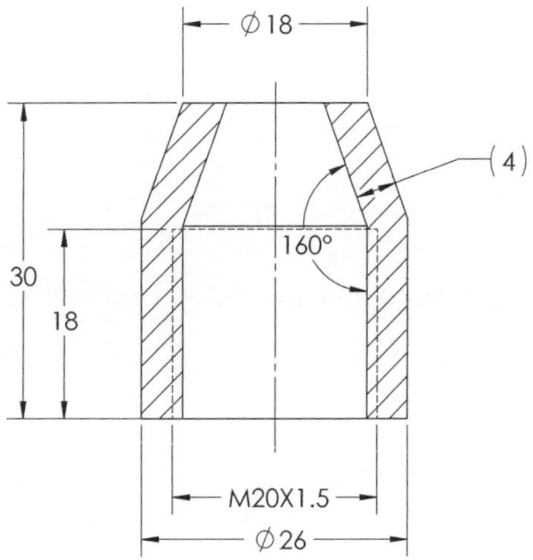

SECTION B-B

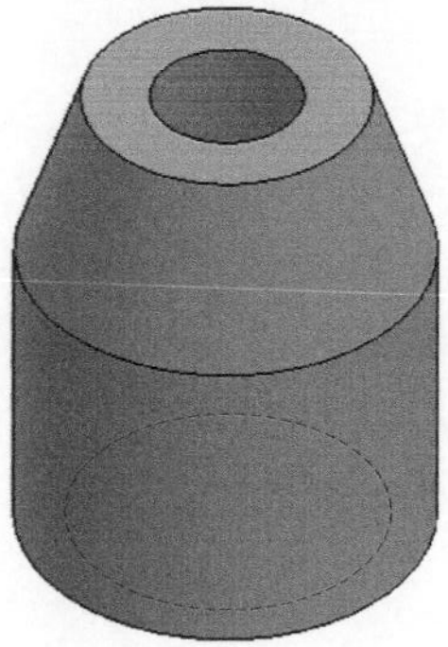

NOTES

1- Material Gray Cast Iron
2- Deburr sharp edges

TOLERANCES UNLESS OTHERWISE SPECIFIED

X------------------------ +/- 1
X.X-------------------- +/- 0.5
X.XX------------------ +/- 0.2
ANGLE--------------- +/- 0.5

ALL DIMENSIONS IN MM

FIRST ISSUED	
DRAWN BY	
CHECKED BY	
APPROVED BY	

CADCIM TECHNOLOGIES

Chuck

SIZE	DRG NO.	SHEET REV
A3	9-010	A
SCALE 2:1		SHEET 12 OF 16

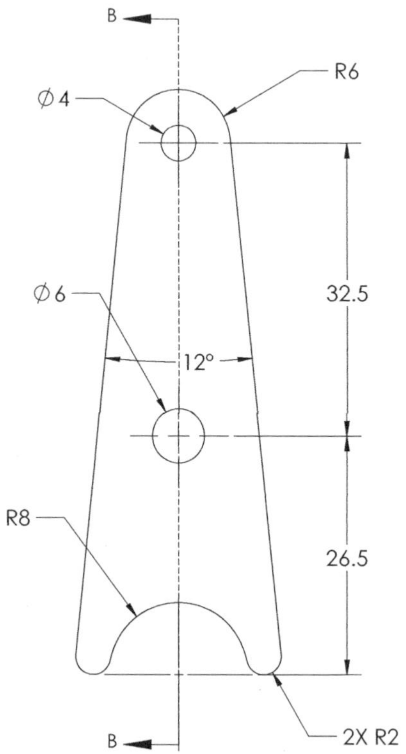

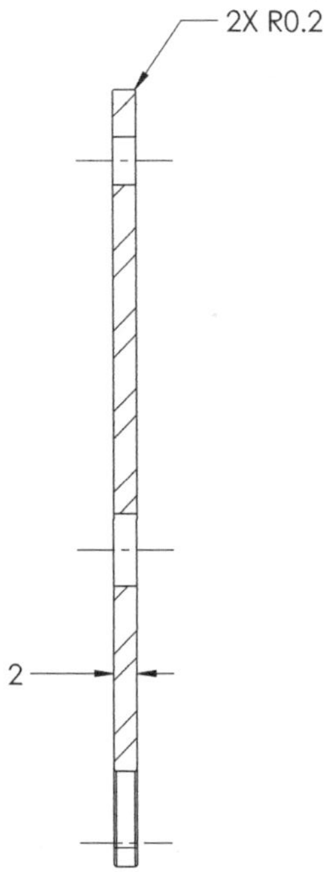

SECTION B-B

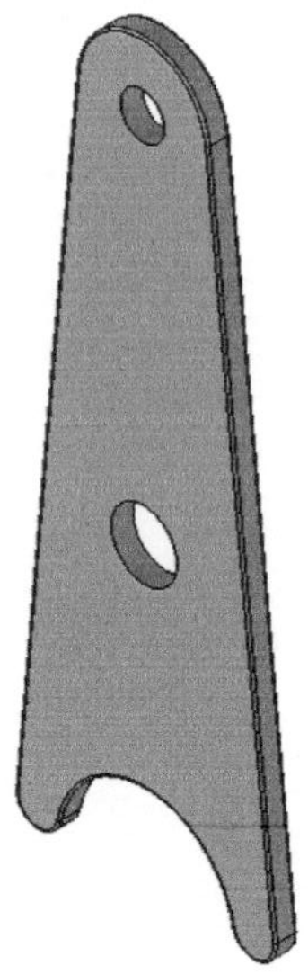

NOTES

1- Material Gray Cast Iron
2- Deburr sharp edges

TOLERANCES UNLESS OTHERWISE SPECIFIED		CADCIM TECHNOLOGIES
X---------- +/- 1 X.X---------- +/- 0.5 X.XX---------- +/- 0.2 ANGLE---------- +/- 0.5	FIRST ISSUED DRAWN BY CHECKED BY APPROVED BY	Crank
ALL DIMENSIONS IN MM		SIZE A3 | DRG NO. 9-011 | SHEET REV A
		SCALE 2:1 | SHEET 13 OF 16

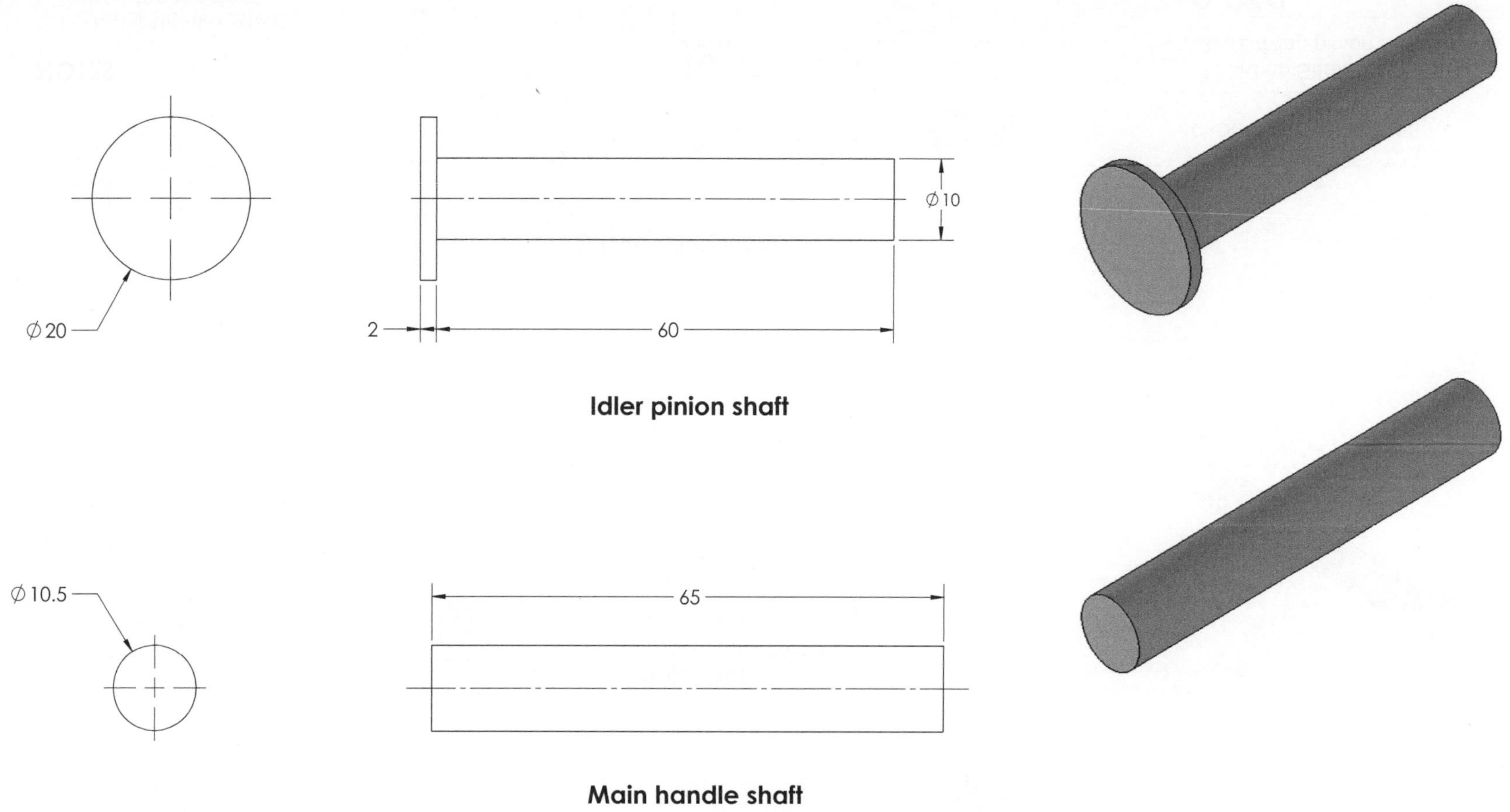

NOTES

1- Material SS
3- Deburr sharp edges

TOLERANCES UNLESS OTHERWISE SPECIFIED		CADCIM TECHNOLOGIES
X---------- +/- 1 X.X---------- +/- 0.5 X.XX---------- +/- 0.2 ANGLE---------- +/- 0.5	FIRST ISSUED DRAWN BY CHECKED BY APPROVED BY	1. Idler pinion Shaft 2. Main Hnadle Shaft
ALL DIMENSIONS IN MM		SIZE A3 · DRG NO. 9-012 · SHEET REV A
		SCALE 2:1 · SHEET 14 OF 16

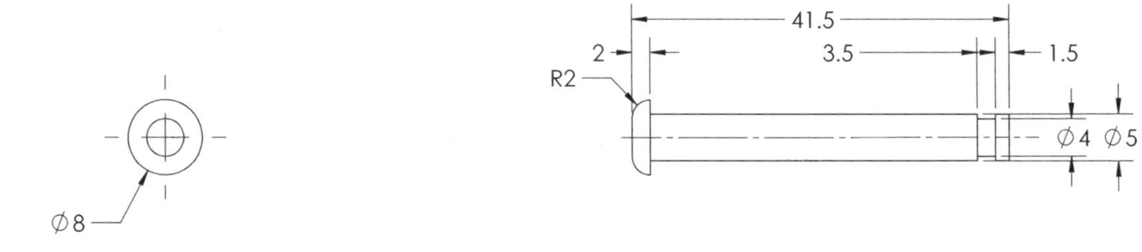

Knob Shaft

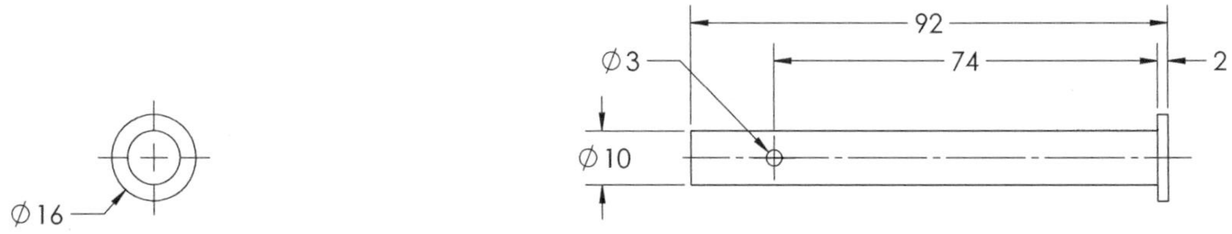

Driving Pinion Shaft

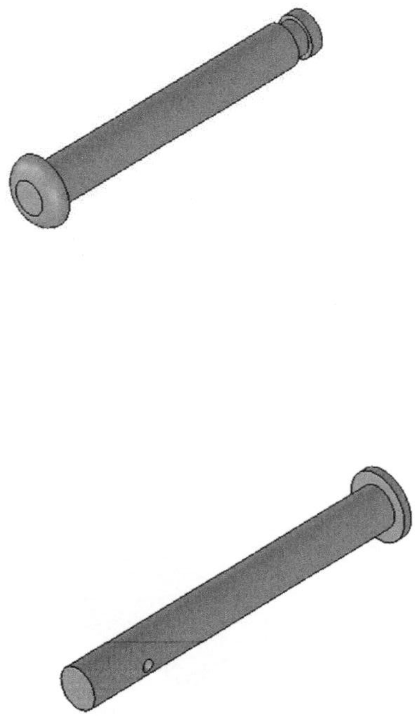

NOTES

1- Material Stainless steel
2- Deburr sharp edges

TOLERANCES UNLESS OTHERWISE SPECIFIED

X---------- +/- 1
X.X---------- +/- 0.5
X.XX---------- +/- 0.2
ANGLE---------- +/- 0.5

ALL DIMENSIONS IN MM

FIRST ISSUED	
DRAWN BY	
CHECKED BY	
APPROVED BY	

CADCIM TECHNOLOGIES

1. Knob Shaft
2. Driving pinion Shaft

SIZE	DRG NO.	SHEET REV
A3	9-013	A
SCALE 2:1		SHEET 15 OF 16

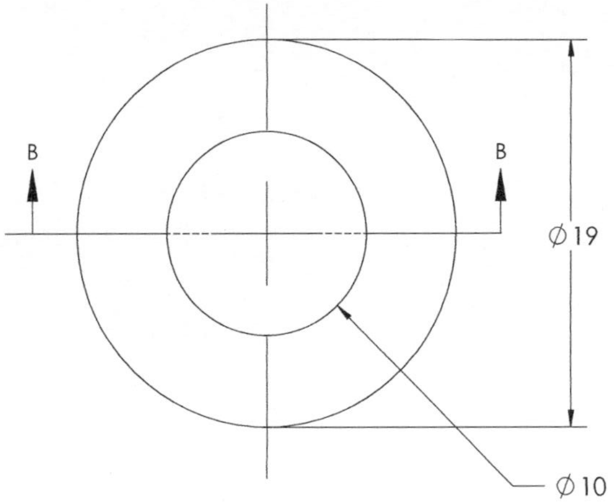

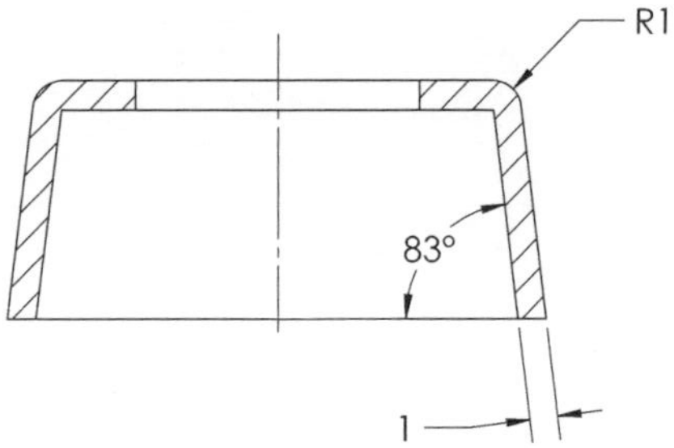

SECTION B-B

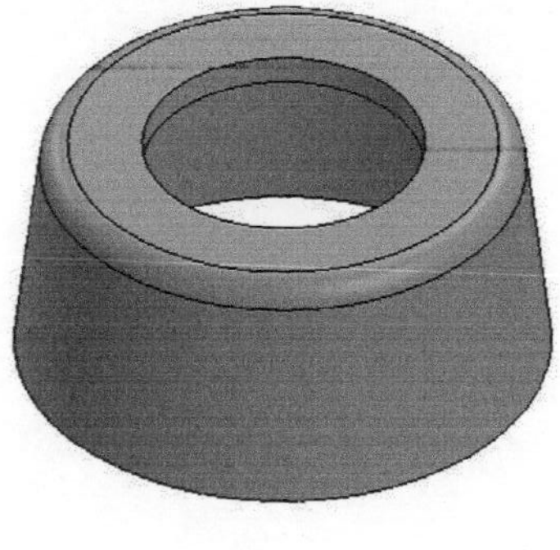

NOTES

1- Material Gray Cast Iron
2- Deburr sharp edges

TOLERANCES UNLESS OTHERWISE SPECIFIED		CADCIM TECHNOLOGIES		
X---------- +/- 1	FIRST ISSUED	Side Handle Cap		
X.X---------- +/- 0.5	DRAWN BY			
X.XX---------- +/- 0.2	CHECKED BY			
ANGLE---------- +/- 0.5	APPROVED BY	SIZE A3	DRG NO. 9-014	SHEET REV A
ALL DIMENSIONS IN MM		SCALE 2:1		SHEET 16 OF 16

This page is intentionally left blank

Project 10

Bending Machine Assembly

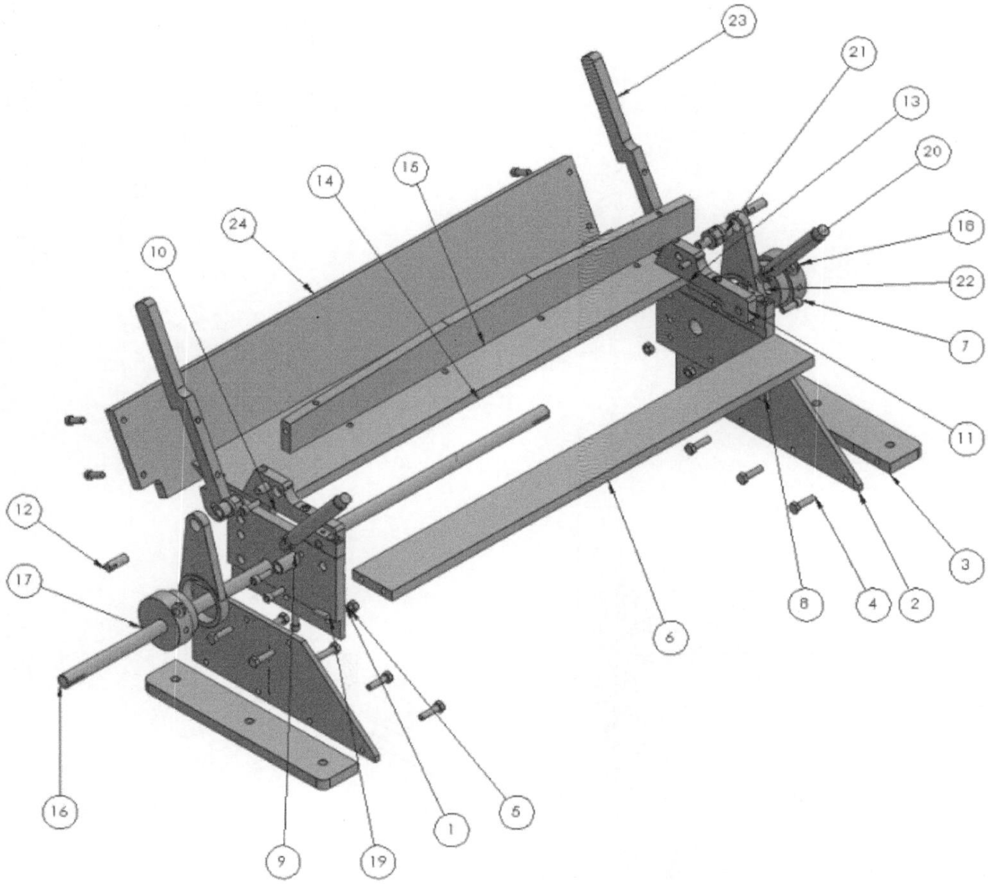

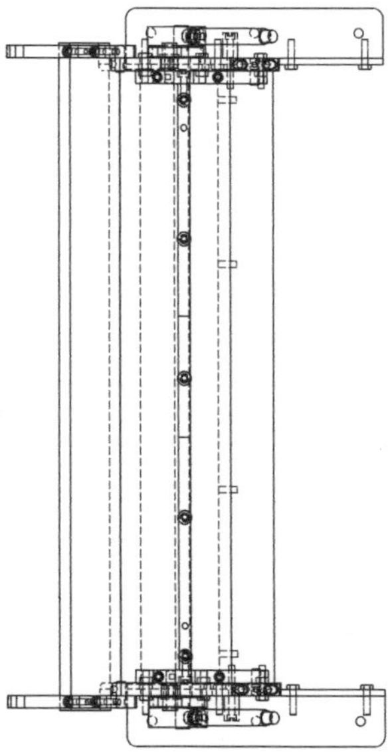

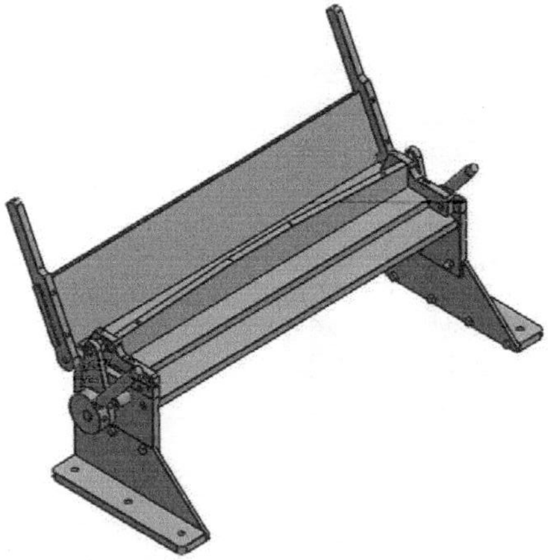

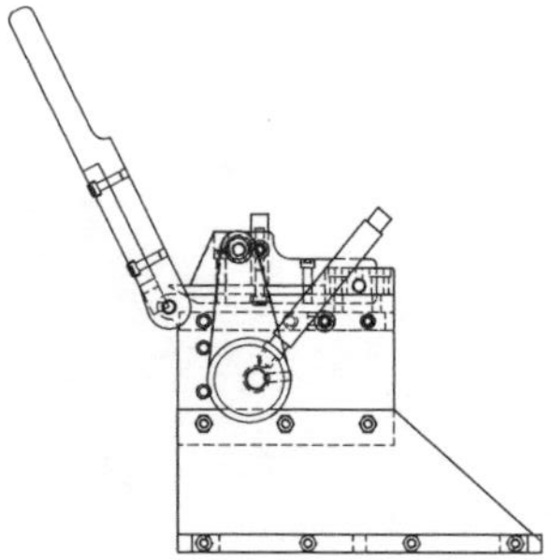

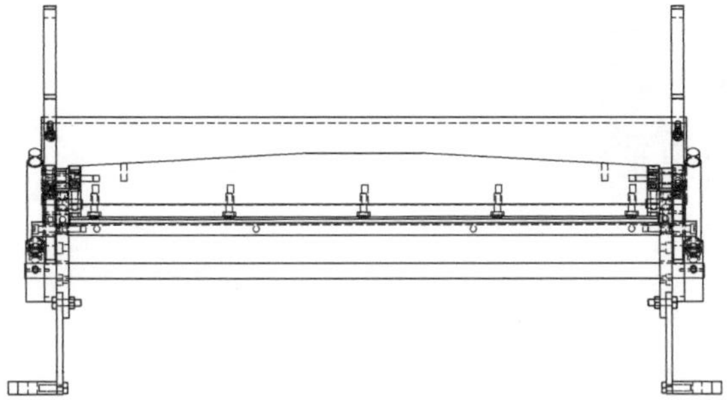

TOLERANCES UNLESS OTHERWISE SPECIFIED		CADCIM TECHNOLOGIES
X-------- +/- 1 X.X-------- +/- 0.05 X.XX-------- +/- 0.02 ANGLE-------- +/- 0.05	FIRST ISSUED DRAWN BY CHECKED BY APPROVED BY	Bending Machine
ALL DIMENSIONS IN INCHES		SIZE A3 · DRG NO. 10-000 · SHEET REV A
		SCALE 1:8 · SHEET 1 OF 21

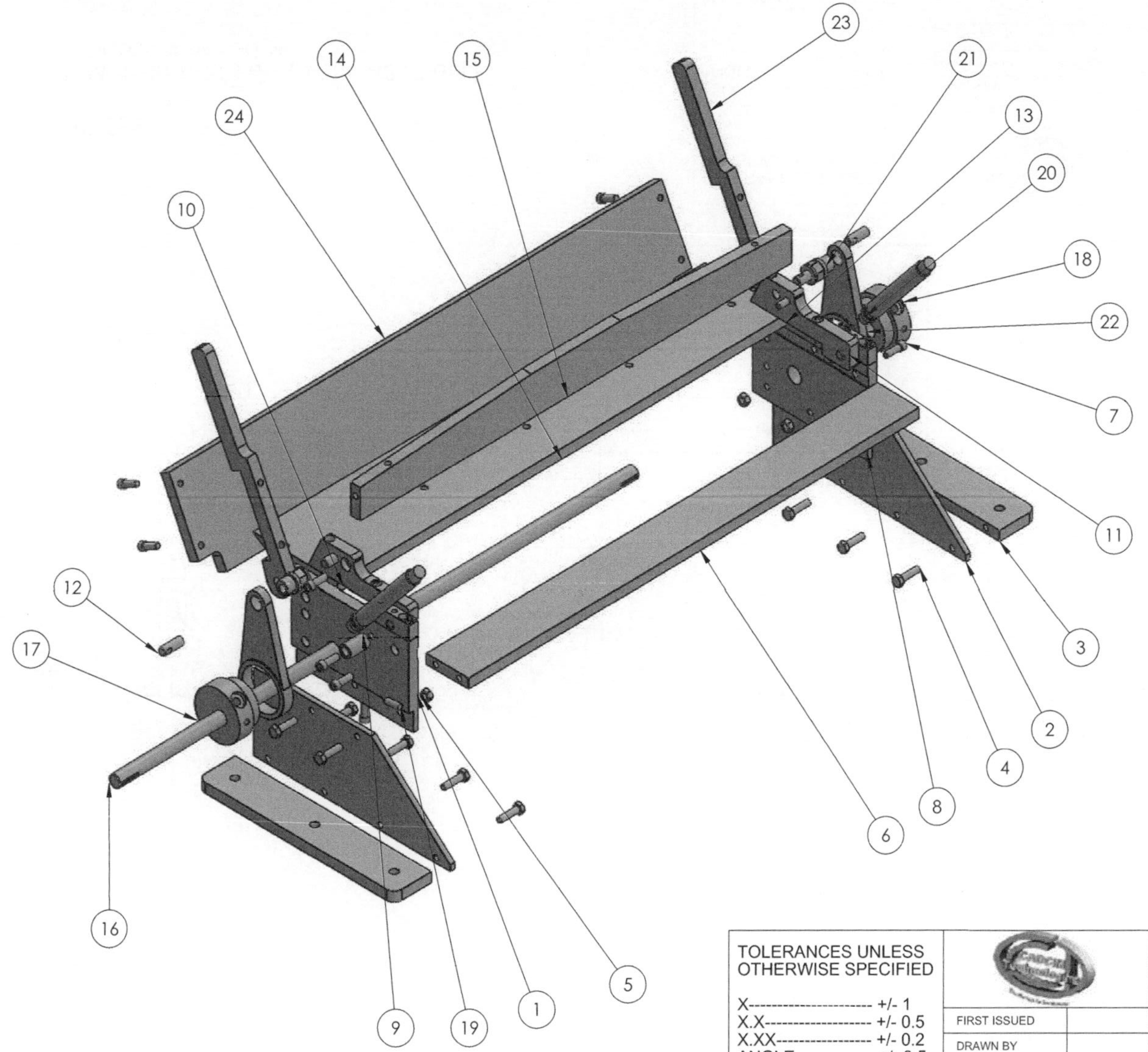

ITEM NO.	PART NUMBER	QTY.
1	Left Side Plate	1
2	foot side	2
3	foot bottom	2
4	1/4-28 Hex Bolt-ANSI	14
5	5/6-18 Hex nut	6
6	Bottom support	1
7	1/4-28 Socket Head Cap Screw- ANSI	19
8	Right Side Plate	1
9	Cam Stop	2
10	Clamp Rocker L	1
11	Thikness Adjustor	2
12	Dowel	6
13	Clamp Rocker R	1
14	Clamp Plate	1
15	Clamp support	1
16	Reach Shaft	1
17	cam L	1
18	cam R	1
19	Shaft Key	2
20	Lever	2
21	Cam adjuster	2
22	Clamp Cam Follower	2
23	Screw adjuster	2
24	Bend over platen	1

TOLERANCES UNLESS OTHERWISE SPECIFIED

X------------------- +/- 1
X.X----------------- +/- 0.5
X.XX---------------- +/- 0.2
ANGLE--------------- +/- 0.5

ALL DIMENSIONS IN MM

FIRST ISSUED	
DRAWN BY	
CHECKED BY	
APPROVED BY	

CADCIM TECHNOLOGIES

Bending machine Exploded

SIZE	DRG NO.	SHEET REV
A3	10-000	A
SCALE 1:4		SHEET 2 OF 21

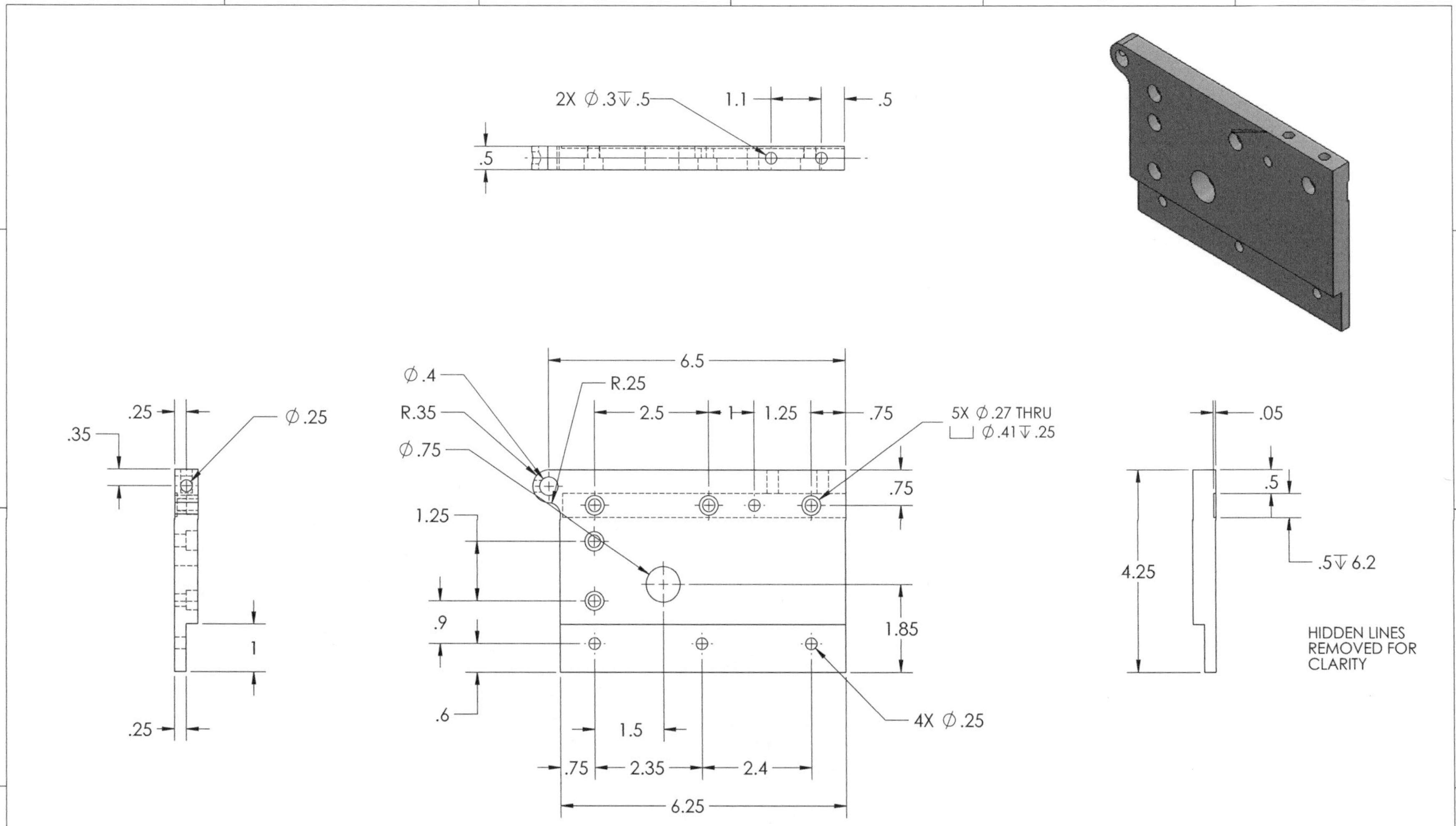

NOTES

1- Material Mild Steel (ASTM A36 Steel)
2- Deburr sharp edges

TOLERANCES UNLESS OTHERWISE SPECIFIED

X---------------------- +/- 0.1
X.X-------------------- +/- 0.05
X.XX------------------ +/- 0.02
ANGLE--------------- +/- 0.05

ALL DIMENSIONS IN INCHES

FIRST ISSUED	
DRAWN BY	
CHECKED BY	
APPROVED BY	

CADCIM TECHNOLOGIES

Left Side Plate

SIZE	DRG NO.	SHEET REV
A3	10-001	A
SCALE 1:2		SHEET 3 OF 21

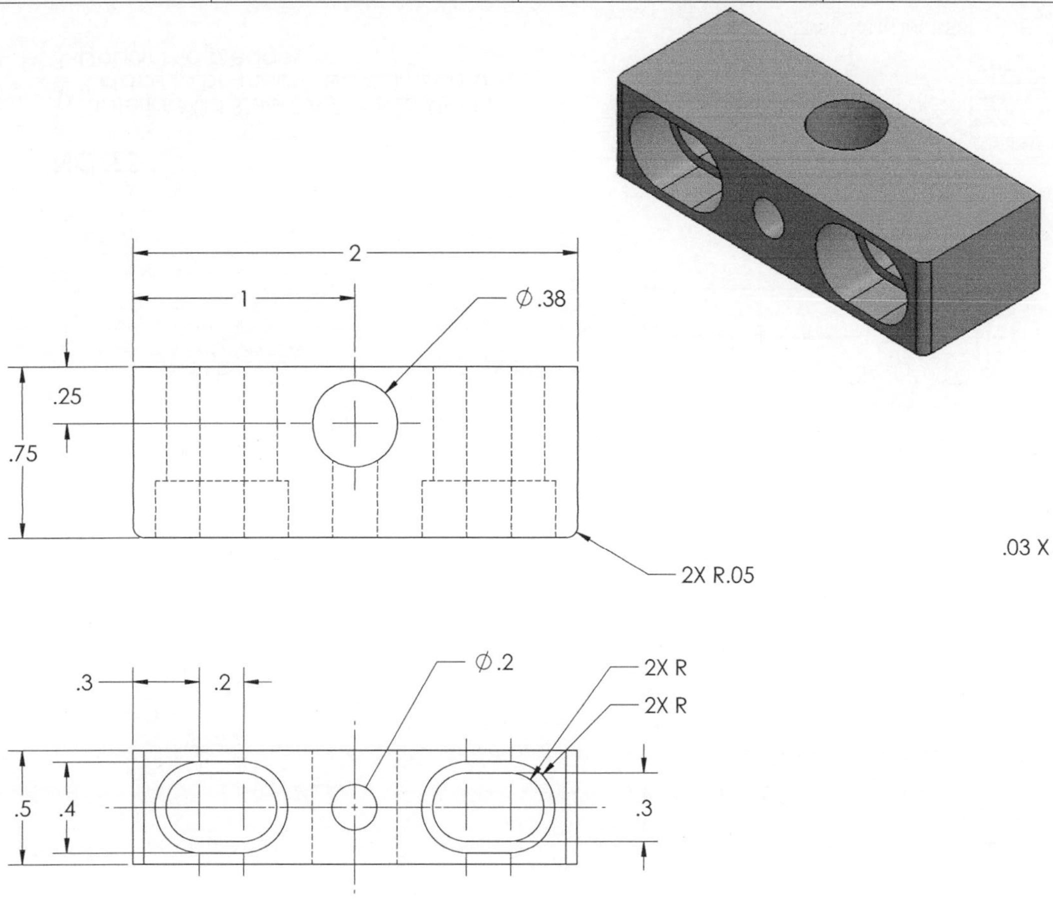

Thickness Adjuster

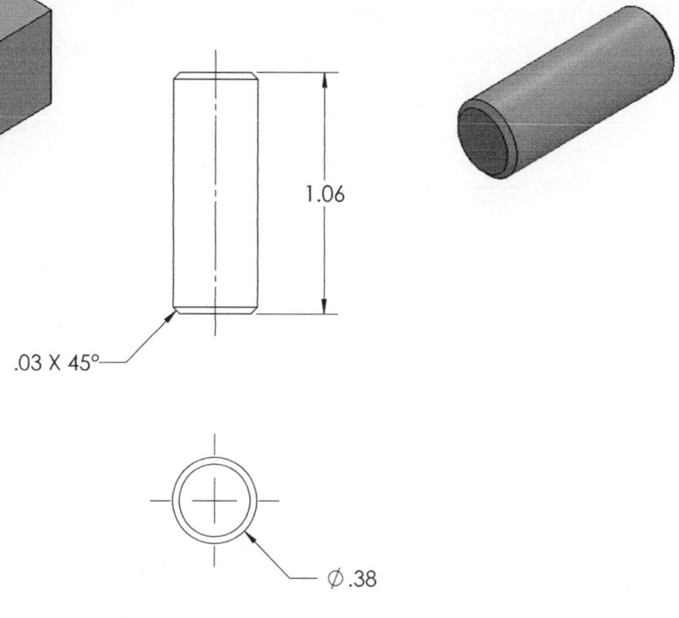

Dowel

NOTES

1- Material Mild Steel (ASTM A36 Steel)
2- Deburr sharp edges

TOLERANCES UNLESS OTHERWISE SPECIFIED		CADCIM TECHNOLOGIES
X---------- +/- 0.1 X.X---------- +/- 0.05 X.XX---------- +/- 0.02 ANGLE---------- +/- 0.05	FIRST ISSUED DRAWN BY CHECKED BY APPROVED BY	1. Thickness Adjuster 2. Dowel
ALL DIMENSIONS IN INCHES		SIZE A3 · DRG NO. 10-002 · SHEET REV A
		SCALE 2:1 · SHEET 4 OF 21

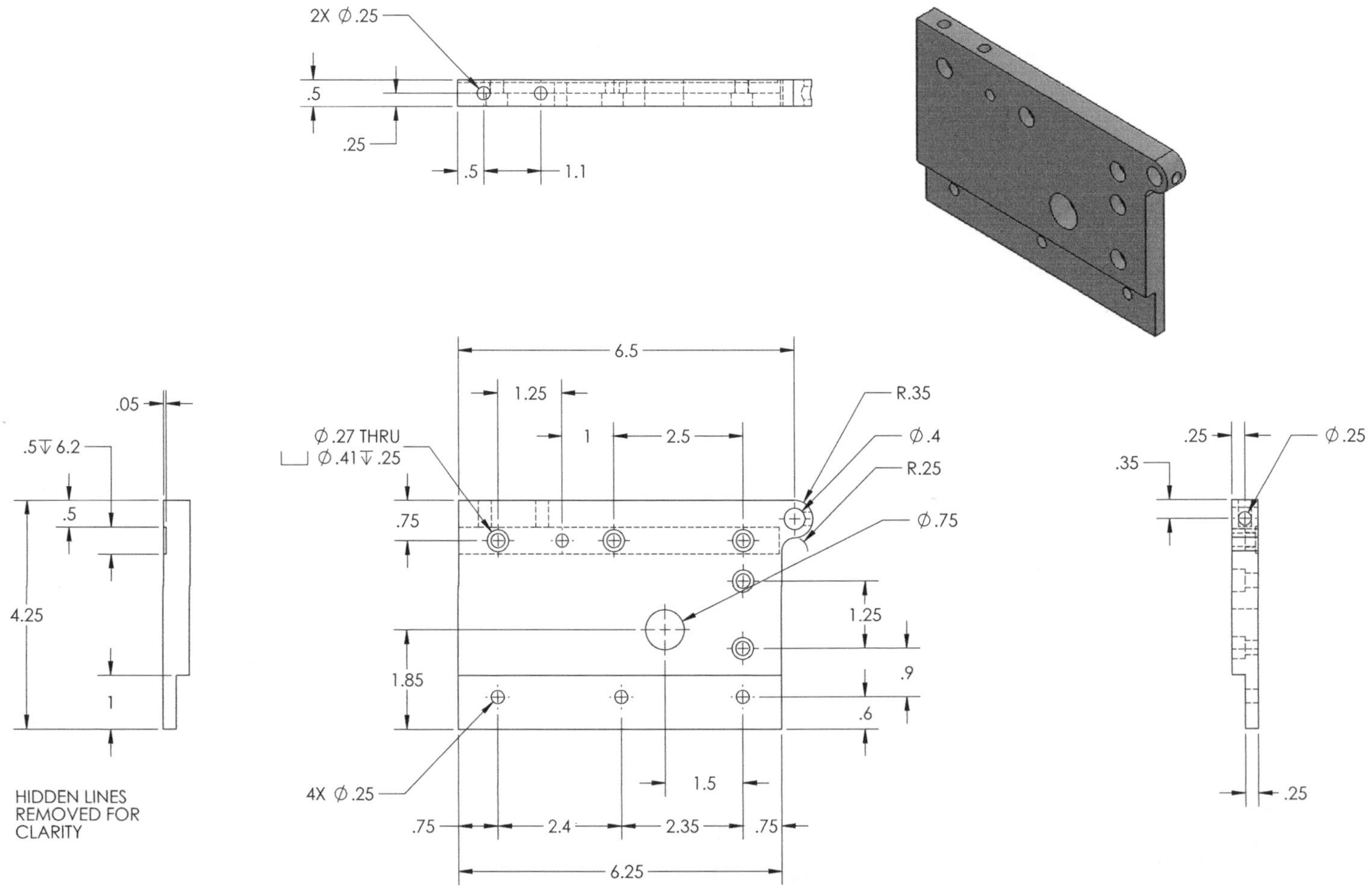

NOTES

1- Material Mild Steel (ASTM A36 Steel)
2- Surface to be machined as indicated
3- Deburr sharp edges

TOLERANCES UNLESS OTHERWISE SPECIFIED	
X	+/- 0.1
X.X	+/- 0.05
X.XX	+/- 0.02
ANGLE	+/- 0.05

ALL DIMENSIONS IN INCHES

FIRST ISSUED	
DRAWN BY	
CHECKED BY	
APPROVED BY	

CADCIM TECHNOLOGIES

Right Side Plate

SIZE	DRG NO.	SHEET REV
A3	10-003	A
SCALE 1:2		SHEET 5 OF 21

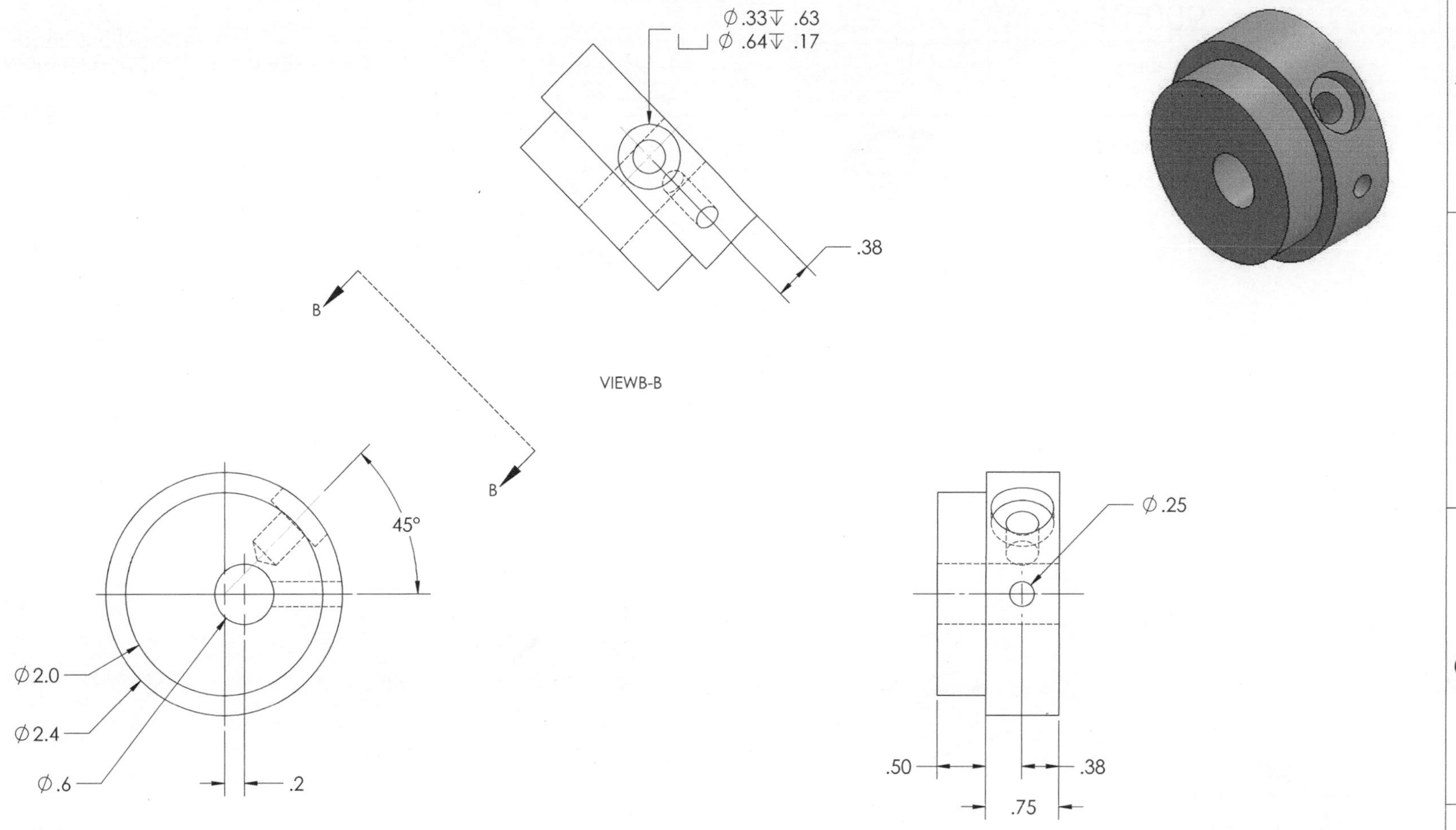

NOTES

1- Material Mild Steel (ASTM A36 Steel)
2- Deburr sharp edges

TOLERANCES UNLESS OTHERWISE SPECIFIED		CADCIM TECHNOLOGIES
X---------- +/- 0.1	FIRST ISSUED	Cam Right
X.X---------- +/- 0.05	DRAWN BY	
X.XX---------- +/- 0.02	CHECKED BY	
ANGLE---------- +/- 0.05	APPROVED BY	SIZE A3 · DRG NO. 10-004 · SHEET REV A
ALL DIMENSIONS IN INCHES		SCALE 1:1 · SHEET 6 OF 21

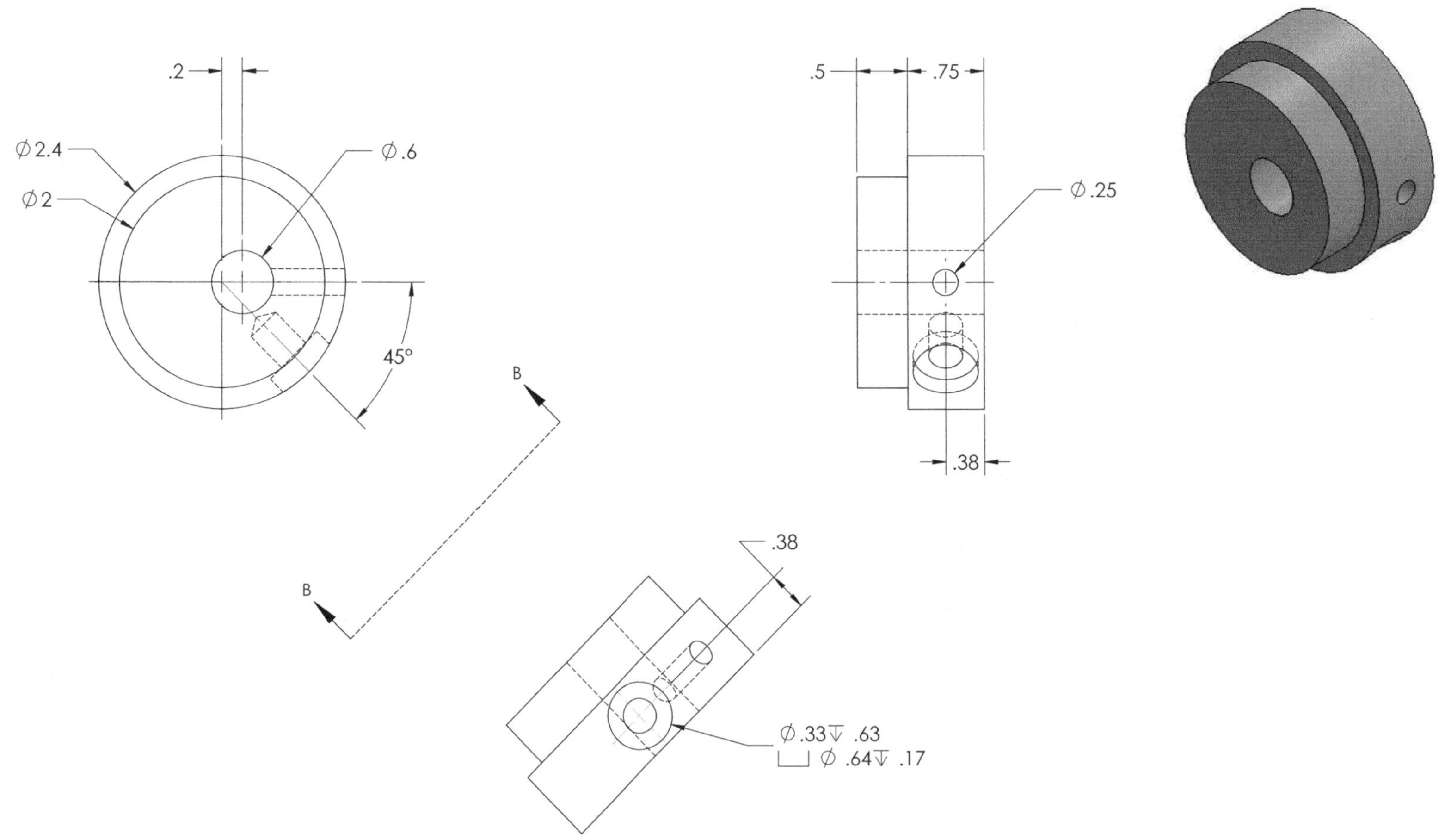

NOTES

1- Material Mild Steel (ASTM A36 Steel)
2- Deburr sharp edges

TOLERANCES UNLESS OTHERWISE SPECIFIED		CADCIM TECHNOLOGIES	
X---------- +/- 1 X.X---------- +/- 0.5 X.XX---------- +/- 0.2 ANGLE---------- +/- 0.5	FIRST ISSUED DRAWN BY CHECKED BY APPROVED BY	Cam Left	
ALL DIMENSIONS IN MM		SIZE A3 · DRG NO. 10-005	SHEET REV A
		SCALE 1:1	SHEET 7 OF 21

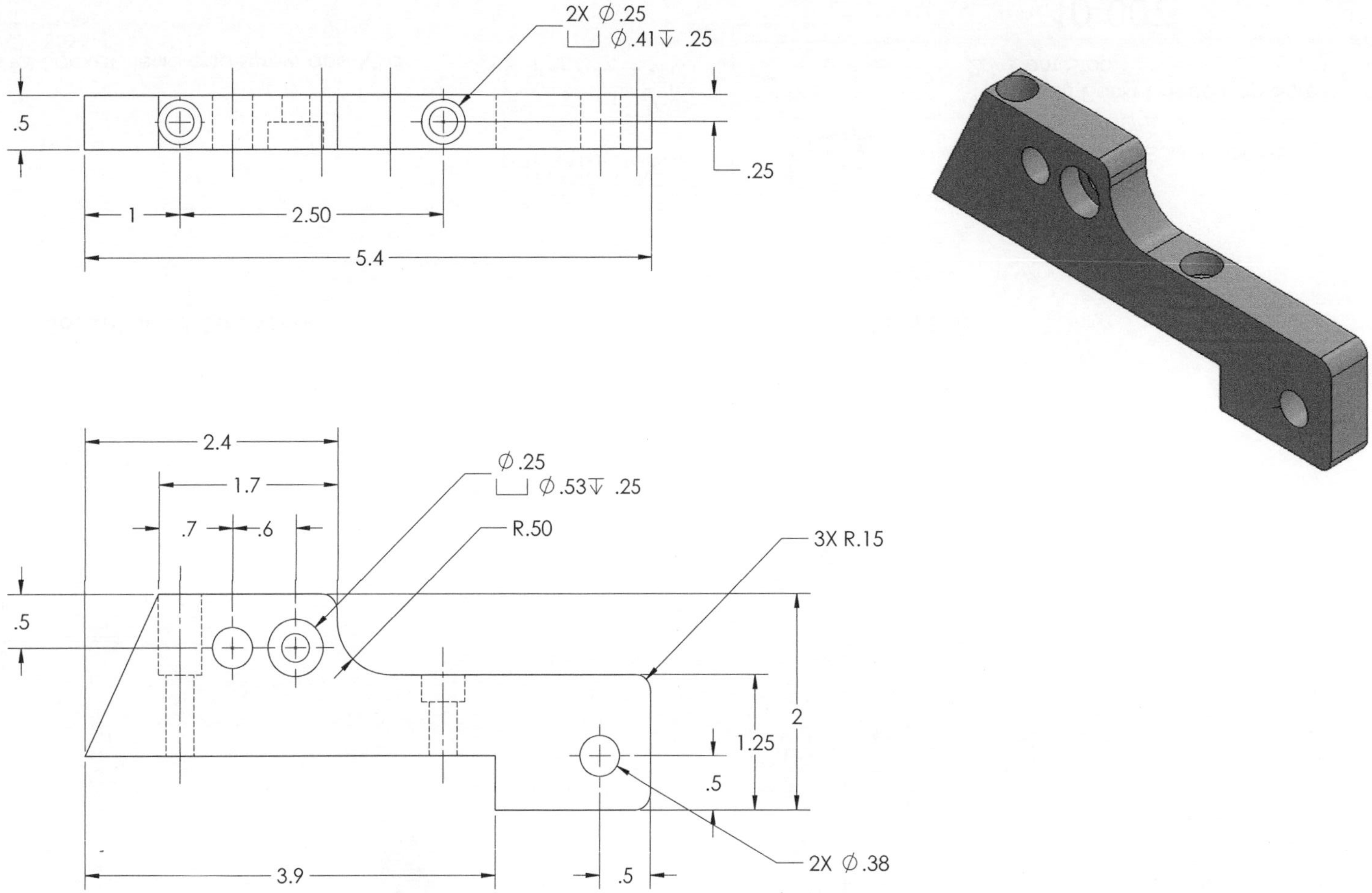

NOTES

1- Material Mild Steel (ASTM A36 Steel)
2- Deburr sharp edges

TOLERANCES UNLESS OTHERWISE SPECIFIED		CADCIM TECHNOLOGIES
X------------------- +/- 0.1	FIRST ISSUED	1. Clamp Rocker Left
X.X----------------- +/- 0.05	DRAWN BY	
X.XX---------------- +/- 0.02	CHECKED BY	
ANGLE------------- +/- 0.05	APPROVED BY	SIZE A3 · DRG NO. 10-006 · SHEET REV A
ALL DIMENSIONS IN INCHES		SCALE 1:1 · SHEET 8 OF 21

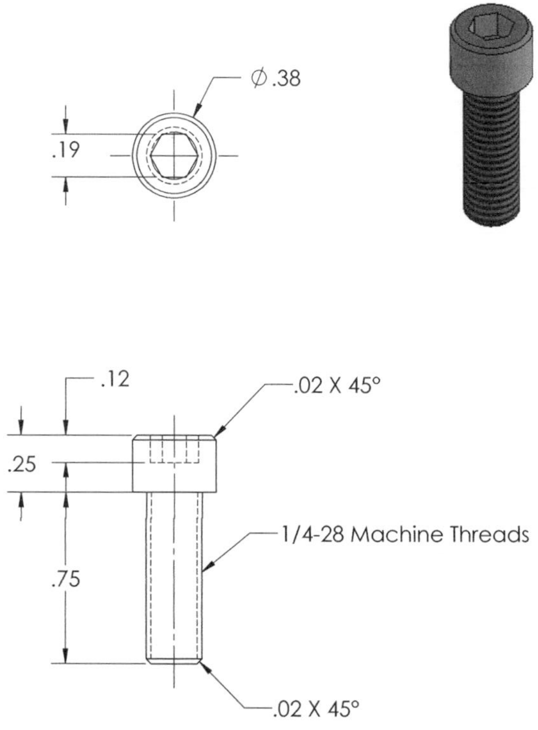

Socket head Cap Screw

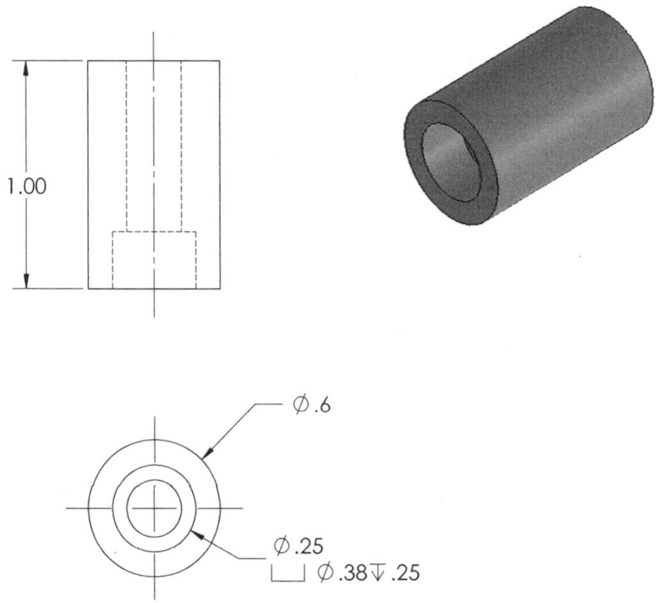

Cam Stop

NOTES

1- Material SS for Socket Head cap screw and Mild Steel (ASTM A36 Steel)
2- Deburr sharp edges

TOLERANCES UNLESS OTHERWISE SPECIFIED		CADCIM TECHNOLOGIES
X---------- +/- 1	FIRST ISSUED	1. 1/4-28 Socket Head Cap Screw- ANSI
X.X---------- +/- 0.5	DRAWN BY	2. Cam Stop
X.XX---------- +/- 0.2	CHECKED BY	SIZE A3 DRG NO. 10-007 SHEET REV A
ANGLE---------- +/- 0.5	APPROVED BY	SCALE 2:1 SHEET 9 OF 21
ALL DIMENSIONS IN MM		

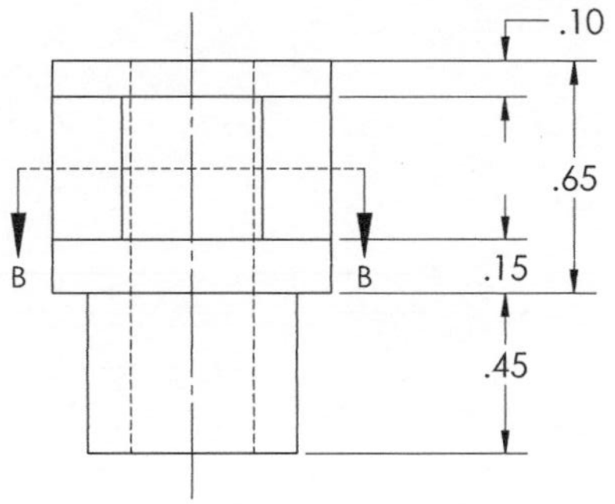

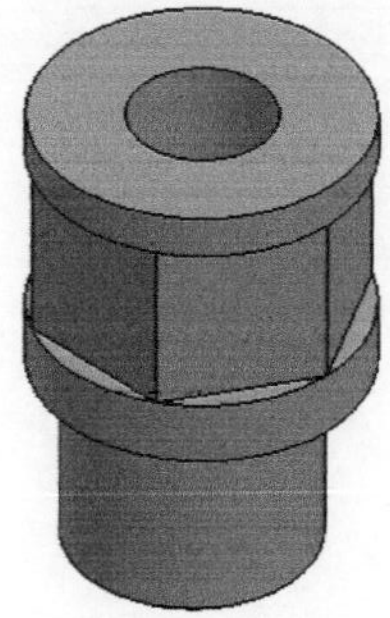

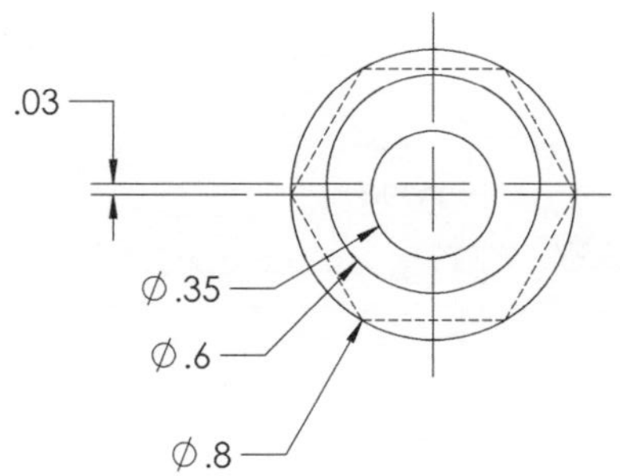

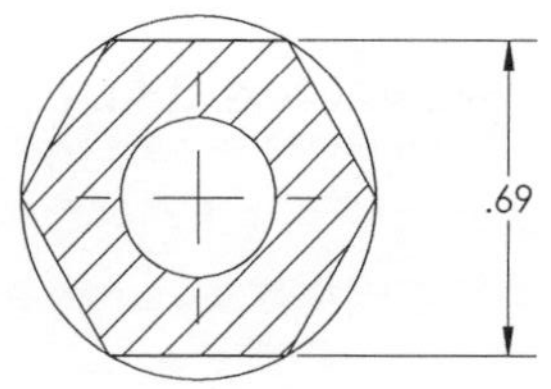

SECTION B-B

NOTES

1- Material Mild Steel (ASTM A36 Steel)
2- Deburr sharp edges

TOLERANCES UNLESS OTHERWISE SPECIFIED		CADCIM TECHNOLOGIES
X---------- +/- 0.1 X.X---------- +/- 0.05 X.XX---------- +/- 0.02 ANGLE---------- +/- 0.05	FIRST ISSUED DRAWN BY CHECKED BY APPROVED BY	Cam Adjuster
ALL DIMENSIONS IN INCHES		SIZE A3	DRG NO. 10-008	SHEET REV A
		SCALE 2:1	SHEET 10 OF 21

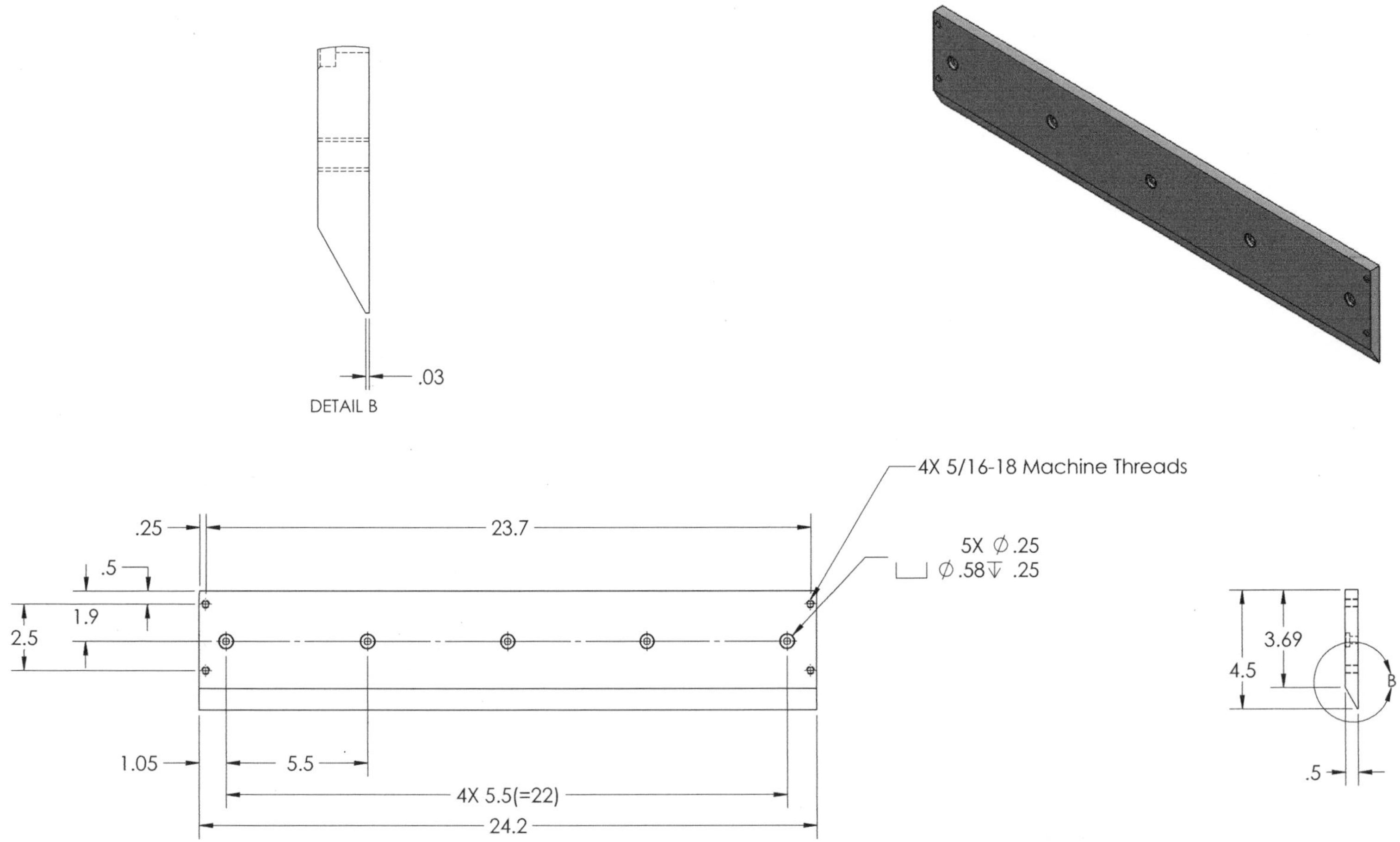

NOTES

1- Material Mild Steel (ASTM A36 Steel)
2- Deburr sharp edges

TOLERANCES UNLESS OTHERWISE SPECIFIED		CADCIM TECHNOLOGIES
X---------- +/- 0.1	FIRST ISSUED	Clamp Plate
X.X---------- +/- 0.05	DRAWN BY	
X.XX---------- +/- 0.02	CHECKED BY	
ANGLE---------- +/- 0.05	APPROVED BY	SIZE A3 DRG NO. 10-009 SHEET REV A
ALL DIMENSIONS IN INCHES		SCALE 1:4 SHEET 11 OF 21

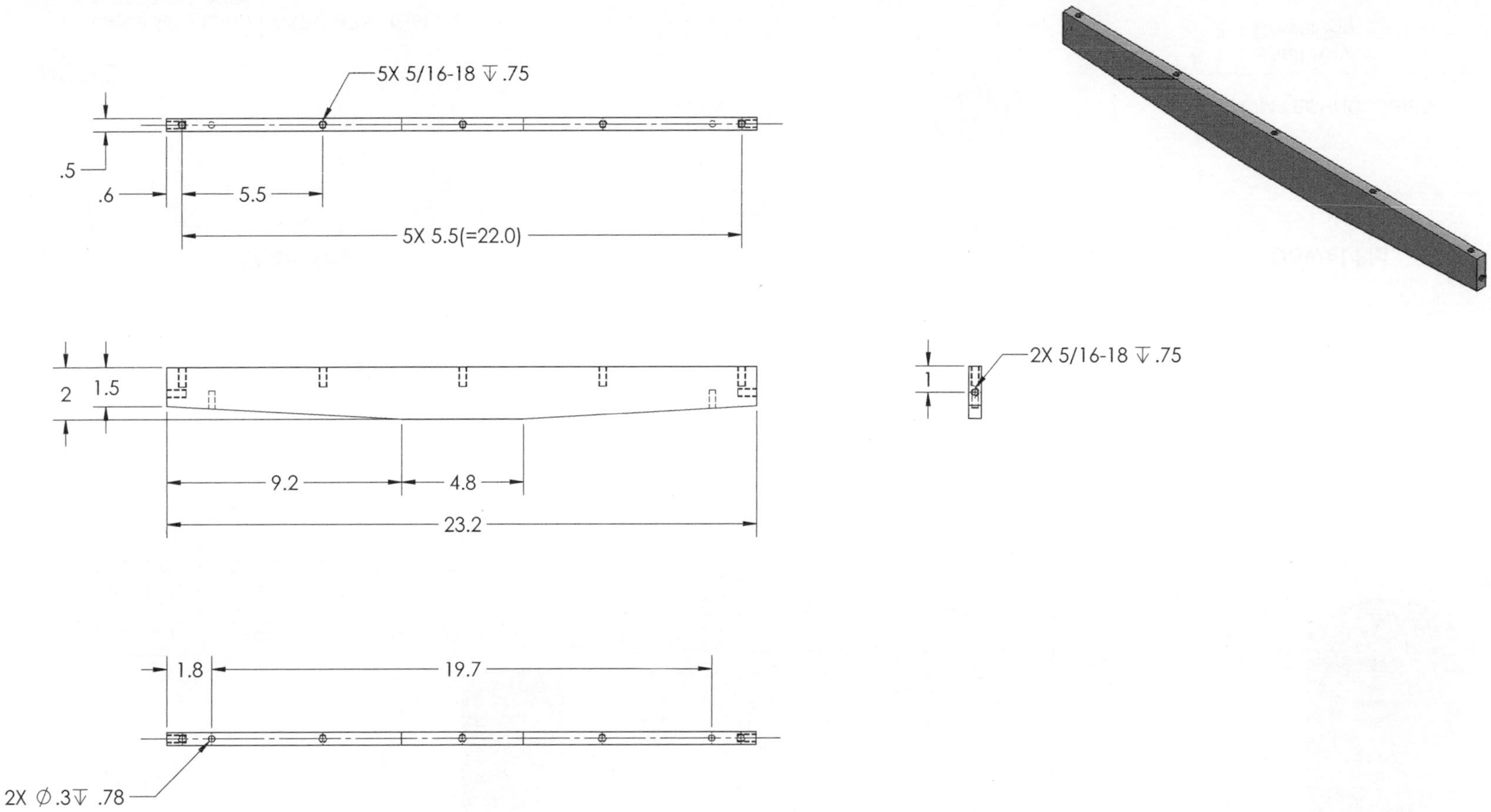

NOTES

1- Material Mild Steel (ASTM A36 Steel)
2- Deburr sharp edges

TOLERANCES UNLESS OTHERWISE SPECIFIED		CADCIM TECHNOLOGIES
X---------------------- +/- 0.1	FIRST ISSUED	Clamp Support
X.X-------------------- +/- 0.05	DRAWN BY	
X.XX------------------ +/- 0.02	CHECKED BY	
ANGLE-------------- +/- 0.05	APPROVED BY	SIZE A3 · DRG NO. 10-010 · SHEET REV A
ALL DIMENSIONS IN INCHES		SCALE 1:4 · SHEET 12 OF 21

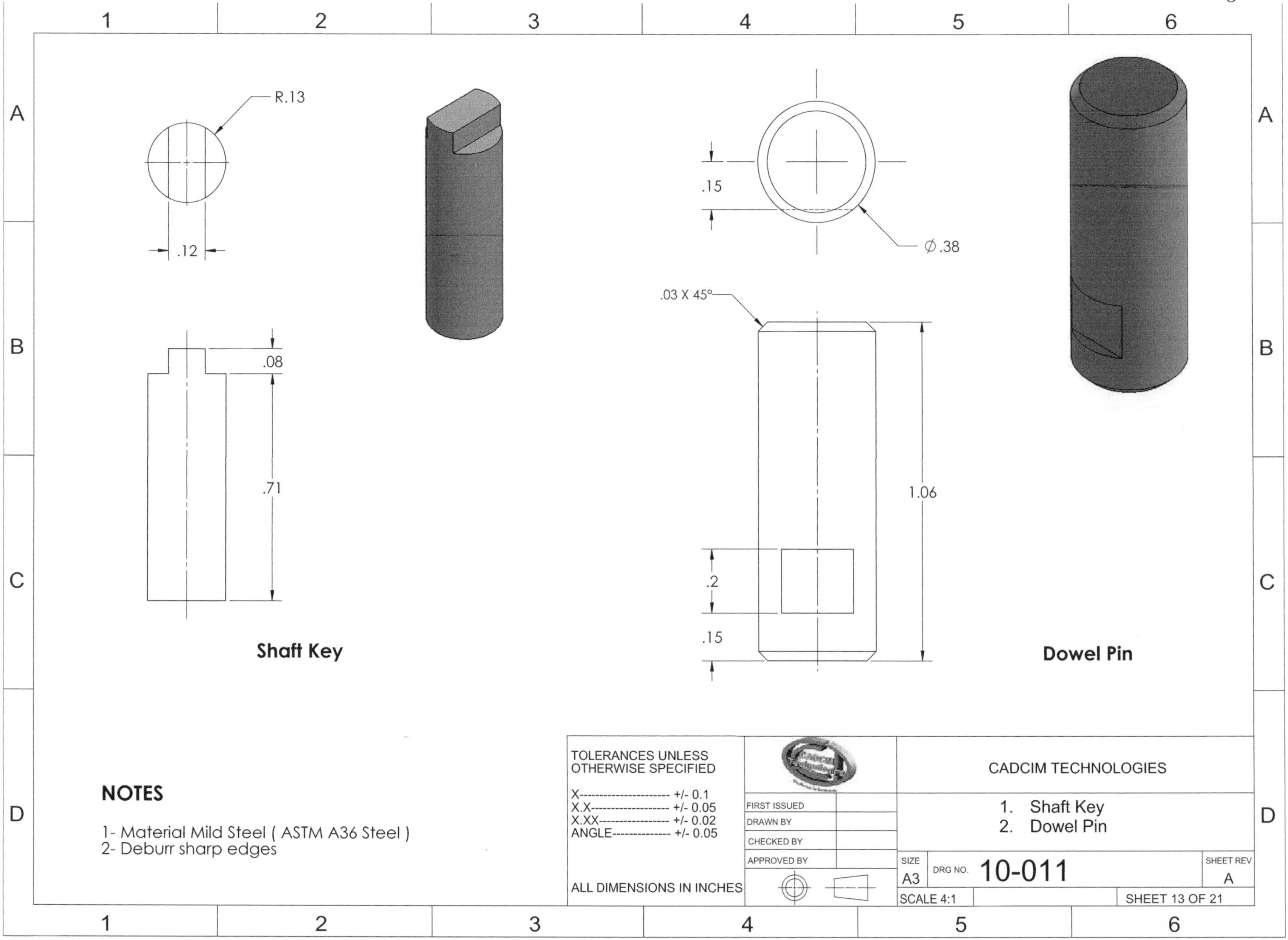

NOTES

1- Material Mild Steel (ASTM A36 Steel)
2- Deburr sharp edges

TOLERANCES UNLESS OTHERWISE SPECIFIED		CADCIM TECHNOLOGIES
X---- +/- 0.1 X.X---- +/- 0.05 X.XX---- +/- 0.02 ANGLE---- +/- 0.05	FIRST ISSUED DRAWN BY CHECKED BY APPROVED BY	1. Shaft Key 2. Dowel Pin
ALL DIMENSIONS IN INCHES		SIZE A3 DRG NO. 10-011 SHEET REV A
		SCALE 4:1 SHEET 13 OF 21

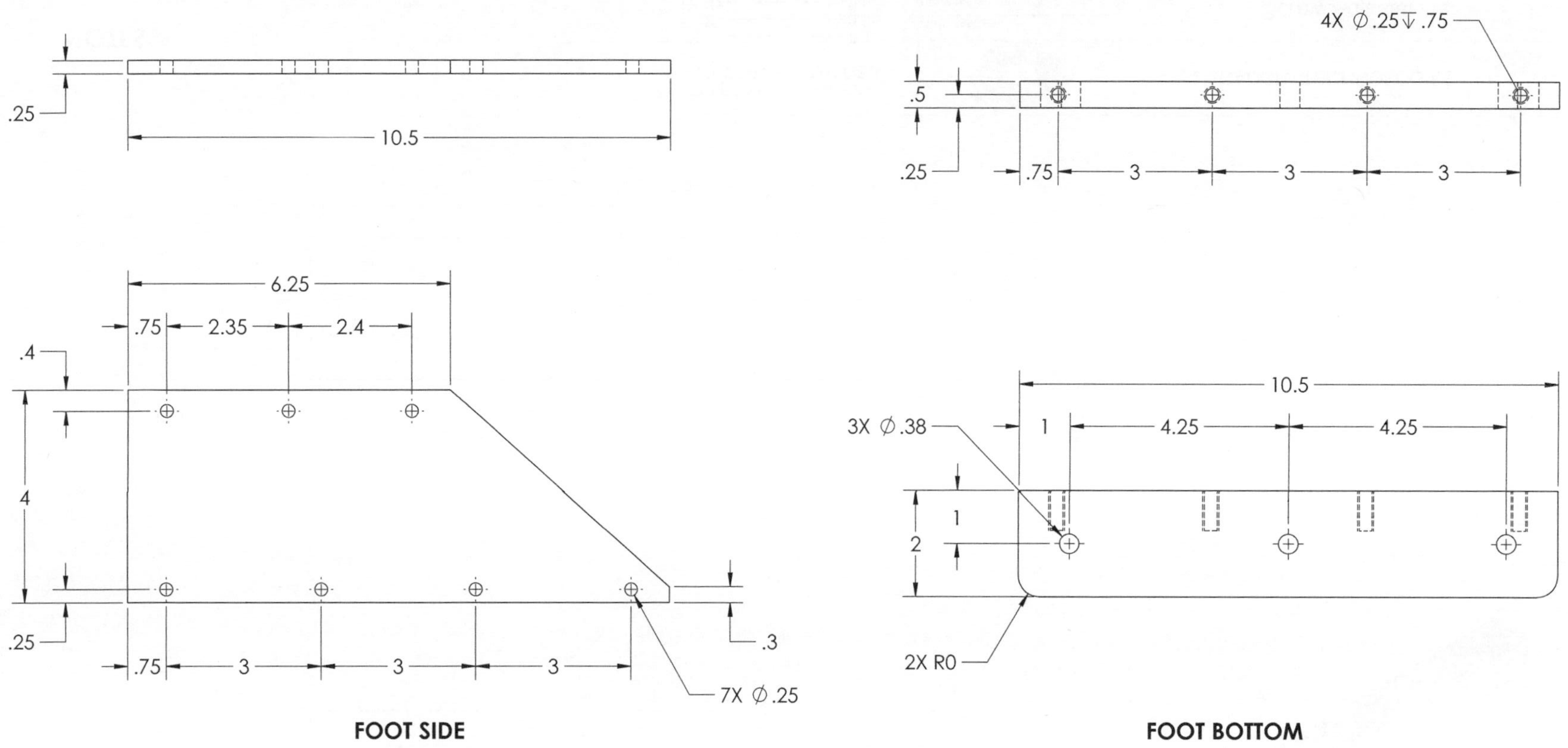

NOTES

1- Material Mild Steel (ASTM A36 Steel)
2- Deburr sharp edges

TOLERANCES UNLESS OTHERWISE SPECIFIED		CADCIM TECHNOLOGIES
X---------- +/- 0.1 X.X---------- +/- 0.05 X.XX---------- +/- 0.02 ANGLE---------- +/- 0.05	FIRST ISSUED DRAWN BY CHECKED BY APPROVED BY	1. Foot Side 2. Foot Bottom
ALL DIMENSIONS IN INCHES		SIZE A3 · DRG NO. 10-012 · SHEET REV A
		SCALE 1:2 · SHEET 14 OF 21

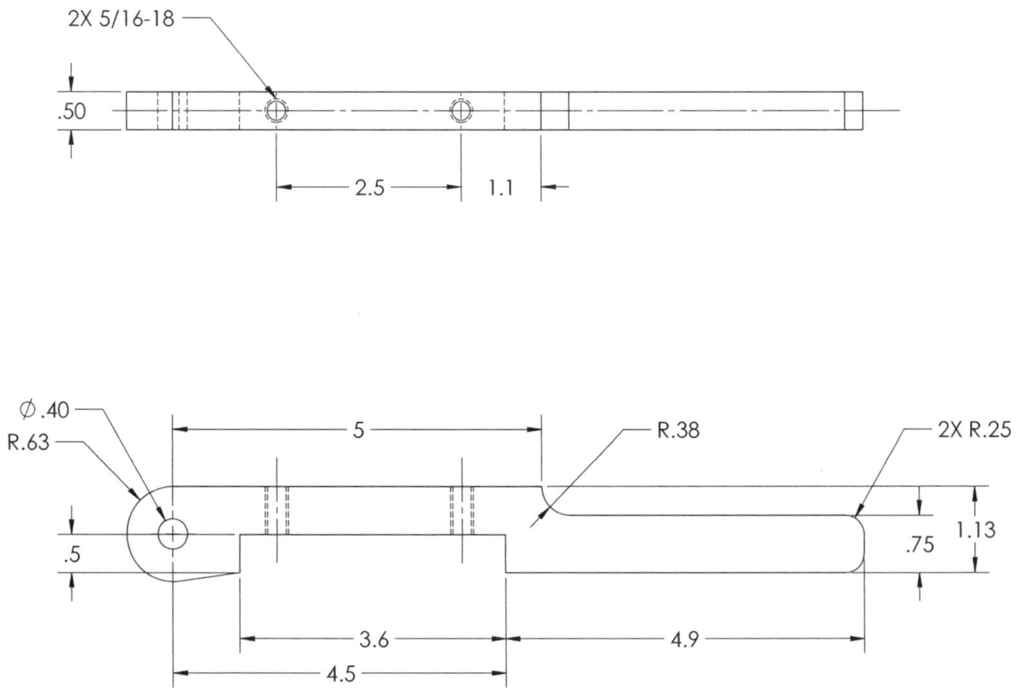

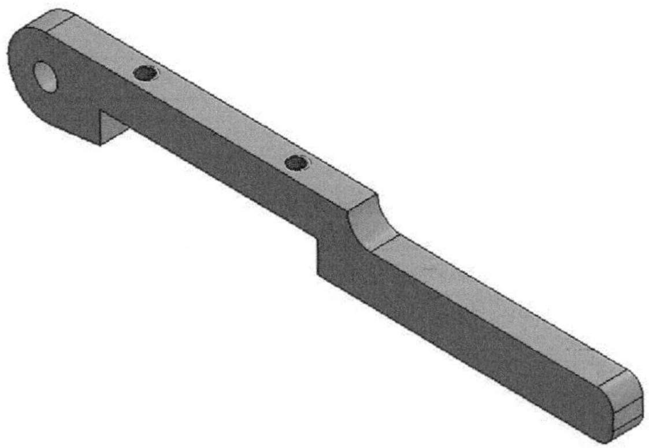

NOTES

1- Material Mild Steel (ASTM A36 Steel)
2- Deburr sharp edges

TOLERANCES UNLESS OTHERWISE SPECIFIED

X---------------------- +/- 0.1
X.X-------------------- +/- 0.05
X.XX------------------ +/- 0.02
ANGLE-------------- +/- 0.05

ALL DIMENSIONS IN INCHES

FIRST ISSUED	
DRAWN BY	
CHECKED BY	
APPROVED BY	

CADCIM TECHNOLOGIES

Screw Adjuster

SIZE	DRG NO.	SHEET REV
A3	10-013	A
SCALE 2:3		SHEET 15 OF 21

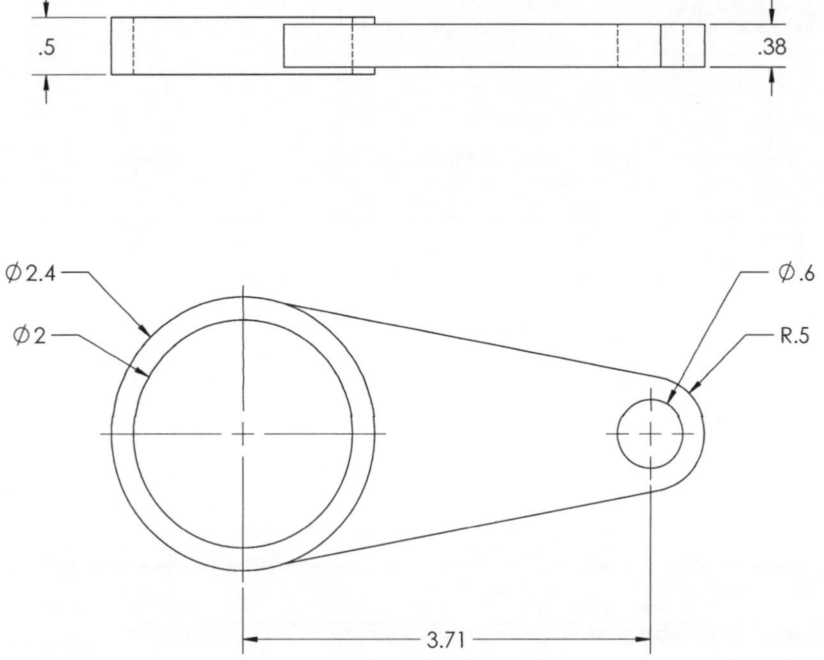

Clamp Cam Follower

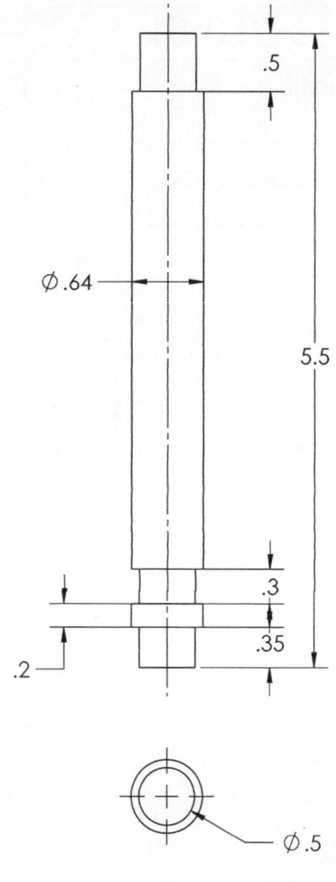

Lever

NOTES

1- Material Mild Steel (ASTM A36 Steel)
2- Deburr sharp edges

TOLERANCES UNLESS OTHERWISE SPECIFIED

X-------------------- +/- 0.1
X.X------------------ +/- 0.05
X.XX---------------- +/- 0.02
ANGLE-------------- +/- 0.05

ALL DIMENSIONS IN INCHES

FIRST ISSUED
DRAWN BY
CHECKED BY
APPROVED BY

CADCIM TECHNOLOGIES

1. Clamp Cam Follower
2. Lever

SIZE A3 | DRG NO. 10-014 | SHEET REV A

SCALE 1:1 | SHEET 16 OF 21

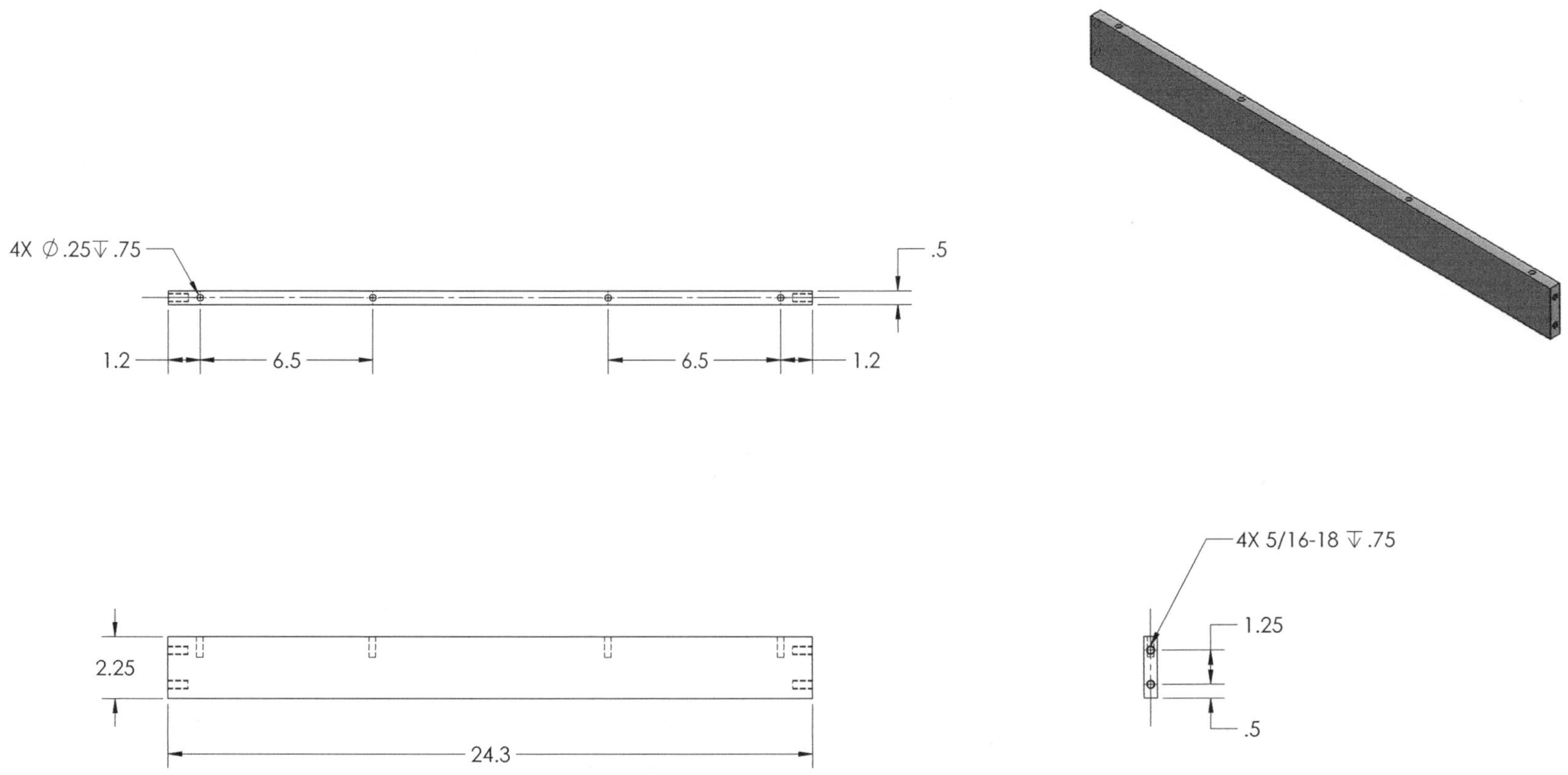

NOTES

1- Material Mild Steel (ASTM A36 Steel)
2- Deburr sharp edges

TOLERANCES UNLESS OTHERWISE SPECIFIED		CADCIM TECHNOLOGIES
X---------- +/- 0.1 X.X---------- +/- 0.05 X.XX---------- +/- 0.02 ANGLE---------- +/- 0.05	FIRST ISSUED DRAWN BY CHECKED BY APPROVED BY	Bottom Support
ALL DIMENSIONS IN INCHES		SIZE A3 · DRG NO. 10-015 · SHEET REV A
		SCALE 1:4 · SHEET 17 OF 21

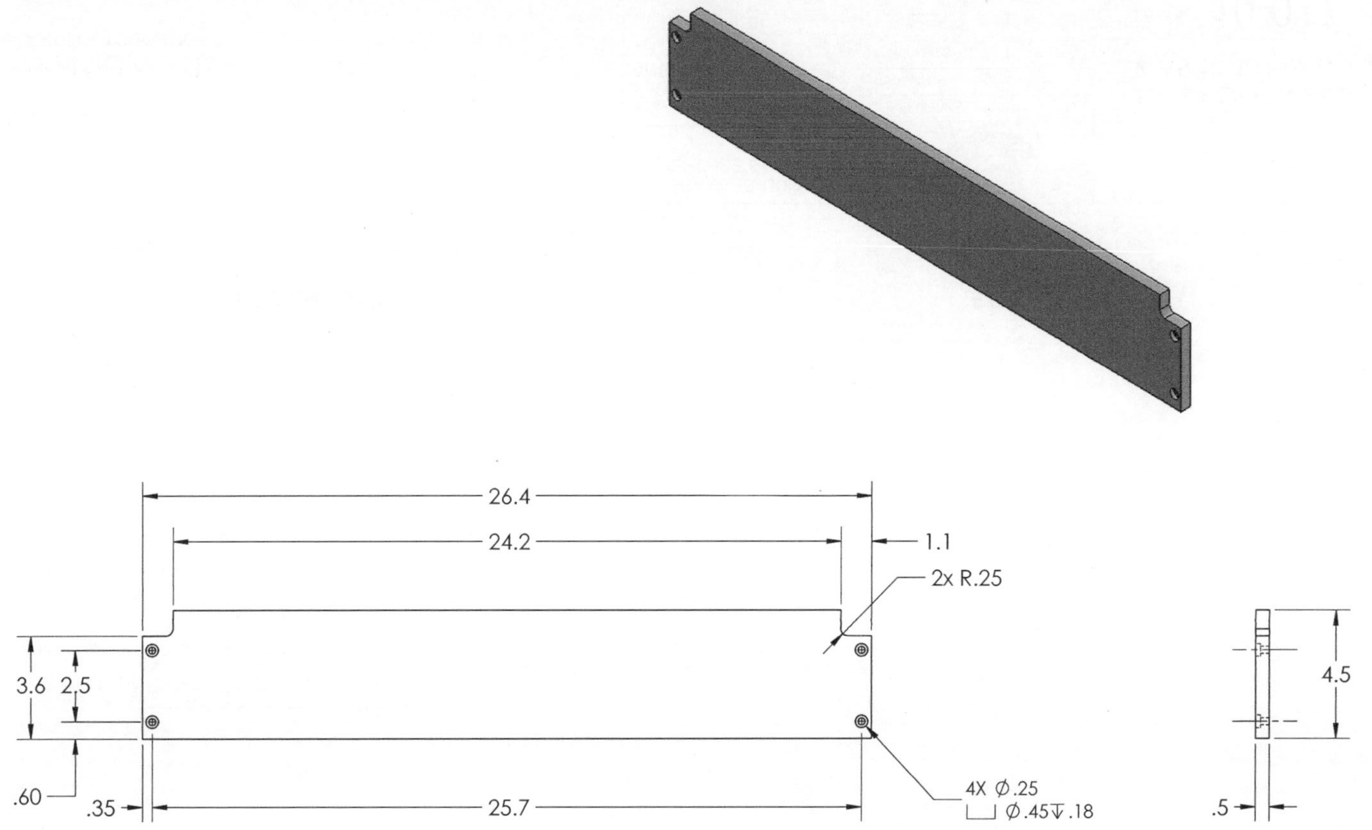

NOTES

1- Material Mild Steel (ASTM A36 Steel)
2- Deburr sharp edges

TOLERANCES UNLESS OTHERWISE SPECIFIED		CADCIM TECHNOLOGIES
X---------- +/- 0.1	FIRST ISSUED	Bend Over Platen
X.X---------- +/- 0.05	DRAWN BY	
X.XX---------- +/- 0.02	CHECKED BY	
ANGLE---------- +/- 0.05	APPROVED BY	SIZE A3 · DRG NO. 10-016 · SHEET REV A
ALL DIMENSIONS IN INCHES		SCALE 1:4 · SHEET 18 OF 21

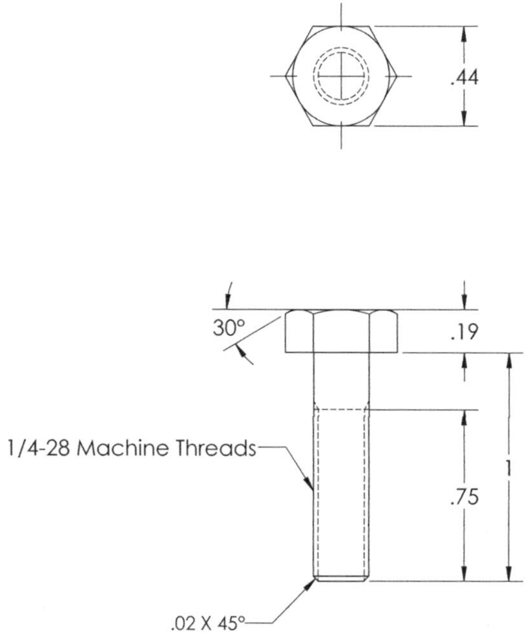

1/4-28 Hex Bolt

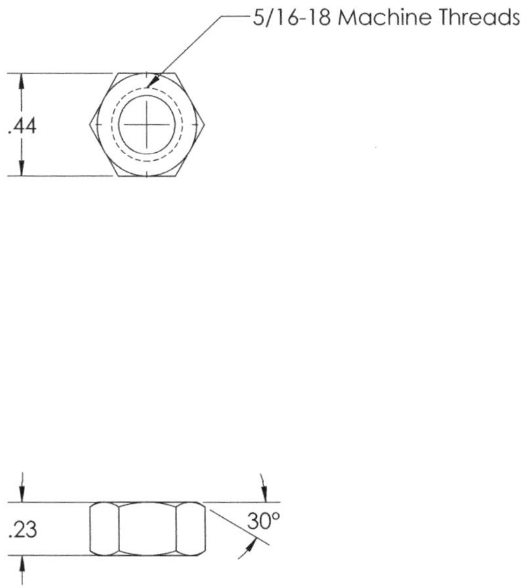

5/16-18 Hex Nut

NOTES

1- Material Stainless Steel
2- Deburr sharp edges

TOLERANCES UNLESS OTHERWISE SPECIFIED

X---------------------- +/- 1
X.X-------------------- +/- 0.5
X.XX------------------ +/- 0.2
ANGLE-------------- +/- 0.5

ALL DIMENSIONS IN MM

FIRST ISSUED	
DRAWN BY	
CHECKED BY	
APPROVED BY	

CADCIM TECHNOLOGIES

1. 1/4-28 Hex Bolt- ANSI
2. 5/16-18 Hex Nut-ANSI

SIZE	DRG NO.	SHEET REV
A3	10-017	A
SCALE 2:1		SHEET 19 OF 21

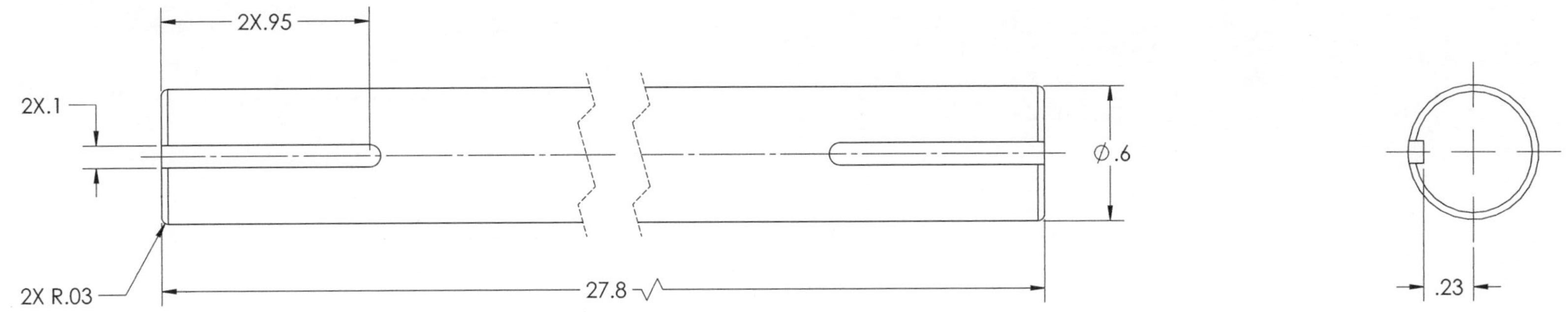

NOTES

1- Material Mild Steel (ASTM A36 Steel)
2- Deburr sharp edges

TOLERANCES UNLESS OTHERWISE SPECIFIED		CADCIM TECHNOLOGIES	
X---------- +/- 1	FIRST ISSUED	Reach Shaft	
X.X---------- +/- 0.5	DRAWN BY		
X.XX---------- +/- 0.2	CHECKED BY		
ANGLE---------- +/- 0.5	APPROVED BY	SIZE A3 DRG NO. 10-018	SHEET REV A
ALL DIMENSIONS IN MM		SCALE 2:1	SHEET 20 OF 21

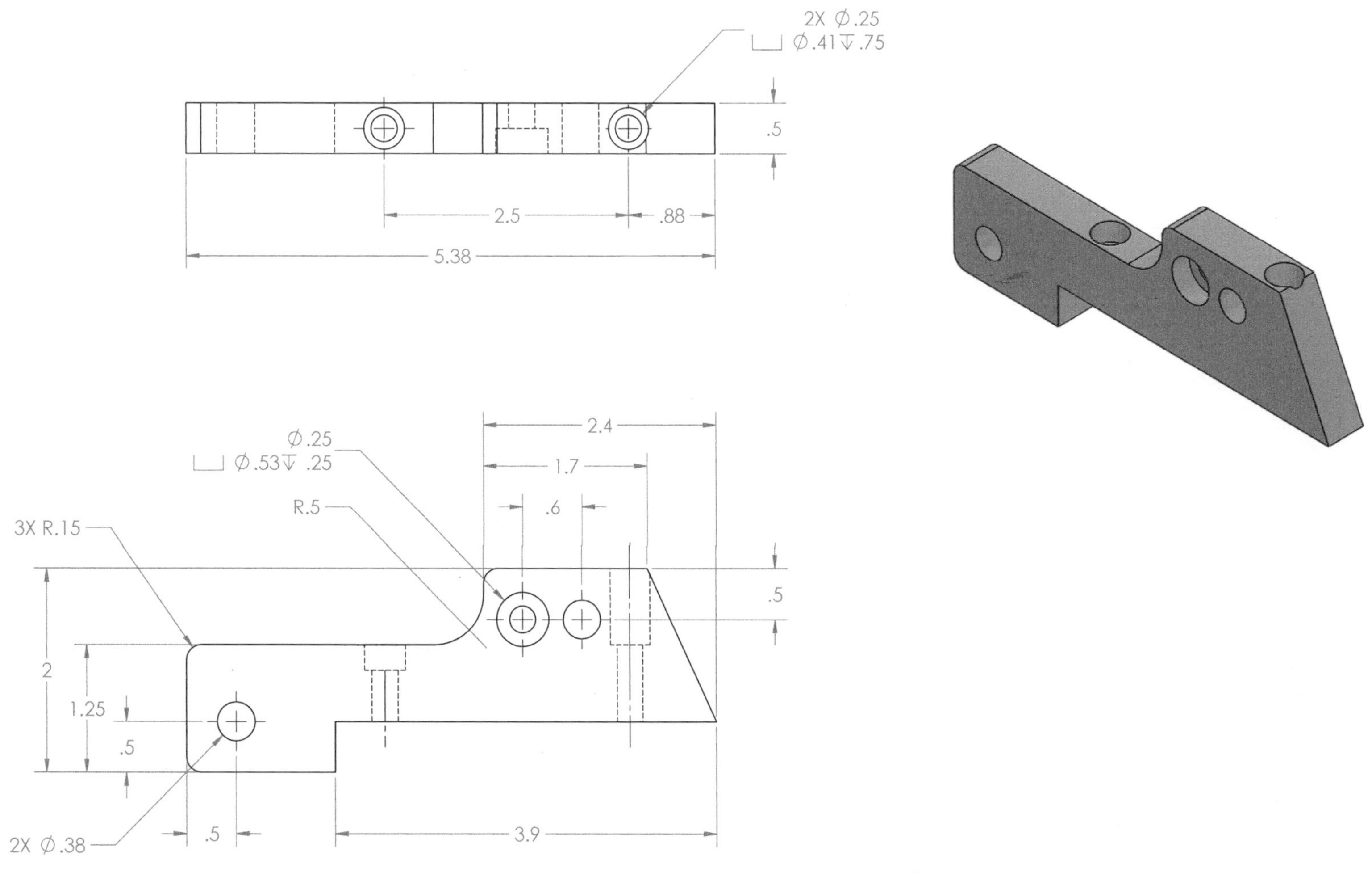

NOTES

1- Material Mild Steel (ASTM A36 Steel)
2- Deburr sharp edges

TOLERANCES UNLESS OTHERWISE SPECIFIED		
X	+/- 0.1	
X.X	+/- 0.05	
X.XX	+/- 0.02	
ANGLE	+/- 0.05	

ALL DIMENSIONS IN INCHES

FIRST ISSUED	
DRAWN BY	
CHECKED BY	
APPROVED BY	

CADCIM TECHNOLOGIES

Clamp Rocker Right

SIZE	DRG NO.	SHEET REV
A3	10-019	A
SCALE 1:1		SHEET 21 OF 21

Project 11

Reduction Gear Box Assembly

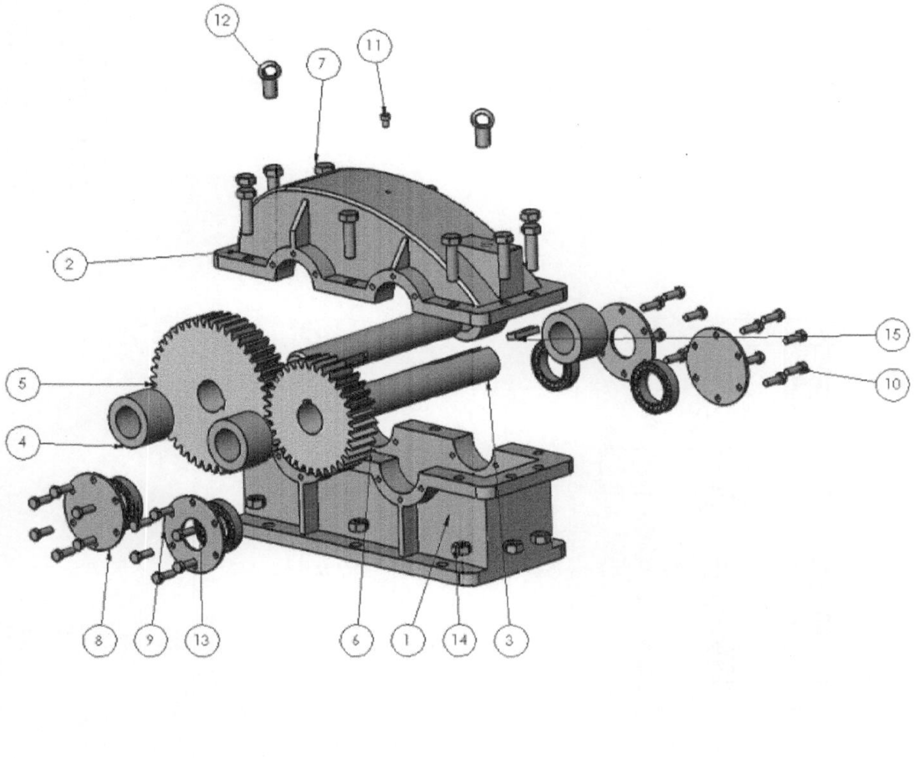

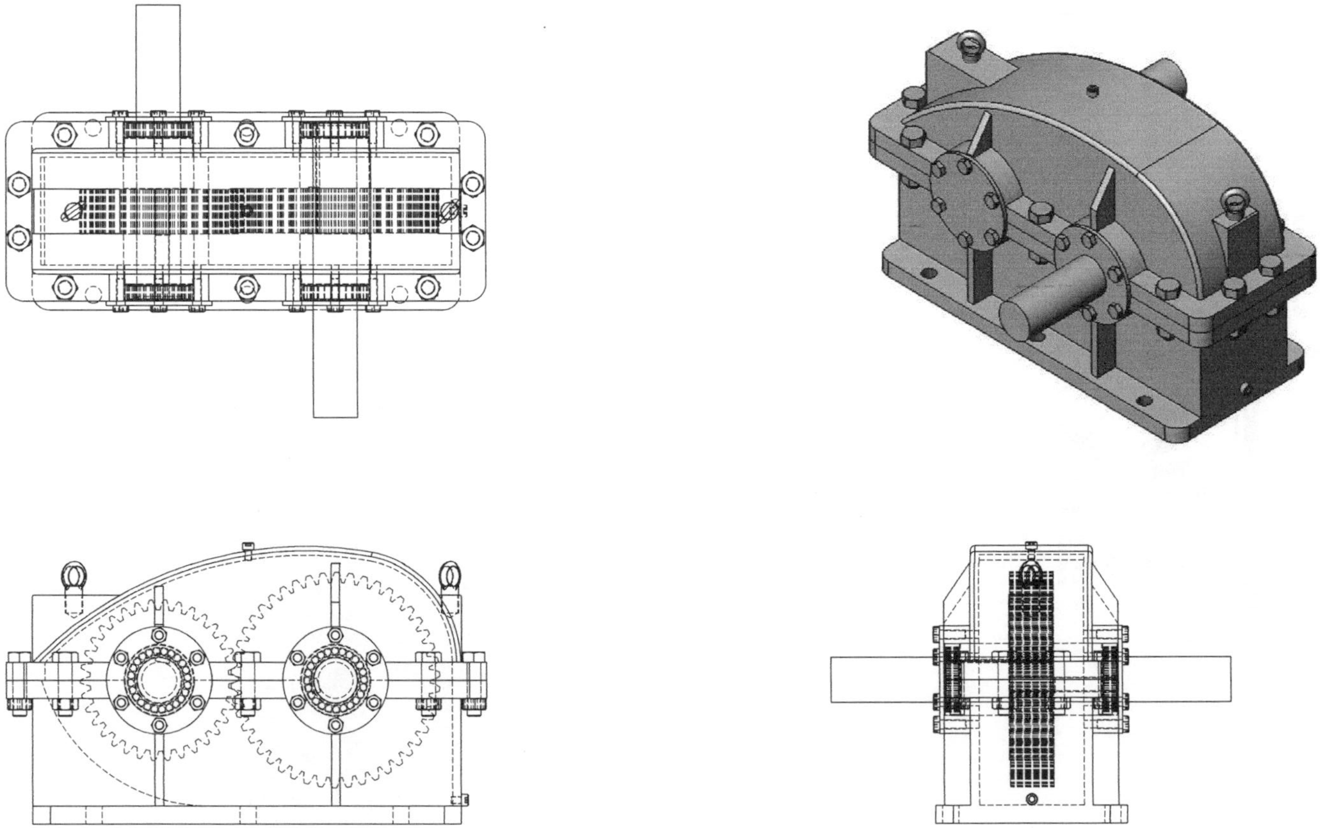

TOLERANCES UNLESS OTHERWISE SPECIFIED	
X	+/- 1
X.X	+/- 0.5
X.XX	+/- 0.2
ANGLE	+/- 0.5

ALL DIMENSIONS IN MM

FIRST ISSUED	
DRAWN BY	
CHECKED BY	
APPROVED BY	

CADCIM TECHNOLOGIES

Reduction gear box

SIZE	DRG NO.	SHEET REV
A3	11-000	A
SCALE 2:1		SHEET 1 OF 12

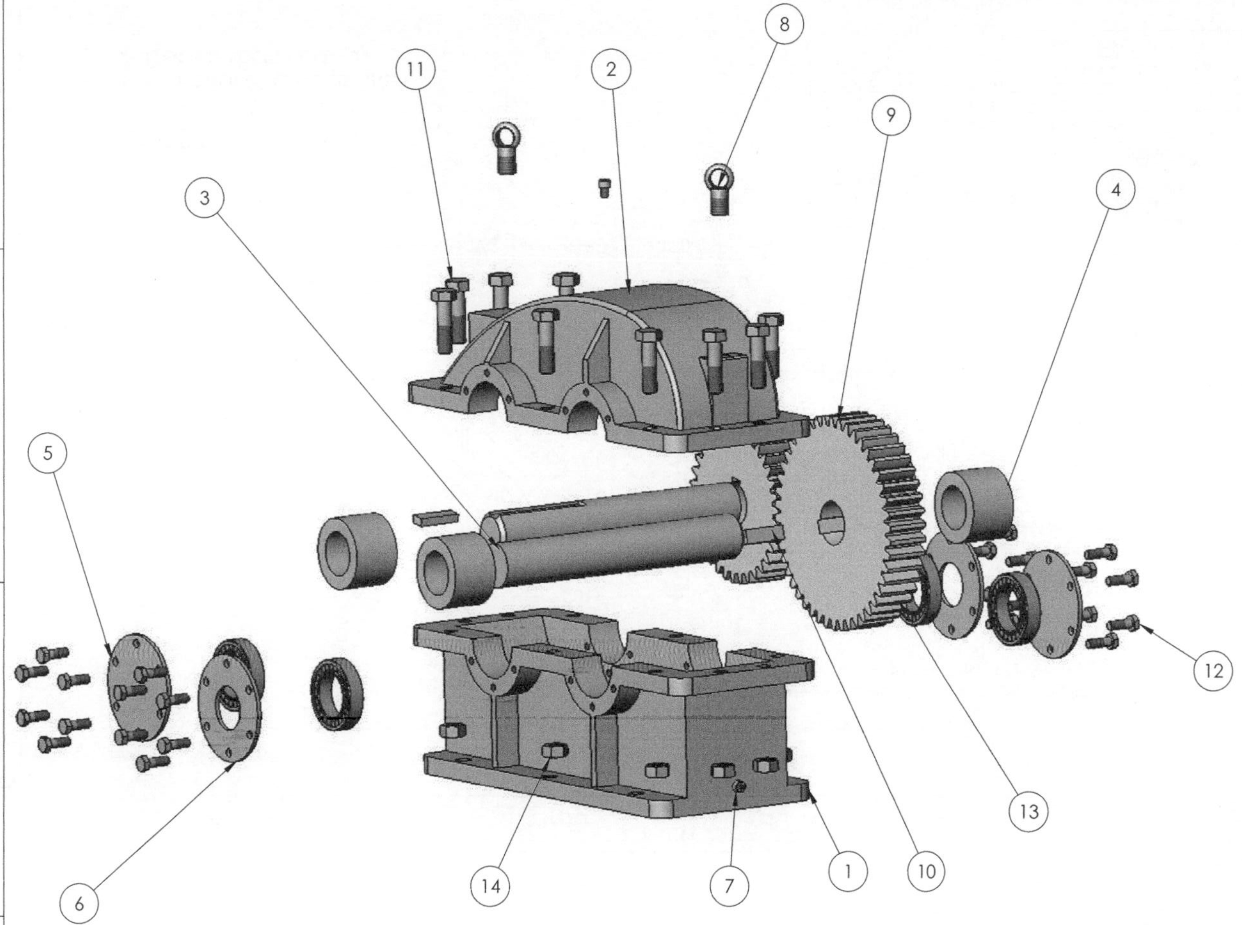

ITEM NO.	PART NUMBER	QTY.
1	LOWER CASE	1
2	UPPER CASE	1
3	SHAFT	2
4	SPACER	4
5	CAP COVER	2
6	CAP	2
7	SOCKET HEAD SCREW 8X1.25	2
8	GRIPPER	2
9	Metric Spur gear -5M 46T 20PA 50FW	1
10	Metric Spur gear -5M 34T 20PA 50FW	1
11	M16X2 Hex Bolt-ANSI B18.2.3.5M	10
12	M10X1.5 Hex Bolt- ANSI B18.2.3.5M	24
13	RADIAL CYLINDRICAL ROLLER BEARING AFBMA 20.1, SIZE20-50	4
14	NUT M16X2NUT-ANSI B18.2.4.2M	10
15	Key	2

TOLERANCES UNLESS OTHERWISE SPECIFIED

X---------------------- +/- 1
X.X------------------- +/- 0.5
X.XX----------------- +/- 0.2
ANGLE-------------- +/- 0.5

ALL DIMENSIONS IN MM

FIRST ISSUED
DRAWN BY
CHECKED BY
APPROVED BY

TICKOO INSTITUTE OF EMERGING TECHNOLOGIES

Reduction gear box exploded

SIZE	DRG NO.	SHEET REV
A3	11-000	A
SCALE 1:8		SHEET 2 OF 12

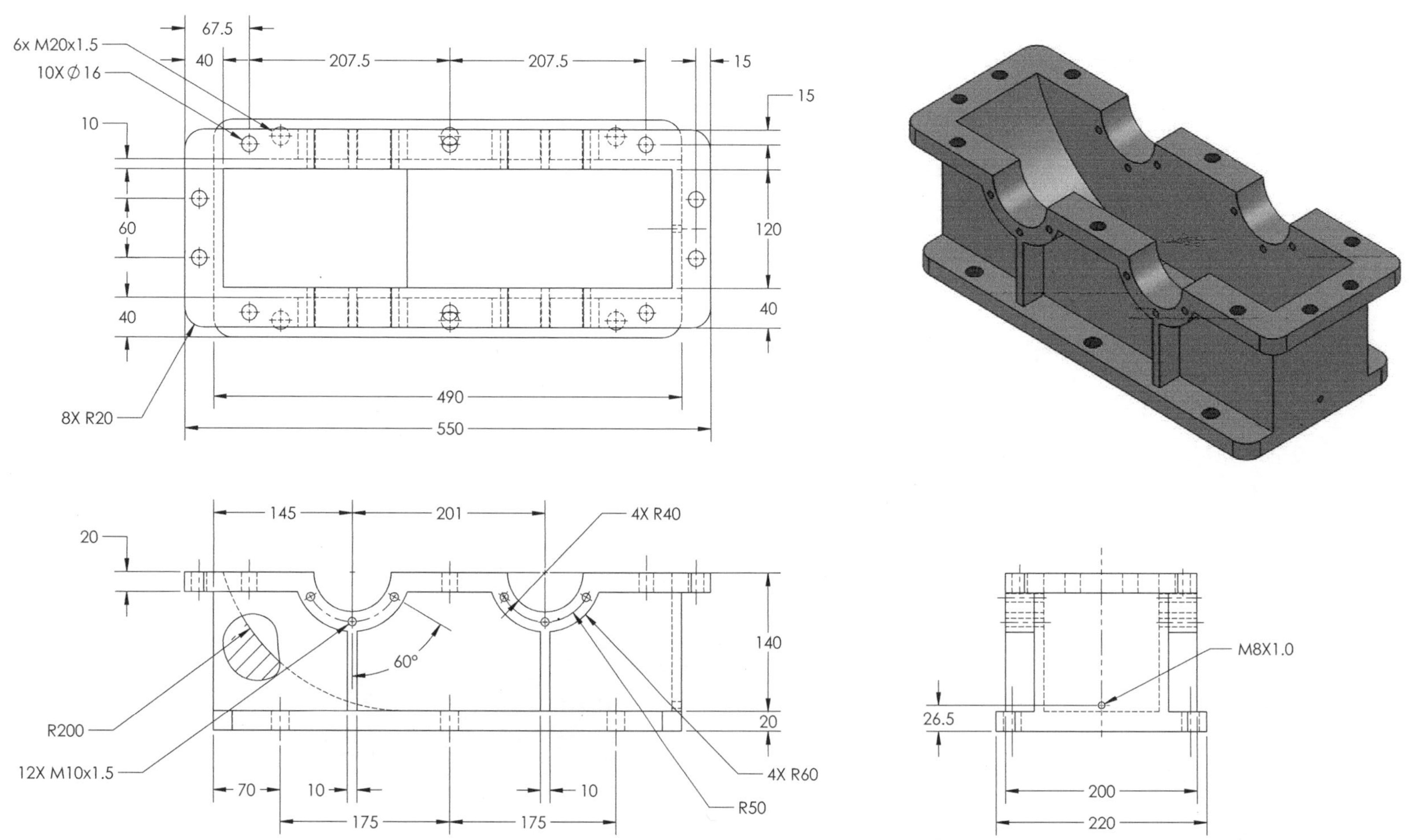

NOTES

1- Material Gray Cast Iron
2- Deburr sharp edges

TOLERANCES UNLESS OTHERWISE SPECIFIED		CADCIM TECHNOLOGIES		
X---------- +/- 1	FIRST ISSUED	Reductor Lower case		
X.X---------- +/- 0.5	DRAWN BY			
X.XX---------- +/- 0.2	CHECKED BY			
ANGLE---------- +/- 0.5	APPROVED BY	SIZE A3	DRG NO. 11-001	SHEET REV A
ALL DIMENSIONS IN MM		SCALE 1:4		SHEET 3 OF 12

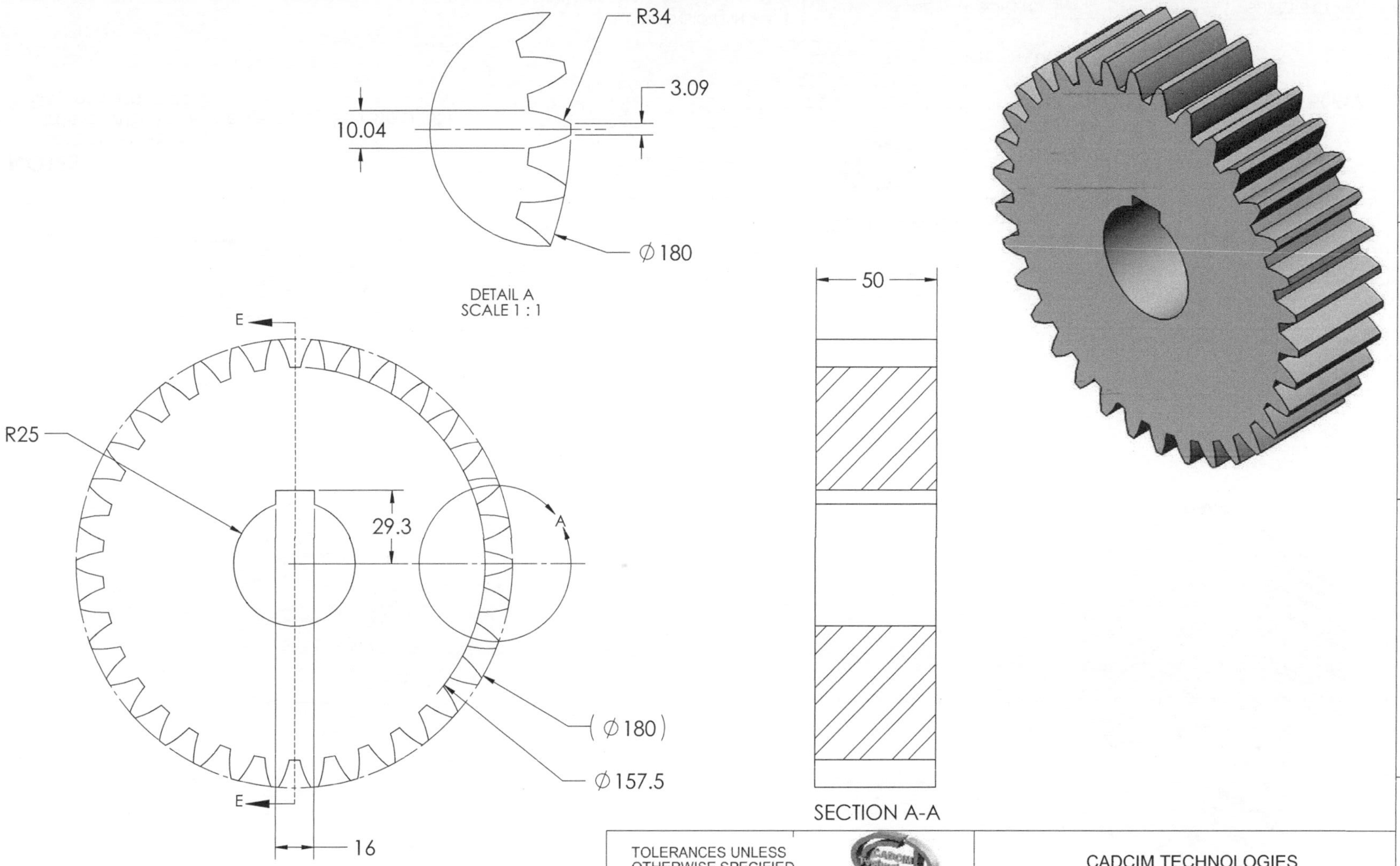

NOTES

1- Number of teeths 34
2- Material AISI 347 Annealed Stainless Steel (SS)
3- Deburr sharp edges

TOLERANCES UNLESS OTHERWISE SPECIFIED		CADCIM TECHNOLOGIES		
X---------- +/- 1	FIRST ISSUED	Metric- Spur gear 5M 34T 20PA 50FW		
X.X---------- +/- 0.5	DRAWN BY			
X.XX---------- +/- 0.2	CHECKED BY			
ANGLE---------- +/- 0.5	APPROVED BY	SIZE A3	DRG NO. 11-002	SHEET REV A
AI ALL DIMENSIONS IN MM		SCALE 1:2		SHEET 4 OF 12

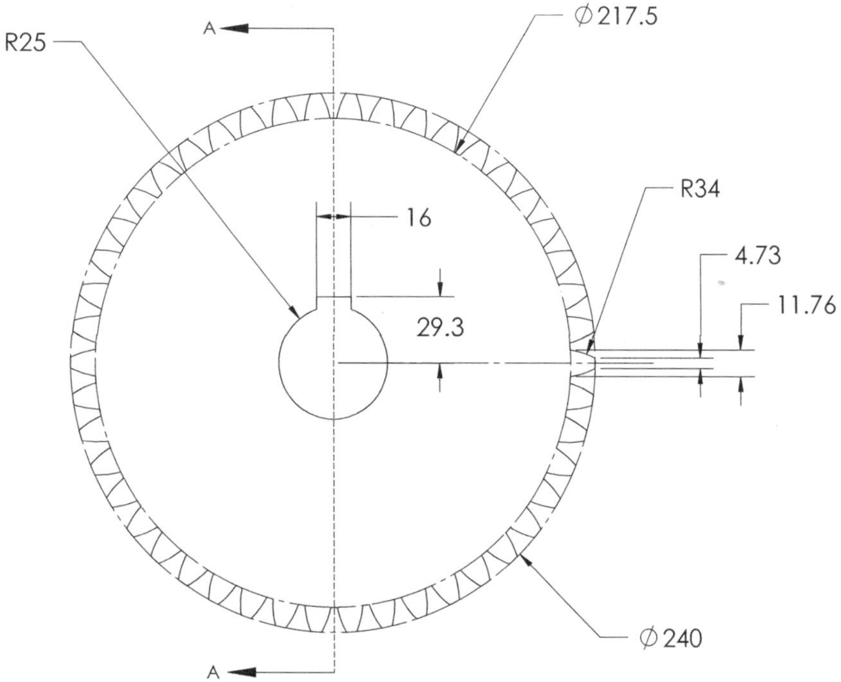

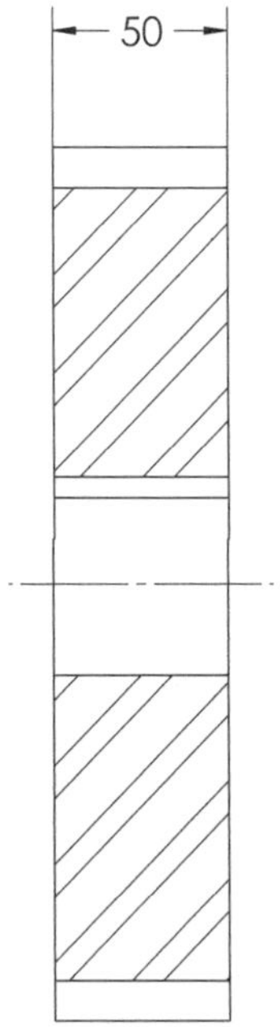

SECTION A-A

NOTES
1- Number of teeths 46
2- Material AISI 347 Annealed Stainless Steel (SS)
3- Deburr sharp edges

TOLERANCES UNLESS OTHERWISE SPECIFIED

X---------------------- +/- 1
X.X-------------------- +/- 0.5
X.XX------------------ +/- 0.2
ANGLE--------------- +/- 0.5

ALL DIMENSIONS IN MM

FIRST ISSUED	
DRAWN BY	
CHECKED BY	
APPROVED BY	

CADCIM TECHNOLOGIES

Metric-Spur Gear 5M 46T 20PA 50FW

SIZE	DRG NO.	SHEET REV
A3	11-003	A
SCALE 1:2		SHEET 5 OF 12

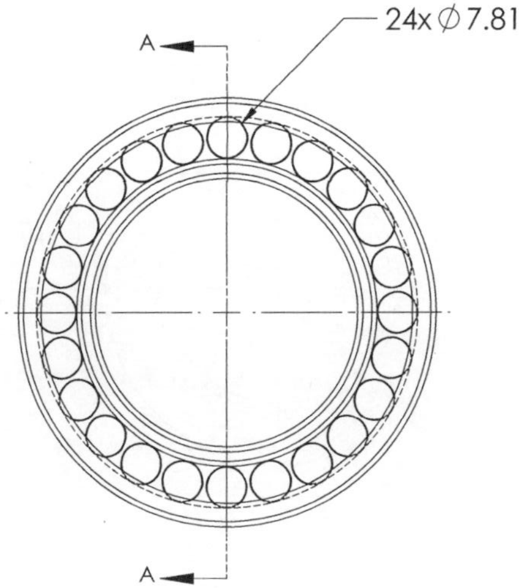

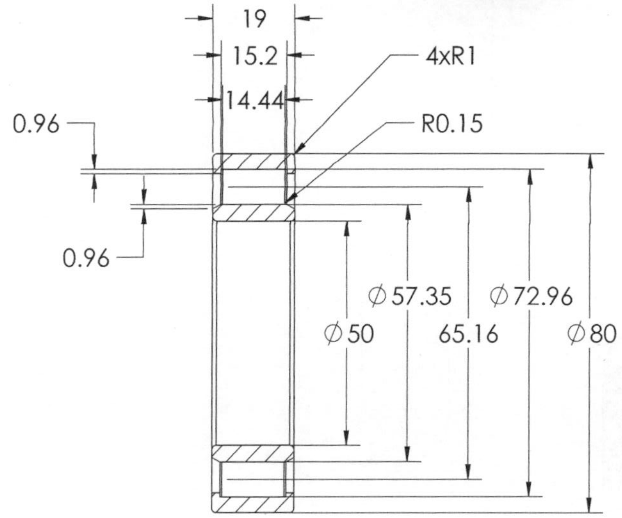

SECTION A-A

NOTES

1- Material Carbon Alloy Steel
2- Deburr sharp edges

TOLERANCES UNLESS OTHERWISE SPECIFIED

X------------------ +/- 1
X.X---------------- +/- 0.5
X.XX--------------- +/- 0.2
ANGLE-------------- +/- 0.5

ALL DIMENSIONS IN MM

FIRST ISSUED	
DRAWN BY	
CHECKED BY	
APPROVED BY	

CADCIM TECHNOLOGIES

Radial Cylindrical Roller BearingAFBMA 20.1, Size 20-50

SIZE	DRG NO.	SHEET REV
A3	11-004	A
SCALE 1:1		SHEET 6 OF 12

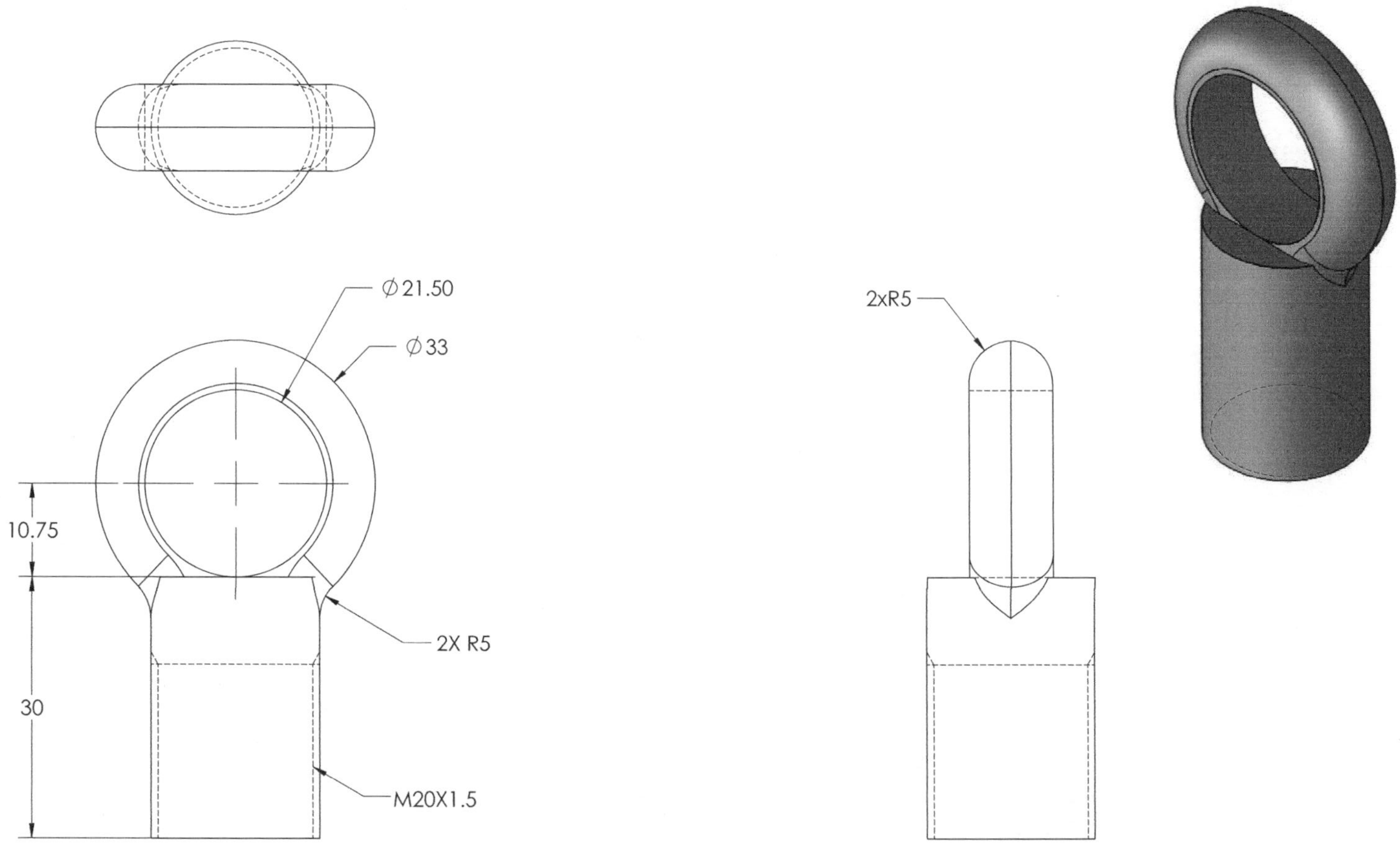

NOTES

1- Material Alloy steel
2- Deburr sharp edges

TOLERANCES UNLESS OTHERWISE SPECIFIED		CADCIM TECHNOLOGIES
X------------ +/- 1	FIRST ISSUED	Gripper
X.X---------- +/- 0.5	DRAWN BY	
X.XX--------- +/- 0.2	CHECKED BY	
ANGLE-------- +/- 0.5	APPROVED BY	SIZE A3 · DRG NO. 11-005 · SHEET REV A
ALL DIMENSIONS IN MM		SCALE 2:1 · SHEET 7 OF 12

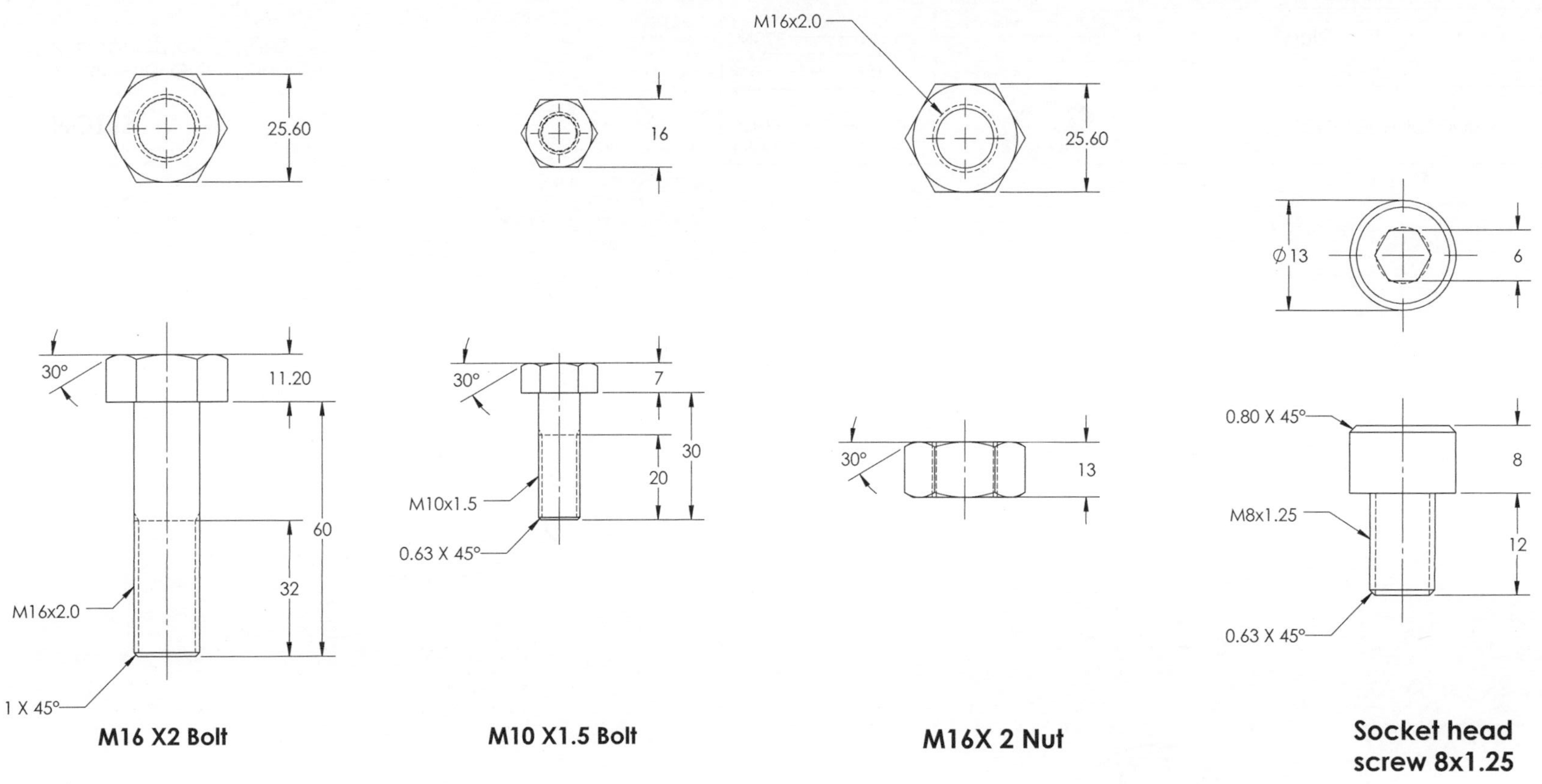

NOTES

1- Material Stainless Steel
2- Deburr sharp edges

TOLERANCES UNLESS OTHERWISE SPECIFIED

X------------------ +/- 1
X.X---------------- +/- 0.5
X.XX--------------- +/- 0.2
ANGLE-------------- +/- 0.5

ALL DIMENSIONS IN MM

FIRST ISSUED	
DRAWN BY	
CHECKED BY	
APPROVED BY	

CADCIM TECHNOLOGIES

1. M16 X 2 Hex Bolt- ANSI B18.2.3.5M
2. M10 X1.5 Hex Bolt- ANSI B18.2.3.5M
3. M16 X 2 NUT-ANSI B18.2.4.2M
4. Socket HeaScrew M8 X 1.25

SIZE	DRG NO.	SHEET REV
A3	11-006	A
SCALE 2:1		SHEET 8 OF 12

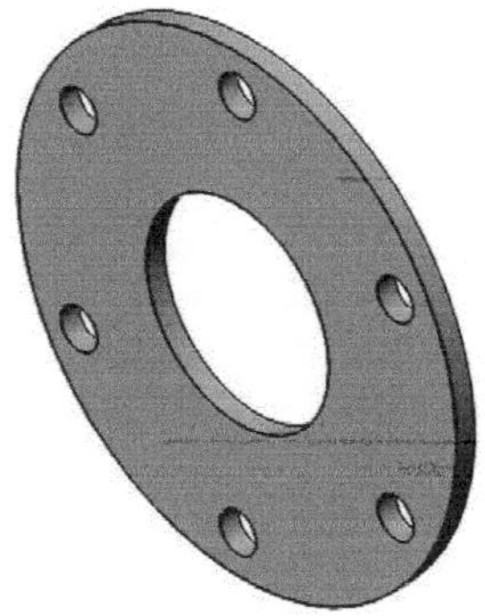

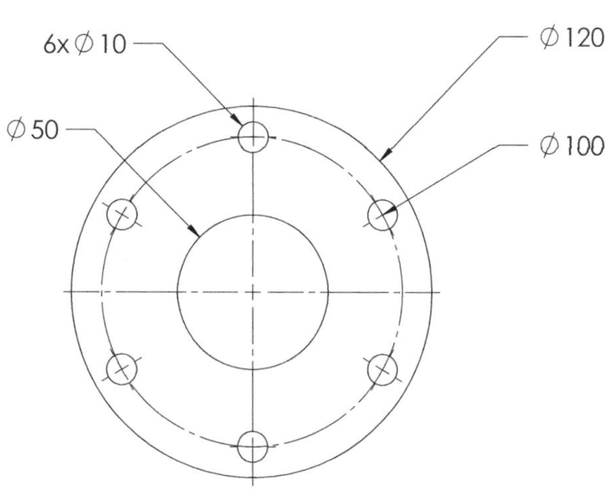

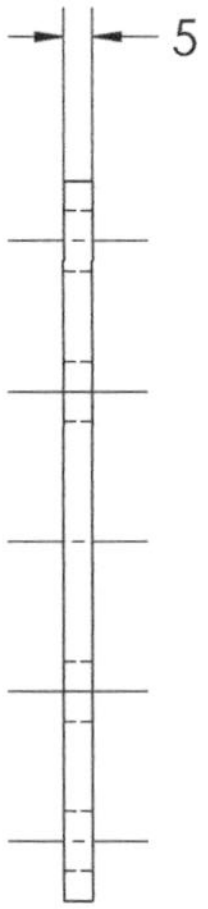

NOTES

1- Material Gray Cast Iron
2- Deburr sharp edges

TOLERANCES UNLESS OTHERWISE SPECIFIED

X	+/- 1
X.X	+/- 0.5
X.XX	+/- 0.2
ANGLE	+/- 0.5

ALL DIMENSIONS IN MM

FIRST ISSUED	
DRAWN BY	
CHECKED BY	
APPROVED BY	

CADCIM TECHNOLOGIES

Cap

SIZE	DRG NO.	SHEET REV
A3	11-007	A
SCALE 2:3		SHEET 9 OF 12

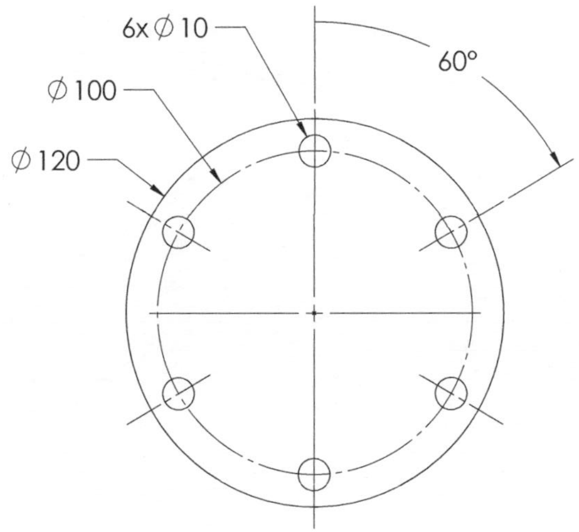

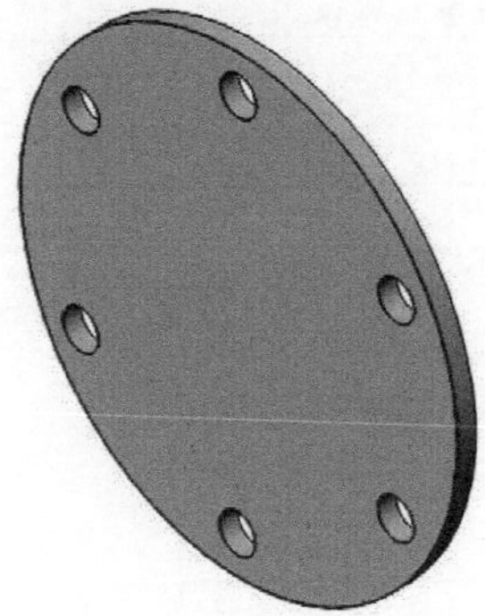

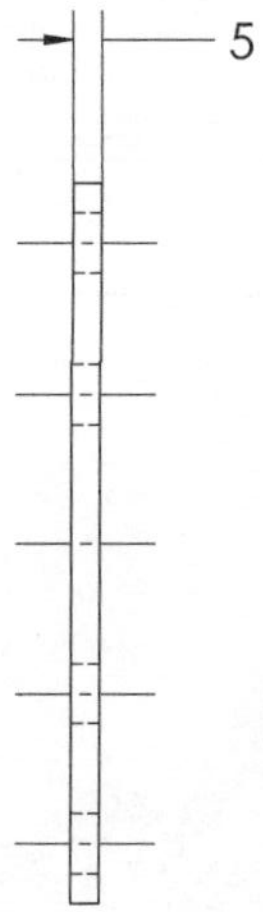

NOTES

1- Material Gray Cast Iron
2- Deburr sharp edges

TOLERANCES UNLESS OTHERWISE SPECIFIED

X---------------------- +/- 1
X.X-------------------- +/- 0.5
X.XX------------------ +/- 0.2
ANGLE-------------- +/- 0.5

ALL DIMENSIONS IN MM

FIRST ISSUED	
DRAWN BY	
CHECKED BY	
APPROVED BY	

CADCIM TECHNOLOGIES

Cap Cover

SIZE	DRG NO.	SHEET REV
A3	11-008	A
SCALE 2:3		SHEET 10 OF 12

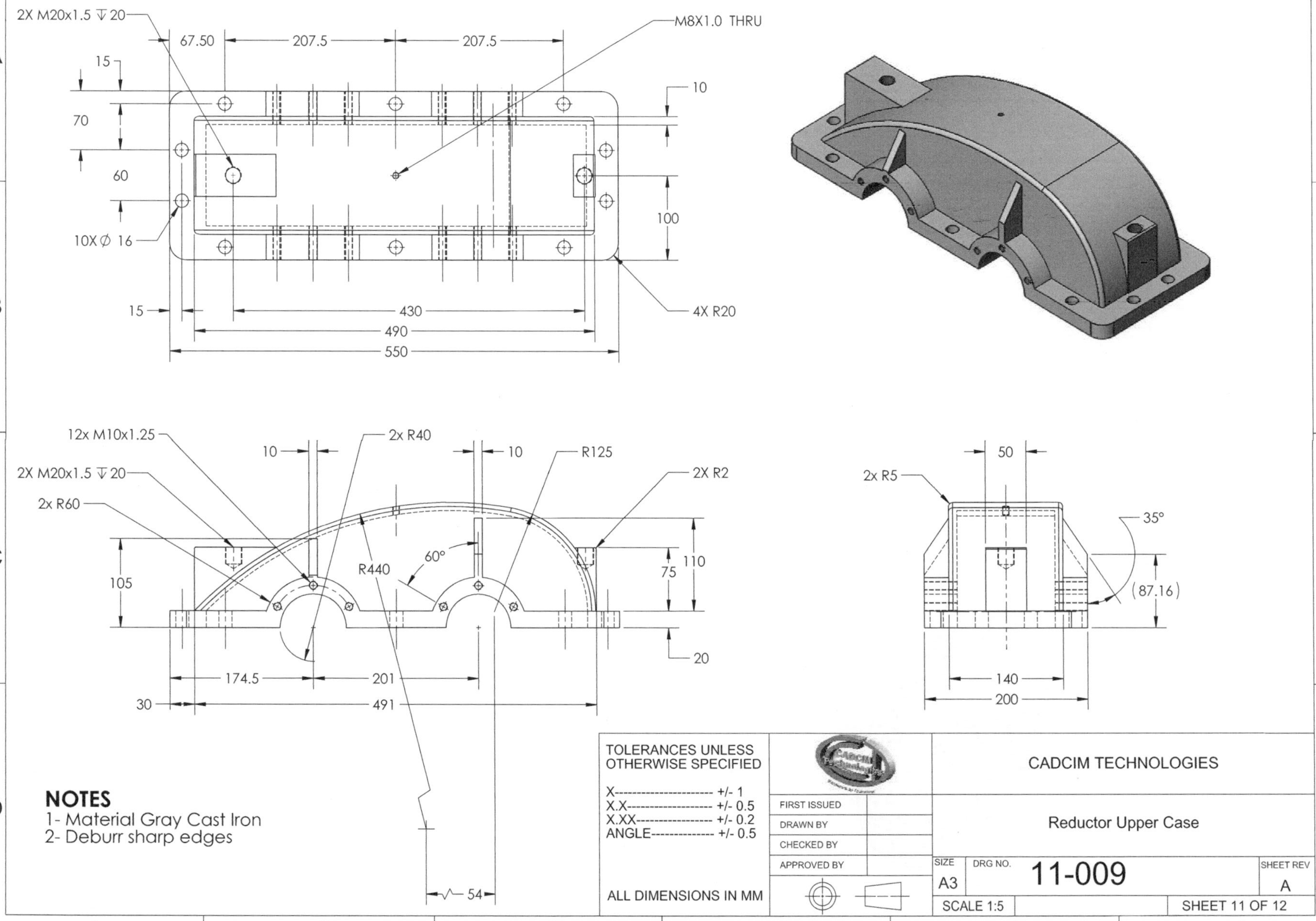

NOTES
1- Material Gray Cast Iron
2- Deburr sharp edges

TOLERANCES UNLESS OTHERWISE SPECIFIED		CADCIM TECHNOLOGIES			
X---- +/- 1	FIRST ISSUED	Reductor Upper Case			
X.X---- +/- 0.5	DRAWN BY				
X.XX---- +/- 0.2	CHECKED BY				
ANGLE---- +/- 0.5	APPROVED BY	SIZE A3	DRG NO. 11-009		SHEET REV A
ALL DIMENSIONS IN MM		SCALE 1:5		SHEET 11 OF 12	

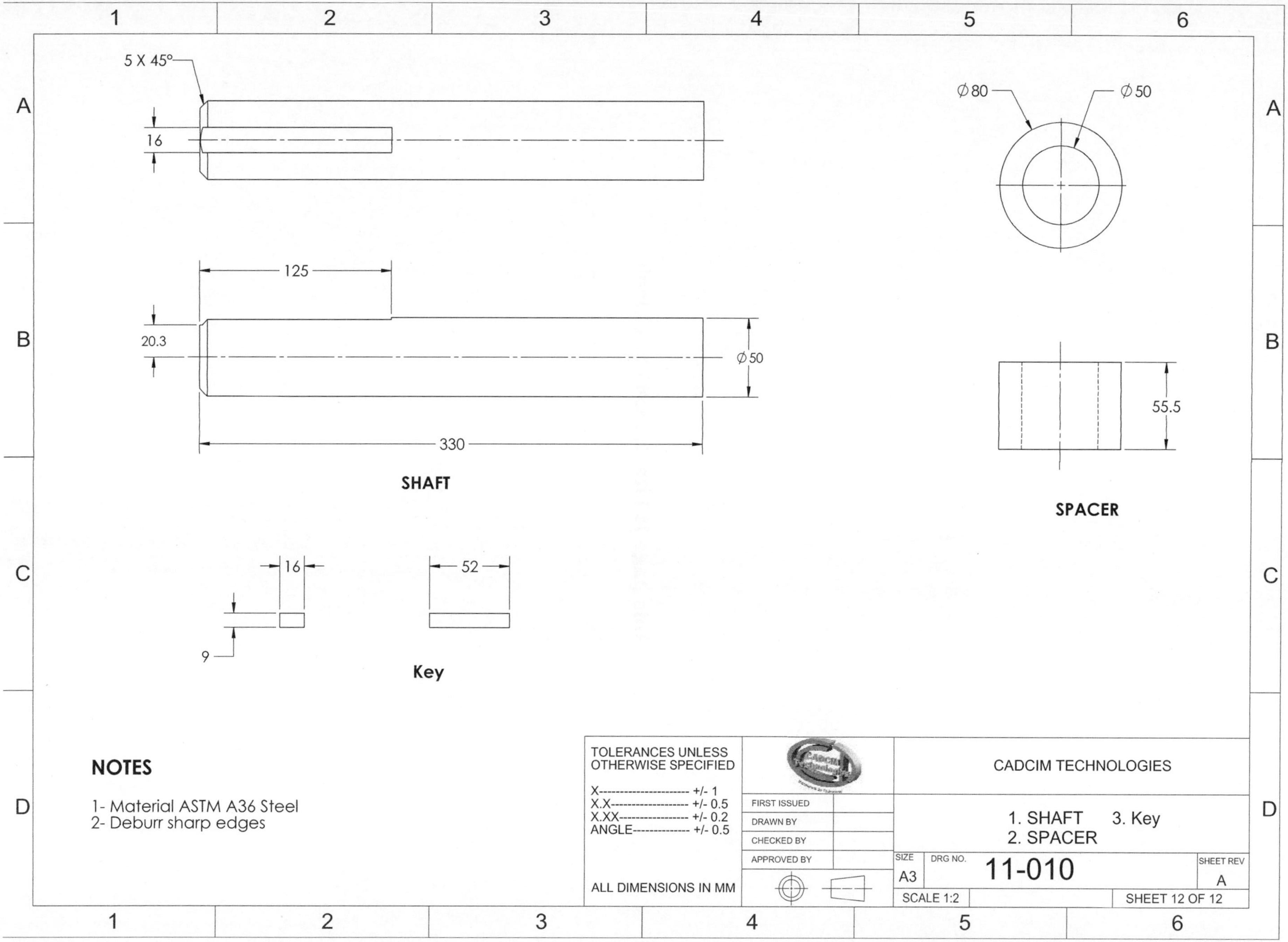
5 X 45°
16
125
20.3
Ø 50
330
SHAFT
Ø 80
Ø 50
55.5
SPACER
16
52
9
Key
NOTES
1- Material ASTM A36 Steel
2- Deburr sharp edges
TOLERANCES UNLESS OTHERWISE SPECIFIED
X---------------------- +/- 1
X.X------------------- +/- 0.5
X.XX----------------- +/- 0.2
ANGLE-------------- +/- 0.5
ALL DIMENSIONS IN MM
FIRST ISSUED
DRAWN BY
CHECKED BY
APPROVED BY
CADCIM TECHNOLOGIES
1. SHAFT 3. Key
2. SPACER
SIZE
A3
DRG NO.
11-010
SHEET REV
A
SCALE 1:2
SHEET 12 OF 12

This page is intentionally left blank

Project 12

Single Stage Centrifugal Pump Assembly

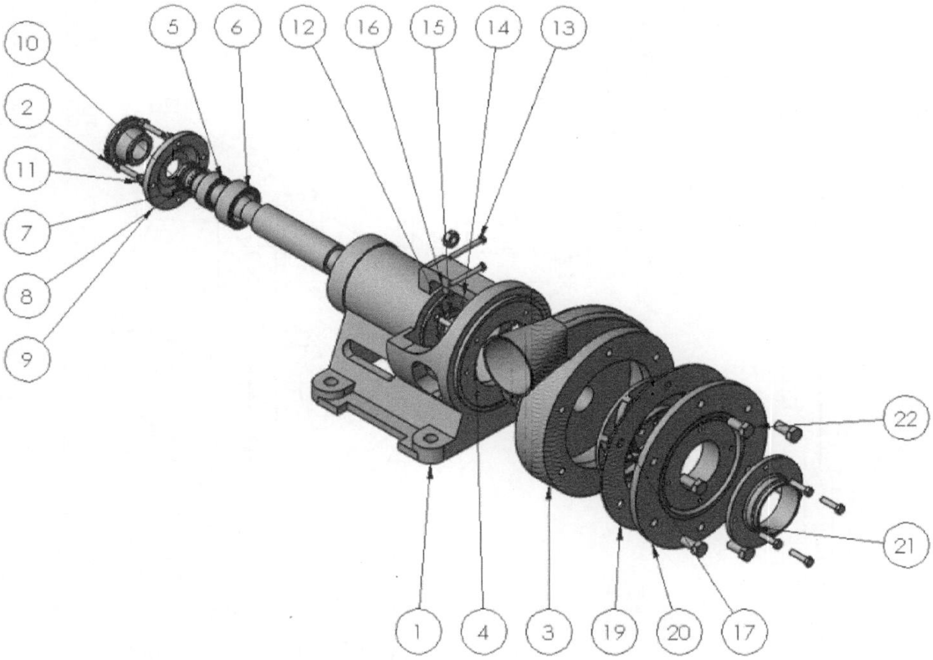

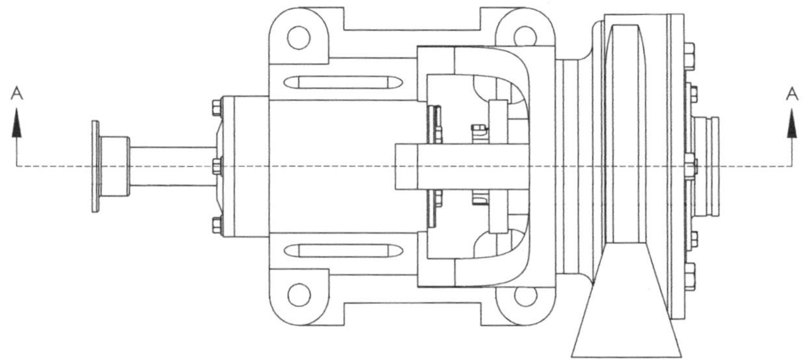

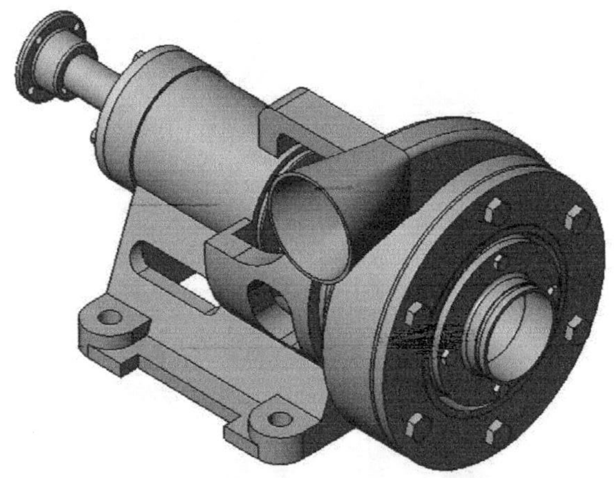

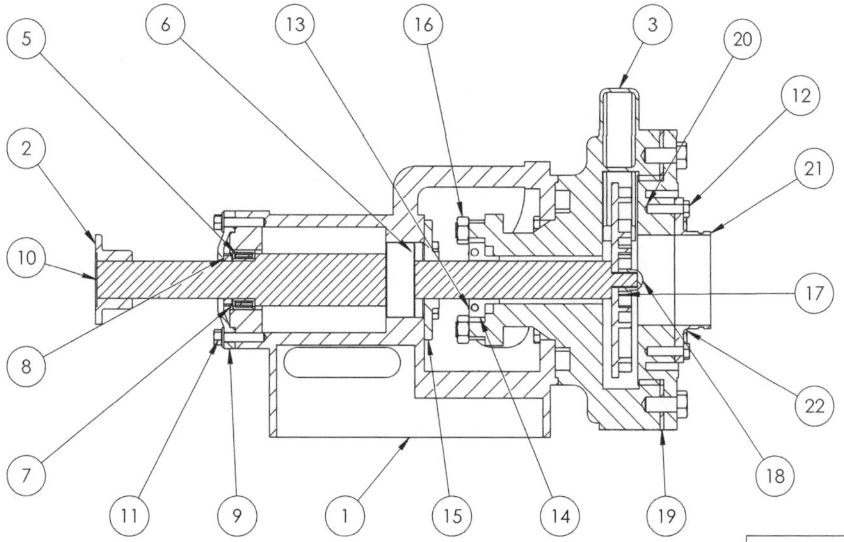

SECTION A-A

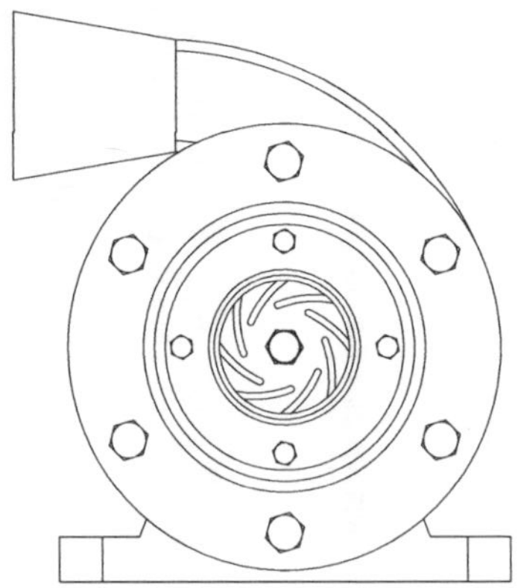

TOLERANCES UNLESS OTHERWISE SPECIFIED

X---------------------- +/- 1
X.X-------------------- +/- 0.5
X.XX------------------ +/- 0.2
ANGLE--------------- +/- 0.5

ALL DIMENSIONS IN MM

FIRST ISSUED	
DRAWN BY	
CHECKED BY	
APPROVED BY	

CADCIM TECHNOLOGIES

Single Stage Centirfugal Pump

SIZE	DRG NO.	SHEET REV
A3	12-000	A
SCALE 1:6		SHEET 1 OF 18

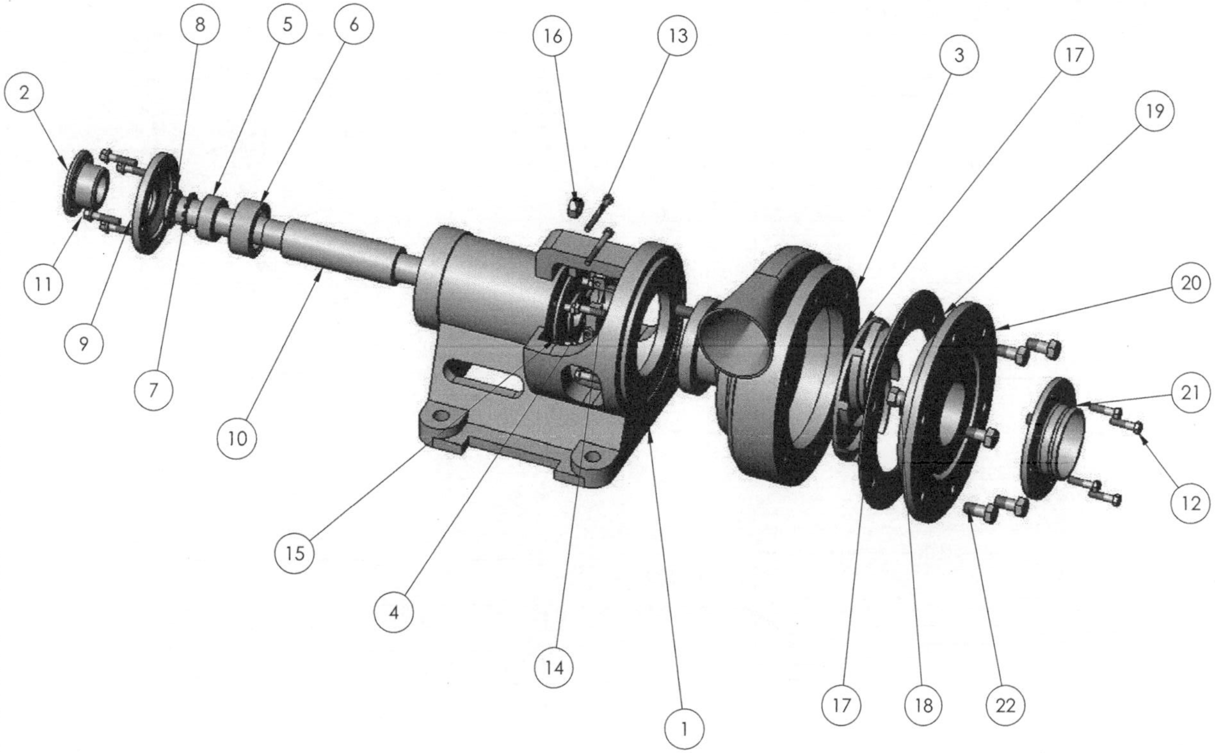

ITEM NO.	PART NUMBER	QTY.
1	Bearing_Housing	1
2	Coupling _	1
3	Volute_Casing	1
4	Stuffing_box gland Lower	1
5	RADIAL CYLINDRICAL ROLLER BEARING AFBMA 20.1, Size 20-50	1
6	RADIAL CYLINDRICAL ROLLER BEARING Bore AFBMA 20.1, SIZE 59-70	1
7	Bearing LockWaher	1
8	Bearing_Nut	1
9	Bearing_Housing End Cap	1
10	shaft	1
11	M12X1.75 Hex Flange Screw- ANSI B18.2.3.4M	4
12	M12x1.75 Hex bolt-ANSI B18.2.3.5M	14
13	M10x1.5 Hex Bolt-ANSI B18.2.35M	2
14	Stuffing_box_gland_Upper	1
15	Bearing_Housing End Cap2	1
16	M20X 2.5 Hex Nut-ANSI B18.2.4.1M	2
17	Impeller	1
18	CAP SCREW M20	1
19	Volute_Casing Gasket	1
20	Volute_Casing Cover	1
21	Suction_Nozzle	1
22	M20X 2.5 Hex Bolt-ANSI B18.2.3.5M	6

TOLERANCES UNLESS OTHERWISE SPECIFIED		CADCIM TECHNOLOGIES
X---------- +/- 1 X.X---------- +/- 0.5 X.XX---------- +/- 0.2 ANGLE---------- +/- 0.5	FIRST ISSUED DRAWN BY CHECKED BY APPROVED BY	Single Stage Centrifugal Pump Exploded
ALL DIMENSIONS IN MM		SIZE A3 · DRG NO. 12-000 · SHEET REV A SCALE 1:8 · SHEET 2 OF 18

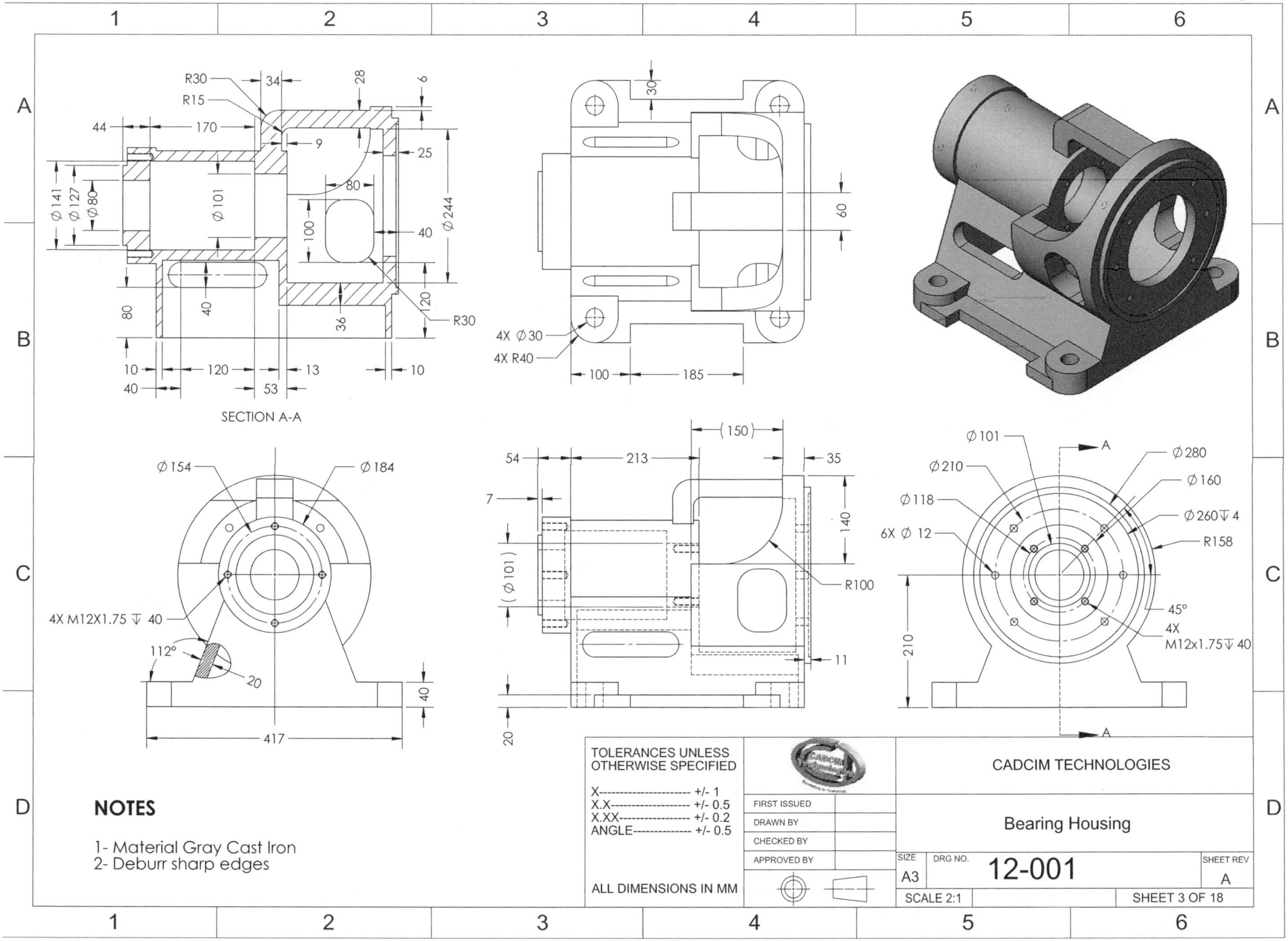
SECTION A-A
TOLERANCES UNLESS OTHERWISE SPECIFIED
X---------- +/- 1
X.X---------- +/- 0.5
X.XX---------- +/- 0.2
ANGLE---------- +/- 0.5
ALL DIMENSIONS IN MM
FIRST ISSUED
DRAWN BY
CHECKED BY
APPROVED BY
CADCIM TECHNOLOGIES
Bearing Housing
SIZE A3
DRG NO. 12-001
SHEET REV A
SCALE 2:1
SHEET 3 OF 18
NOTES
1- Material Gray Cast Iron
2- Deburr sharp edges

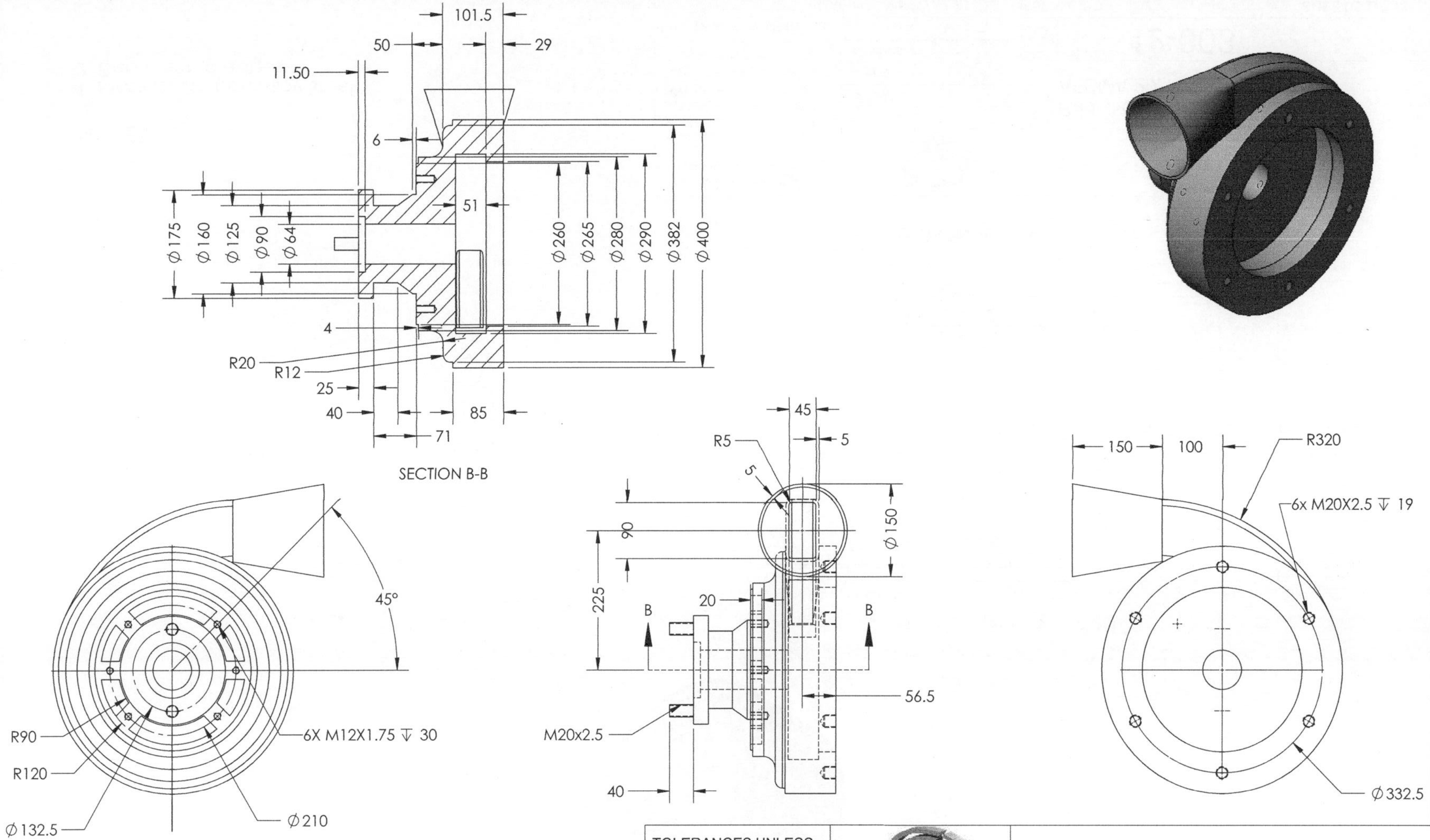

NOTES

1- Material Gray Cast Iron
2- Deburr sharp edges

TOLERANCES UNLESS OTHERWISE SPECIFIED		CADCIM TECHNOLOGIES
X---------- +/- 1	FIRST ISSUED	
X.X---------- +/- 0.5	DRAWN BY	Volute Casing
X.XX---------- +/- 0.2	CHECKED BY	
ANGLE---------- +/- 0.5	APPROVED BY	SIZE A3	DRG NO. 12-002	SHEET REV A
ALL DIMENSIONS IN MM		SCALE 1:6	SHEET 4 OF 18

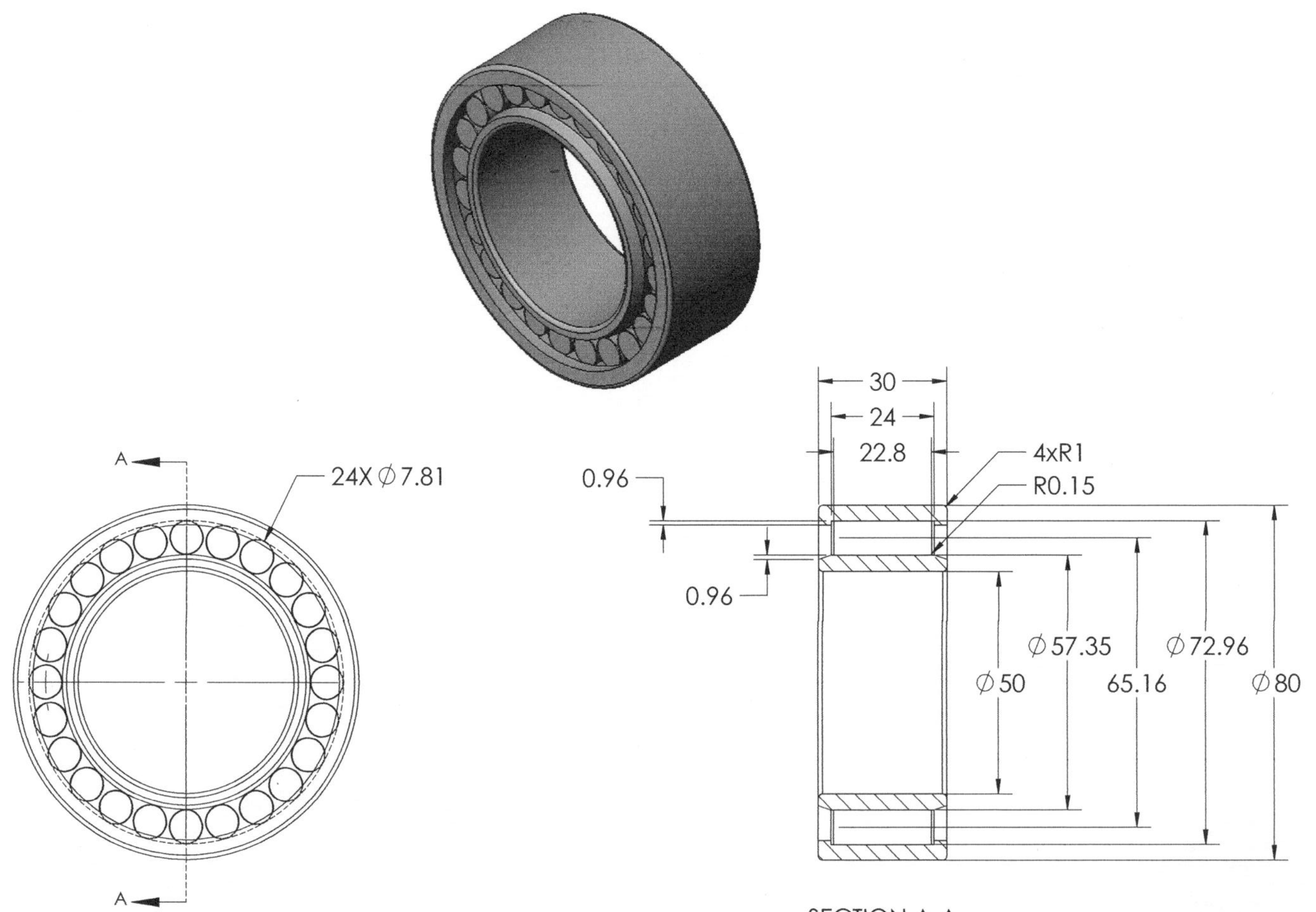

SECTION A-A

NOTES

1- Material Carbon Alloy Steel
2- Deburr sharp edges

TOLERANCES UNLESS OTHERWISE SPECIFIED		CADCIM TECHNOLOGIES
X---------------------- +/- 1	FIRST ISSUED	Radial Cylindrical Roller Bearing AFBMA 20.1, Size 40-50
X.X------------------- +/- 0.5	DRAWN BY	
X.XX----------------- +/- 0.2	CHECKED BY	
ANGLE--------------- +/- 0.5	APPROVED BY	SIZE A3 · DRG NO. 12-003 · SHEET REV A
ALL DIMENSIONS IN MM		SCALE 1:1 · SHEET 5 OF 18

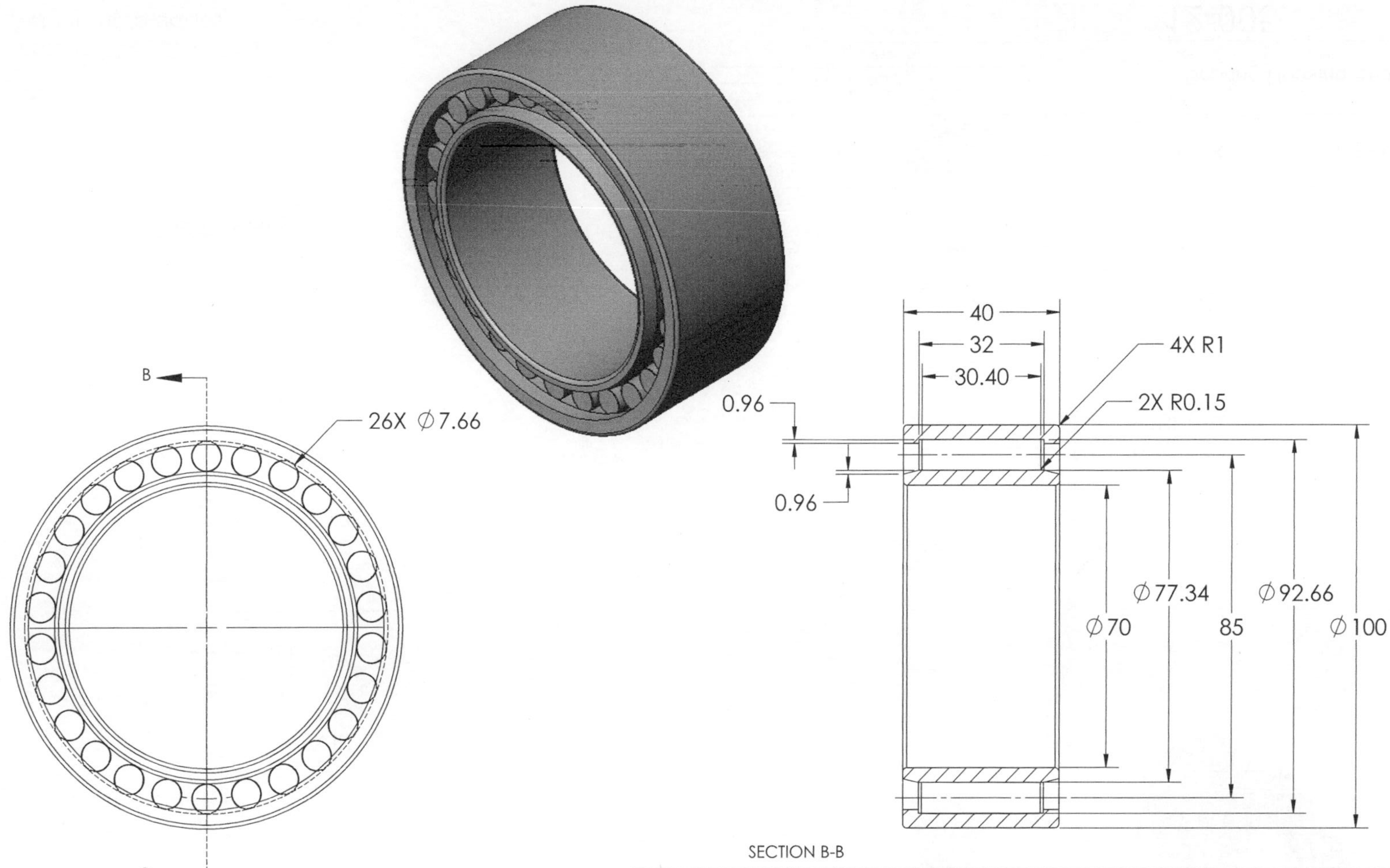

TOLERANCES UNLESS OTHERWISE SPECIFIED		CADCIM TECHNOLOGIES
X---------- +/- 1 X.X---------- +/- 0.5 X.XX---------- +/- 0.2 ANGLE---------- +/- 0.5	FIRST ISSUED DRAWN BY CHECKED BY APPROVED BY	Radial Cylindrical Roller Bearing AFBMA 20.1, Size 59-70
ALL DIMENSIONS IN MM		SIZE A3 · DRG NO. 12-004 · SHEET REV A
		SCALE 2:1 · SHEET 6 OF 18

NOTES

1- Material Carbon Alloy Steel
2- Debure sharp edges

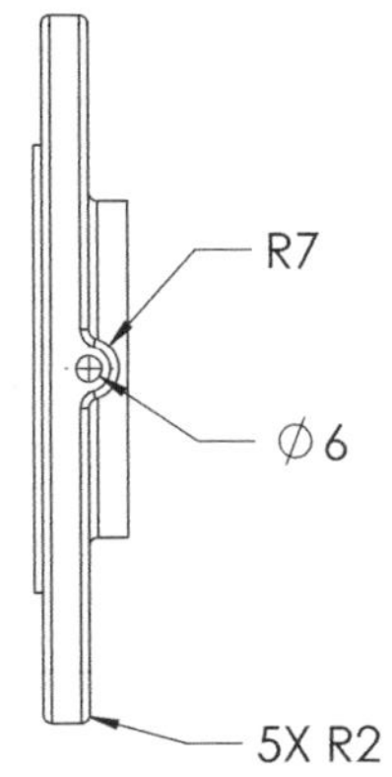

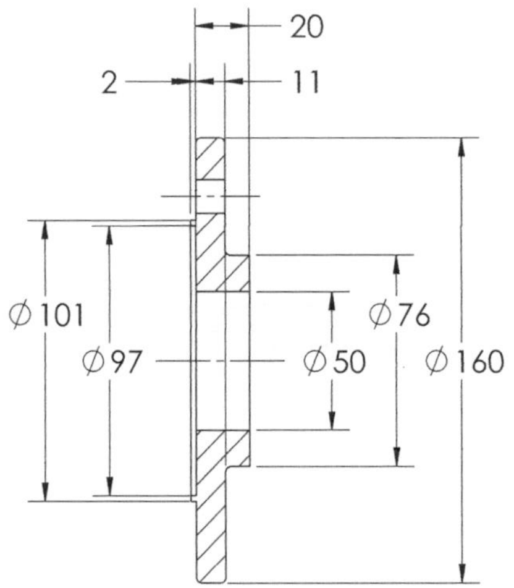

SECTION A-A

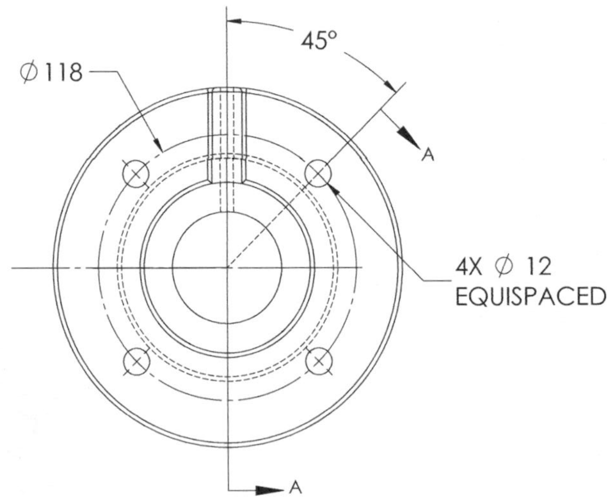

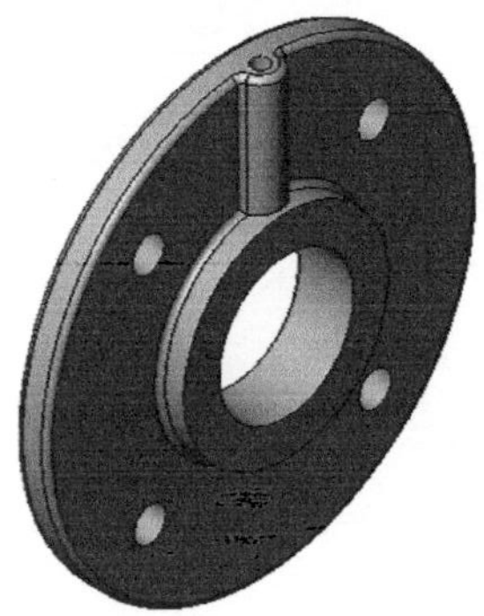

NOTES

1- Material Gray Cast Iron
2- Deburr sharp edges

TOLERANCES UNLESS OTHERWISE SPECIFIED		CADCIM TECHNOLOGIES
X---------- +/- 1 X.X---------- +/- 0.5 X.XX---------- +/- 0.2 ANGLE---------- +/- 0.5	FIRST ISSUED DRAWN BY CHECKED BY APPROVED BY	Bearing Housing End CAP2
ALL DIMENSIONS IN MM		SIZE A3 · DRG NO. 12-005 · SHEET REV A
		SCALE 1:2 · SHEET 7 OF 18

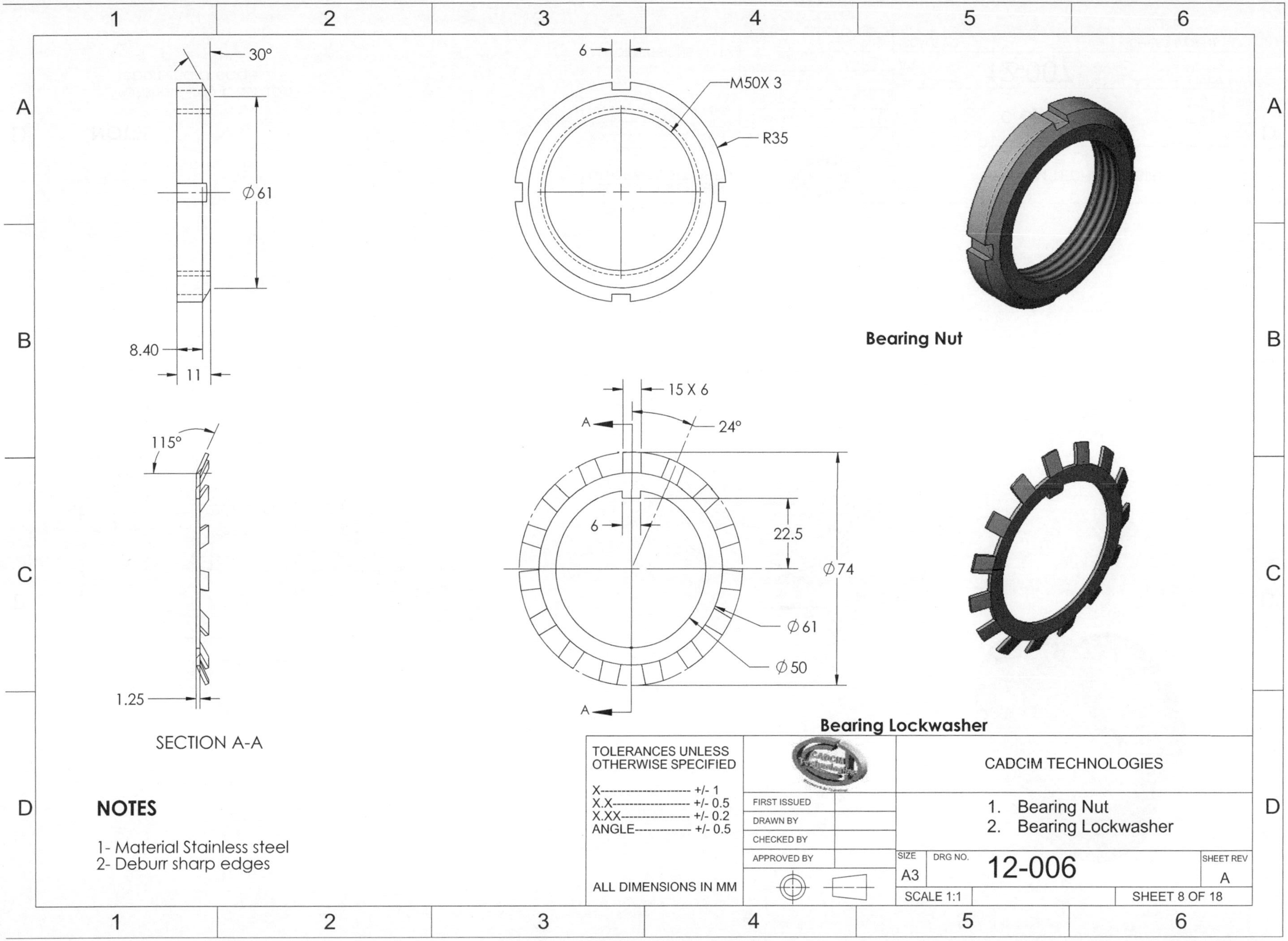
30°
6
M50X 3
R35
Ø61
8.40
11
Bearing Nut
15 X 6
24°
115°
6
22.5
Ø74
Ø61
Ø50
1.25
A
SECTION A-A
Bearing Lockwasher
NOTES
1- Material Stainless steel
2- Deburr sharp edges
TOLERANCES UNLESS OTHERWISE SPECIFIED
X---------- +/- 1
X.X---------- +/- 0.5
X.XX---------- +/- 0.2
ANGLE---------- +/- 0.5
ALL DIMENSIONS IN MM
FIRST ISSUED
DRAWN BY
CHECKED BY
APPROVED BY
CADCIM TECHNOLOGIES
1. Bearing Nut
2. Bearing Lockwasher
SIZE A3
DRG NO. 12-006
SHEET REV A
SCALE 1:1
SHEET 8 OF 18

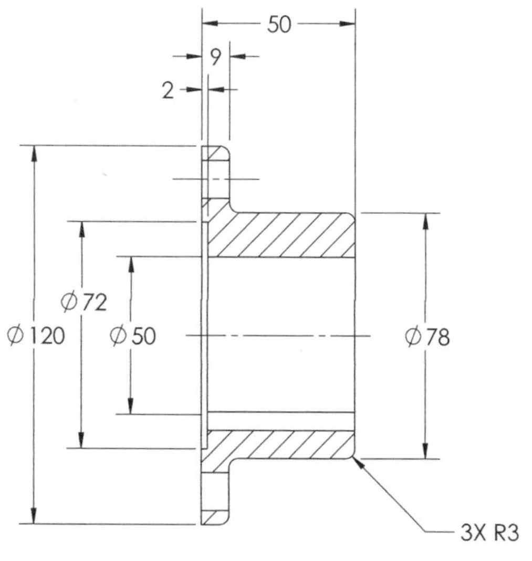

SECTION B-B

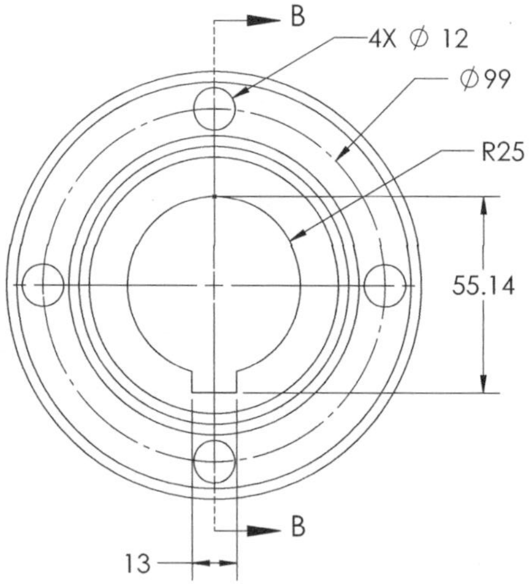

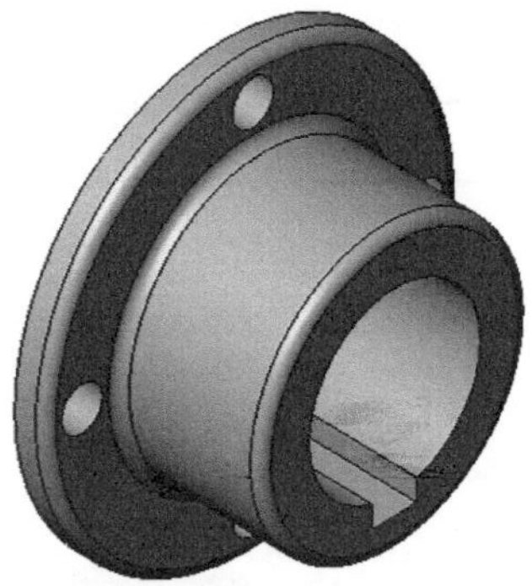

NOTES

1- Material Gray Cast Iron
2- Deburr sharp edges

TOLERANCES UNLESS OTHERWISE SPECIFIED		CADCIM TECHNOLOGIES
X---- +/- 1 X.X---- +/- 0.5 X.XX---- +/- 0.2 ANGLE---- +/- 0.5	FIRST ISSUED DRAWN BY CHECKED BY APPROVED BY	Coupling
ALL DIMENSIONS IN MM		SIZE A3 · DRG NO. 12-007 · SHEET REV A
		SCALE 2:3 · SHEET 9 OF 18

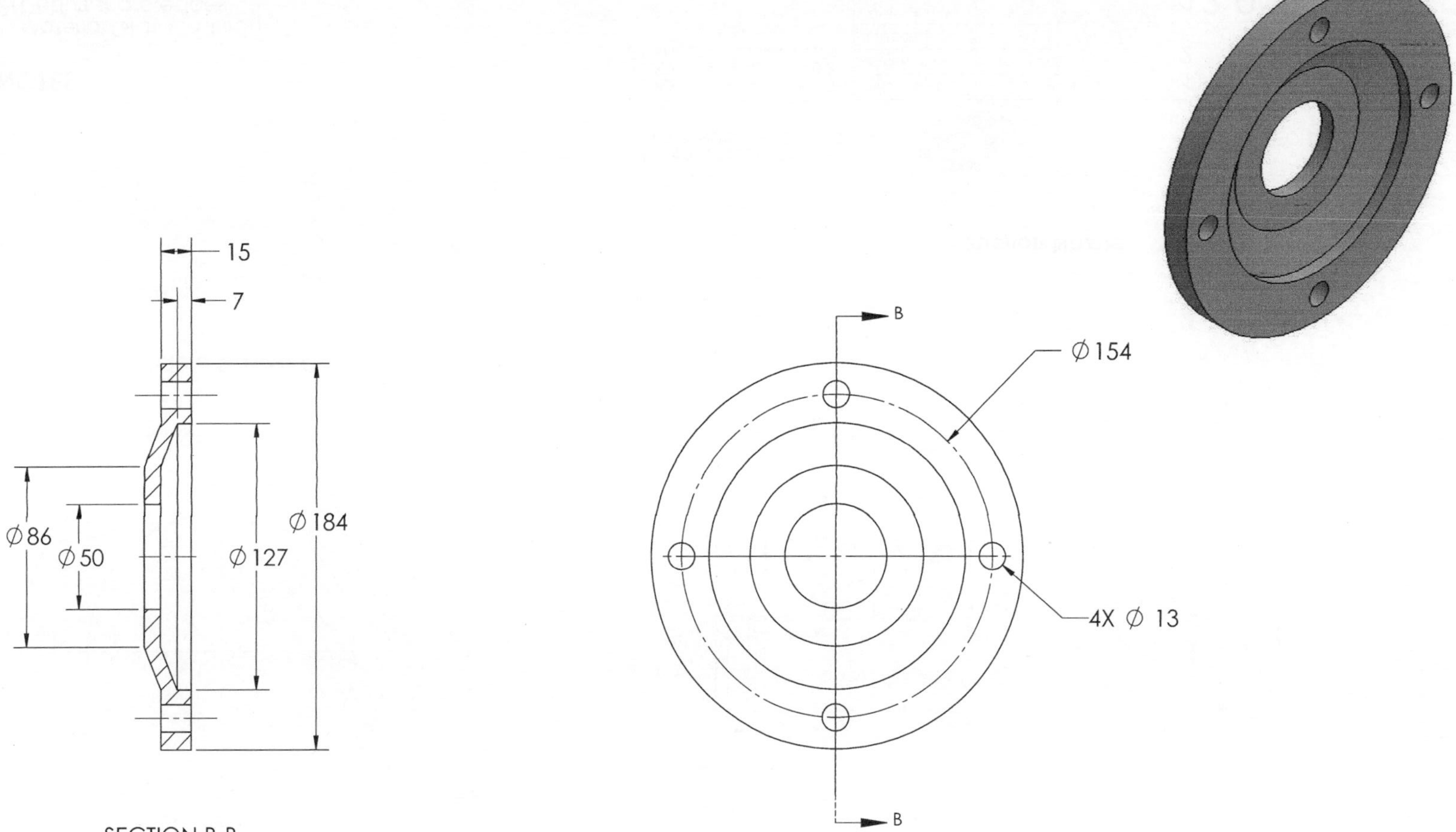

SECTION B-B

NOTES

1- Material Gray Cast Iron
2- Deburr sharp edges

TOLERANCES UNLESS OTHERWISE SPECIFIED		CADCIM TECHNOLOGIES		
X---------- +/- 1	FIRST ISSUED	Bearing House End Cap		
X.X---------- +/- 0.5	DRAWN BY			
X.XX---------- +/- 0.2	CHECKED BY			
ANGLE---------- +/- 0.5	APPROVED BY	SIZE A3	DRG NO. 12-008	SHEET REV A
ALL DIMENSIONS IN MM		SCALE 1:2		SHEET 10 OF 18

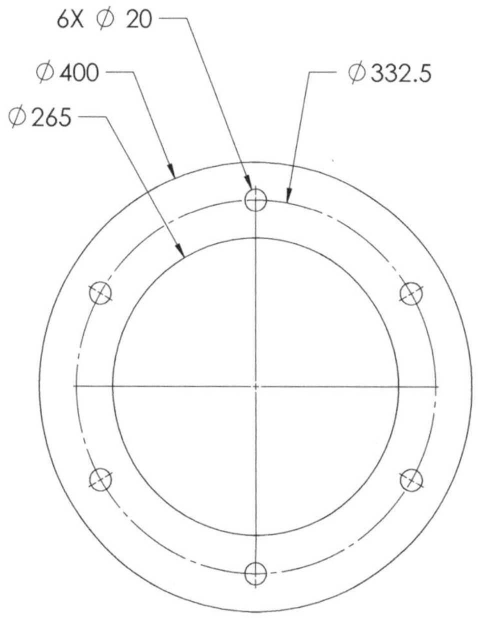

Thickness 5mm

Volute Casing Gasket

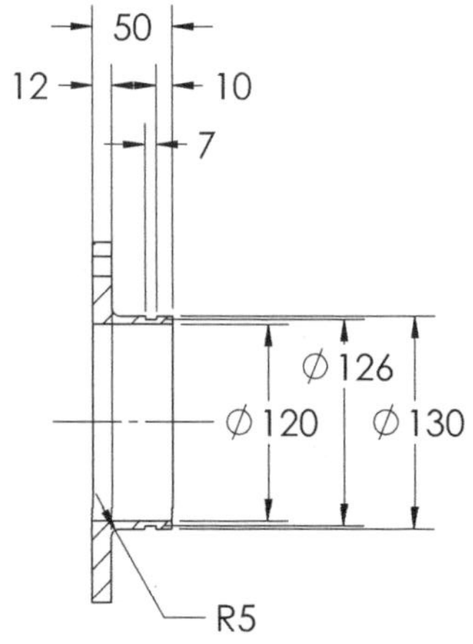

SECTION D-D

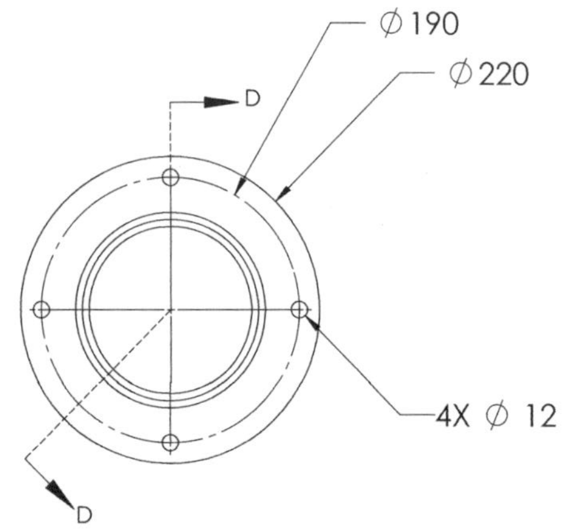

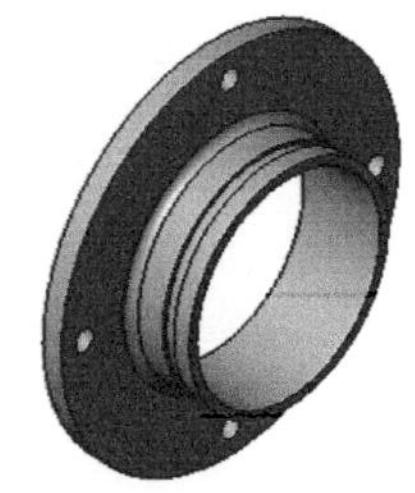

Suction Nozzle

NOTES

1- Material Gray Cast Iron
2- Deburr sharp edges

TOLERANCES UNLESS OTHERWISE SPECIFIED
X---------- +/- 1
X.X---------- +/- 0.5
X.XX---------- +/- 0.2
ANGLE---------- +/- 0.5

ALL DIMENSIONS IN MM

FIRST ISSUED
DRAWN BY
CHECKED BY
APPROVED BY

CADCIM TECHNOLOGIES

1. Volute Casing Gasket
2. Suction Nozle

SIZE	DRG NO.	SHEET REV
A3	12-009	A
SCALE 1:4		SHEET 11 OF 18

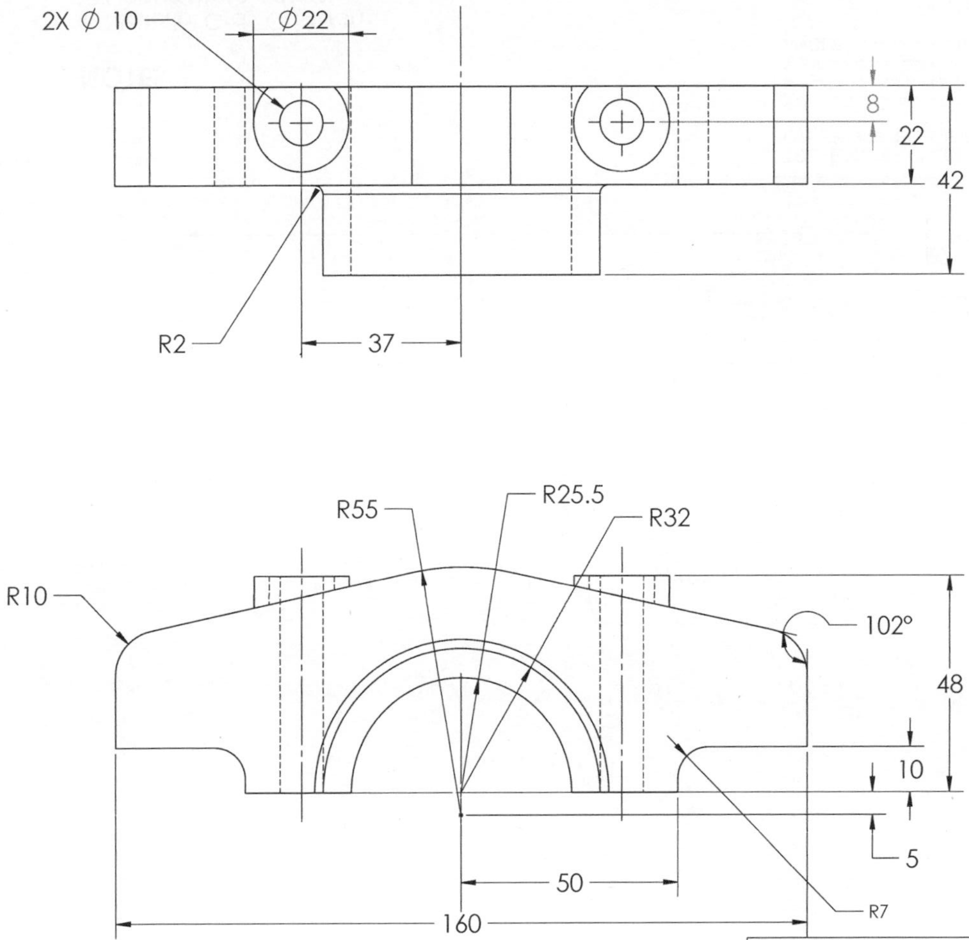

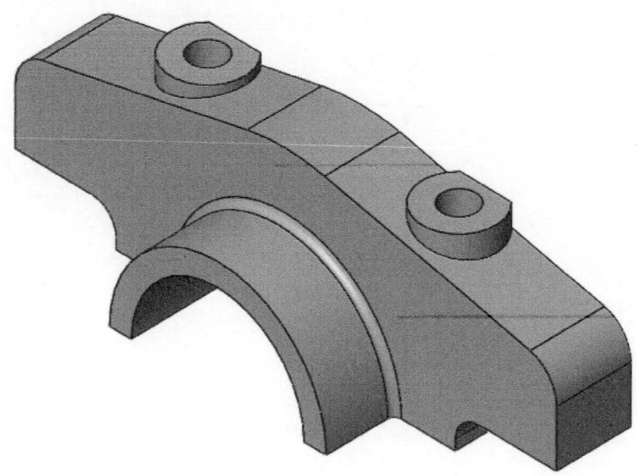

NOTES

1- Material Gray Cast Iron
2- Deburr sharp edges

TOLERANCES UNLESS OTHERWISE SPECIFIED

X------------------- +/- 1
X.X----------------- +/- 0.5
X.XX---------------- +/- 0.2
ANGLE--------------- +/- 0.5

ALL DIMENSIONS IN MM

FIRST ISSUED	
DRAWN BY	
CHECKED BY	
APPROVED BY	

CADCIM TECHNOLOGIES

Stuffing Box gland upper

SIZE	DRG NO.	SHEET REV
A3	12-010	A
SCALE 1:1		SHEET 12 OF 18

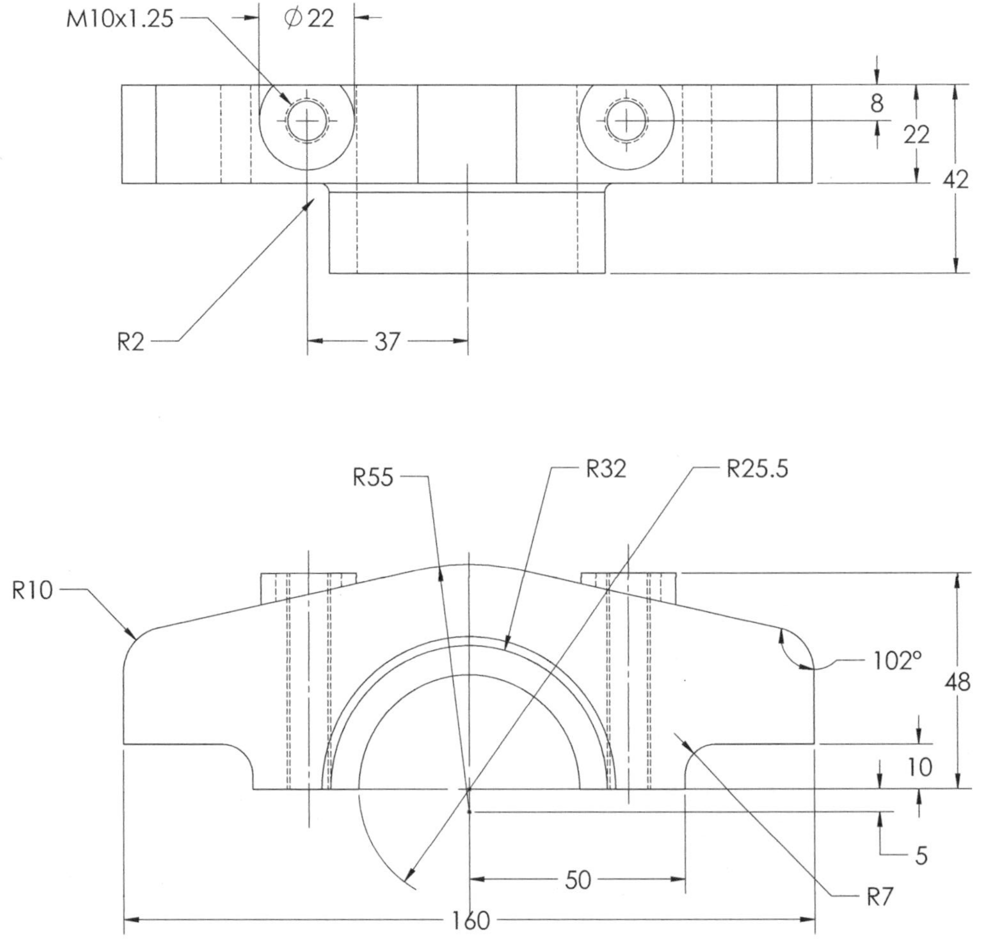

NOTES

1- Material Gray Cast Iron
2- Deburr sharp edges

TOLERANCES UNLESS OTHERWISE SPECIFIED

X---------------------- +/- 1
X.X-------------------- +/- 0.5
X.XX------------------- +/- 0.2
ANGLE----------------- +/- 0.5

ALL DIMENSIONS IN MM

FIRST ISSUED	
DRAWN BY	
CHECKED BY	
APPROVED BY	

CADCIM TECHNOLOGIES

Stuffing box gland Lower

SIZE	DRG NO.	SHEET REV
A3	12-011	A
SCALE 1:1		SHEET 13 OF 18

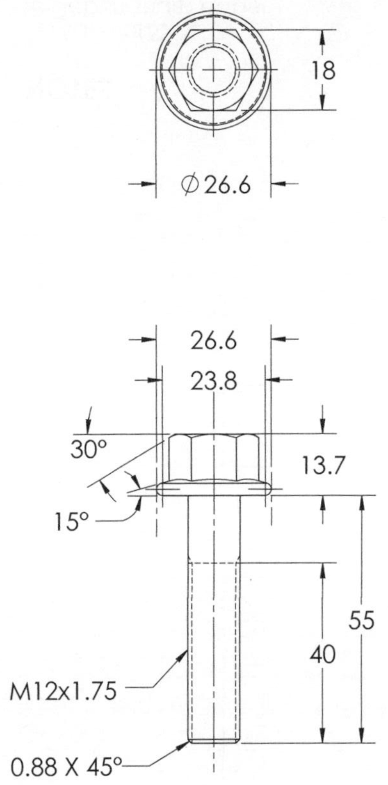

M12X 1.75 Flange Screw

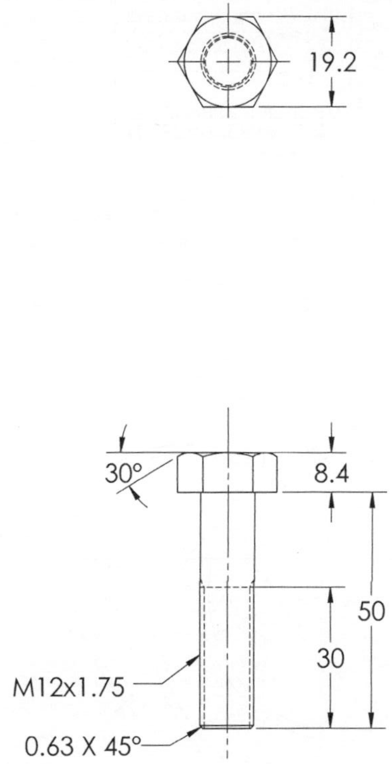

M12X 1.75 Hex Bolt

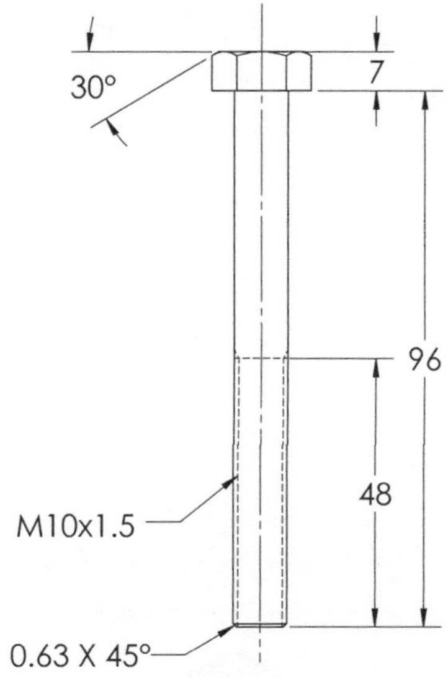

M10X 1.5 Hex-Bolt

NOTES

1- Material Stainless steel
2- Deburr sharp edges

TOLERANCES UNLESS OTHERWISE SPECIFIED

X---------- +/- 1
X.X---------- +/- 0.5
X.XX---------- +/- 0.2
ANGLE---------- +/- 0.5

ALL DIMENSIONS IN MM

FIRST ISSUED	
DRAWN BY	
CHECKED BY	
APPROVED BY	

CADCIM TECHNOLOGIES

1. M12x1.75 Hex Flange Screw- ANSI B18.2.3.4M
2. M12 X 1.75 Hex Bolt-ANSI B18.2.3.5M
3. M10X1.5 Hex Bolt-ANSI B18.2.3.5M

SIZE	DRG NO.	SHEET REV
A3	12-012	A
SCALE 1:1		SHEET 14 OF 18

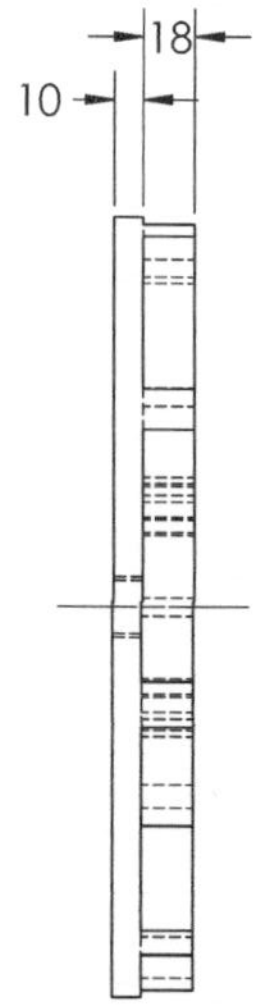

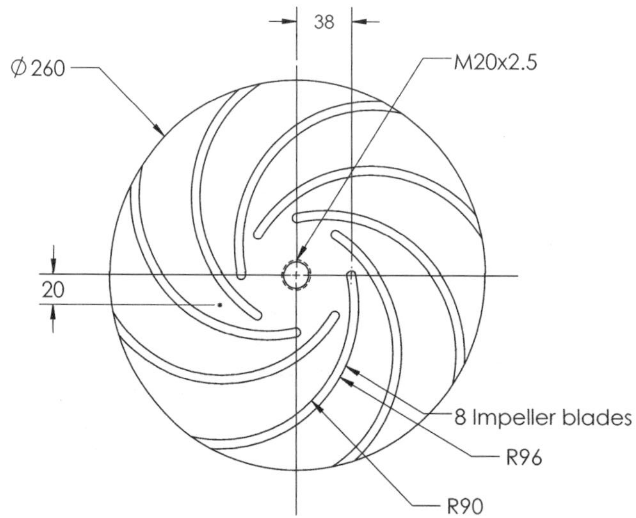

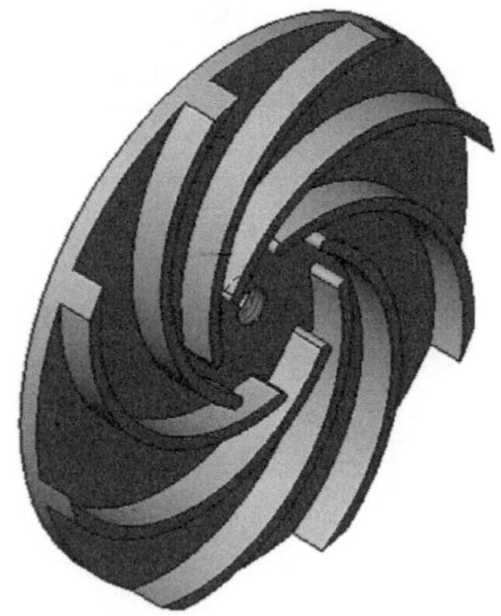

NOTES

1- Material SS
2- Deburr sharp edges

TOLERANCES UNLESS OTHERWISE SPECIFIED		CADCIM TECHNOLOGIES		
X---------- +/- 1	FIRST ISSUED	Impeller		
X.X---------- +/- 0.5	DRAWN BY			
X.XX---------- +/- 0.2	CHECKED BY			
ANGLE---------- +/- 0.5	APPROVED BY	SIZE A3	DRG NO. 12-013	SHEET REV A
ALL DIMENSIONS IN MM		SCALE 1:3		SHEET 15 OF 18

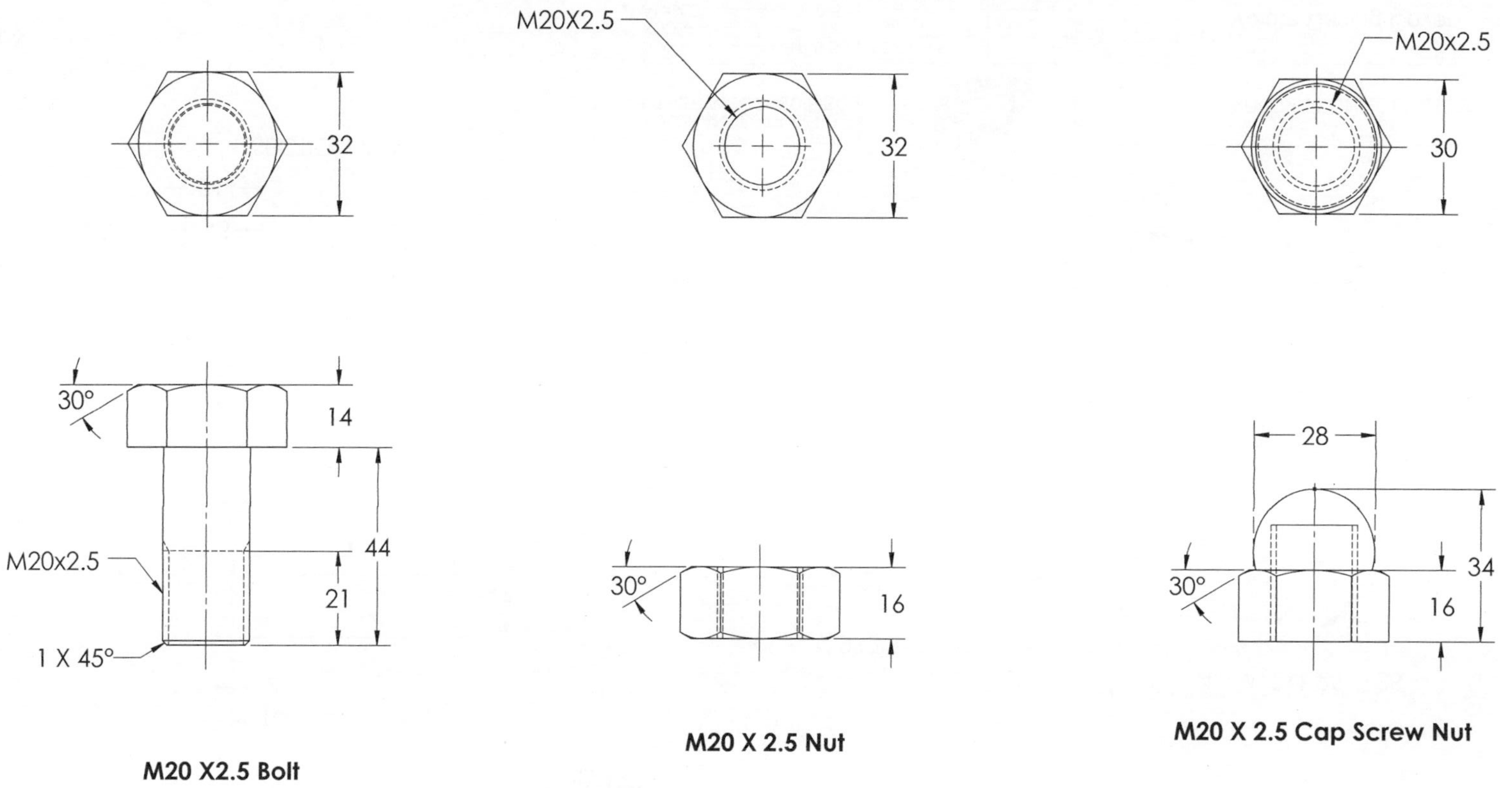

NOTES

1- Material Stainless Steel
2- Debure sharp edges

TOLERANCES UNLESS OTHERWISE SPECIFIED		CADCIM TECHNOLOGIES
X---------- +/- 1	FIRST ISSUED	1. M20 X 2.5 Hex Bolt-ANSI B18.2.3.5M
X.X---------- +/- 0.5	DRAWN BY	2. M20 x 2.5 NUT-ANSI B18.2.4.2M
X.XX---------- +/- 0.2	CHECKED BY	3. M20 x 2.5 Nut Cap Screw
ANGLE---------- +/- 0.5	APPROVED BY	SIZE A3 DRG NO. 12-014 SHEET REV A
ALL DIMENSIONS IN MM		SCALE 1:1 SHEET 16 OF 18

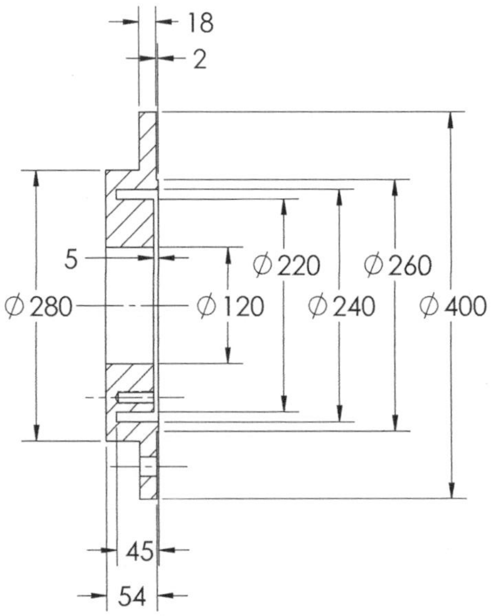

SECTION A-A

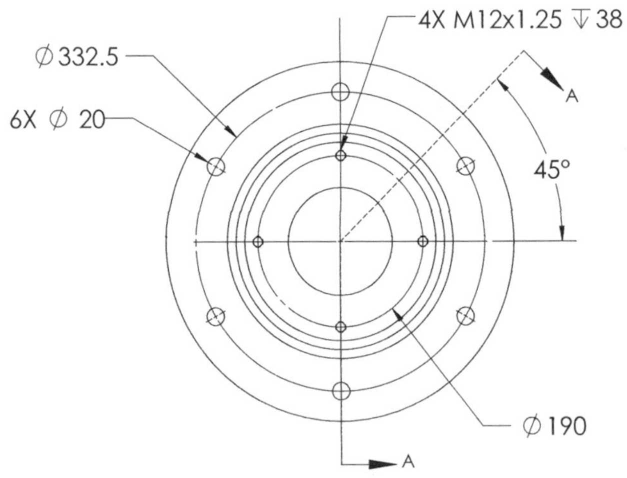

NOTES

1- Material Gray Cast Iron
2- Deburr sharp edges

TOLERANCES UNLESS OTHERWISE SPECIFIED

X---------------------- +/- 1
X.X-------------------- +/- 0.5
X.XX------------------ +/- 0.2
ANGLE--------------- +/- 0.5

ALL DIMENSIONS IN MM

FIRST ISSUED	
DRAWN BY	
CHECKED BY	
APPROVED BY	

CADCIM TECHNOLOGIES

Volute Casing Cover

SIZE	DRG NO.	SHEET REV
A3	12-015	A
SCALE 1:5		SHEET 17 OF 18

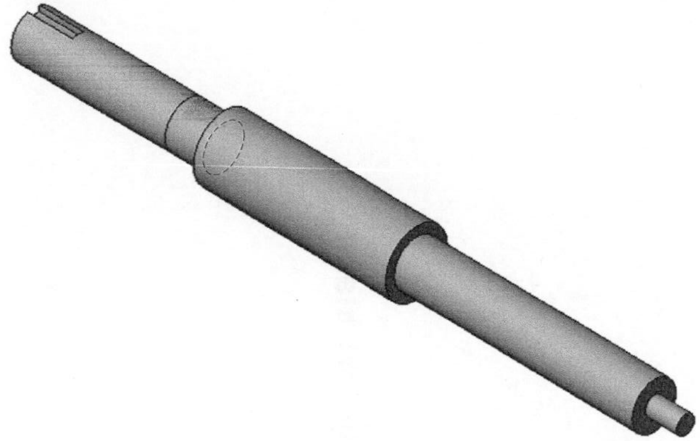

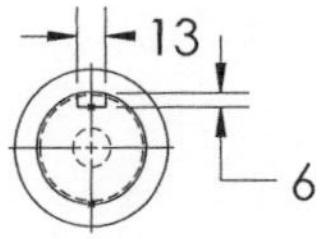

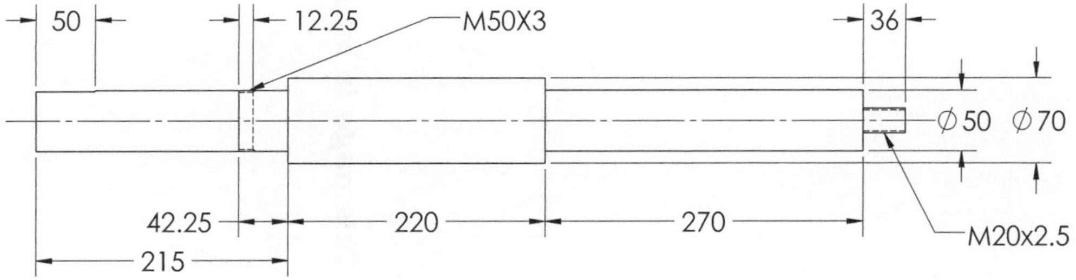

NOTES

1- Material SS
2- Deburr sharp edges

TOLERANCES UNLESS OTHERWISE SPECIFIED		CADCIM TECHNOLOGIES	
X---------- +/- 1 X.X---------- +/- 0.5 X.XX---------- +/- 0.2 ANGLE---------- +/- 0.5	FIRST ISSUED DRAWN BY CHECKED BY APPROVED BY	Shaft	
ALL DIMENSIONS IN MM		SIZE A3 / DRG NO. 12-016	SHEET REV A
		SCALE 1:4	SHEET 18 OF 18

This page is intentionally left blank

Project 13

Single Plate Clutch Assembly

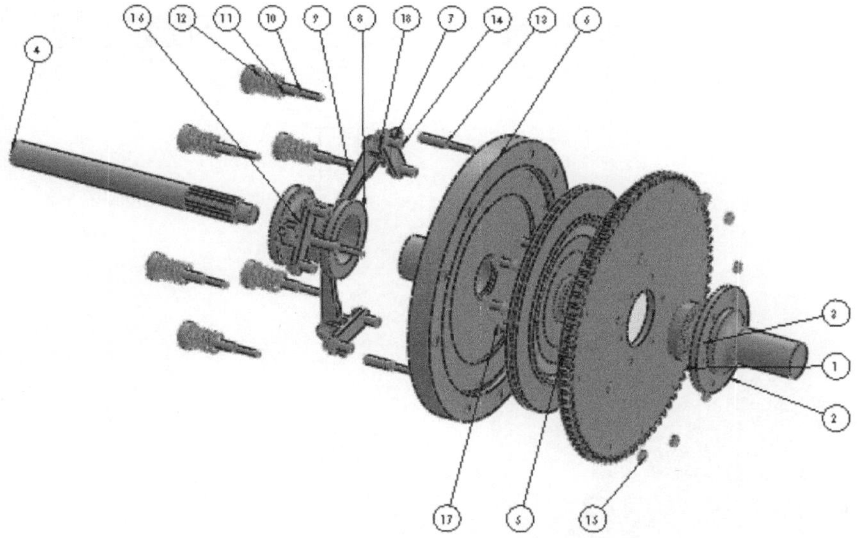

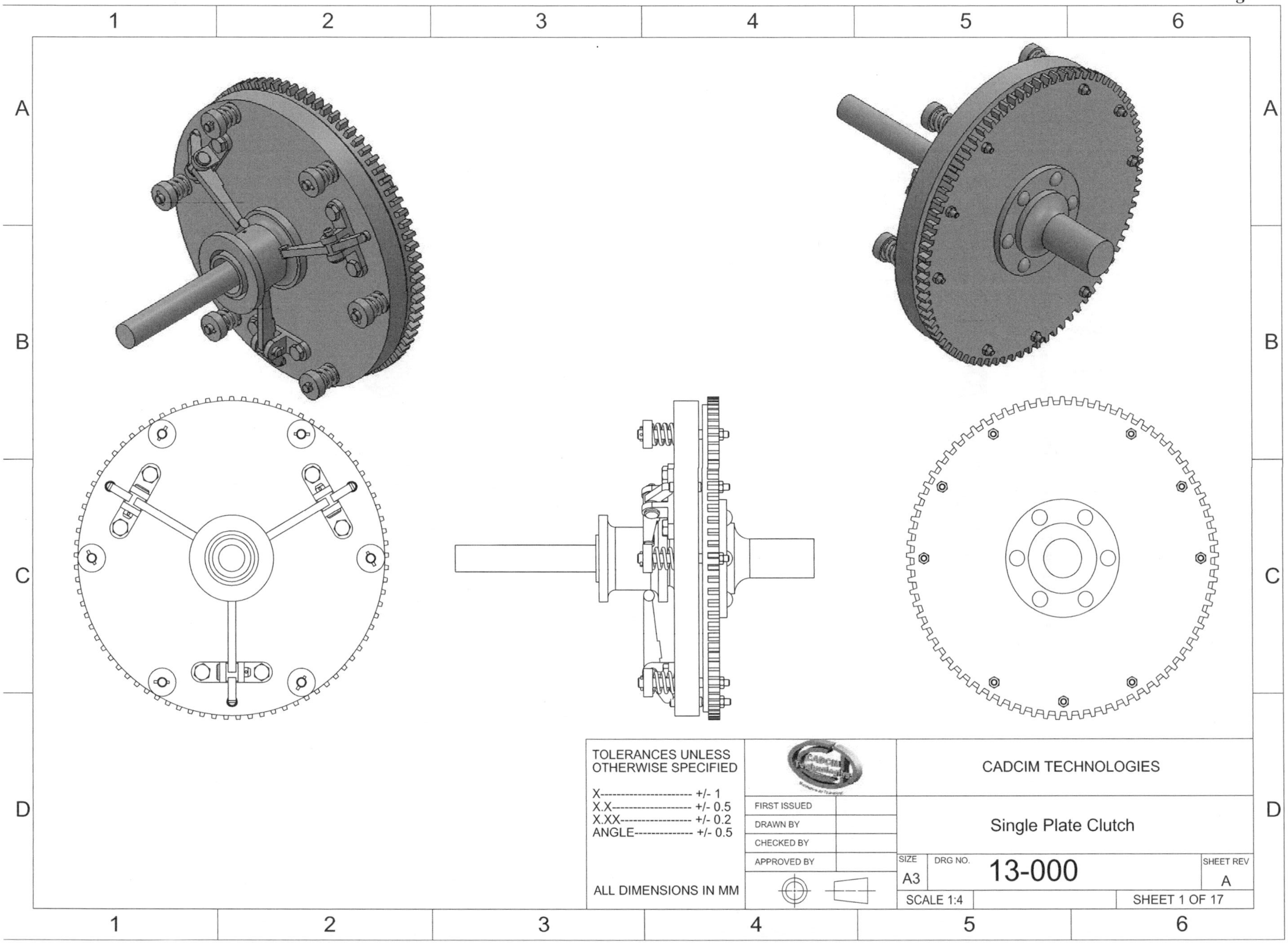
1
2
3
4
5
6
A
B
C
D
TOLERANCES UNLESS OTHERWISE SPECIFIED
X---------------------- +/- 1
X.X------------------- +/- 0.5
X.XX------------------ +/- 0.2
ANGLE-------------- +/- 0.5
ALL DIMENSIONS IN MM
FIRST ISSUED
DRAWN BY
CHECKED BY
APPROVED BY
CADCIM TECHNOLOGIES
Single Plate Clutch
SIZE
A3
DRG NO.
13-000
SHEET REV
A
SCALE 1:4
SHEET 1 OF 17

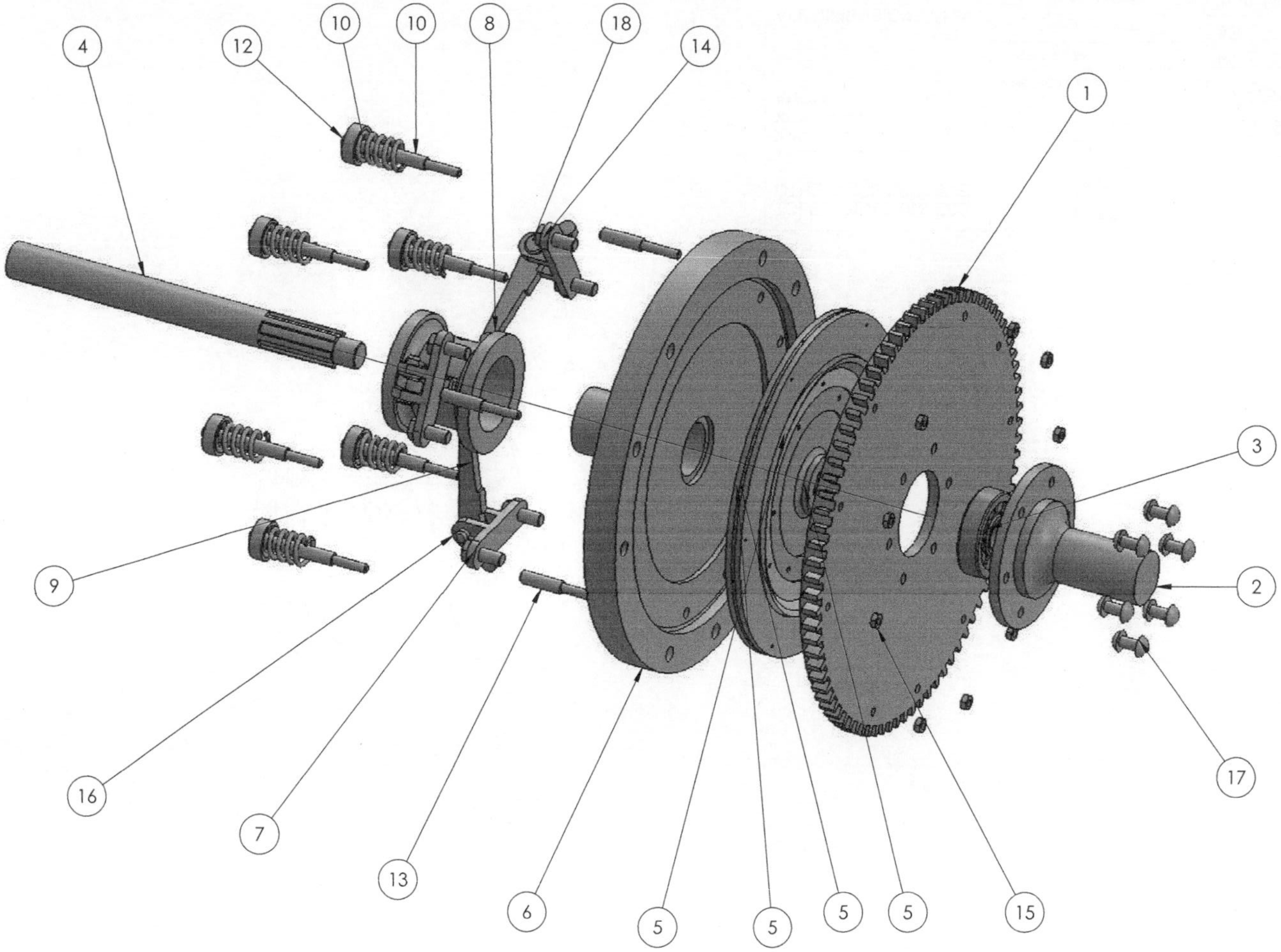

ITEM NO.	PART NUMBER	QTY.
1	Flywheel	1
2	Driving_Shaft	1
3	RADIAL CYLINDRICAL ROLLER BEARING AFBMA 20.1, Size 4-25	1
4	Drlven Shaft	1
5	Clutch and Friction disc assem	1
	Friction disc	2
	Oil through ring	2
	Support plate	1
	Clutch Plate	1
6	Driving Flange	1
7	Bracket toggle lever	3
8	Release Bearing	1
9	Togglelever_	3
10	Pin for spring	6
11	Spring	6
12	Seating for spring	6
13	Pin for toggle lever	3
14	M12X1.75 Hex Bolt-ANSI B18.2.3.5M	6
15	M8X1.25 Hex Nut-ANSI B18.2.4.1M_	9
16	Slotpin	9
17	rivet	6
18	Celvis Pin12X40X3.2-ISO 2341_	3

TOLERANCES UNLESS OTHERWISE SPECIFIED

X---------------------- +/- 1
X.X-------------------- +/- 0.5
X.XX------------------ +/- 0.2
ANGLE-------------- +/- 0.5

ALL DIMENSIONS IN MM

FIRST ISSUED
DRAWN BY
CHECKED BY
APPROVED BY

CADCIM TECHNOLOGIES

Single Plate Clutch

SIZE A3 | DRG NO. 13-000 | SHEET REV A

SCALE 1:4 | SHEET 2 OF 17

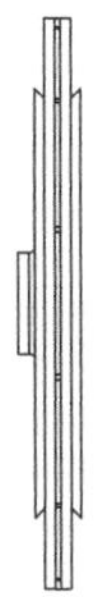

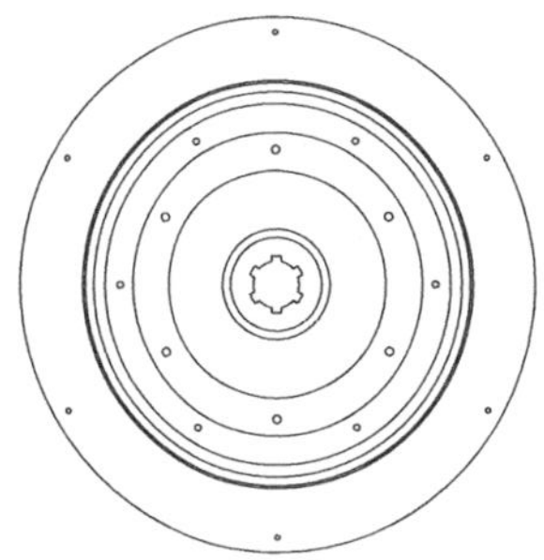

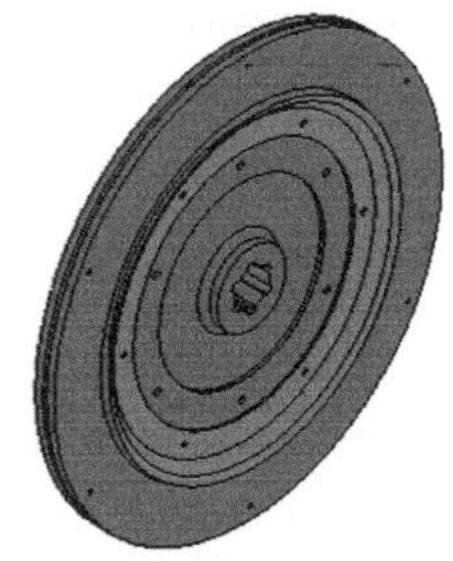

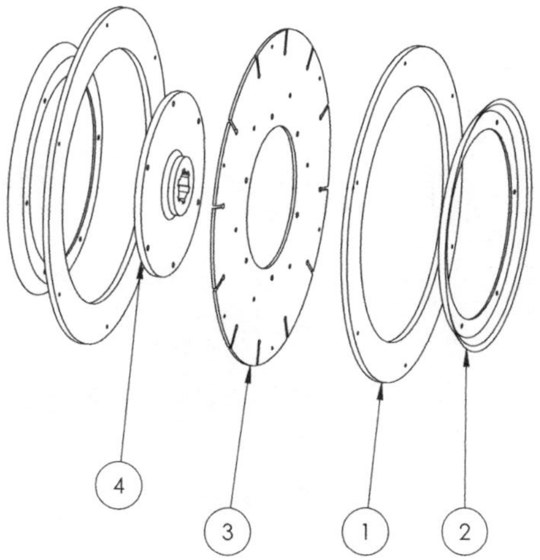

ITEM NO.	PART NUMBER	QTY.
1	Friction disc	2
2	Oil through ring	2
3	Support plate	1
4	Clutch Plate	1

TOLERANCES UNLESS OTHERWISE SPECIFIED

X---------- +/- 1
X.X---------- +/- 0.5
X.XX---------- +/- 0.2
ANGLE---------- +/- 0.5

ALL DIMENSIONS IN MM

FIRST ISSUED
DRAWN BY
CHECKED BY
APPROVED BY

CADCIM TECHNOLOGIES

Clutch plate and Friction disc Assembly

SIZE A3 | DRG NO. 13-000 | SHEET REV A

SCALE 1:5 | SHEET 3 OF 17

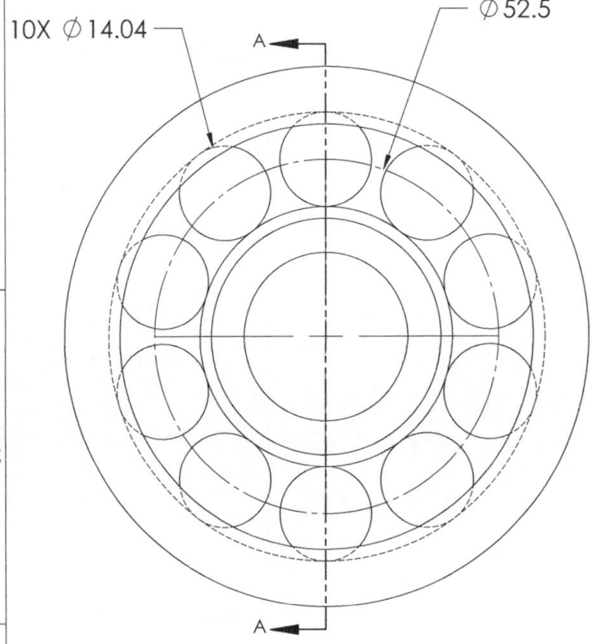

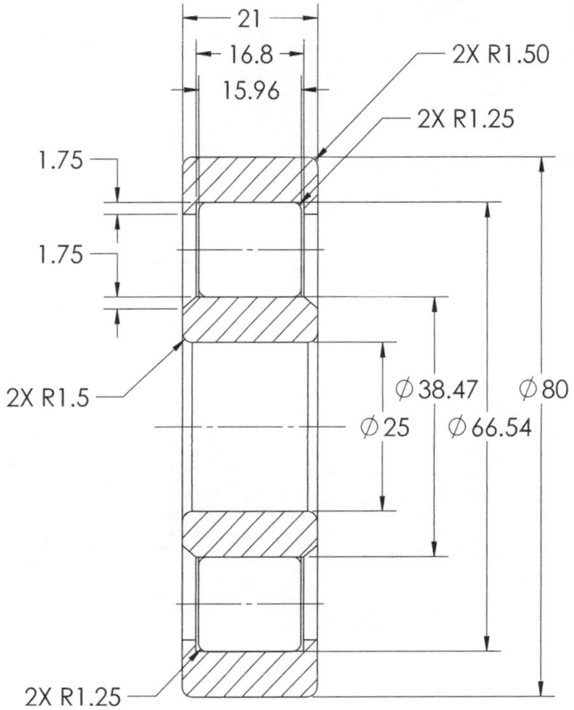

SECTION A-A

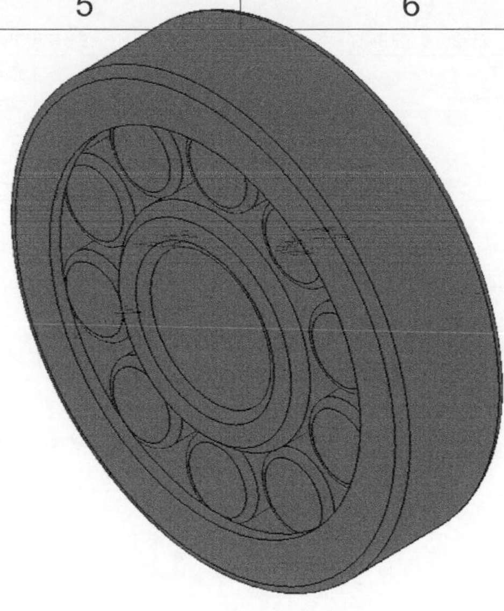

NOTES

1- Material Carbon Alloy Steel
2- Deburr sharp edges

TOLERANCES UNLESS OTHERWISE SPECIFIED		CADCIM TECHNOLOGIES
X---------- +/- 1	FIRST ISSUED	Radial Cylindrical Roller Bearing AFBMA 20.1, Size 04-25
X.X---------- +/- 0.5	DRAWN BY	
X.XX---------- +/- 0.2	CHECKED BY	
ANGLE---------- +/- 0.5	APPROVED BY	SIZE A3 · DRG NO. 13-001 · SHEET REV A
ALL DIMENSIONS IN MM		SCALE 3:2 · SHEET 4 OF 17

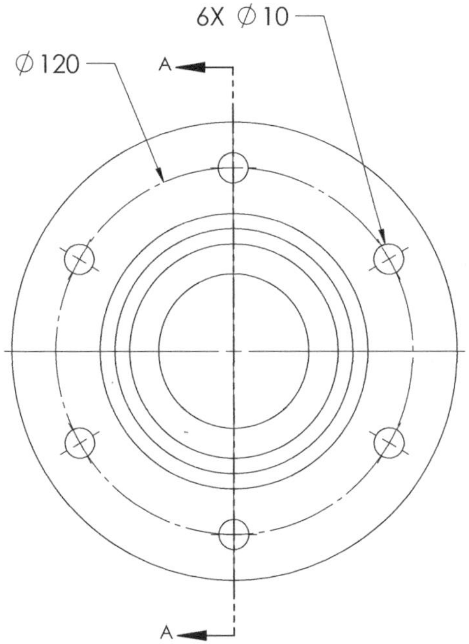

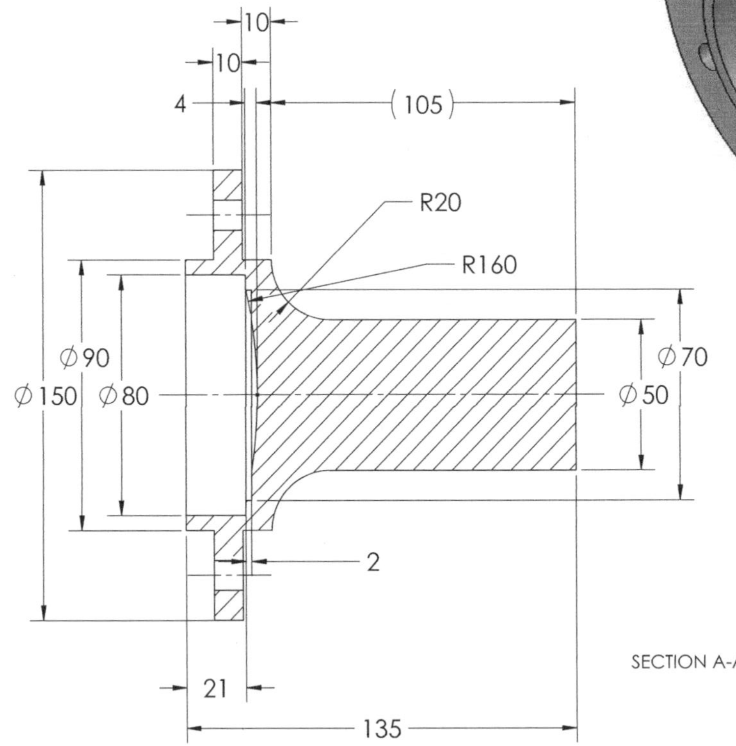

SECTION A-A

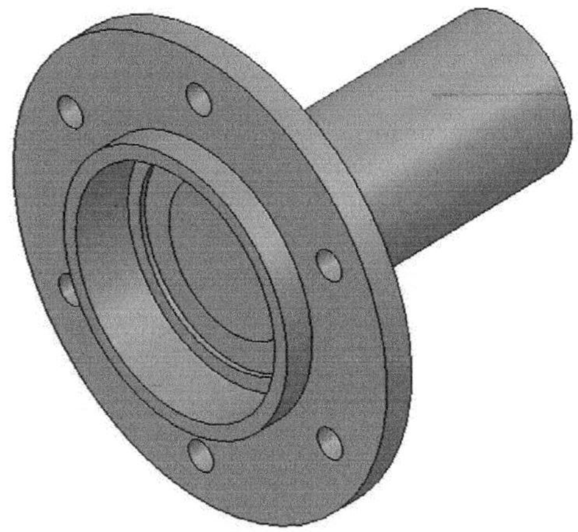

NOTES

1- Material ASTM A36 Steel
2- Deburr sharp edges

TOLERANCES UNLESS OTHERWISE SPECIFIED		CADCIM TECHNOLOGIES
X-------- +/- 1 X.X-------- +/- 0.5 X.XX-------- +/- 0.2 ANGLE-------- +/- 0.5	FIRST ISSUED DRAWN BY CHECKED BY APPROVED BY	Driving Shaft
ALL DIMENSIONS IN MM		SIZE A3	DRG NO. 13-002	SHEET REV A
		SCALE 2:3	SHEET 5 OF 17

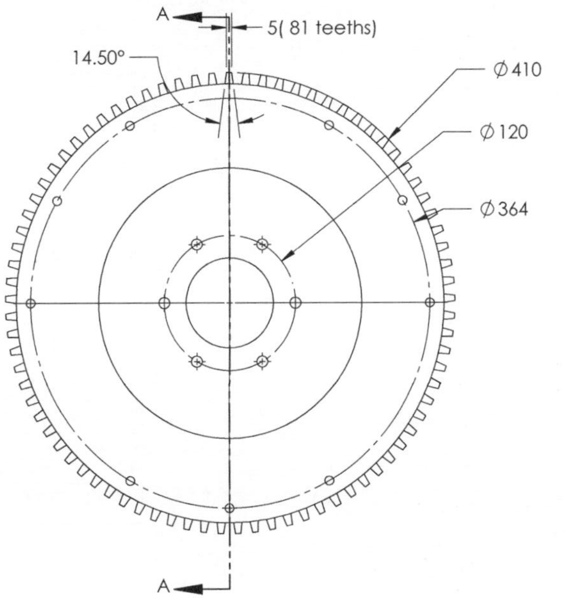

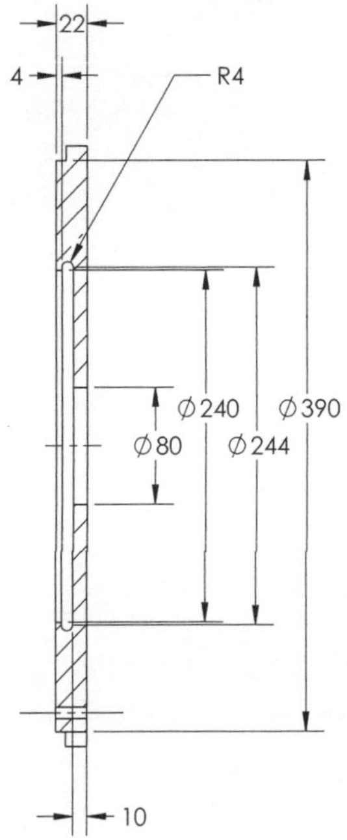

SECTION A-A

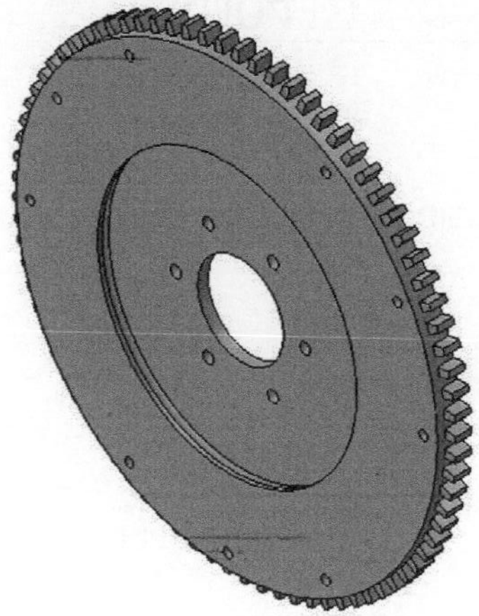

NOTES

1- Material High Strength steel
2- Deburr sharp edges

TOLERANCES UNLESS OTHERWISE SPECIFIED		CADCIM TECHNOLOGIES	
X---------- +/- 1 X.X---------- +/- 0.5 X.XX---------- +/- 0.2 ANGLE---------- +/- 0.5	FIRST ISSUED	Flywheel	
	DRAWN BY		
	CHECKED BY		
	APPROVED BY	SIZE A3 / DRG NO. 13-003	SHEET REV A
ALL DIMENSIONS IN MM		SCALE 2:1	SHEET 6 OF 17

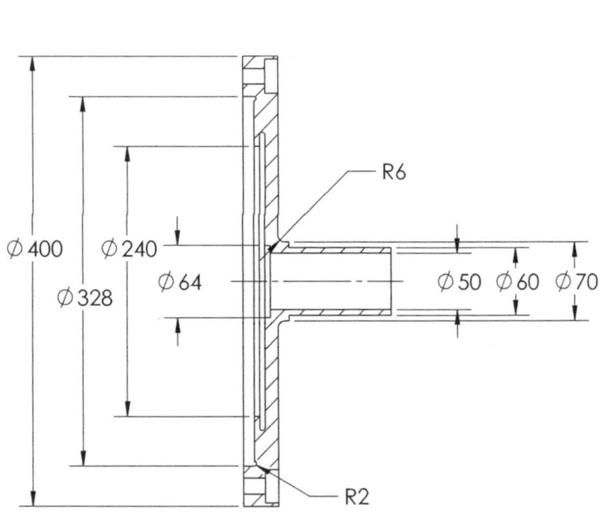

SECTION A-A

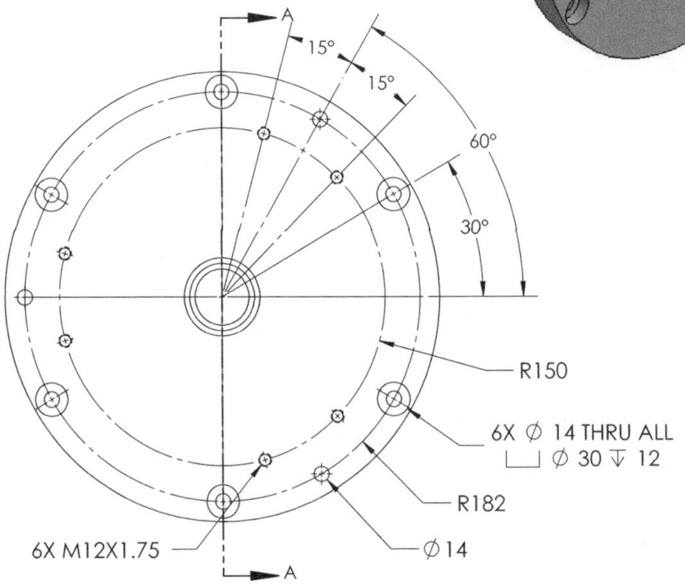

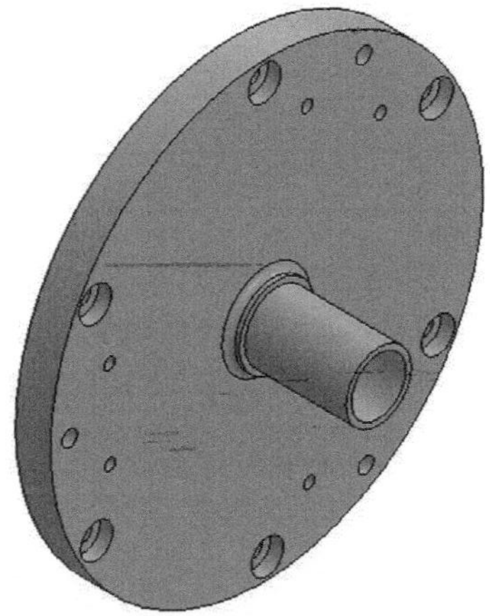

NOTES

1- Material ASTM A36 Steel
2- Deburr sharp edges

TOLERANCES UNLESS OTHERWISE SPECIFIED

X---------- +/- 1
X.X---------- +/- 0.5
X.XX---------- +/- 0.2
ANGLE---------- +/- 0.5

ALL DIMENSIONS IN MM

FIRST ISSUED
DRAWN BY
CHECKED BY
APPROVED BY

CADCIM TECHNOLOGIES

Driving Flange

SIZE A3 | DRG NO. 13-004 | SHEET REV A

SCALE 2:1 | SHEET 7 OF 17

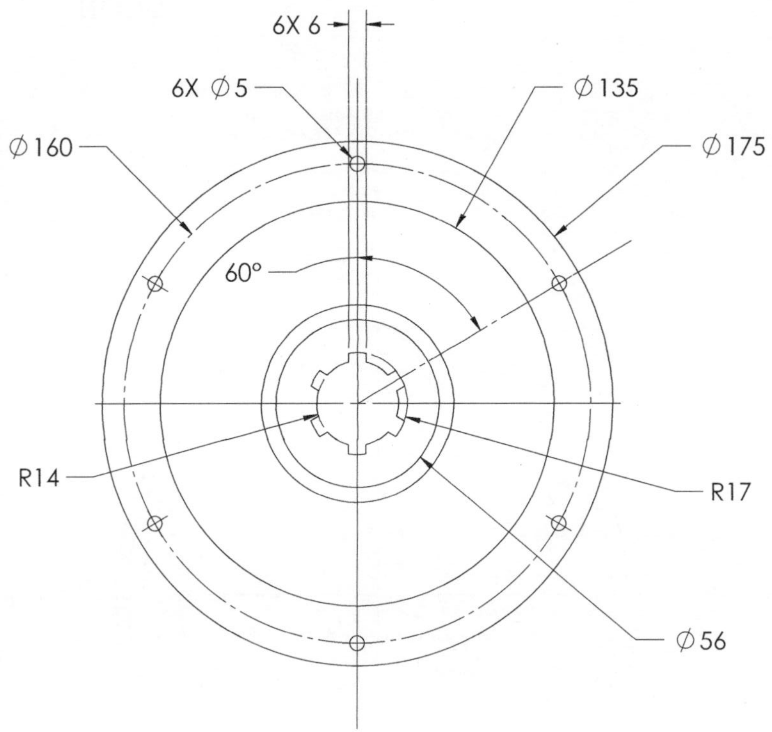

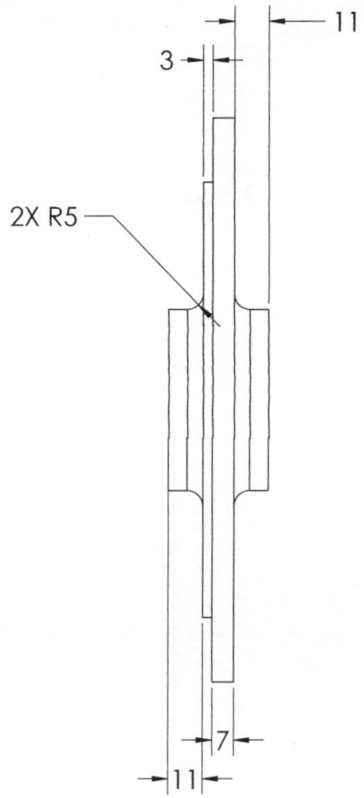

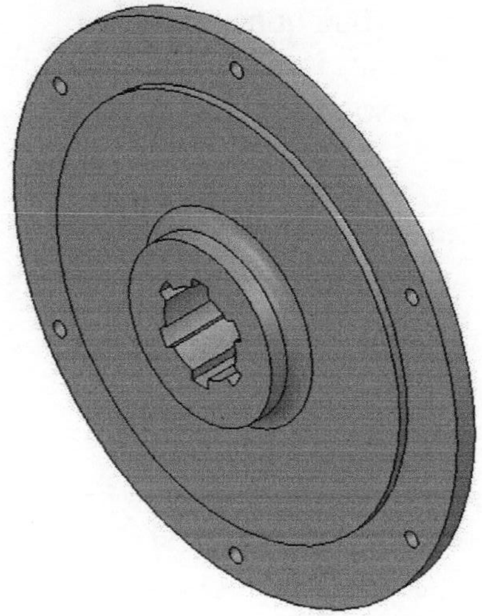

NOTES

1- Material Gray Cast Iron
2- Deburr sharp edges

TOLERANCES UNLESS OTHERWISE SPECIFIED		CADCIM TECHNOLOGIES
X---------- +/- 1 X.X---------- +/- 0.5 X.XX---------- +/- 0.2 ANGLE---------- +/- 0.5	FIRST ISSUED DRAWN BY CHECKED BY APPROVED BY	Clutch Plate
ALL DIMENSIONS IN MM		SIZE A3 — DRG NO. 13-005 — SHEET REV A
		SCALE 2:3 — SHEET 8 OF 17

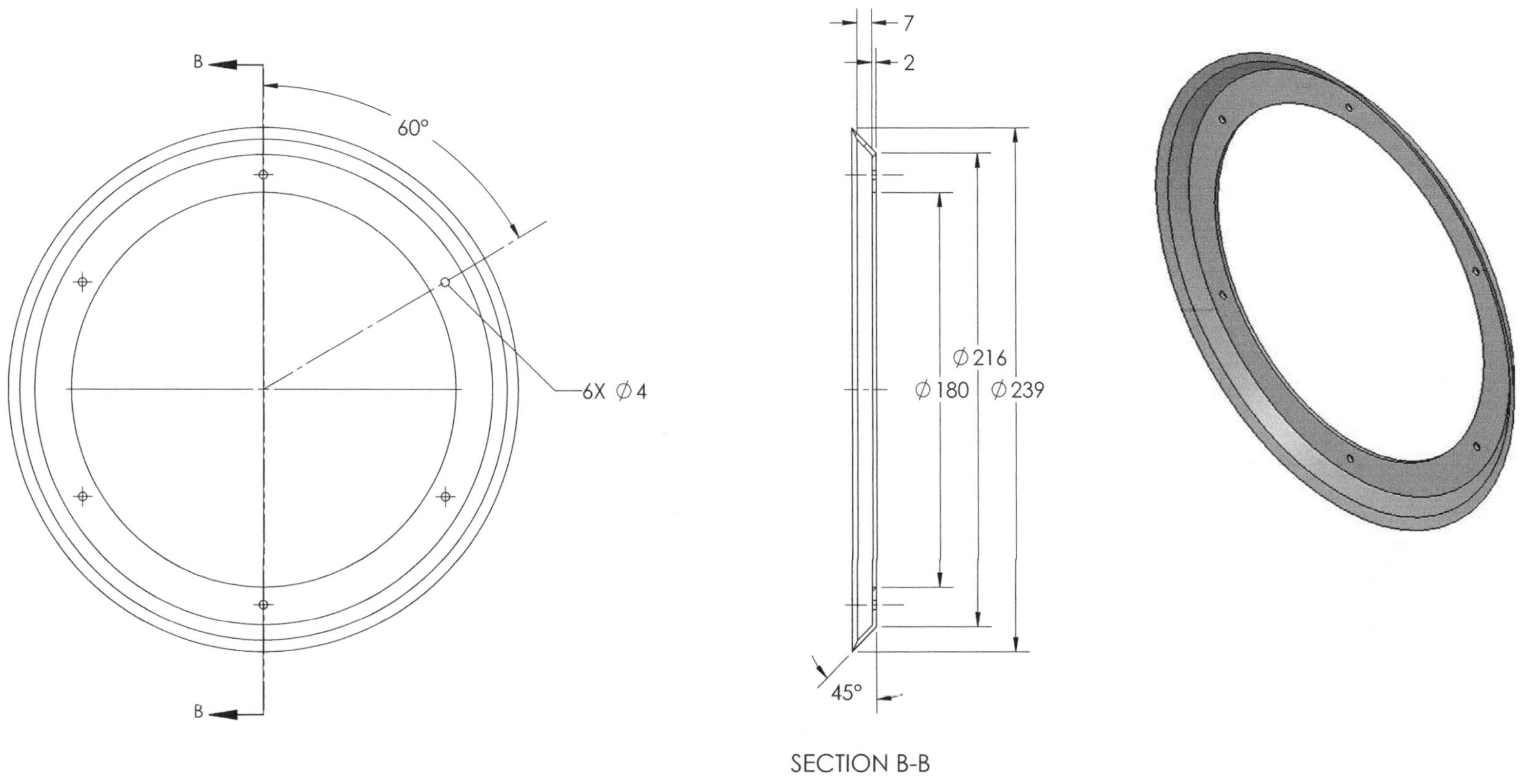

NOTES

1- Material Gray Cast Iron
2- Deburr sharp edges

TOLERANCES UNLESS OTHERWISE SPECIFIED		CADCIM TECHNOLOGIES
X---------- +/- 1	FIRST ISSUED	Oil Through ring
X.X---------- +/- 0.5	DRAWN BY	
X.XX---------- +/- 0.2	CHECKED BY	
ANGLE---------- +/- 0.5	APPROVED BY	SIZE A3 DRG NO. 13-006 SHEET REV A
ALL DIMENSIONS IN MM		SCALE 1:2 SHEET 9 OF 17

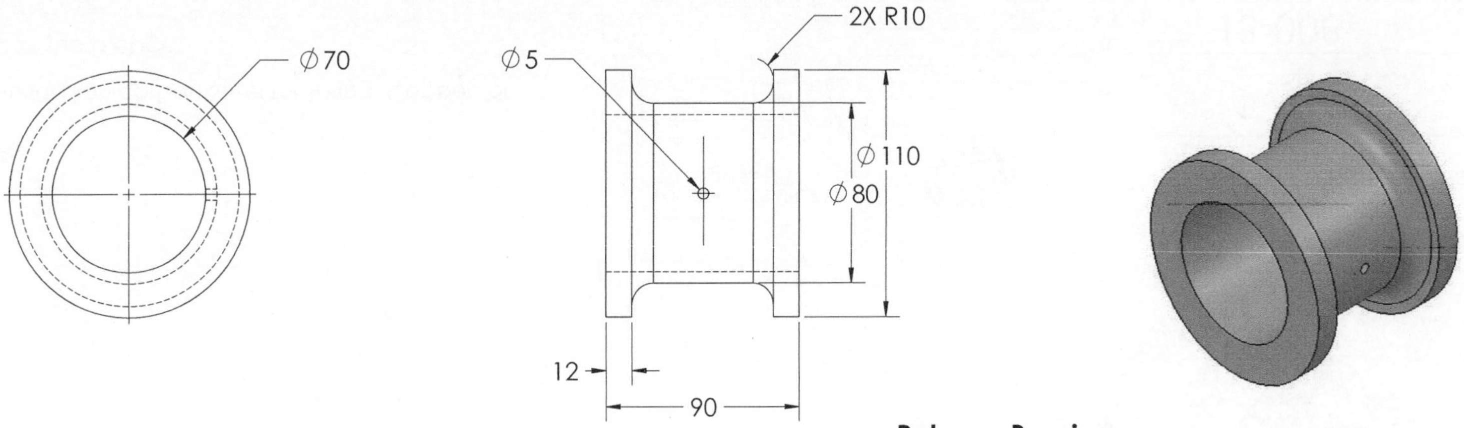

Release Bearing

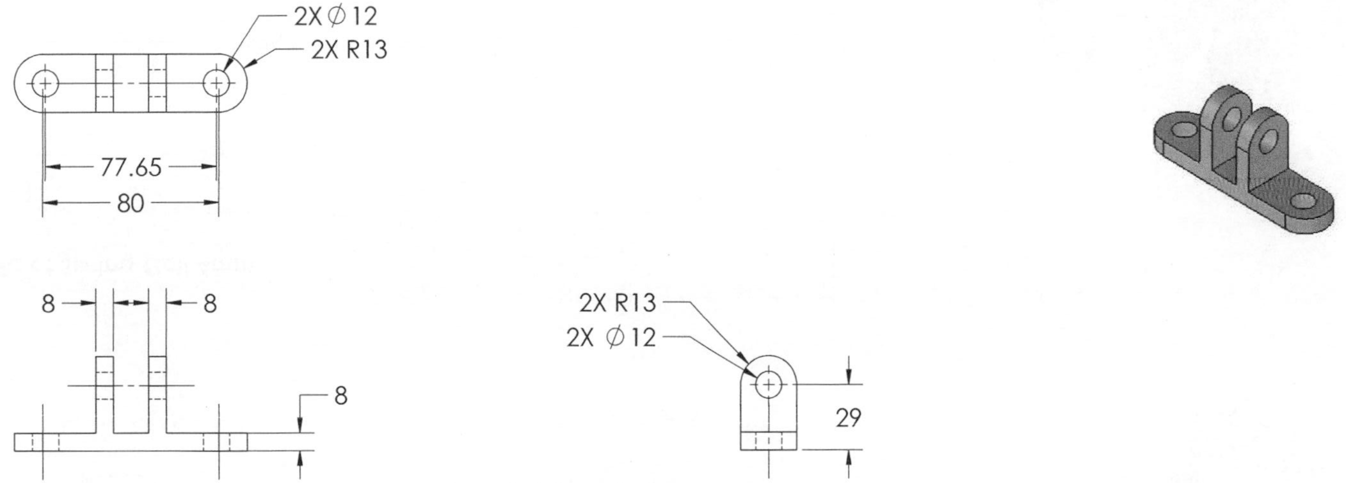

Bracket toggle lever

NOTES

1- Material Gray Cast Iron
2- Deburr sharp edges

TOLERANCES UNLESS OTHERWISE SPECIFIED		CADCIM TECHNOLOGIES		
X------- +/- 1 X.X------- +/- 0.5 X.XX------- +/- 0.2 ANGLE------- +/- 0.5	FIRST ISSUED DRAWN BY CHECKED BY APPROVED BY	1. Withdrawal Sleeve 2. Bracket toggle lever		
ALL DIMENSIONS IN MM		SIZE A3	DRG NO. 13-007	SHEET REV A
		SCALE 1:2		SHEET 10 OF 17

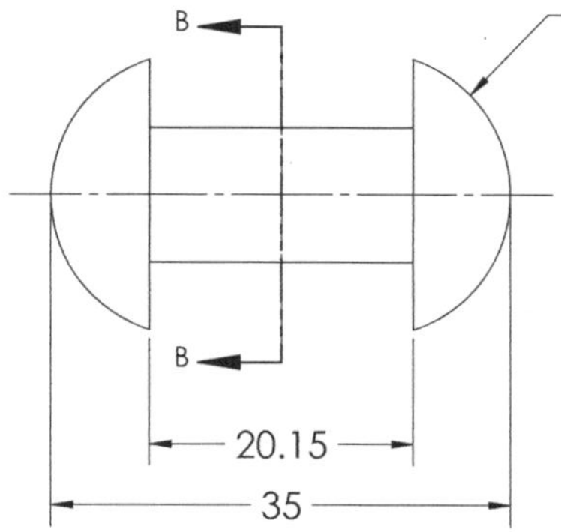

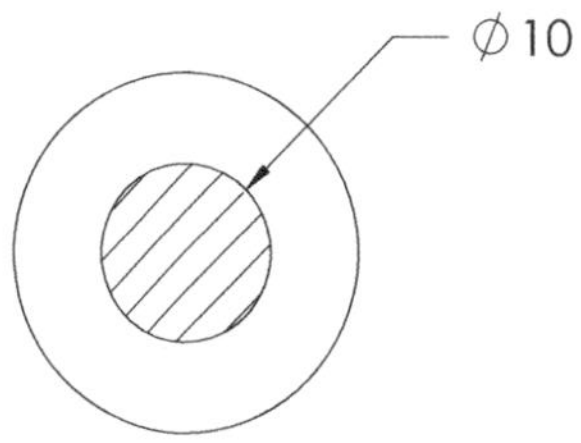

SECTION B-B

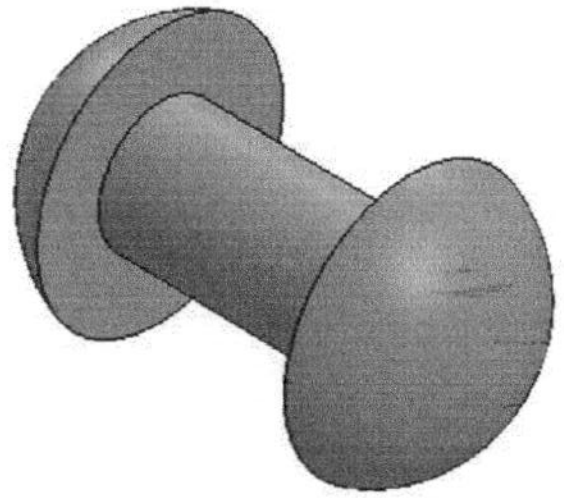

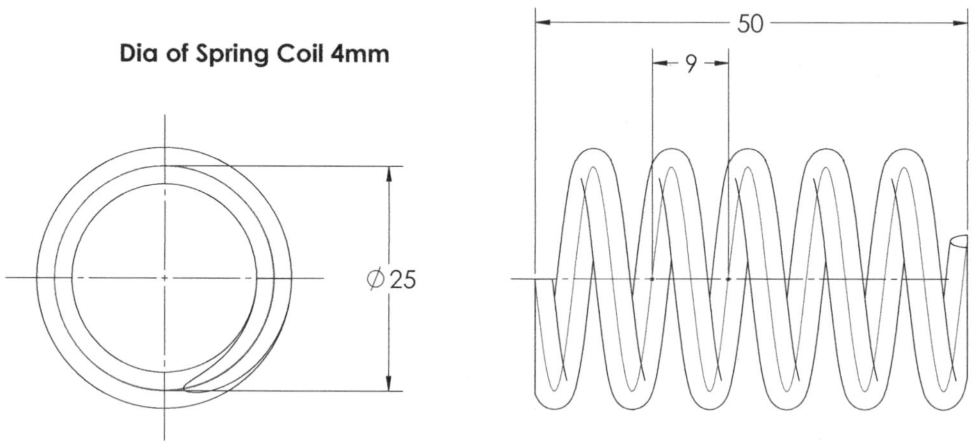

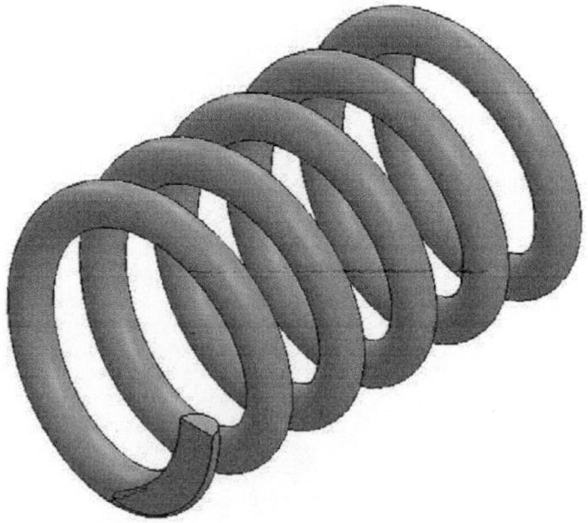

NOTES

1- Material High carbon Steel for spring, Copper for Rivet
2- Deburr sharp edges

TOLERANCES UNLESS OTHERWISE SPECIFIED

X---------------------- +/- 1
X.X-------------------- +/- 0.5
X.XX------------------ +/- 0.2
ANGLE--------------- +/- 0.5

ALL DIMENSIONS IN MM

FIRST ISSUED	
DRAWN BY	
CHECKED BY	
APPROVED BY	

CADCIM TECHNOLOGIES

1. Rivet
2. Spring

SIZE	DRG NO.	SHEET REV
A3	13-008	A
SCALE 2:1		SHEET 11 OF 17

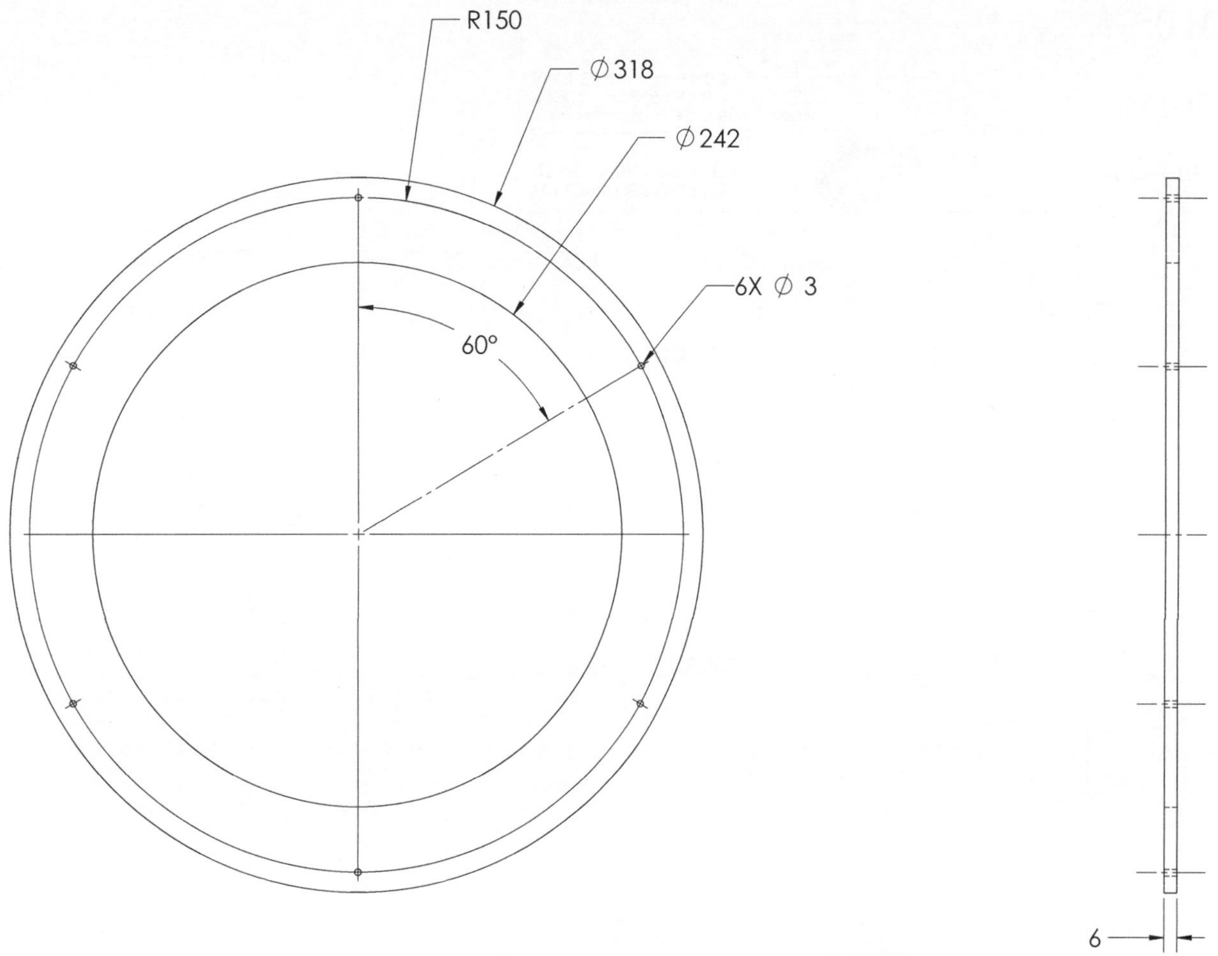

NOTES

1- Material Ceramic
2- Deburr sharp edges

TOLERANCES UNLESS OTHERWISE SPECIFIED		CADCIM TECHNOLOGIES		
X---------------------- +/- 1	FIRST ISSUED	Friction Disc		
X.X-------------------- +/- 0.5	DRAWN BY			
X.XX------------------- +/- 0.2	CHECKED BY			
ANGLE------------------ +/- 0.5	APPROVED BY	SIZE A3	DRG NO. 13-009	SHEET REV A
ALL DIMENSIONS IN MM		SCALE 1:2		SHEET 12 OF 17

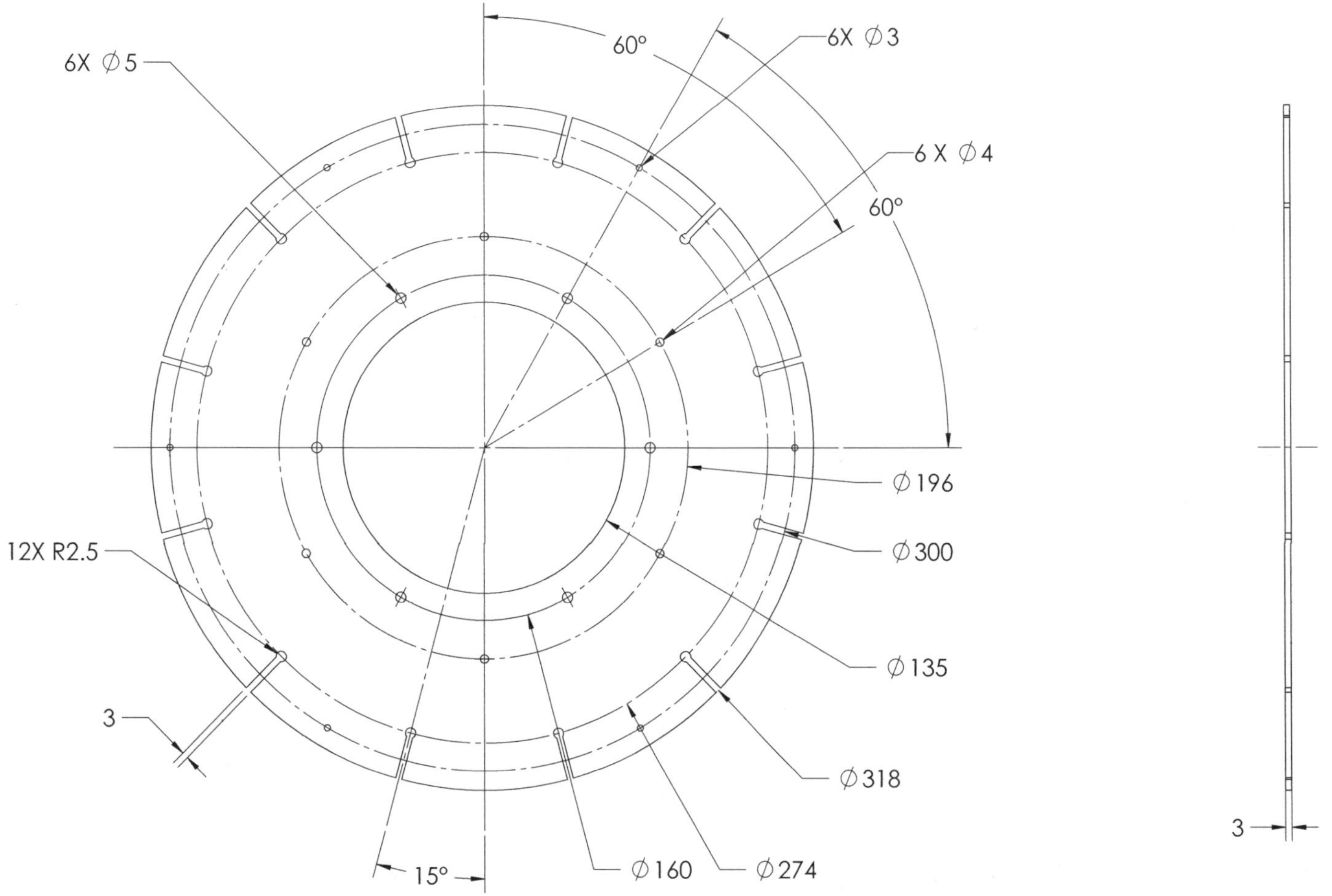

NOTES

1- Material Mild Steel
2- Deburr sharp edges

TOLERANCES UNLESS OTHERWISE SPECIFIED

X---------- +/- 1
X.X---------- +/- 0.5
X.XX---------- +/- 0.2
ANGLE---------- +/- 0.5

ALL DIMENSIONS IN MM

FIRST ISSUED
DRAWN BY
CHECKED BY
APPROVED BY

CADCIM TECHNOLOGIES

Support Plate

SIZE A3 | DRG NO. 13-010 | SHEET REV A

SCALE 1:2 | SHEET 13 OF 17

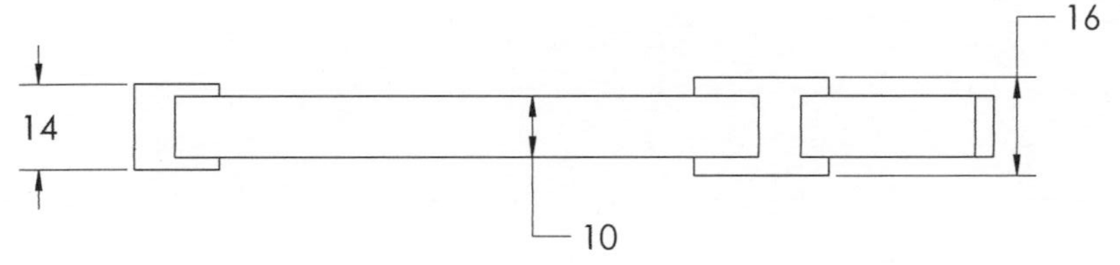

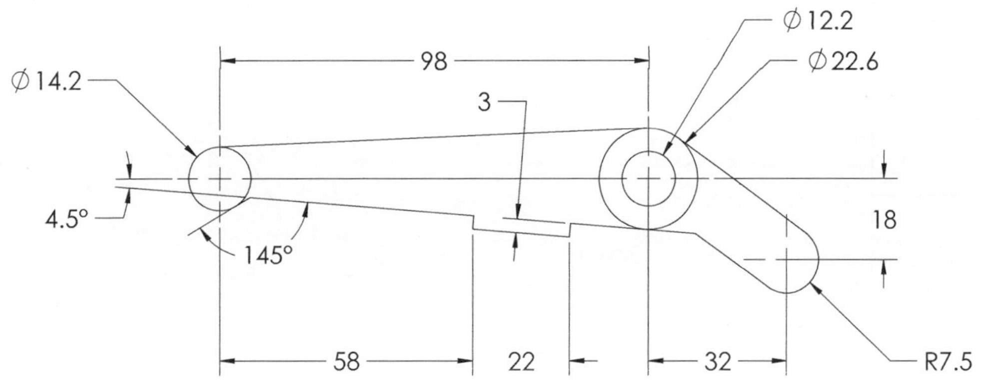

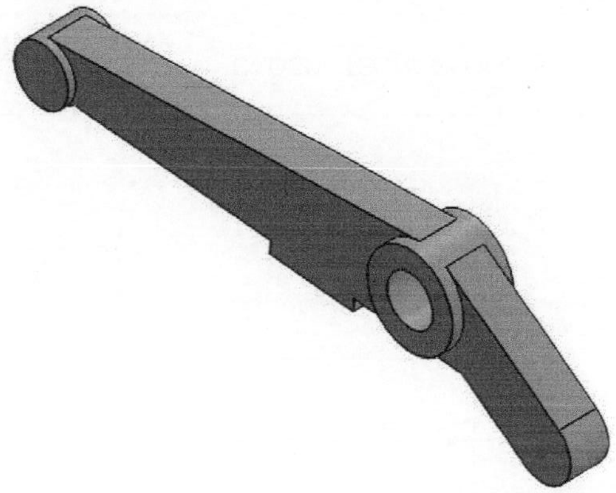

NOTES

1- Material Cast Iron
2- Deburr sharp edges

TOLERANCES UNLESS OTHERWISE SPECIFIED		CADCIM TECHNOLOGIES
X---------- +/- 1	FIRST ISSUED	Toggle Lever
X.X---------- +/- 0.5	DRAWN BY	
X.XX---------- +/- 0.2	CHECKED BY	
ANGLE---------- +/- 0.5	APPROVED BY	SIZE A3 · DRG NO. 13-011 · SHEET REV A
ALL DIMENSIONS IN MM		SCALE 1:1 · SHEET 14 OF 17

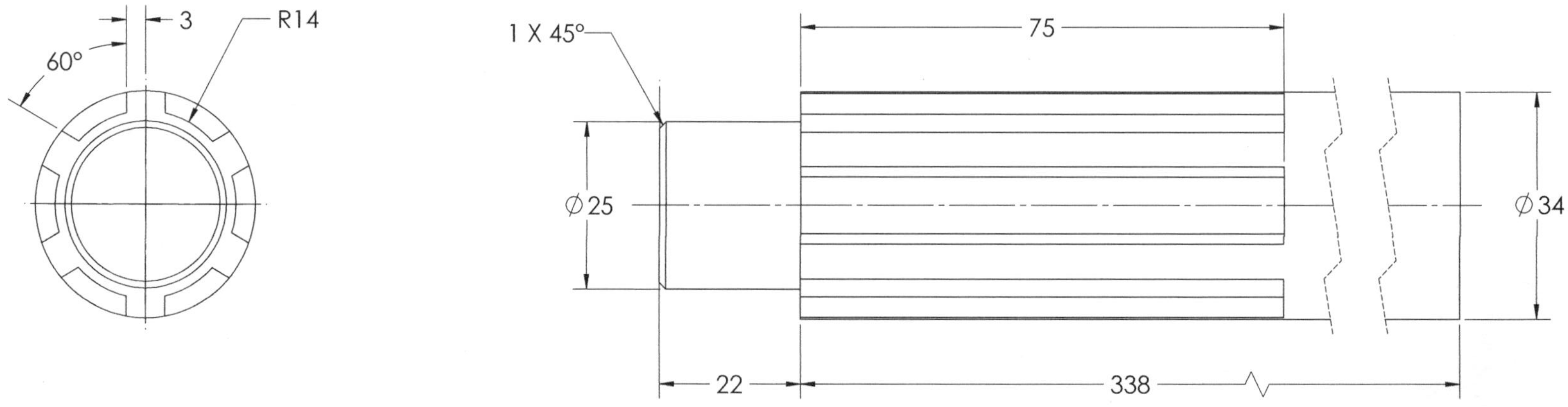

NOTES

1- Material Stainless Steel
2- Deburr sharp edges

TOLERANCES UNLESS OTHERWISE SPECIFIED		CADCIM TECHNOLOGIES
X---------- +/- 1 X.X---------- +/- 0.5 X.XX---------- +/- 0.2 ANGLE---------- +/- 0.5	FIRST ISSUED DRAWN BY CHECKED BY APPROVED BY	Driven Shaft
ALL DIMENSIONS IN MM		SIZE A3 / DRG NO. 13-012 / SHEET REV A
		SCALE 2:1 / SHEET 15 OF 17

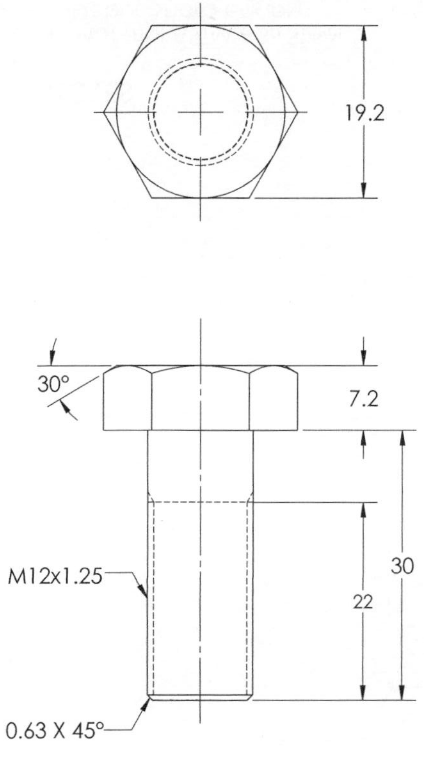

M12 x 1.75 Bolt

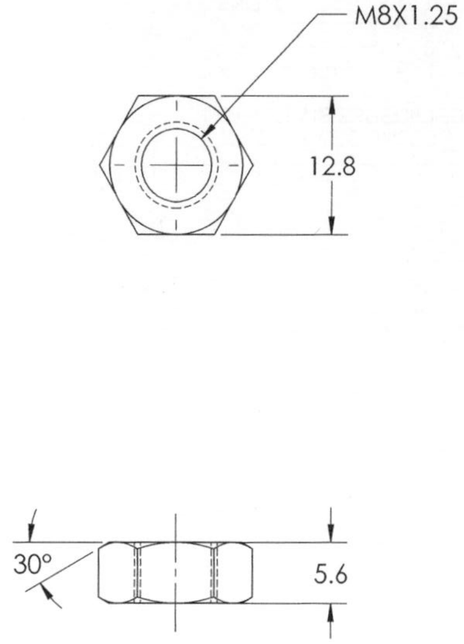

M8 x 1.25 Nut

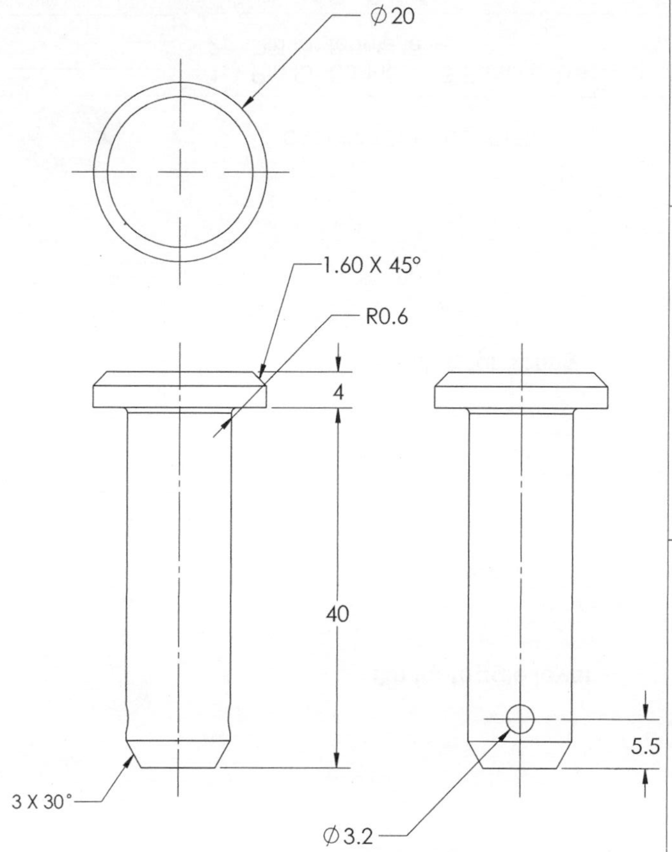

Celvis Pin

NOTES

1- Material Stainless Steel
2- Deburr sharp edges

TOLERANCES UNLESS OTHERWISE SPECIFIED

X---------------------- +/- 1
X.X------------------- +/- 0.5
X.XX----------------- +/- 0.2
ANGLE--------------- +/- 0.5

ALL DIMENSIONS IN MM

FIRST ISSUED
DRAWN BY
CHECKED BY
APPROVED BY

CADCIM TECHNOLOGIES

1. M12X 1.25 Hex Bolt- ANSI B18.2.3.5M
2. M8 X 1.0 Hex Nut- ANSI B18.2.4.1M
3. Clevis Pin 12 X 40 X3.20 -ISO 2341

SIZE	DRG NO.	SHEET REV
A3	13-013	A
SCALE 2:1		SHEET 16 OF 17

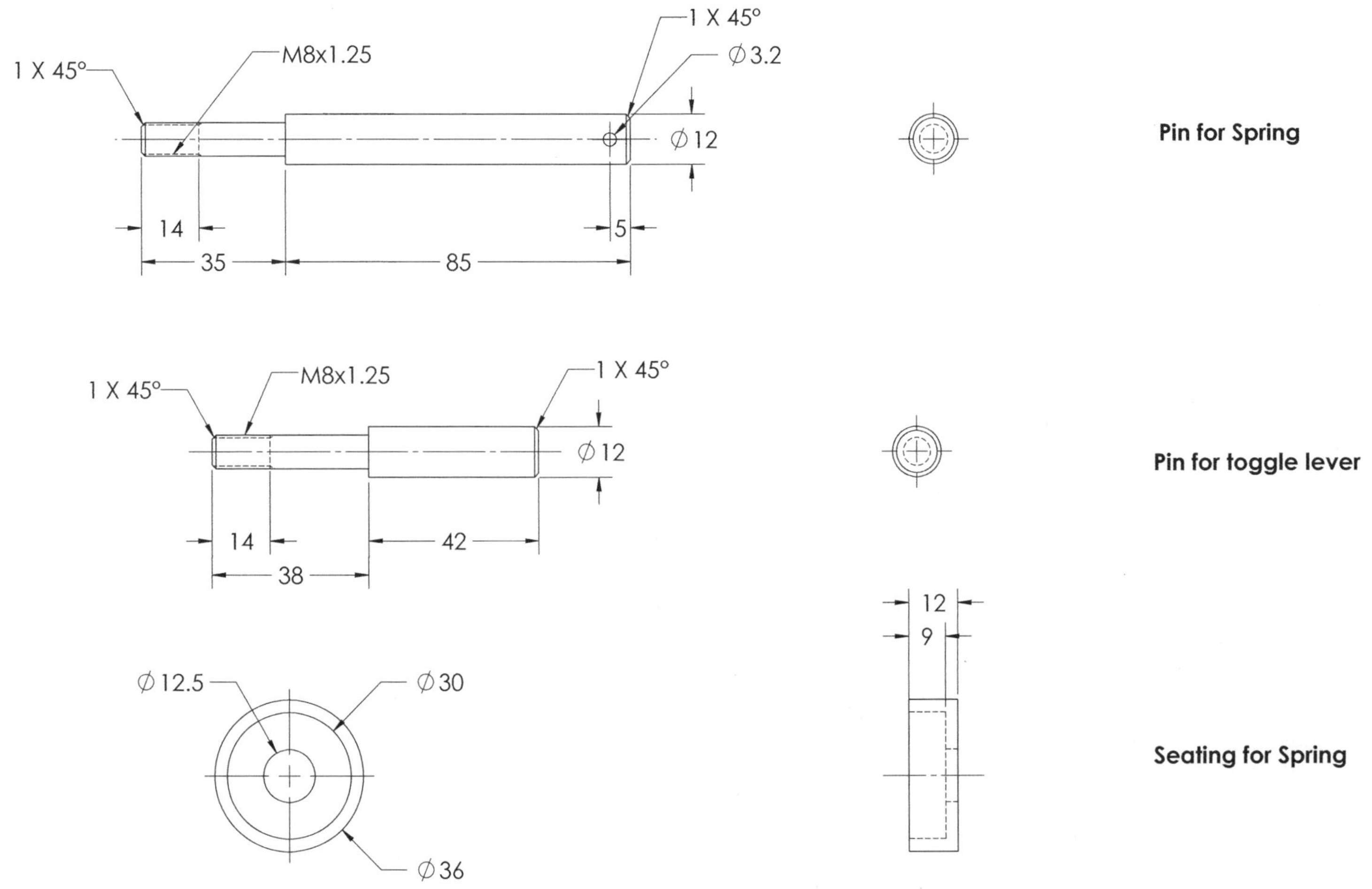

NOTES

1- Material ASTM A36 Steel
2- Deburr sharp edges

TOLERANCES UNLESS OTHERWISE SPECIFIED

X---------------------- +/- 1
X.X-------------------- +/- 0.5
X.XX------------------ +/- 0.2
ANGLE-------------- +/- 0.5

ALL DIMENSIONS IN MM

FIRST ISSUED	
DRAWN BY	
CHECKED BY	
APPROVED BY	

CADCIM TECHNOLOGIES

1. Pin for Spring 3.Seating fo spring
2. Pin for toggle lever

SIZE	DRG NO.	SHEET REV
A3	13-014	A
SCALE 1:1		SHEET 17 OF 17

Project 14

Vertical Steam Engine

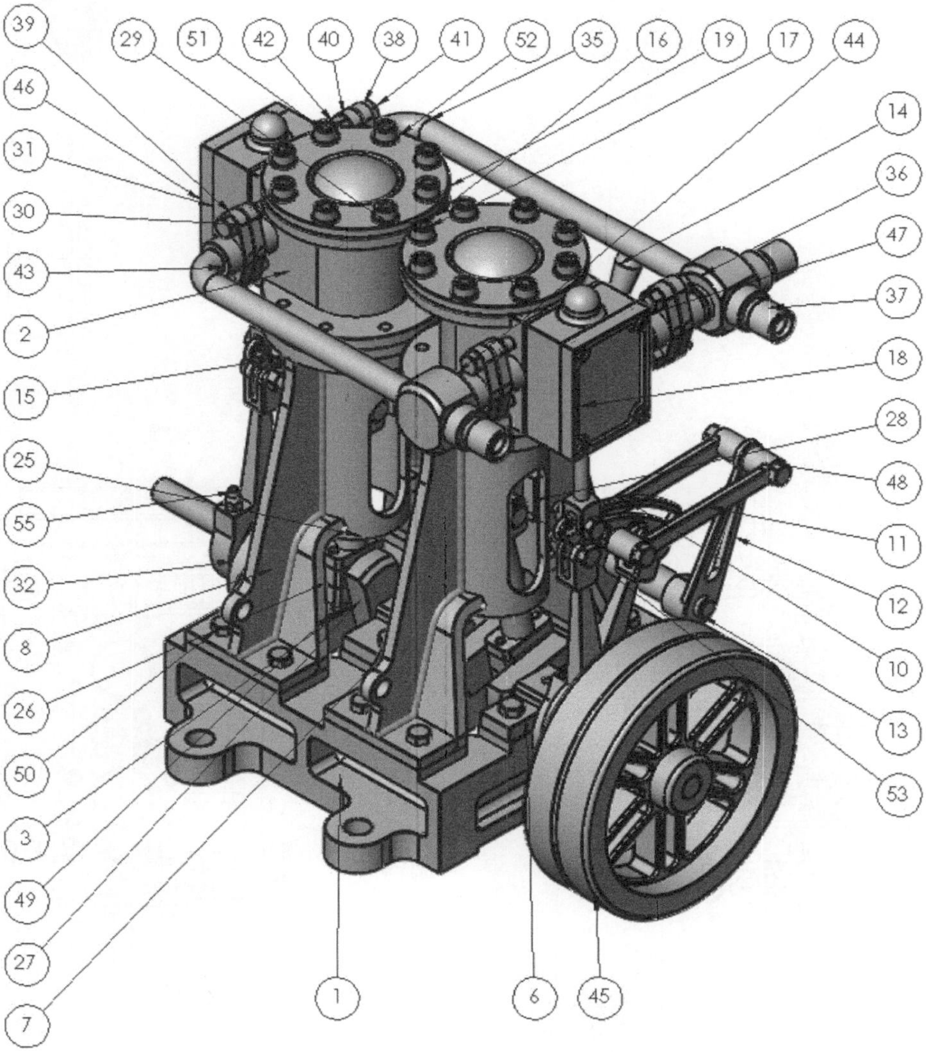

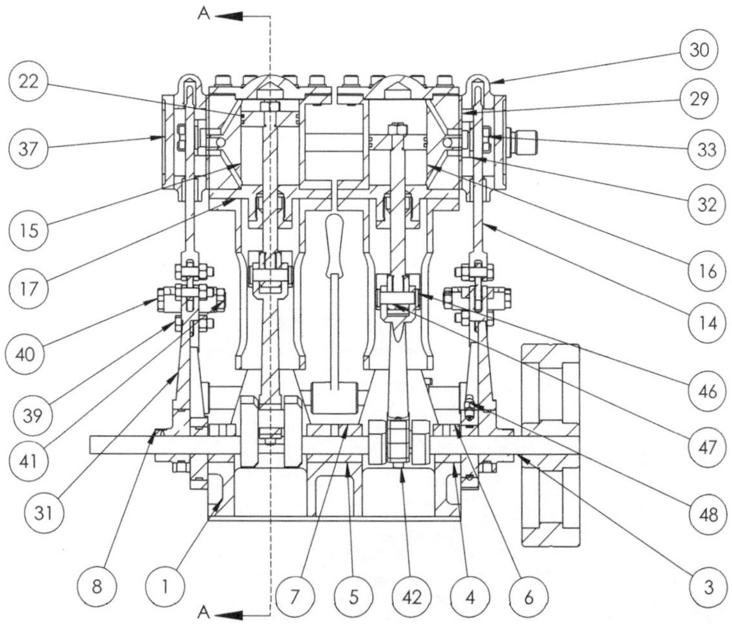

Section B-B

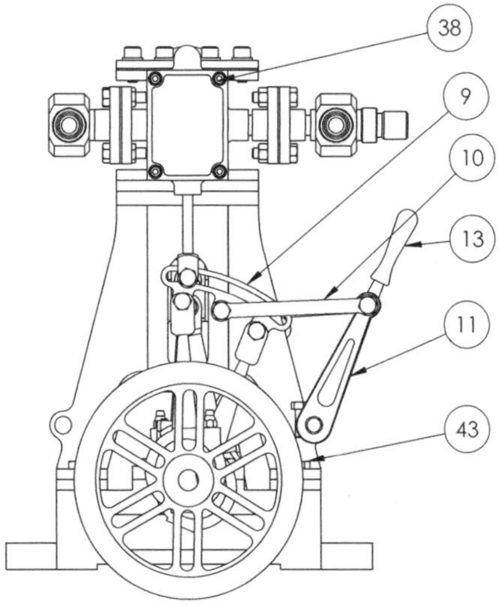

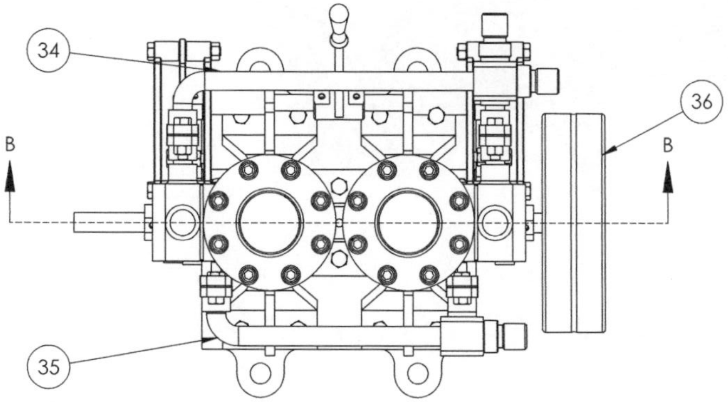

TOLERANCES UNLESS OTHERWISE SPECIFIED

X------------------- +/- 1
X.X----------------- +/- 0.5
X.XX---------------- +/- 0.2
ANGLE-------------- +/- 0.5

ALL DIMENSIONS IN MM

FIRST ISSUED	
DRAWN BY	
CHECKED BY	
APPROVED BY	

CADCIM TECHNOLOGIES

Vertical Twin Steam Turbine Assembly

SIZE	DRG NO.	SHEET REV
A3	14-000	A
SCALE 1:3		SHEET 1 OF 36

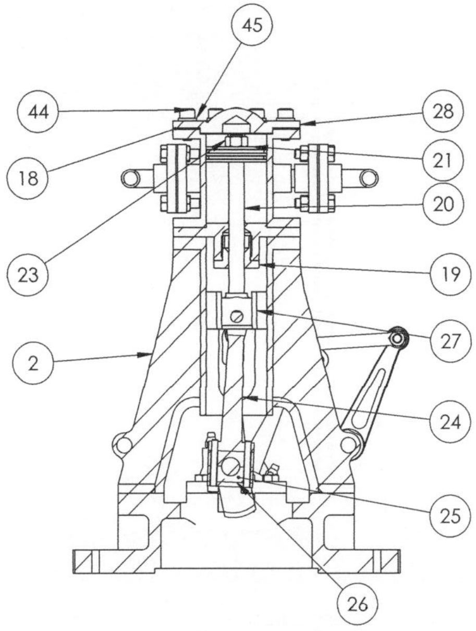

SECTION A-A

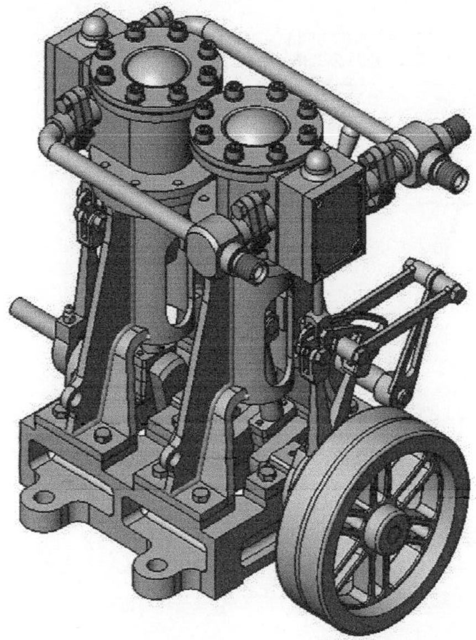

ITEM NO.	PART NUMBER	QTY.
1	BASE	1
2	Welding Assembly Standard	2
3	CRANKSHAFT_	1
4	LOWER BASE BEARING HOLDER 1	2
5	LOWER BASE BEARING HOLDER 2	1
6	UPPER BASE BEARING HOLDER 1	2
7	UPPER BASE BEARING HOLDER 2	1
8	Assembly Eccentric	2
9	REVERSE GEAR LINK	2
10	REVERSE GEAR DRAG LINK	4
11	REVERSE GEAR LEVER LINK	2
12	REVERSE GEAR LEVER ROD	1
13	REVERSE GEAR LEVER	1
14	STEAM CHEST SLIDE VALVE ROD	2
15	CYLINDER LEFT	1
16	CYLINDER RIGHT	1
17	CYLINDER COVER LOWER	2
18	CYLINDER PACKING	2
19	CYLINDER PACKNUT	2
20	STEAM PISTON ROD	2
21	STEAM PISTON	2
22	STEAM PISTON RING	4
23	M8X1.0 Hex Nut-ANSI B18.2.4.1M	2
24	CRANKROD	2
25	CONNECTING ROD CAP	4
26	BEARING KEEPER	2

ITEM NO.	PART NUMBER	QTY.
27	CROSSHEAD	2
28	UPPER CYLINDER COVER	2
29	VALVE PLATE	2
30	STEAMCHEST	2
31	ECCENTRIC ROD	4
32	SLIDE VALVE	2
33	SLIDE VALVE HOLDER	2
34	Assembly cylinder piping Entry	1
35	Assembly cylinder piping EXIT	1
36	FLYWHEEL	1
37	STEAMCHEST COVER	2
38	M4X 0.7 X40 Socket Head Cap Screws-ANSI B18.3.1M	8
39	M6 X 1 X 22 Hex Bolt- ANSI B18.2.3.5M	6
40	M6 X 1 X 42-Hex Bolt- ANSI B18.2.3.5M	4
41	M6 X 1Hex NUT-ANSI B18.2.4.1M	10
42	M4X 0.7 X30 Socket Head Cap Screws-ANSI B18.3.1M	4
43	M6 X 1 X16 Hex Bolt-ANSI B18.2.3.5M	15
44	M6X 1.0 X14 Socket Head Cap Screws-ANSI B18.3.1M	32
45	M6 Plain Washer Grade A- ISO 7086	16
46	CRANKROD BOLT	2
47	CRANKROD PIN	2
48	LUBRICATING NIPPLE	4

TOLERANCES UNLESS OTHERWISE SPECIFIED

X---------------------- +/- 1
X.X-------------------- +/- 0.5
X.XX------------------ +/- 0.2
ANGLE-------------- +/- 0.5

ALL DIMENSIONS IN MM

FIRST ISSUED
DRAWN BY
CHECKED BY
APPROVED BY

CADCIM TECHNOLOGIES

Vertical Twin Steam Turbine Assembly

SIZE A3 | DRG NO. 14-000 | SHEET REV A

SCALE 1:3 | SHEET 2 OF 36

ITEM NO.	PART NUMBER	QTY.
1	Standard Cylinder	1
2	Standard Rib	2
3	Standard Foot	2
4	Standard Socle	2

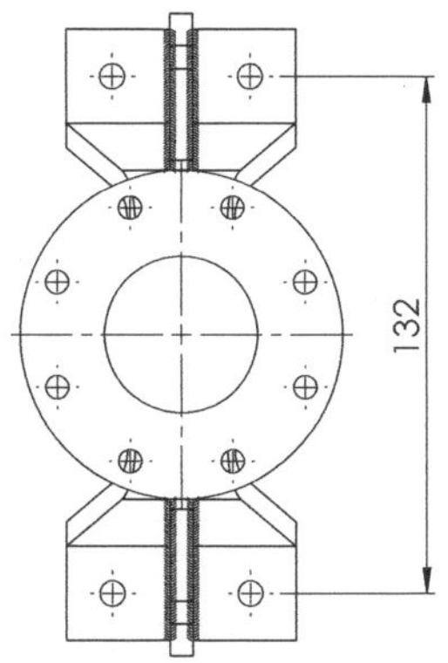

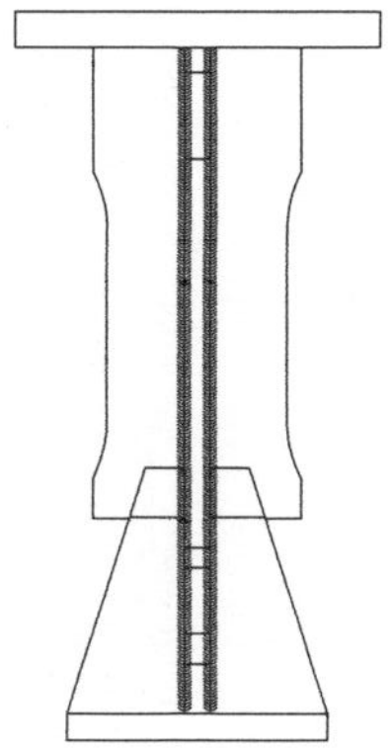

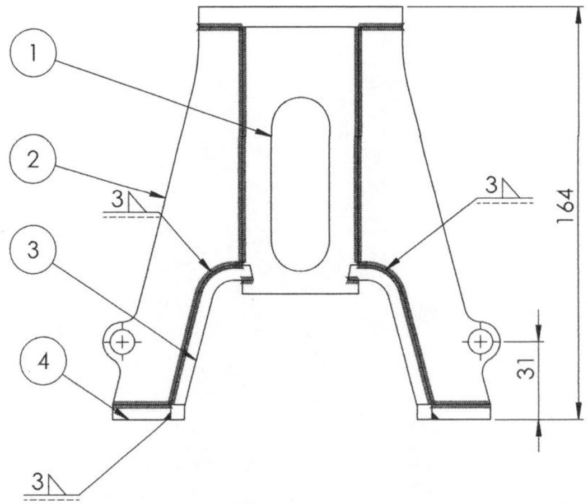

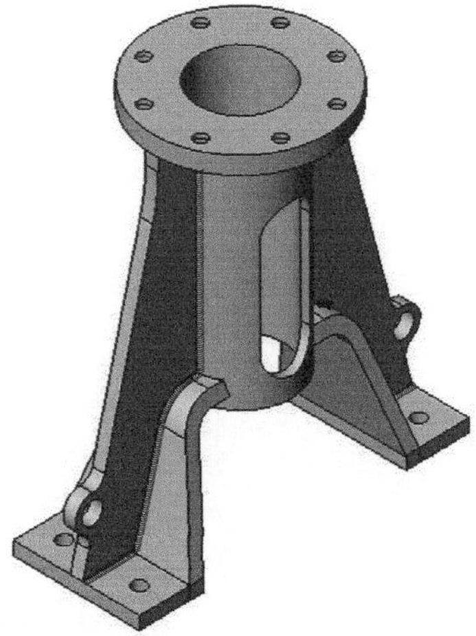

TOLERANCES UNLESS OTHERWISE SPECIFIED

X---------------------- +/- 1
X.X-------------------- +/- 0.5
X.XX------------------ +/- 0.2
ANGLE--------------- +/- 0.5

ALL DIMENSIONS IN MM

FIRST ISSUED	
DRAWN BY	
CHECKED BY	
APPROVED BY	

CADCIM TECHNOLOGIES

Welding Assembly Standard

SIZE	DRG NO.	SHEET REV
A3	14-000	A
SCALE 1:2		SHEET 3 OF 36

ITEM NO.	PART NUMBER	QTY.
1	CYLINDER PIPING TUBE ENTRY	1
2	CYLINDER PIPING COLLECTOR ENTRY	1
3	CYLINDER PIPING CONNECTOR	2
4	CYLINDER PIPING TUBE GLANSE	1
5	CYLINDER PIPING TUBE GLANSE PACKING	2
6	CYLINDER PIPING COLLECTOR GLANSE	3
7	M6 X 1 X 22 Hex Bolt- ANSI B18.2.3.5M	4
8	M6 X 1Hex NUT- ANSI B18.2.4.1M	4

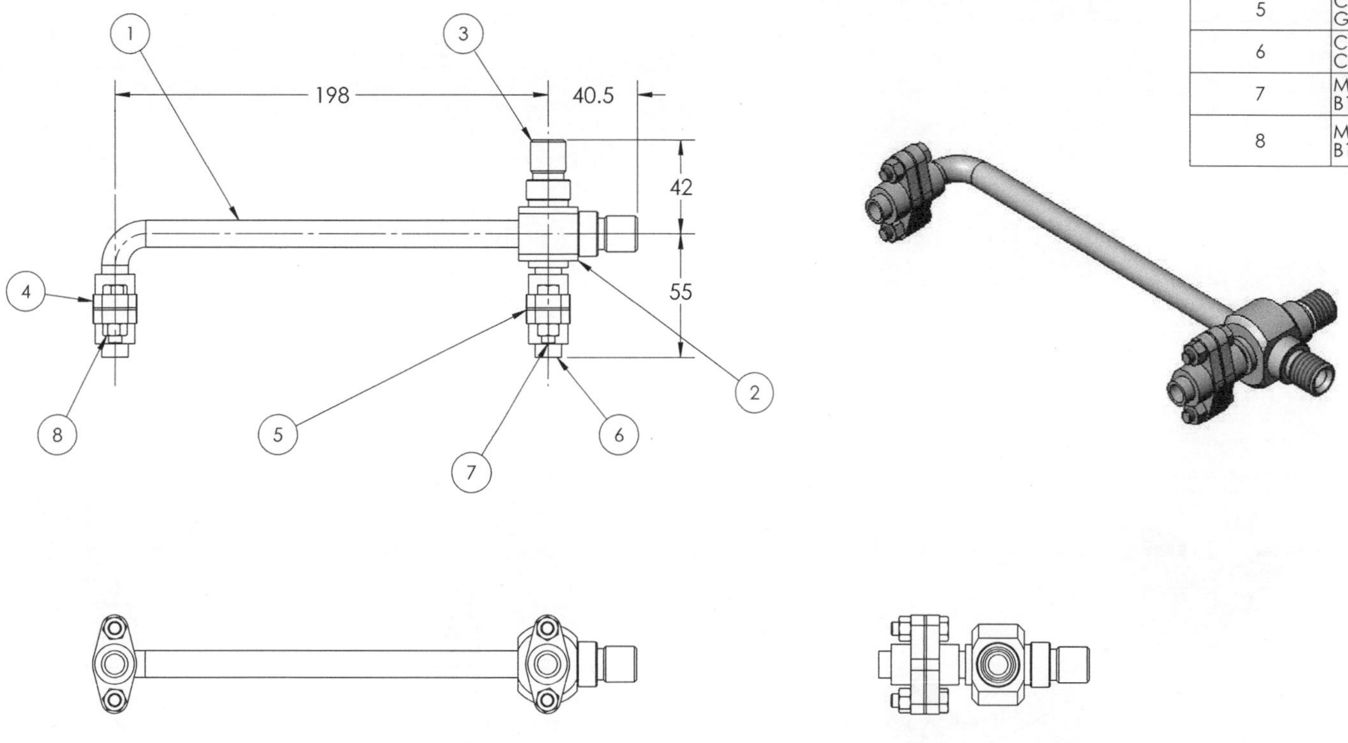

TOLERANCES UNLESS OTHERWISE SPECIFIED

X---------------------- +/- 1
X.X------------------- +/- 0.5
X.XX----------------- +/- 0.2
ANGLE-------------- +/- 0.5

ALL DIMENSIONS IN MM

FIRST ISSUED
DRAWN BY
CHECKED BY
APPROVED BY

CADCIM TECHNOLOGIES

Assembly cylinder Piping Entry

SIZE	DRG NO.	SHEET REV
A3	14-000	A
SCALE 1:2		SHEET 4 OF 36

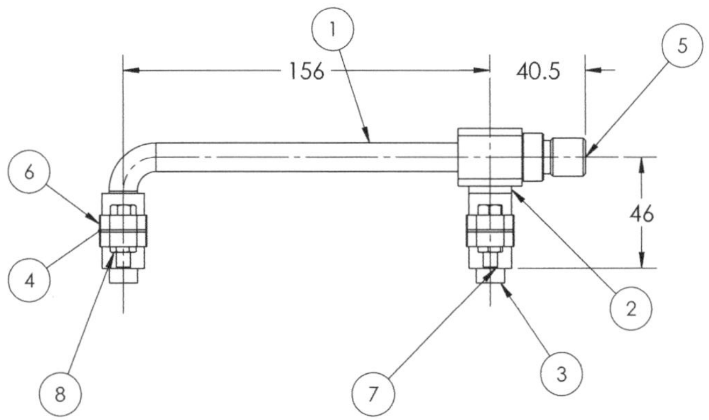

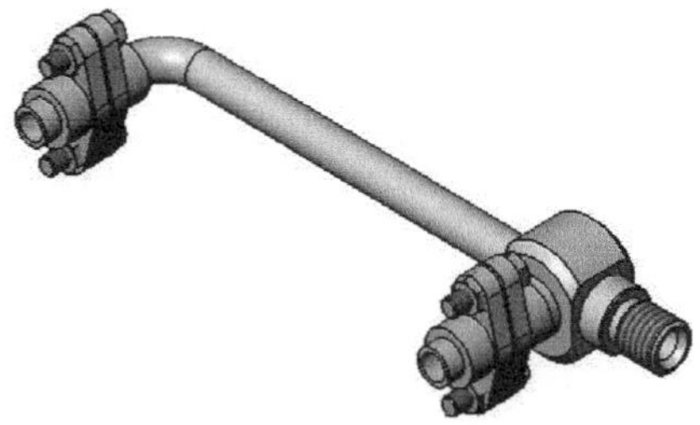

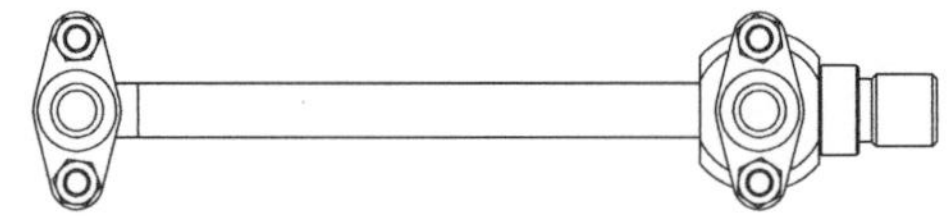

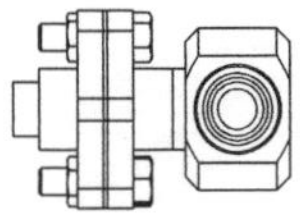

ITEM NO.	PART NUMBER	QTY.
1	CYLINDER PIPING TUBE EXIT	1
2	CYLINDER PIPING COLLECTOR EXIT	1
3	CYLINDER PIPING COLLECTOR GLANSE	3
4	CYLINDER PIPING TUBE GLANSE PACKING	2
5	CYLINDER PIPING CONNECTOR	1
6	CYLINDER PIPING TUBE GLANSE	1
7	M6 X 1 X 22 Hex Bolt-ANSI B18.2.3.5M	4
8	M6 X 1Hex NUT- ANSI B18.2.4.1M	4

TOLERANCES UNLESS OTHERWISE SPECIFIED

X---------------------- +/- 1
X.X-------------------- +/- 0.5
X.XX------------------ +/- 0.2
ANGLE-------------- +/- 0.5

ALL DIMENSIONS IN MM

FIRST ISSUED	
DRAWN BY	
CHECKED BY	
APPROVED BY	

CADCIM TECHNOLOGIES

Assembly Cylinder Piping Exit

SIZE	DRG NO.	SHEET REV
A3	14-000	A
SCALE 1:2		SHEET 5 OF 36

ITEM NO.	PART NUMBER	QTY.
1	ECCENTRIC 01	1
2	ECCENTRIC 02	1

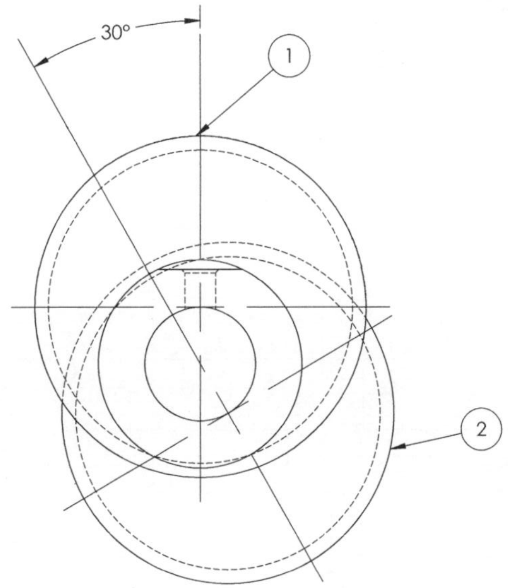

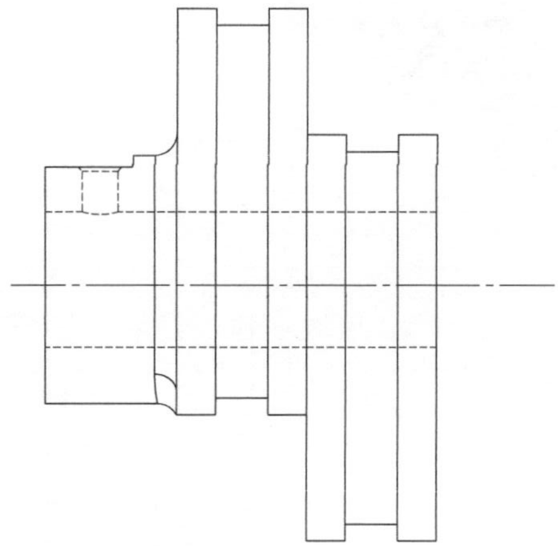

TOLERANCES UNLESS OTHERWISE SPECIFIED		CADCIM TECHNOLOGIES
X---------- +/- 1 X.X---------- +/- 0.5 X.XX---------- +/- 0.2 ANGLE---------- +/- 0.5	FIRST ISSUED DRAWN BY CHECKED BY APPROVED BY	Assembly Eccentric
ALL DIMENSIONS IN MM		SIZE A3 · DRG NO. 14-000 · SHEET REV A
		SCALE 2:1 · SHEET 6 OF 36

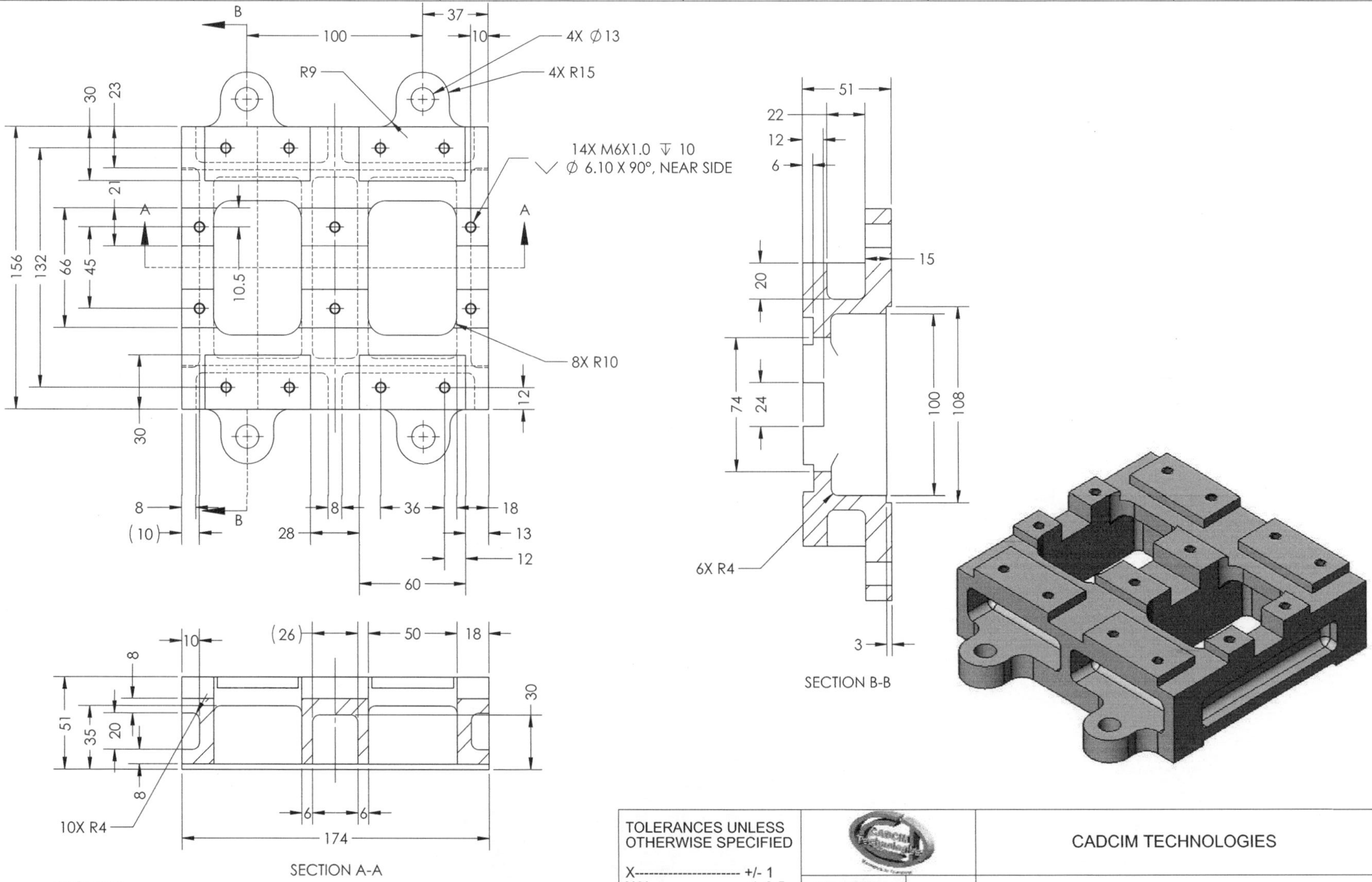

NOTES

1- Material Mild Steel
2- Deburr sharp edges

TOLERANCES UNLESS OTHERWISE SPECIFIED

X---------------------- +/- 1
X.X-------------------- +/- 0.5
X.XX------------------- +/- 0.2
ANGLE------------------ +/- 0.5

ALL DIMENSIONS IN MM

FIRST ISSUED	
DRAWN BY	
CHECKED BY	
APPROVED BY	

CADCIM TECHNOLOGIES

BASE

SIZE	DRG NO.	SHEET REV
A3	14-001	A
SCALE 1:2		SHEET 7 OF 36

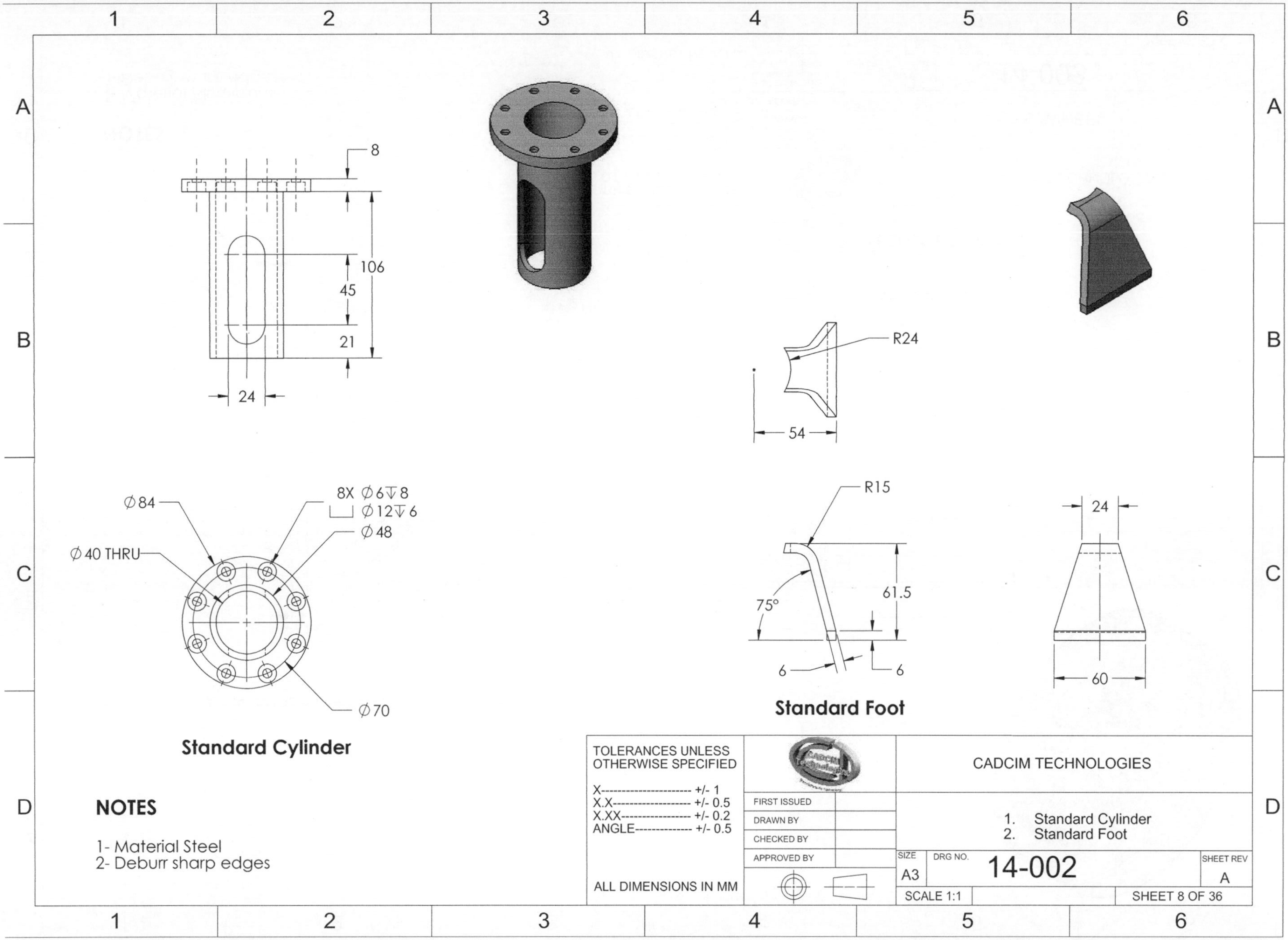

8
106
45
21
24
8X ⌀6↧8
⌴ ⌀12↧6
⌀48
⌀84
⌀40 THRU
⌀70
Standard Cylinder
R24
54
R15
61.5
75°
6
6
24
60
Standard Foot
NOTES
1- Material Steel
2- Deburr sharp edges
TOLERANCES UNLESS OTHERWISE SPECIFIED
X---------- +/- 1
X.X---------- +/- 0.5
X.XX---------- +/- 0.2
ANGLE---------- +/- 0.5
ALL DIMENSIONS IN MM
FIRST ISSUED
DRAWN BY
CHECKED BY
APPROVED BY
CADCIM TECHNOLOGIES
1. Standard Cylinder
2. Standard Foot
SIZE A3
DRG NO. 14-002
SHEET REV A
SCALE 1:1
SHEET 8 OF 36

ALL THE FILLETS ON THE RIMS HAVING RADIUS 1MM

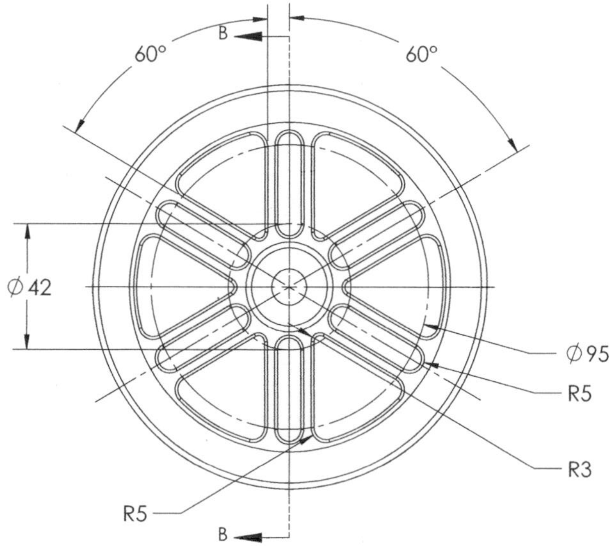

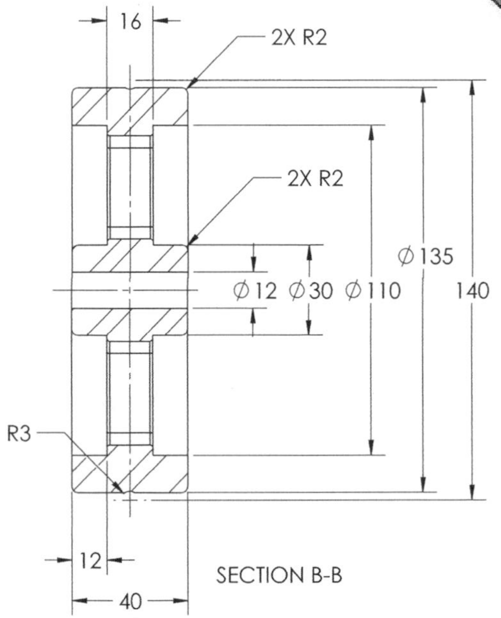

SECTION B-B

NOTES

1- Material Aluminium
3- Deburr sharp edges

TOLERANCES UNLESS OTHERWISE SPECIFIED		
X---------- +/- 1	FIRST ISSUED	
X.X---------- +/- 0.5	DRAWN BY	
X.XX---------- +/- 0.2	CHECKED BY	
ANGLE---------- +/- 0.5	APPROVED BY	
ALL DIMENSIONS IN MM		

CADCIM TECHNOLOGIES

FLYWHEEL

SIZE	DRG NO.	SHEET REV
A3	14-003	A
SCALE 2:3		SHEET 9 OF 36

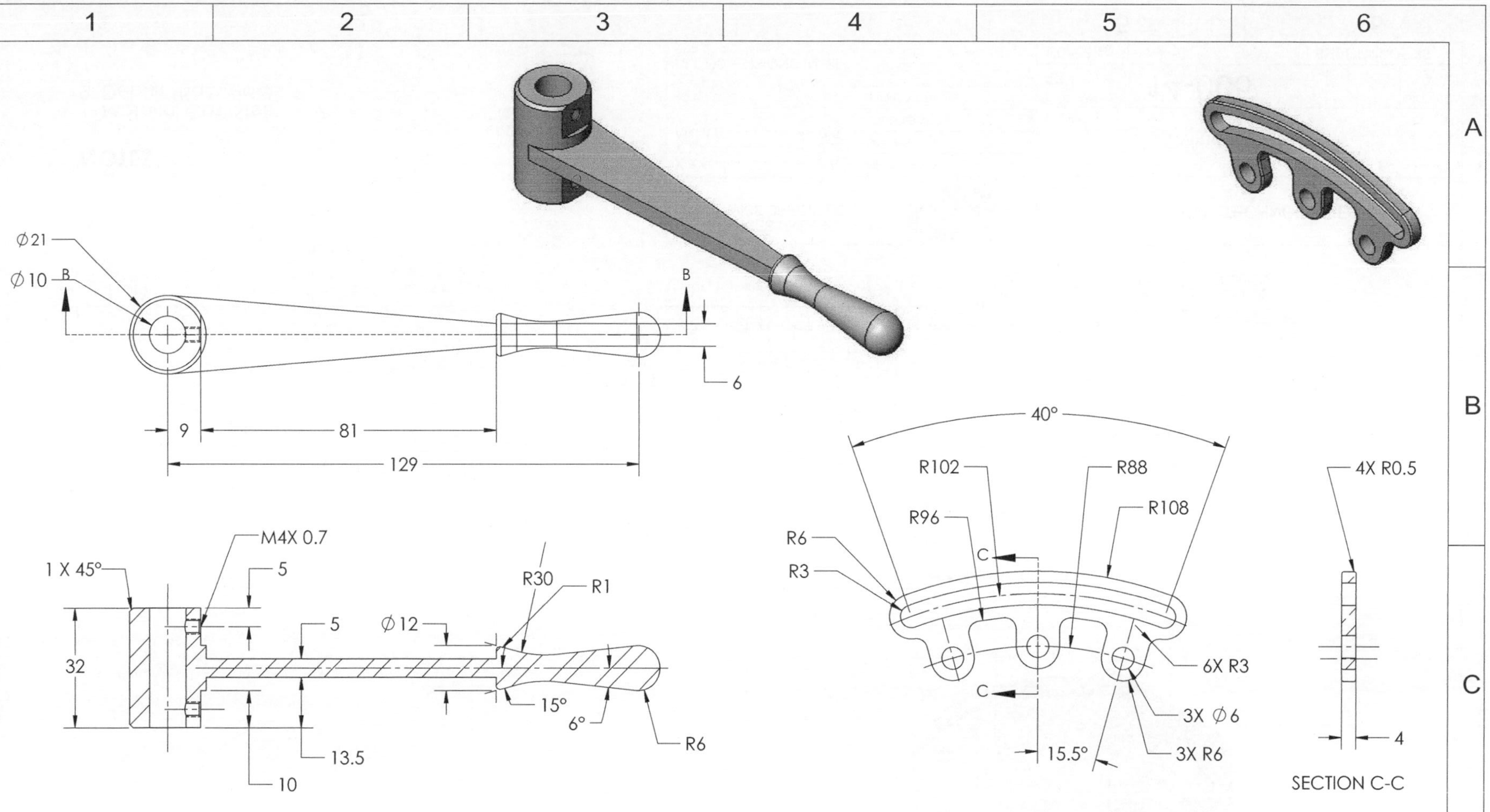

Reverse Gear Lever

Reverse Gear LINK

NOTES

1- Material Steel for 1, Copper alloy for 2
2- Deburr sharp edges

TOLERANCES UNLESS OTHERWISE SPECIFIED		CADCIM TECHNOLOGIES
X---------- +/- 1 X.X---------- +/- 0.5 X.XX---------- +/- 0.2 ANGLE---------- +/- 0.5	FIRST ISSUED DRAWN BY CHECKED BY APPROVED BY	1. Reverse Gear Lever 2. Reverse Gear Link
ALL DIMENSIONS IN MM		SIZE A3 · DRG NO. 14-004 · SHEET REV A
		SCALE 1:1 · SHEET 10 OF 36

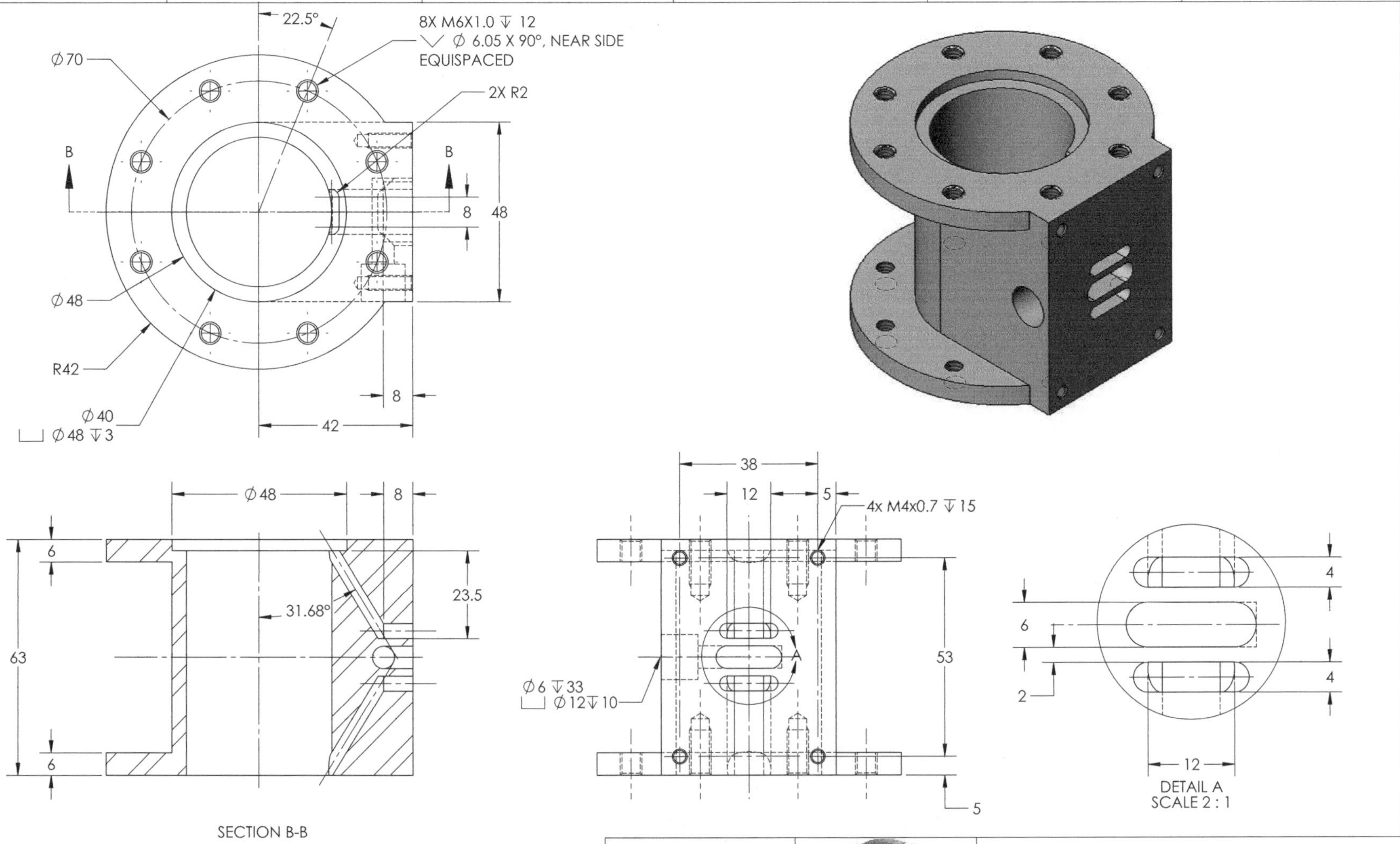

NOTES

1- Material Cast Steel
2- Deburr sharp edges

TOLERANCES UNLESS OTHERWISE SPECIFIED		CADCIM TECHNOLOGIES
X---------- +/- 1	FIRST ISSUED	Cylinder Right
X.X---------- +/- 0.5	DRAWN BY	
X.XX---------- +/- 0.2	CHECKED BY	
ANGLE---------- +/- 0.5	APPROVED BY	SIZE A3 · DRG NO. 14-005 · SHEET REV A
ALL DIMENSIONS IN MM		SCALE 1:1 · SHEET 11 OF 36

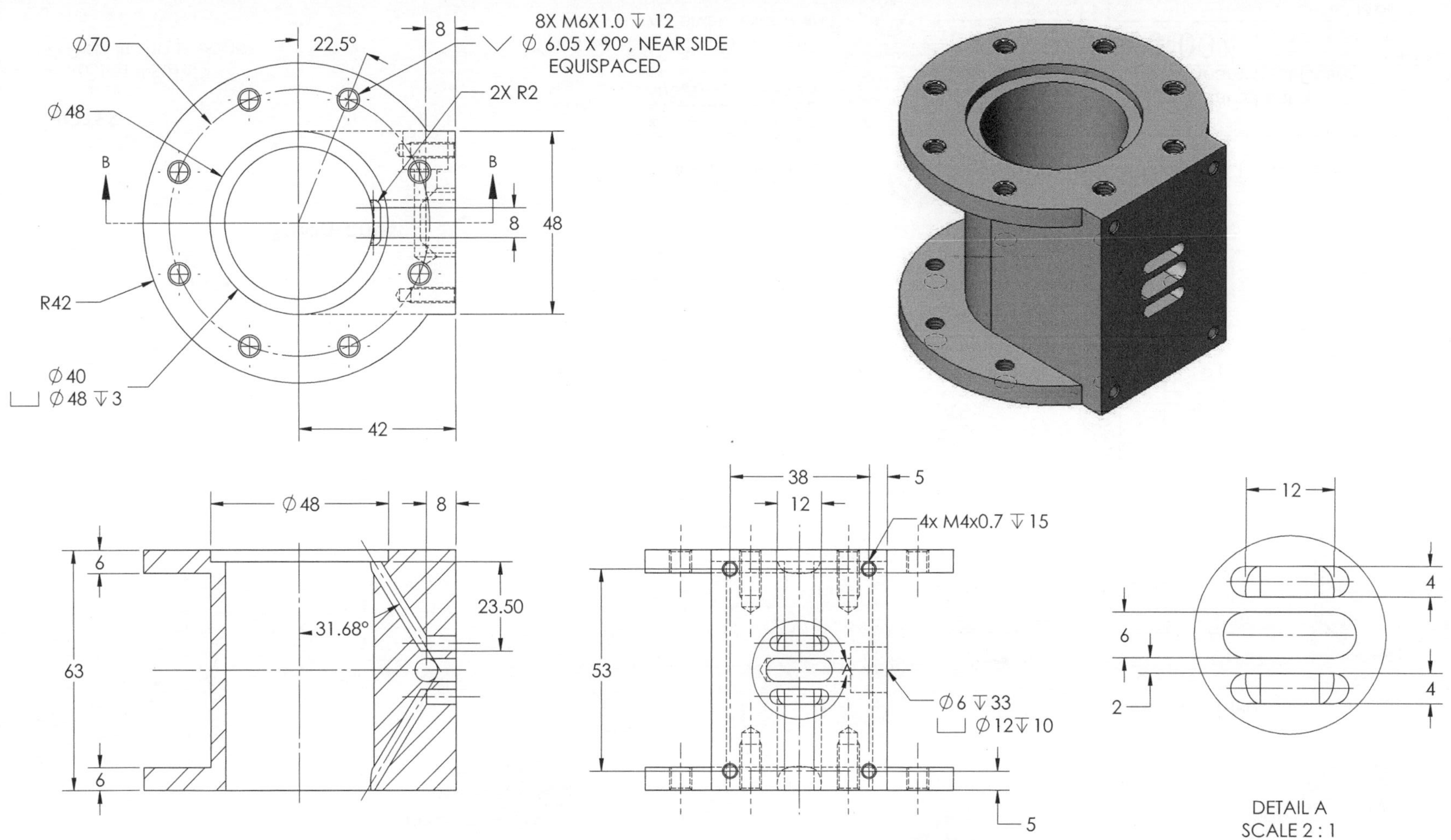

SECTION B-B

NOTES

1- Material Cast Steel
2- Deburr sharp edges

TOLERANCES UNLESS OTHERWISE SPECIFIED		CADCIM TECHNOLOGIES
X---------- +/- 1 X.X---------- +/- 0.5 X.XX---------- +/- 0.2 ANGLE---------- +/- 0.5	FIRST ISSUED DRAWN BY CHECKED BY APPROVED BY	Cylinder Left
ALL DIMENSIONS IN MM		SIZE A3 · DRG NO. 14-006 · SHEET REV A
		SCALE 1:1 · SHEET 12 OF 36

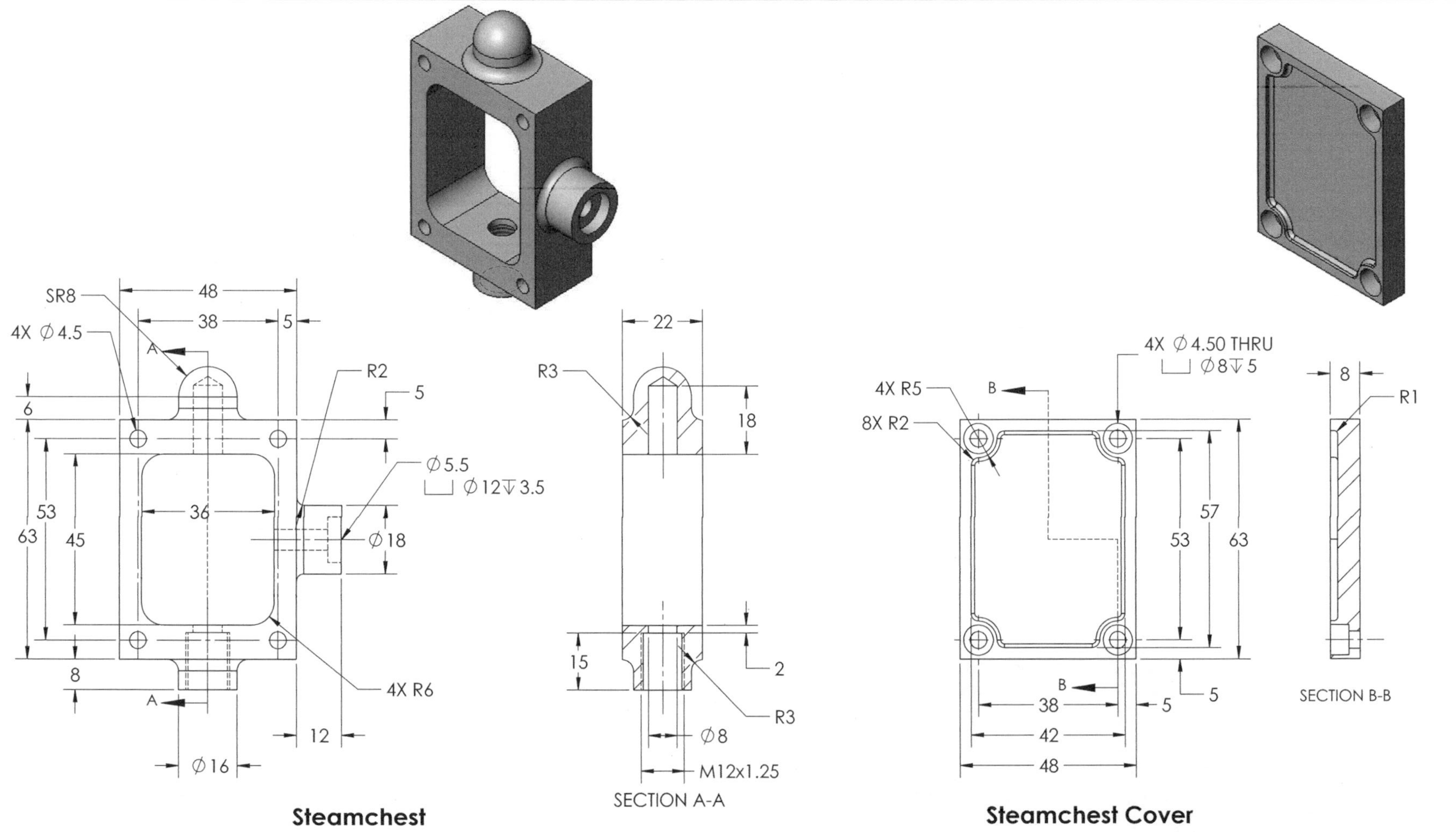

NOTES

1- Material Steel
2- Deburr sharp edges

TOLERANCES UNLESS OTHERWISE SPECIFIED		CADCIM TECHNOLOGIES
X---------- +/- 1 X.X---------- +/- 0.5 X.XX---------- +/- 0.2 ANGLE---------- +/- 0.5	FIRST ISSUED DRAWN BY CHECKED BY APPROVED BY	1. Steamchest 2. Steamchest Cover
ALL DIMENSIONS IN MM		SIZE A3 · DRG NO. 14-007 · SHEET REV A
		SCALE 1:1 · SHEET 13 OF 36

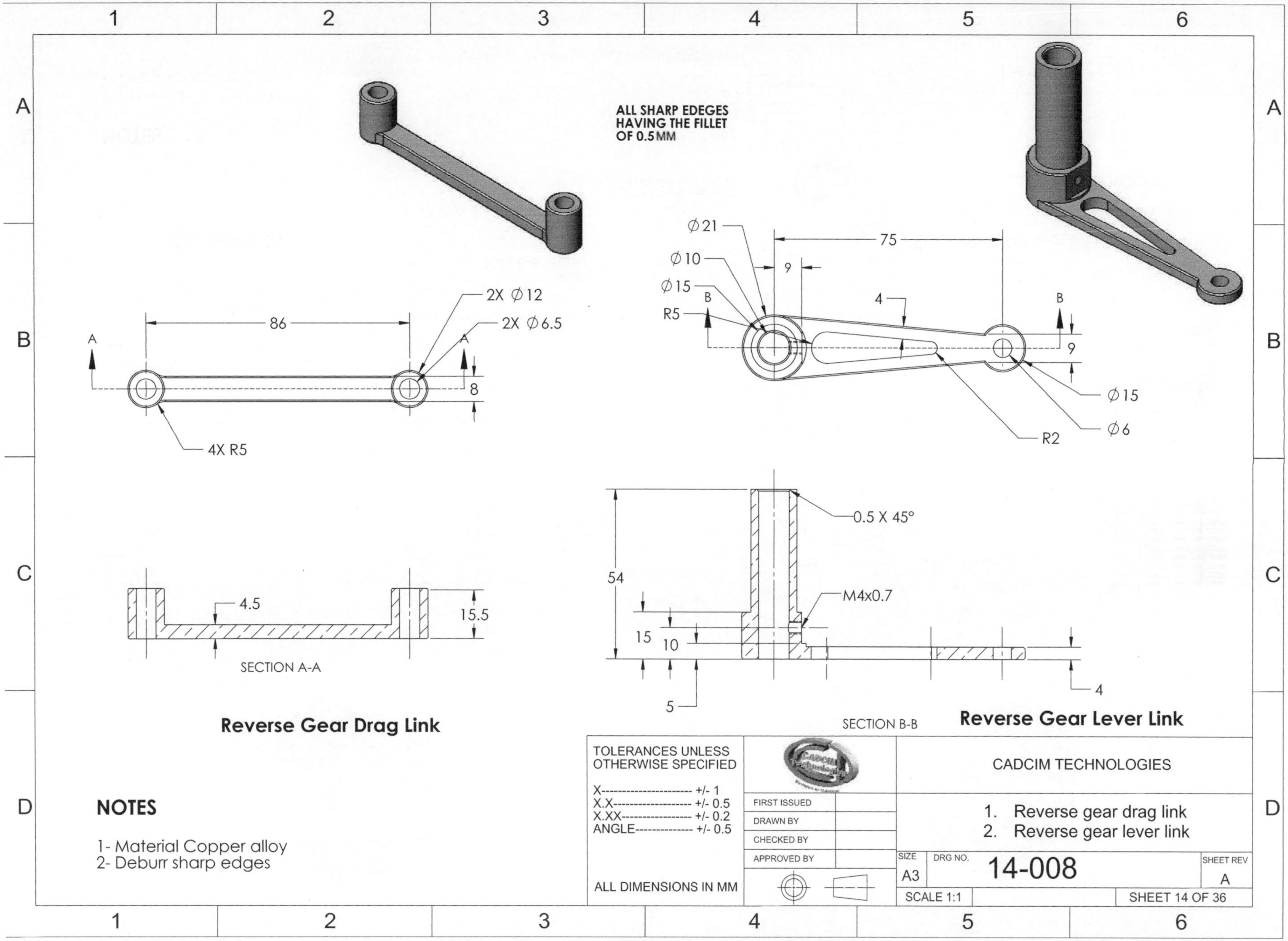
ALL SHARP EDEGES HAVING THE FILLET OF 0.5MM
86
2X ⌀12
2X ⌀6.5
8
4X R5
A
4.5
15.5
SECTION A-A
Reverse Gear Drag Link
⌀21
⌀10
⌀15
R5
75
9
4
B
9
⌀15
⌀6
R2
0.5 X 45°
M4x0.7
54
15
10
5
4
SECTION B-B
Reverse Gear Lever Link
NOTES
1- Material Copper alloy
2- Deburr sharp edges
TOLERANCES UNLESS OTHERWISE SPECIFIED
X-------------------- +/- 1
X.X------------------ +/- 0.5
X.XX---------------- +/- 0.2
ANGLE-------------- +/- 0.5
ALL DIMENSIONS IN MM
FIRST ISSUED
DRAWN BY
CHECKED BY
APPROVED BY
CADCIM TECHNOLOGIES
1. Reverse gear drag link
2. Reverse gear lever link
SIZE
A3
DRG NO.
14-008
SHEET REV
A
SCALE 1:1
SHEET 14 OF 36

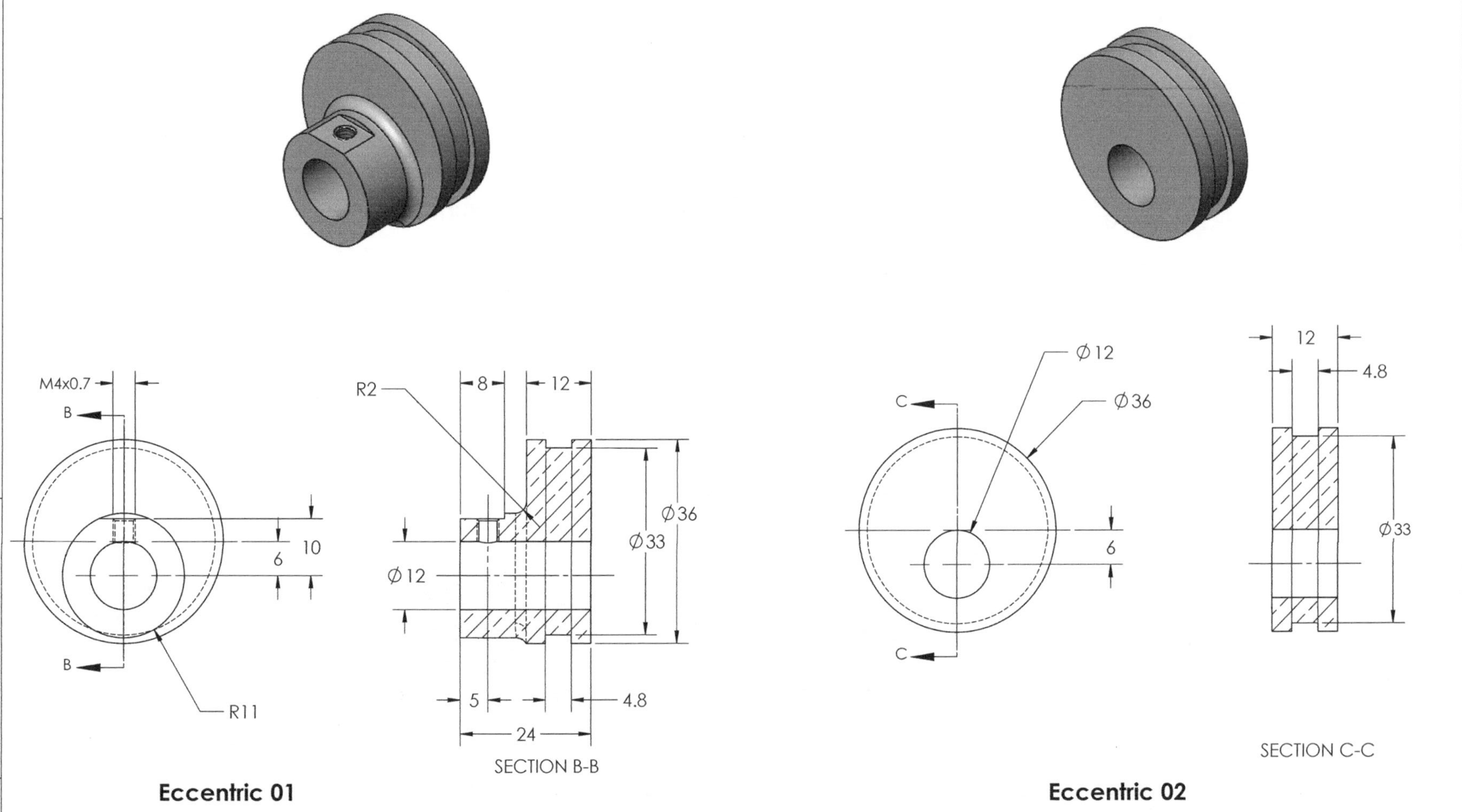

NOTES

1- Material Copper alloy
2- Deburr sharp edges

TOLERANCES UNLESS OTHERWISE SPECIFIED		CADCIM TECHNOLOGIES
X ---- +/- 1 X.X ---- +/- 0.5 X.XX ---- +/- 0.2 ANGLE ---- +/- 0.5	FIRST ISSUED DRAWN BY CHECKED BY APPROVED BY	1. Eccentric 01 2. Eccentric 02
ALL DIMENSIONS IN MM		SIZE A3 · DRG NO. 14-009 · SHEET REV A
		SCALE 3:2 · SHEET 15 OF 36

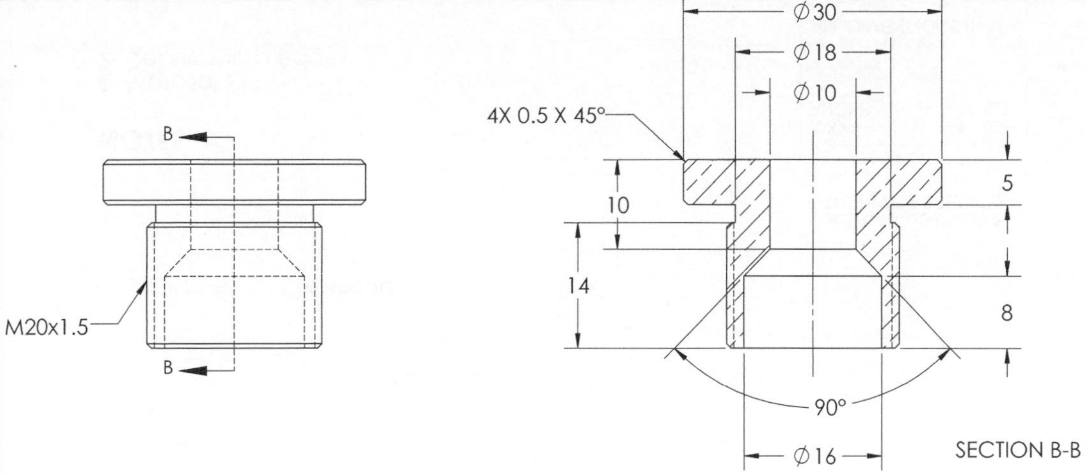

Cylinder Packnut

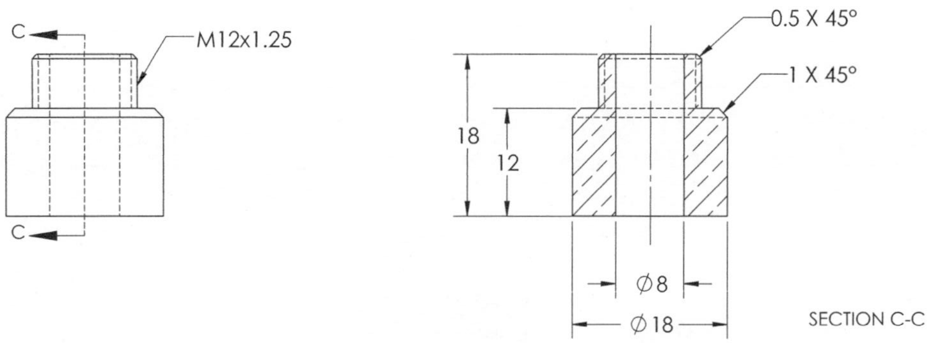

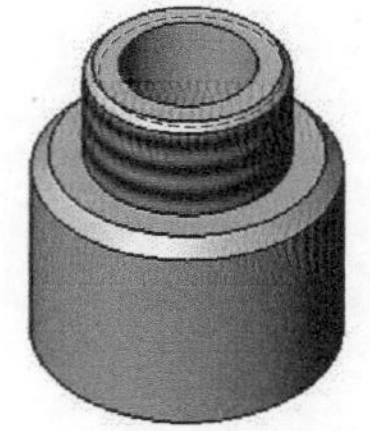

Cylinder Pipe Connector

NOTES

1- Material Brass
2- Deburr sharp edges

TOLERANCES UNLESS OTHERWISE SPECIFIED		CADCIM TECHNOLOGIES	
X---- +/- 1 X.X---- +/- 0.5 X.XX---- +/- 0.2 ANGLE---- +/- 0.5	FIRST ISSUED DRAWN BY CHECKED BY APPROVED BY	1. Cylinder Packnut 2. Cylinder Pipe Connector	
ALL DIMENSIONS IN MM		SIZE A3 / DRG NO. 14-010	SHEET REV A
		SCALE 2:1	SHEET 16 OF 36

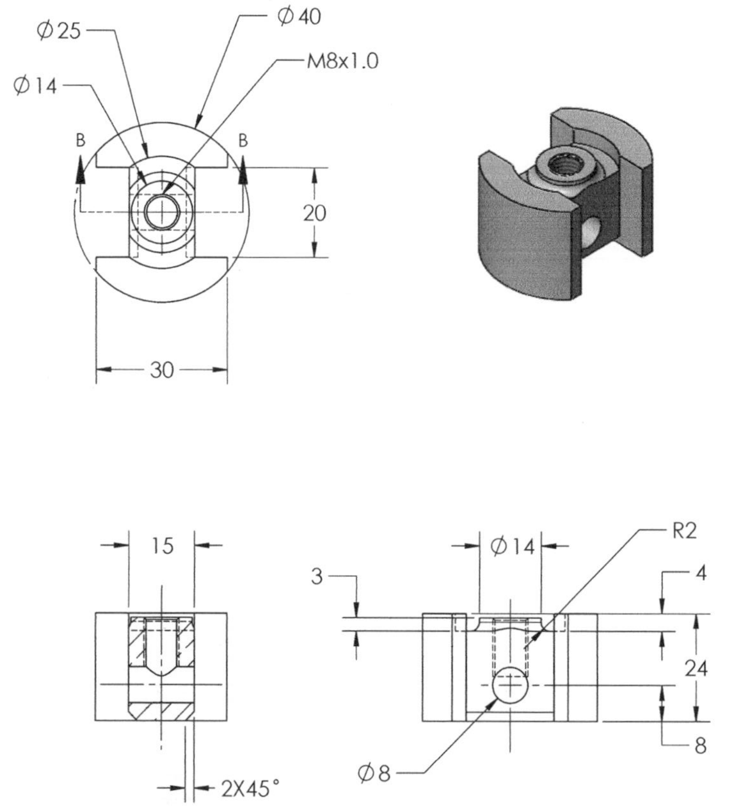

SECTION B-B **Crosshead**

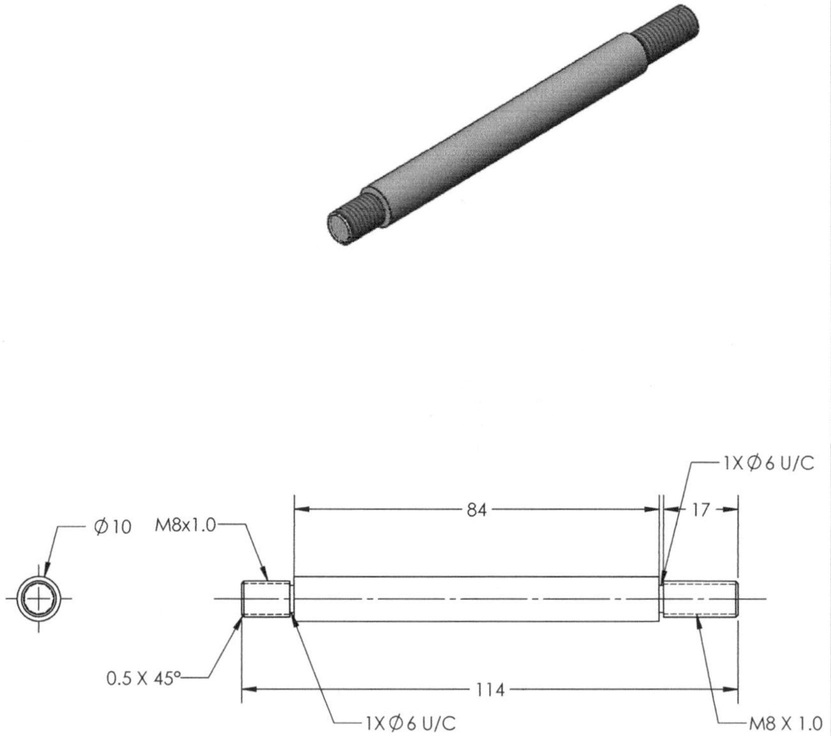

Steam Piston Rod

NOTES

1- Material SS
2- Deburr sharp edges

TOLERANCES UNLESS OTHERWISE SPECIFIED		CADCIM TECHNOLOGIES
X------- +/- 1 X.X------- +/- 0.5 X.XX------- +/- 0.2 ANGLE------- +/- 0.5	FIRST ISSUED DRAWN BY CHECKED BY APPROVED BY	1. Crosshead 2. Steam Piston Rod
ALL DIMENSIONS IN MM		SIZE A3 · DRG NO. 14-011 · SHEET REV A
		SCALE 1:1 · SHEET 17 OF 36

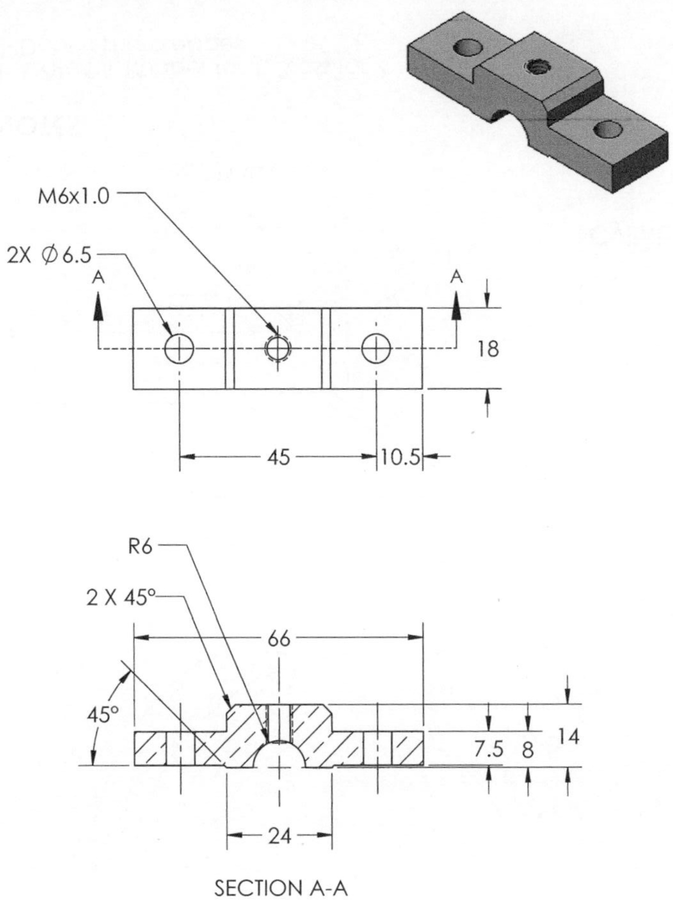

Upper Base Bearing Holder 1

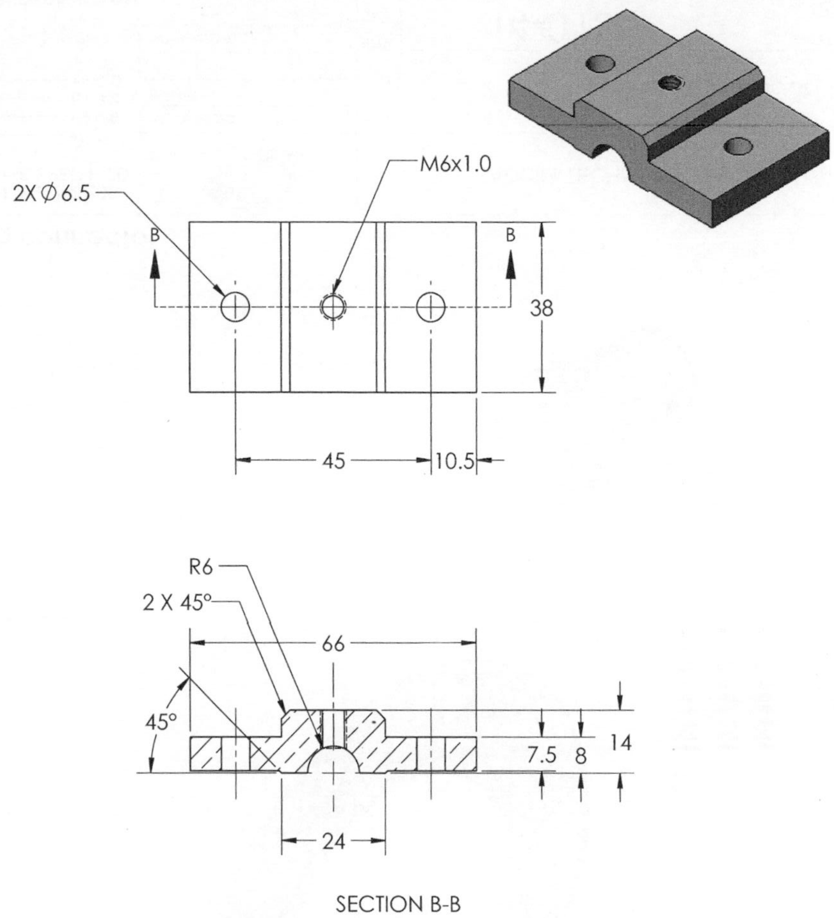

Upper Base Bearing Holder 2

NOTES

1- Material Brass
2- Deburr sharp edges

TOLERANCES UNLESS OTHERWISE SPECIFIED		CADCIM TECHNOLOGIES
X---------- +/- 1 X.X---------- +/- 0.5 X.XX---------- +/- 0.2 ANGLE---------- +/- 0.5	FIRST ISSUED DRAWN BY CHECKED BY APPROVED BY	1. Upper Base Bearing Holder 1 2. Upper Base Bearing Holder 2
ALL DIMENSIONS IN MM		SIZE A3	DRG NO. 14-012	SHEET REV A
		SCALE 1:1	SHEET 18 OF 36

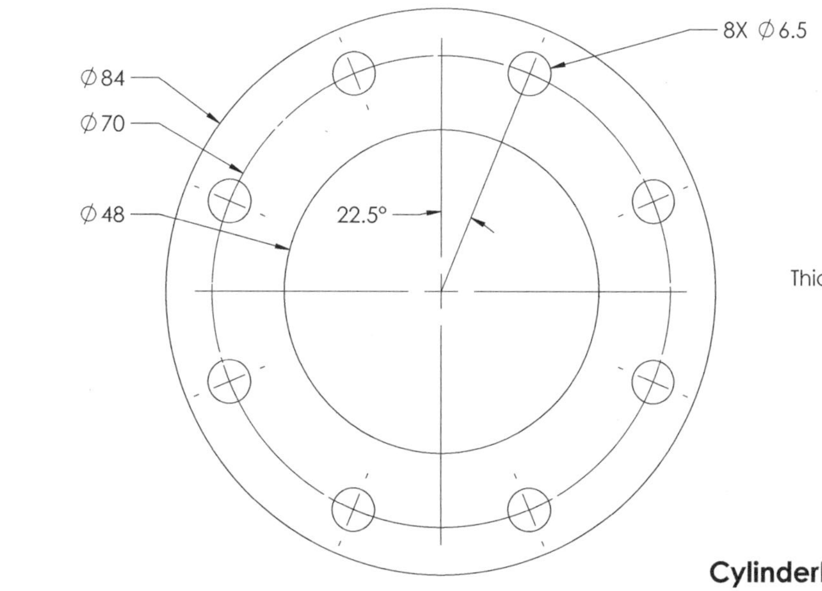

Thickness 1mm

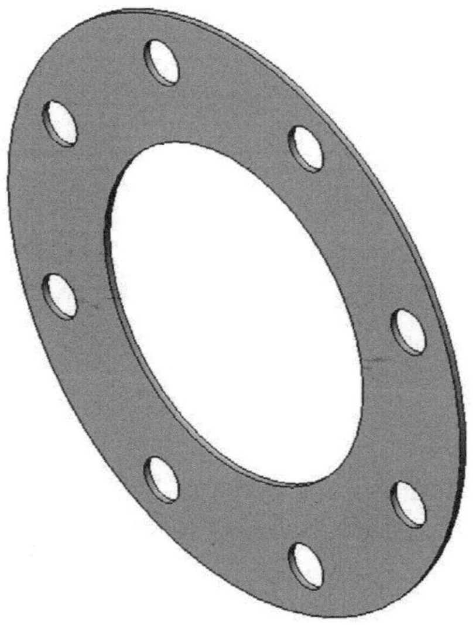

CylinderPacking

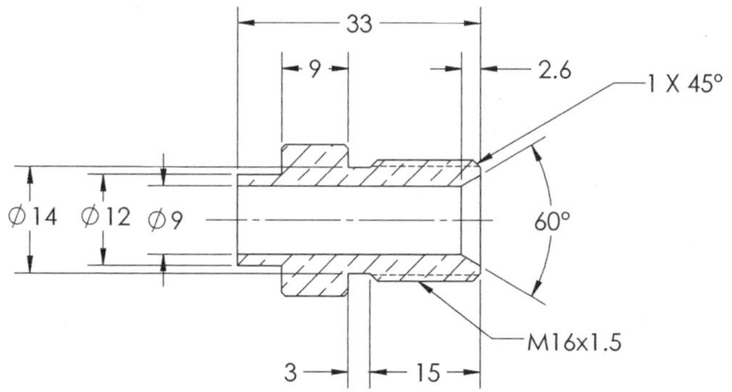

SECTION B-B

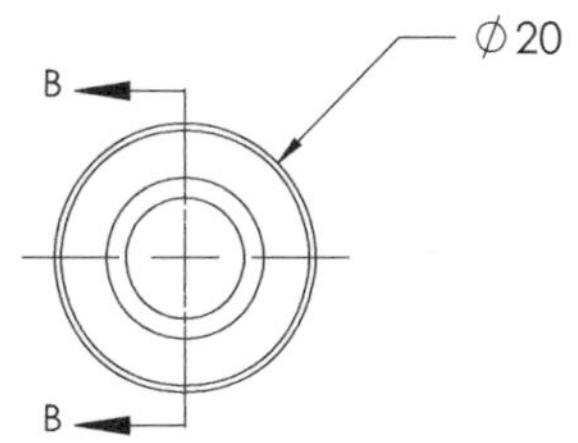

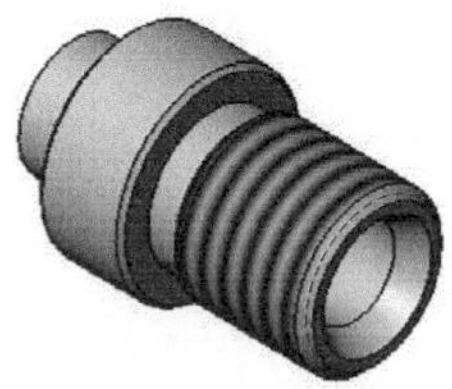

Cylinder Piping connector

NOTES

1- Material Rubber for 1, Brass for 2
2- Deburr sharp edges

TOLERANCES UNLESS OTHERWISE SPECIFIED		CADCIM TECHNOLOGIES		
X---------- +/- 1 X.X---------- +/- 0.5 X.XX---------- +/- 0.2 ANGLE---------- +/- 0.5	FIRST ISSUED DRAWN BY CHECKED BY APPROVED BY	1. Cylinder Packing 2. Cylinder Piping Connector		
ALL DIMENSIONS IN MM		SIZE A3	DRG NO. 14-013	SHEET REV A
		SCALE 3:2		SHEET 19 OF 36

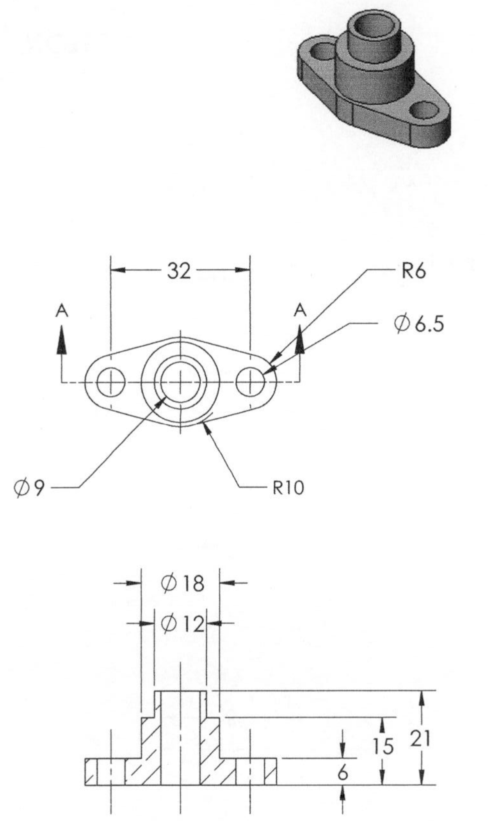

Cylinder Piping collector glanse

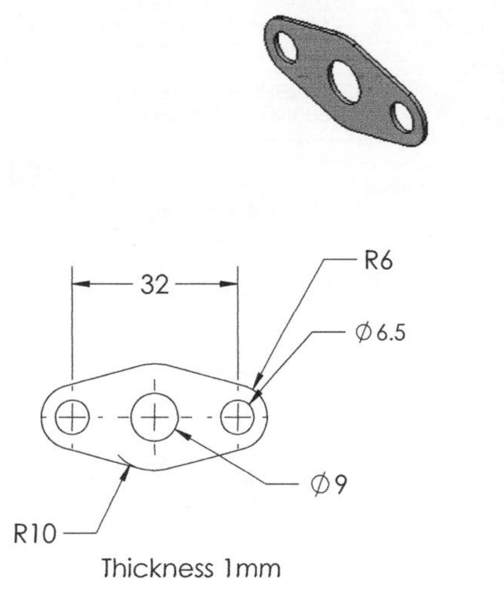

Cylinder Piping tube glanse packing

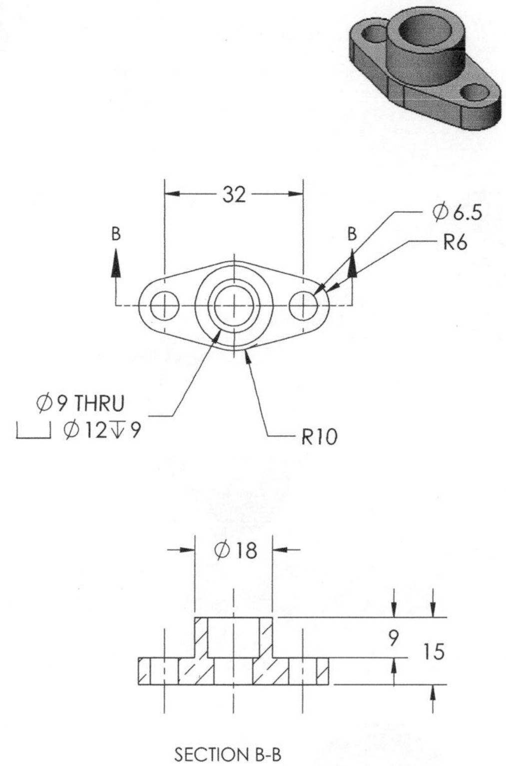

Cylinder Piping tube glanse

NOTES

1- Material Brass for 1,3 and Copper for 2
2- Deburr sharp edges

TOLERANCES UNLESS OTHERWISE SPECIFIED		CADCIM TECHNOLOGIES
X---------- +/- 1 X.X---------- +/- 0.5 X.XX---------- +/- 0.2 ANGLE---------- +/- 0.5	FIRST ISSUED DRAWN BY CHECKED BY APPROVED BY	1. Cylinder piping collector glanse 2. Cylinder piping tube glanse packing 3. Cylinder piping tube glanse
ALL DIMENSIONS IN MM		SIZE A3 · DRG NO. 14-014 · SHEET REV A SCALE 1:1 · SHEET 20 OF 36

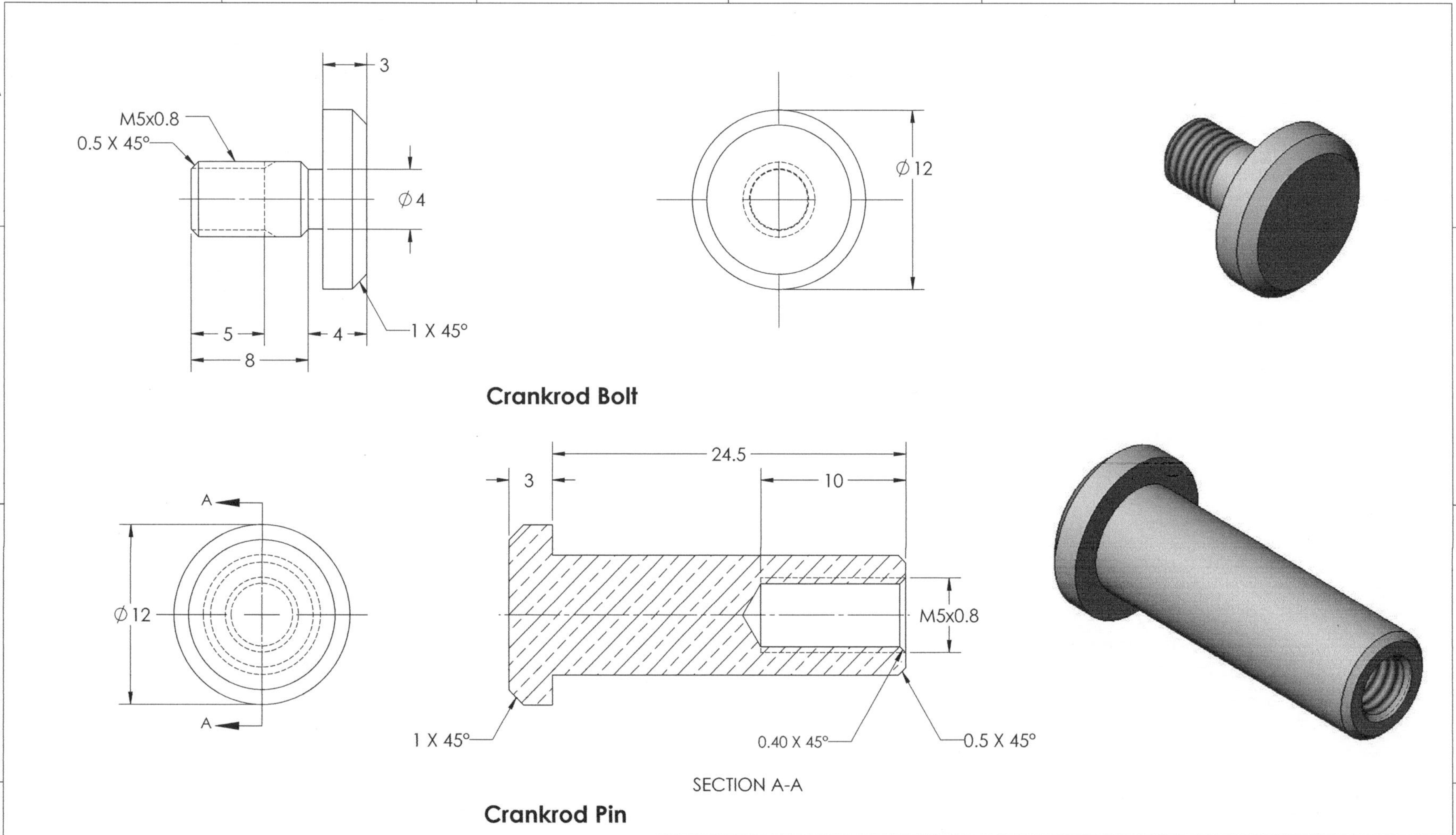

NOTES

1- Material Copper
2- Deburr sharp edges

TOLERANCES UNLESS OTHERWISE SPECIFIED

X------ +/- 1
X.X------ +/- 0.5
X.XX------ +/- 0.2
ANGLE------ +/- 0.5

ALL DIMENSIONS IN MM

FIRST ISSUED
DRAWN BY
CHECKED BY
APPROVED BY

CADCIM TECHNOLOGIES

1. Crankrod Bolt
2. Crankrod Pin

SIZE A3 | DRG NO. 14-015 | SHEET REV A

SCALE 4:1 | SHEET 21 OF 36

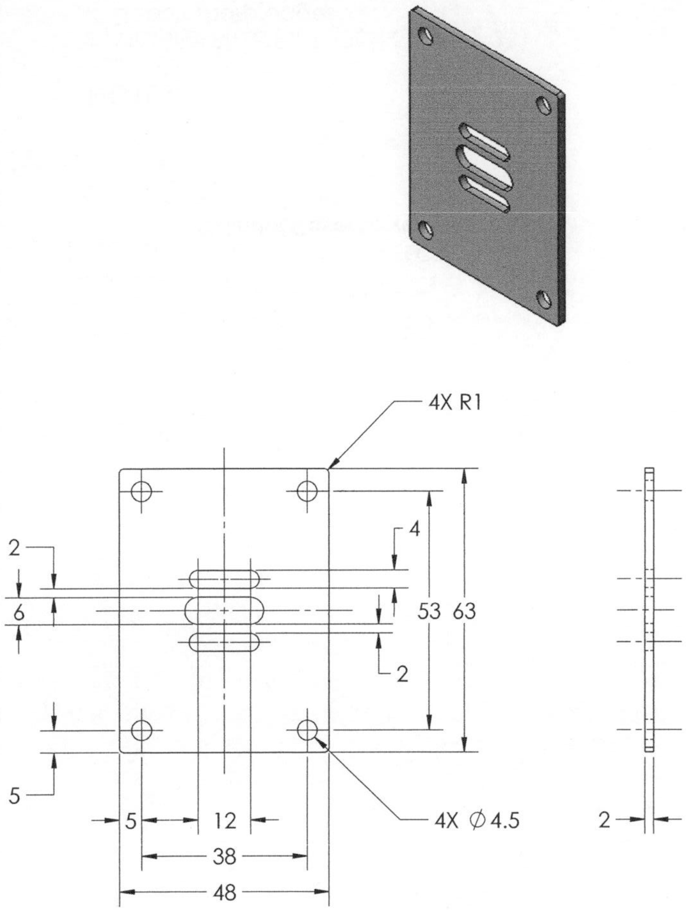

Valve Plate

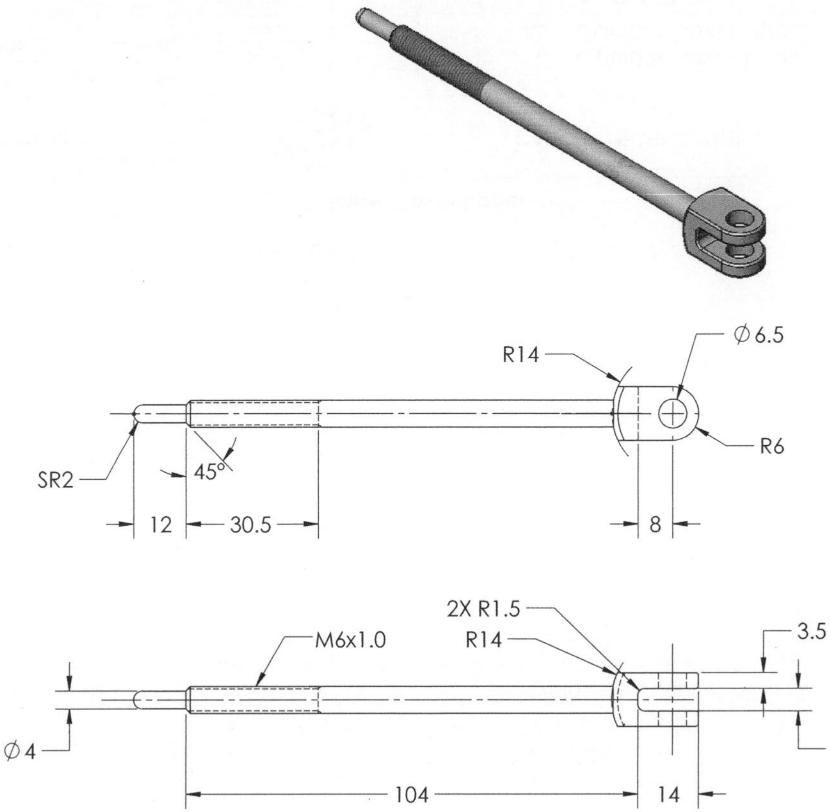

Steam chest slide valve rod

NOTES

1- Material Copper alloy for 1 and Stainless Steel for 2
2- Deburr sharp edges

TOLERANCES UNLESS OTHERWISE SPECIFIED

X---------- +/- 1
X.X---------- +/- 0.5
X.XX---------- +/- 0.2
ANGLE---------- +/- 0.5

ALL DIMENSIONS IN MM

FIRST ISSUED
DRAWN BY
CHECKED BY
APPROVED BY

CADCIM TECHNOLOGIES

1. Valve Plate
2. Steam chest slide valve rod

SIZE	DRG NO.	SHEET REV
A3	14-016	A
SCALE 2:1		SHEET 22 OF 36

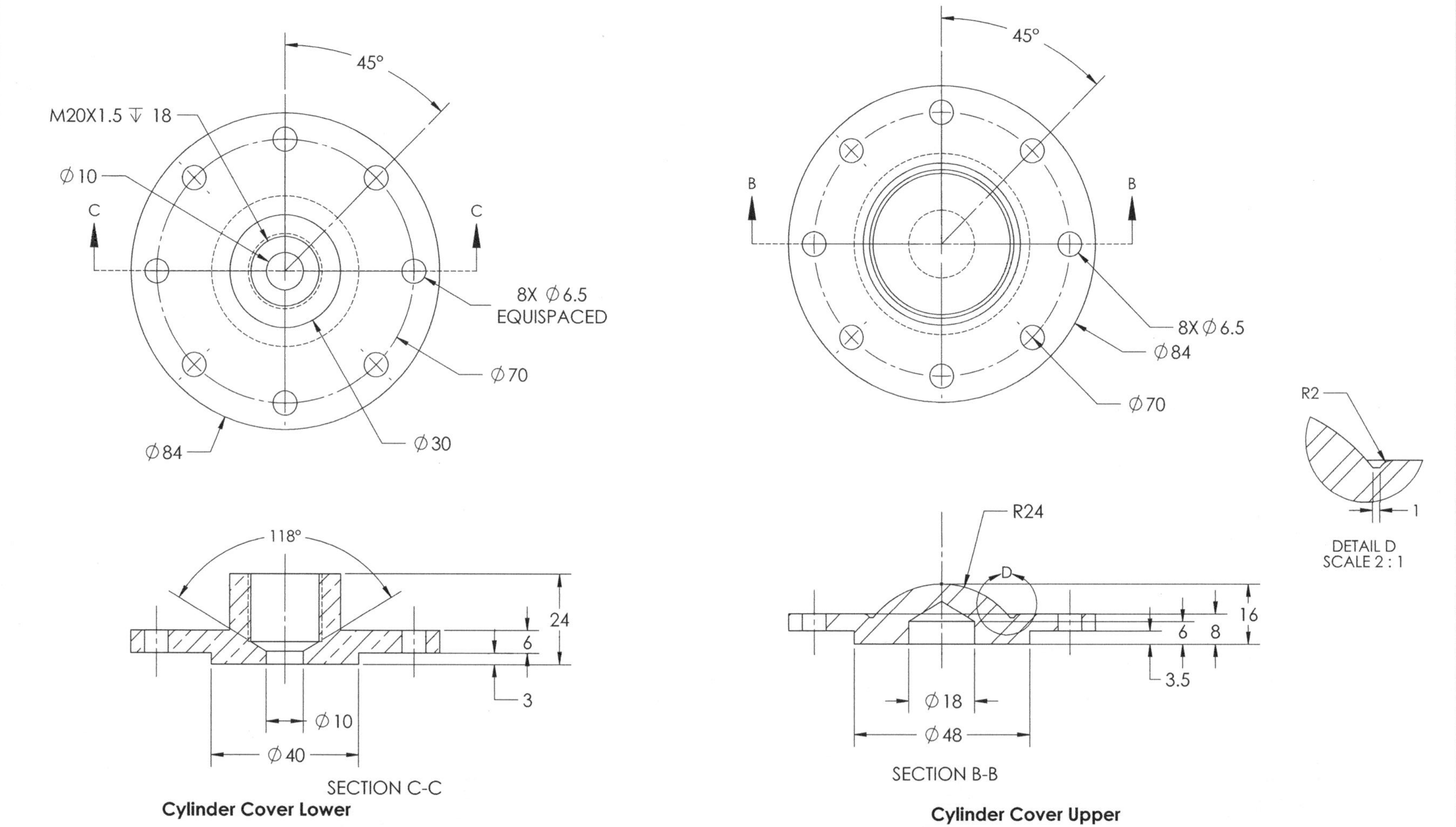

NOTES

1- Material Brass for 1, Cast Steel for 2
2- Deburr sharp edges

TOLERANCES UNLESS OTHERWISE SPECIFIED		CADCIM TECHNOLOGIES
X---------- +/- 1 X.X---------- +/- 0.5 X.XX---------- +/- 0.2 ANGLE---------- +/- 0.5	FIRST ISSUED DRAWN BY CHECKED BY APPROVED BY	1. Cylinder Cover Lower 2. Cylinder Cover Upper
ALL DIMENSIONS IN MM		SIZE A3 · DRG NO. 14-017 · SHEET REV A
		SCALE 1:1 · SHEET 23 OF 36

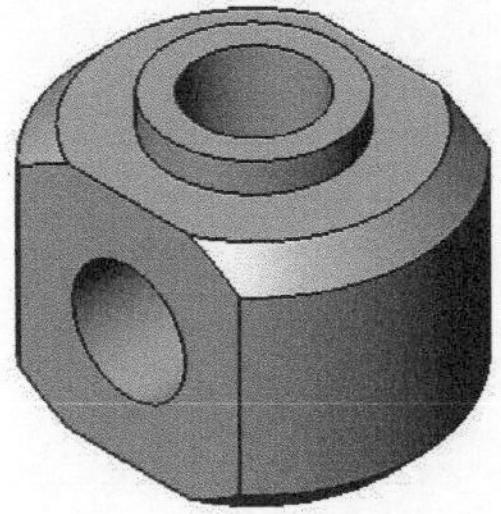

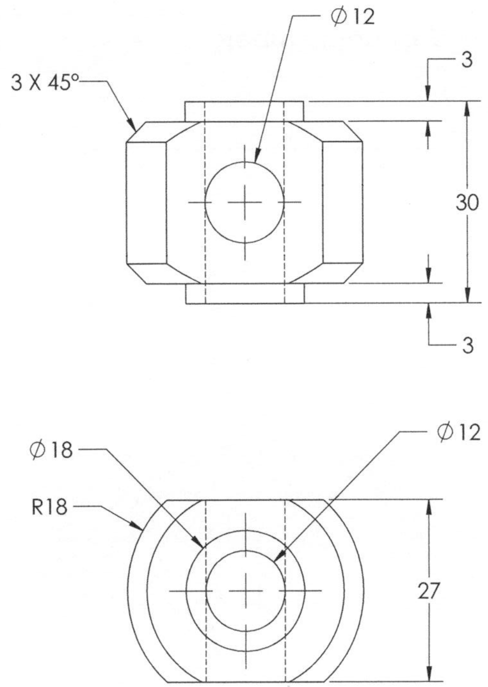

Cylinder Piping collector entry

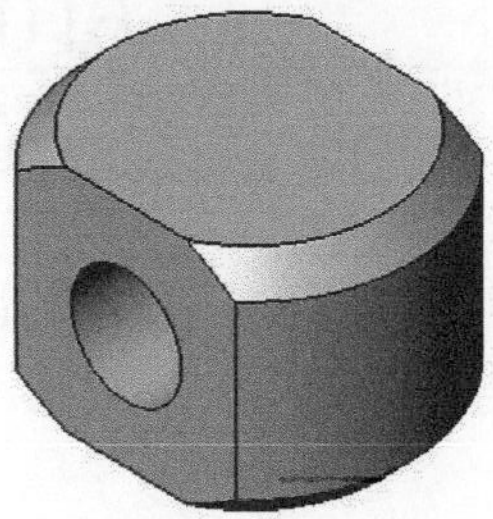

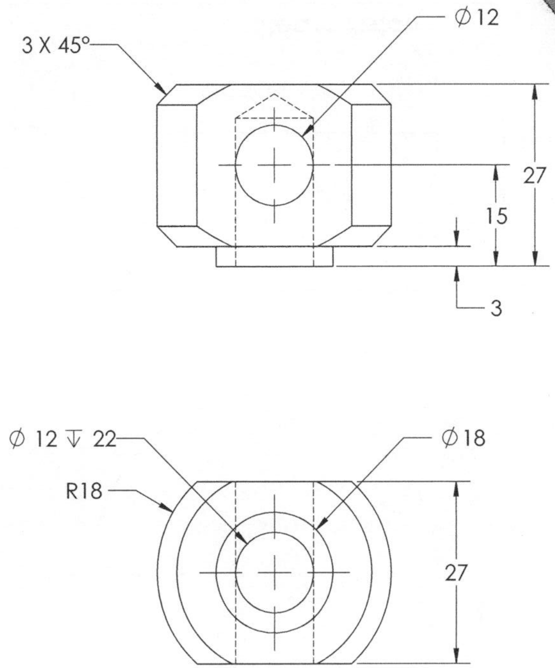

Cylinder Piping collector exit

NOTES

1- Material Brass
2- Deburr sharp edges

TOLERANCES UNLESS OTHERWISE SPECIFIED		CADCIM TECHNOLOGIES
X---------- +/- 1 X.X---------- +/- 0.5 X.XX---------- +/- 0.2 ANGLE---------- +/- 0.5	FIRST ISSUED DRAWN BY CHECKED BY APPROVED BY	1. Cylinder piping collector entry 2. Cylinder piping collector exit
ALL DIMENSIONS IN MM		SIZE A3 · DRG NO. 14-018 · SHEET REV A
		SCALE 3:2 · SHEET 24 OF 36

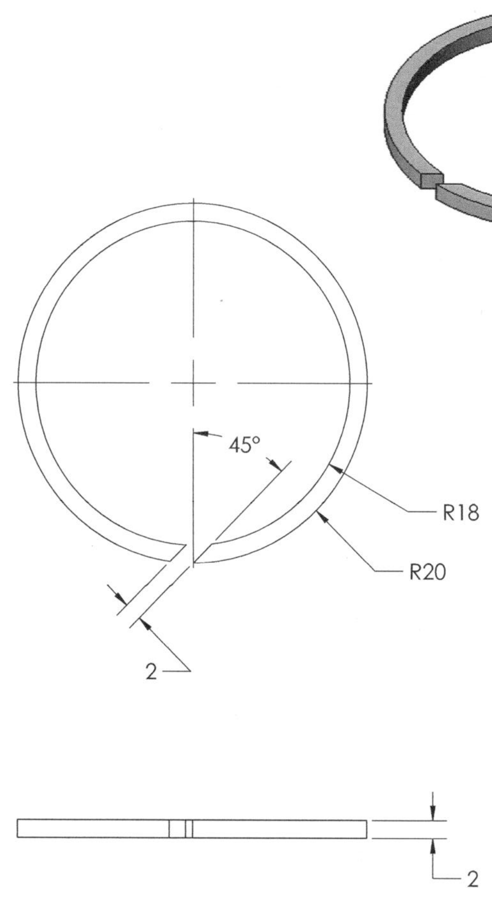

Steam Piston Ring

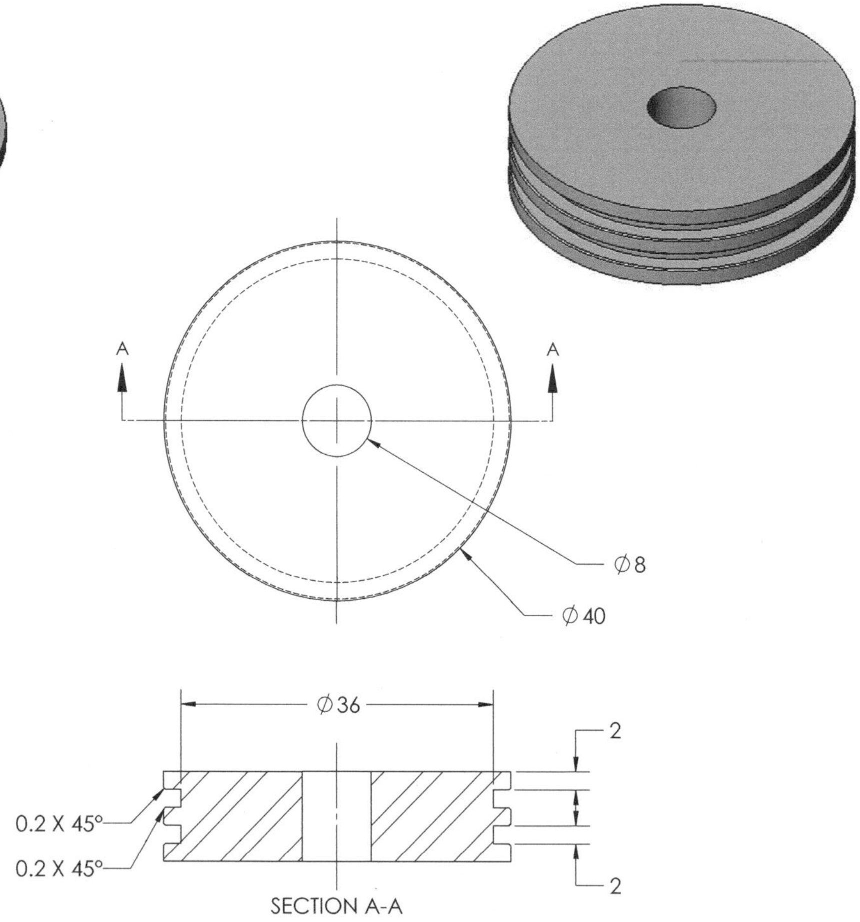

Steam Piston

NOTES

1- Material Stainless Steel
2- Deburr sharp edges

TOLERANCES UNLESS OTHERWISE SPECIFIED		CADCIM TECHNOLOGIES
X---- +/- 1 X.X---- +/- 0.5 X.XX---- +/- 0.2 ANGLE---- +/- 0.5	FIRST ISSUED DRAWN BY CHECKED BY APPROVED BY	1. Steam Piston Ring 2. Steam Piston
ALL DIMENSIONS IN MM		SIZE A3 · DRG NO. 14-019 · SHEET REV A
		SCALE 2:1 · SHEET 25 OF 36

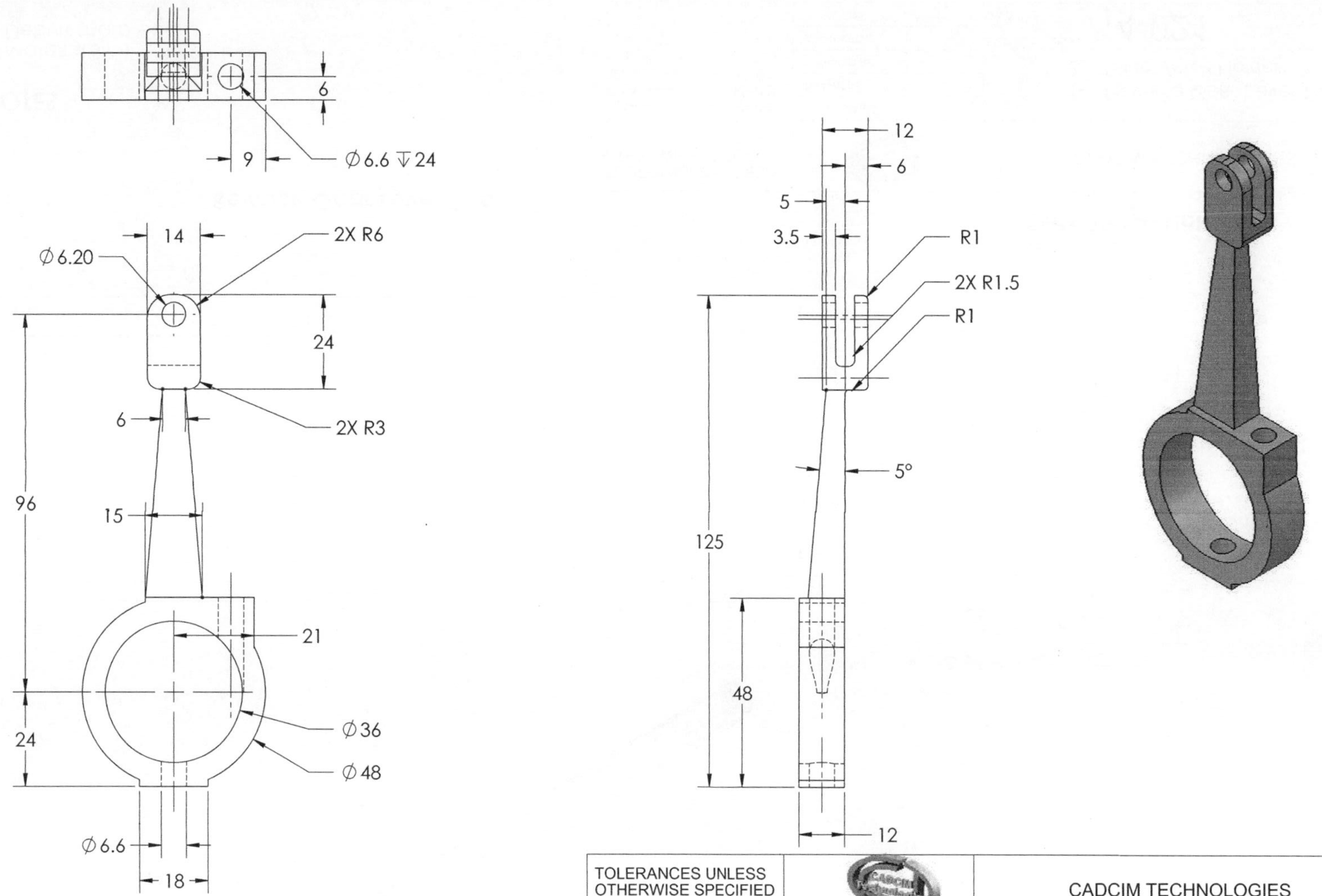

TOLERANCES UNLESS OTHERWISE SPECIFIED		CADCIM TECHNOLOGIES
X------------ +/- 1 X.X---------- +/- 0.5 X.XX--------- +/- 0.2 ANGLE-------- +/- 0.5	FIRST ISSUED DRAWN BY CHECKED BY APPROVED BY	Eccentric Rod
ALL DIMENSIONS IN MM		SIZE A3 · DRG NO. 14-020 · SHEET REV A
		SCALE1:1 · SHEET 26 OF 36

NOTES

1- Material Stainless Steel
2- Deburr sharp edges

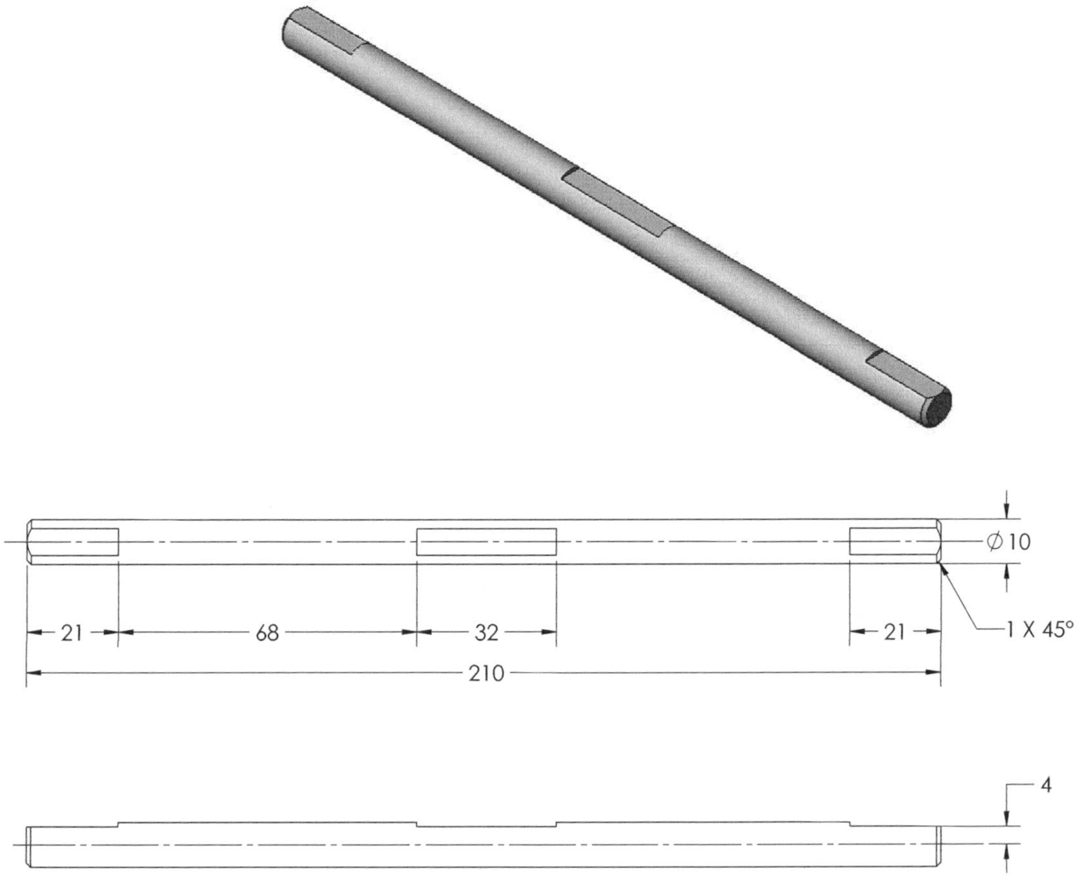

Reverse Gear Lever Rod

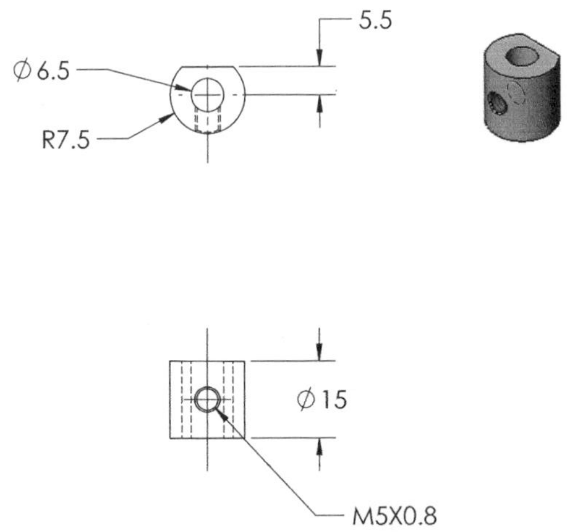

Slide Valve Holder

NOTES

1- Material SS
2- Deburr sharp edges

TOLERANCES UNLESS OTHERWISE SPECIFIED		CADCIM TECHNOLOGIES
X---------- +/- 1 X.X---------- +/- 0.5 X.XX---------- +/- 0.2 ANGLE---------- +/- 0.5	FIRST ISSUED DRAWN BY CHECKED BY APPROVED BY	1. Reverse Gear Lever Rod 2. Slide Valve Holder
ALL DIMENSIONS IN MM		SIZE A3 · DRG NO. 14-021 · SHEET REV A
		SCALE1:1 · SHEET 27 OF 36

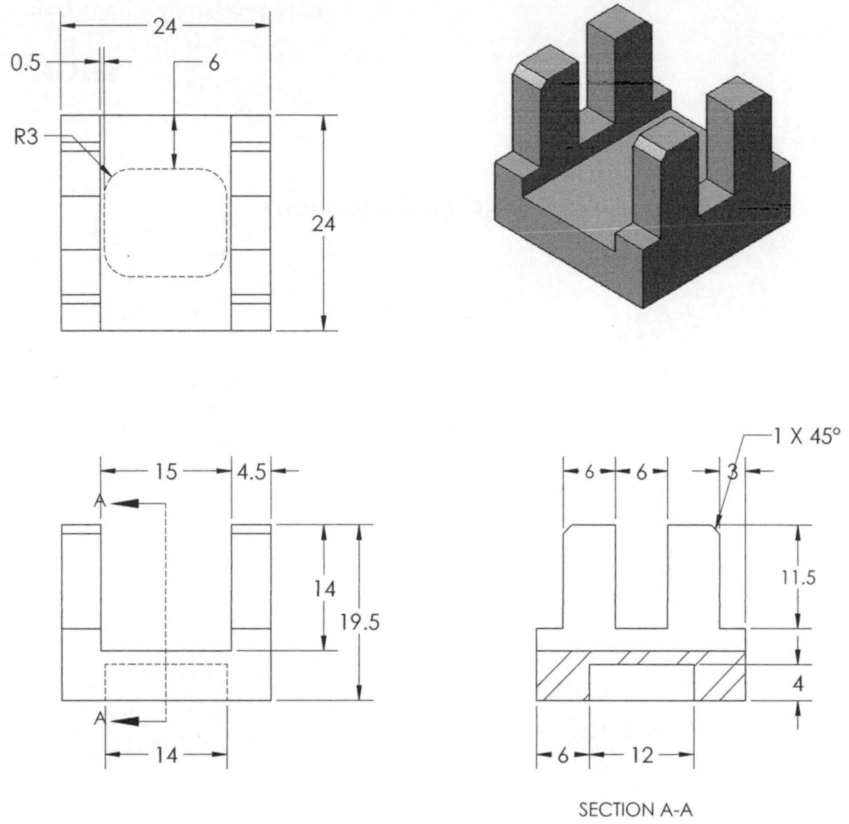

Slide Valve

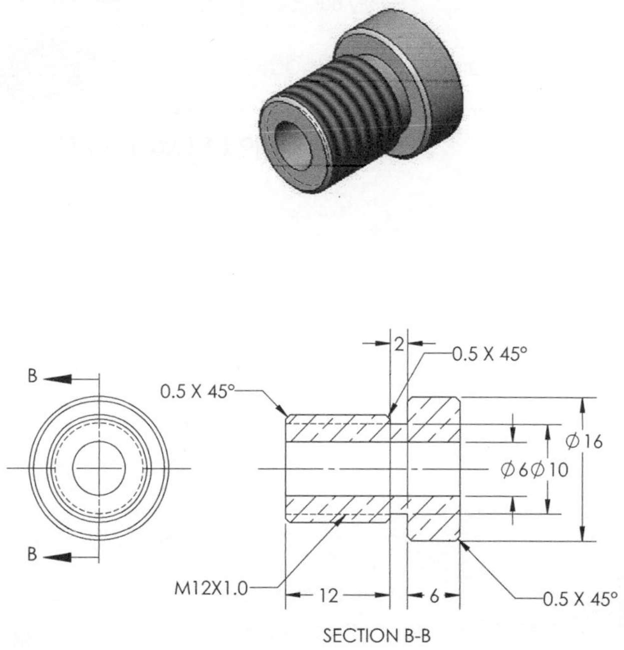

Valve Packnut

NOTES

1- Material SS for 1, Brass for 2
2- Deburr sharp edges

TOLERANCES UNLESS OTHERWISE SPECIFIED		CADCIM TECHNOLOGIES
X---- +/- 1 X.X---- +/- 0.5 X.XX---- +/- 0.2 ANGLE---- +/- 0.5	FIRST ISSUED DRAWN BY CHECKED BY APPROVED BY	1. Slide Valve 2. Valve Packnut
ALL DIMENSIONS IN MM		SIZE A3 · DRG NO. 14-022 · SHEET REV A
		SCALE 2:1 · SHEET 28 OF 36

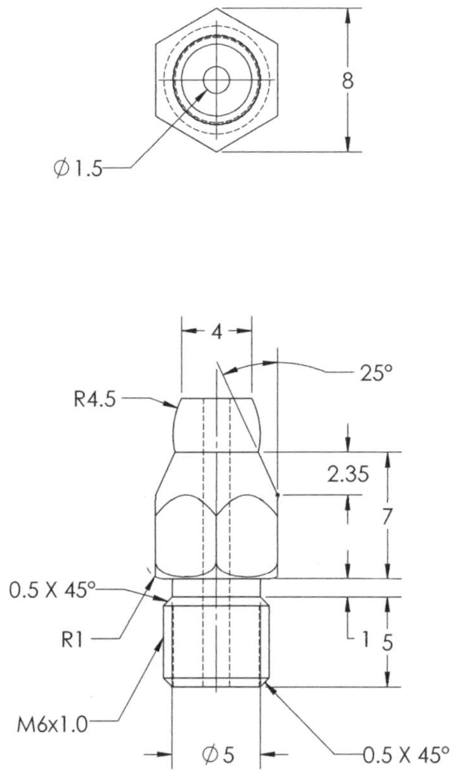

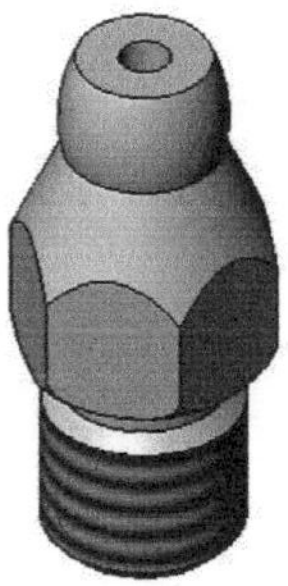

Lubricating Nipple

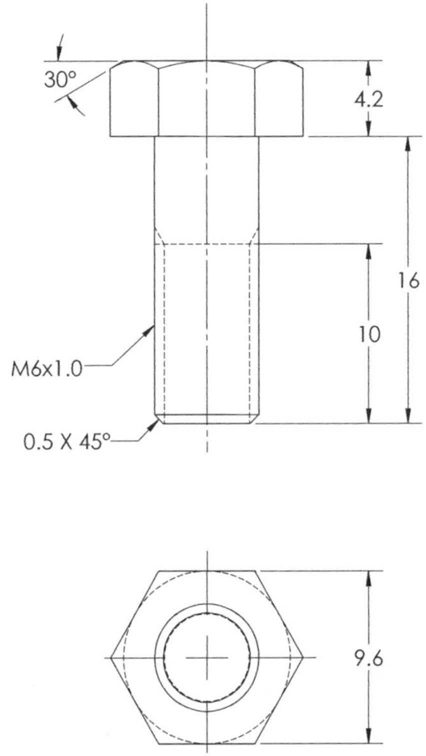

M6X 1.0X16 Bolt

NOTES

1- Material ASTM A36 Steel
2- Deburr sharp edges

TOLERANCES UNLESS OTHERWISE SPECIFIED

X---------- +/- 1
X.X---------- +/- 0.5
X.XX---------- +/- 0.2
ANGLE---------- +/- 0.5

ALL DIMENSIONS IN MM

FIRST ISSUED
DRAWN BY
CHECKED BY
APPROVED BY

CADCIM TECHNOLOGIES

1. Lubricating Nipple
2. M6X1.0 Hex Bolt- ANSI B18.2.4.1M

SIZE	DRG NO.	SHEET REV
A3	14-023	A
SCALE 4:1		SHEET 29 OF 36

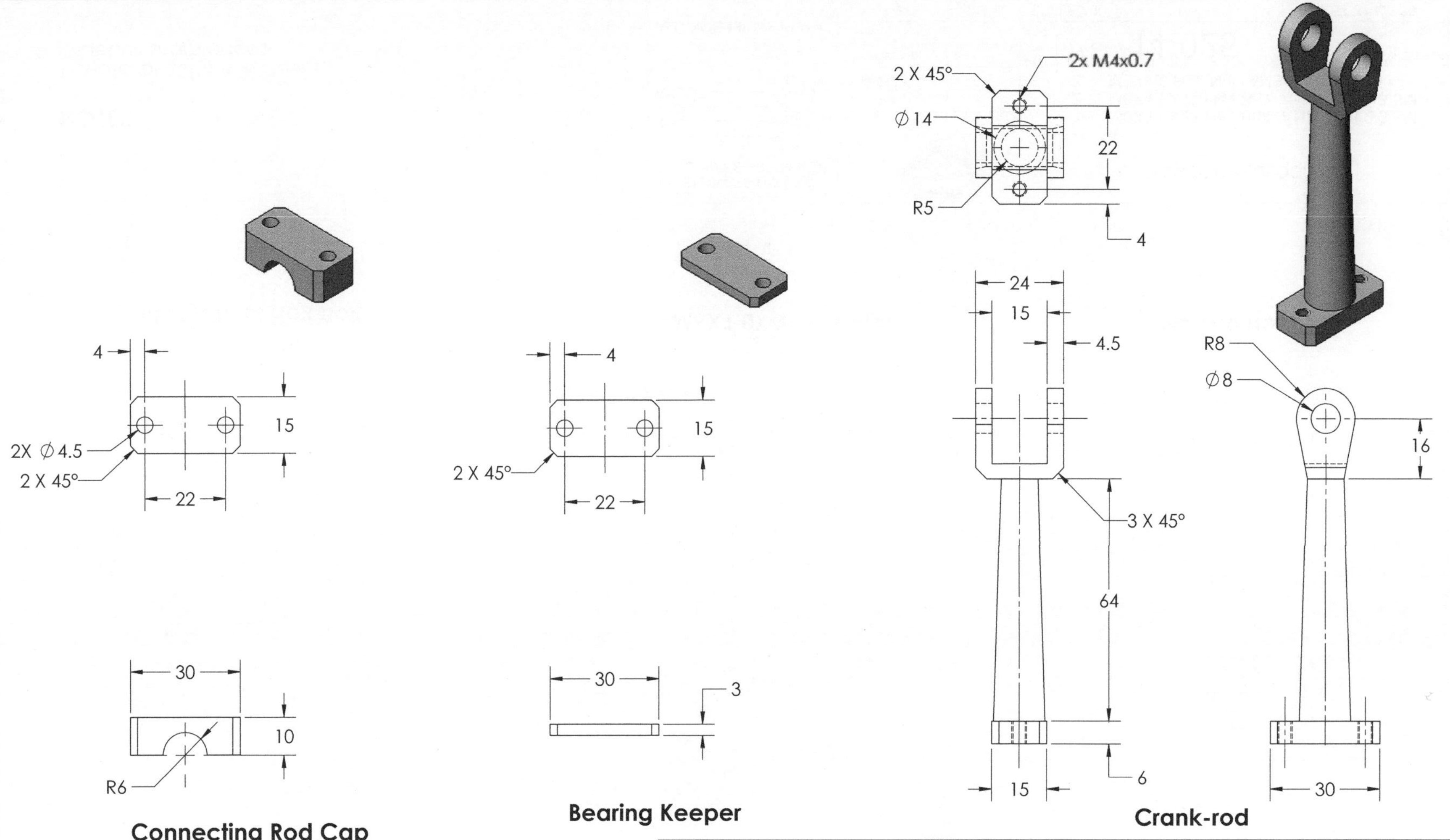

NOTES

1- Material Stainless Steel For 1, Brass for 2 and 3
2- Deburr sharp edges

TOLERANCES UNLESS OTHERWISE SPECIFIED		CADCIM TECHNOLOGIES		
X------------ +/- 1 X.X------------ +/- 0.5 X.XX------------ +/- 0.2 ANGLE------------ +/- 0.5	FIRST ISSUED DRAWN BY CHECKED BY APPROVED BY	1. Connecting rod cap 2. Bearing Keeper 3. Crankrod		
ALL DIMENSIONS IN MM		SIZE A3	DRG NO. 14-024	SHEET REV A
		SCALE 1:1		SHEET 30 OF 36

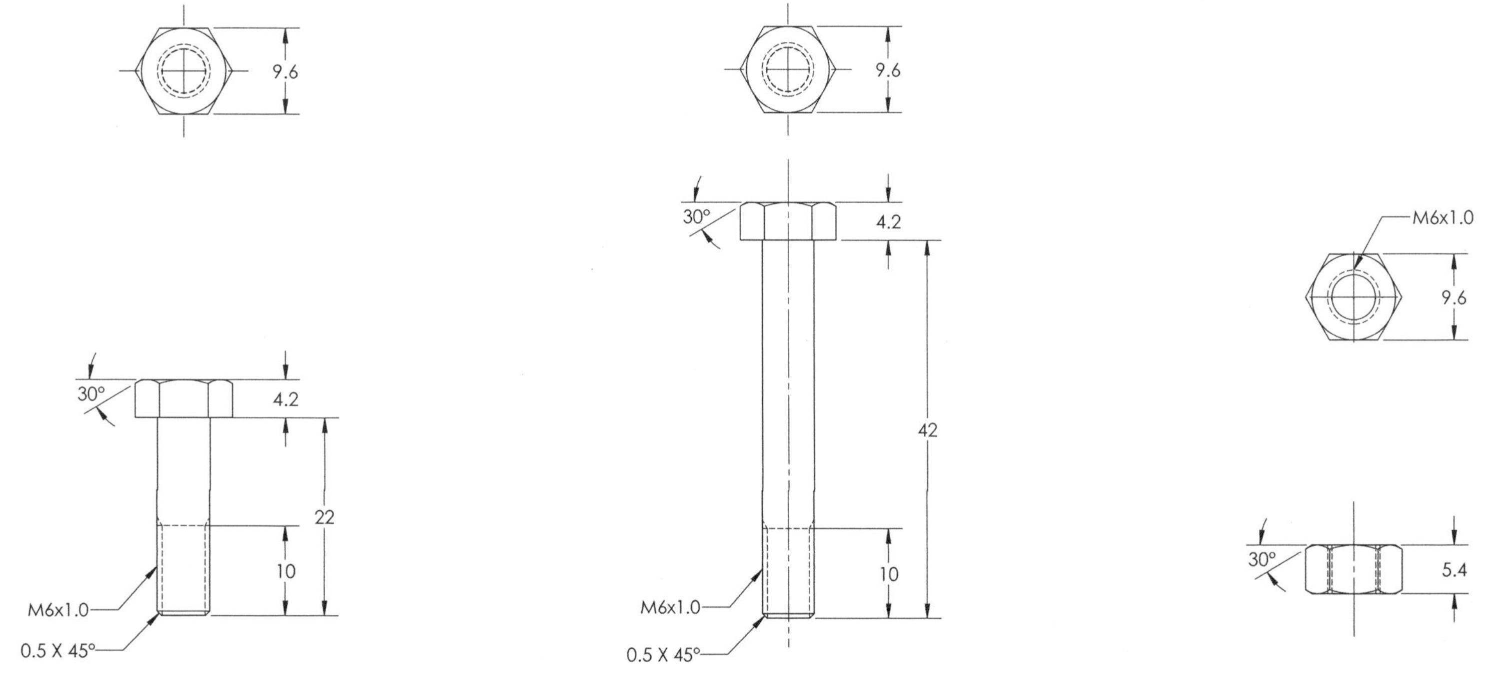

M6X1.0X22 Hex Bolt

M6X1.0X40 Hex Bolt

M6X1.0 Hex Nut

NOTES

1- Material ASTM A36 Steel
2- Deburr sharp edges

TOLERANCES UNLESS OTHERWISE SPECIFIED		CADCIM TECHNOLOGIES
X---------- +/- 1	FIRST ISSUED	1. M6X1.0X22 Hex Bolt- ANSI B18.2.3.5M
X.X---------- +/- 0.5	DRAWN BY	2. M6X1.0X42 Hex Bolt- ANSI B18.2.3.5M
X.XX---------- +/- 0.2	CHECKED BY	3. M6X1.0 Hex Nut- ANSI B18.2.4.1M
ANGLE---------- +/- 0.5	APPROVED BY	SIZE A3 · DRG NO. 14-025 · SHEET REV A
ALL DIMENSIONS IN MM		SCALE 2:1 · SHEET 31 OF 36

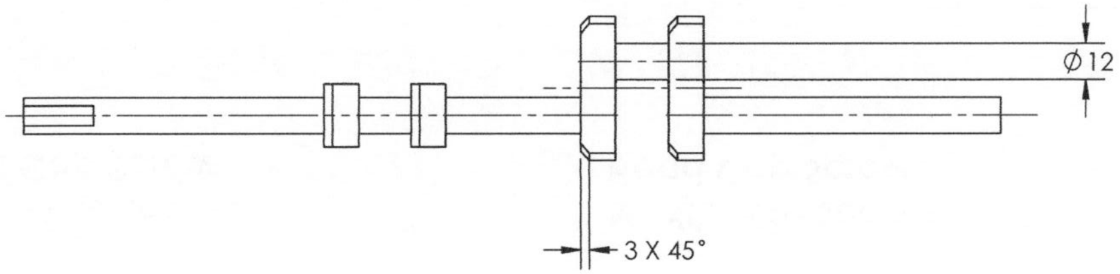

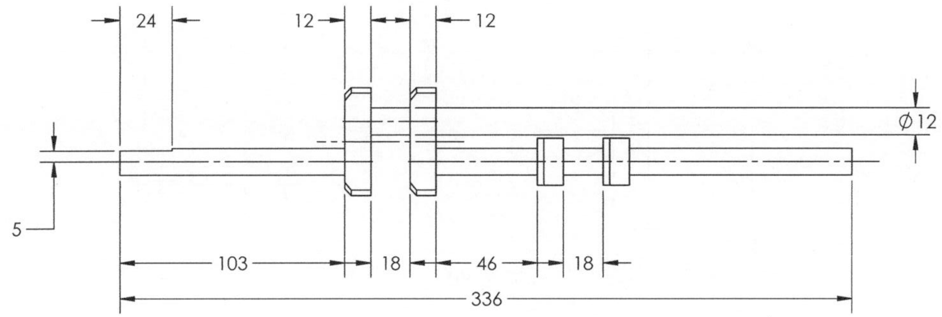

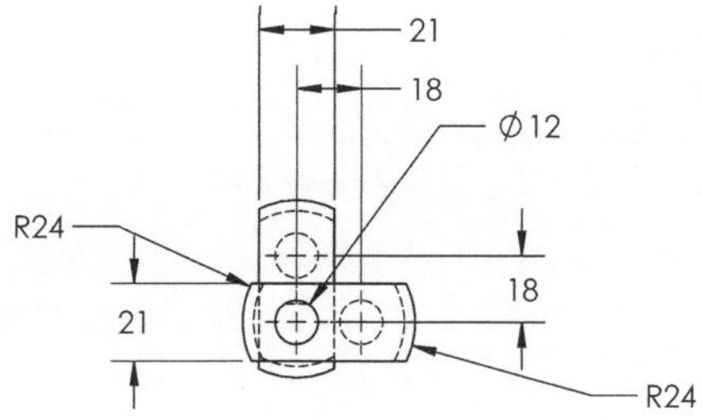

NOTES

1- Material SS
3- Deburr sharp edges

TOLERANCES UNLESS OTHERWISE SPECIFIED		CADCIM TECHNOLOGIES
X---------- +/- 1 X.X---------- +/- 0.5 X.XX---------- +/- 0.2 ANGLE---------- +/- 0.5	FIRST ISSUED DRAWN BY CHECKED BY APPROVED BY	CRANKSHAFT
ALL DIMENSIONS IN MM		SIZE A3 / DRG NO. 14-026 / SHEET REV A
		SCALE 1:2 / SHEET 32 OF 36

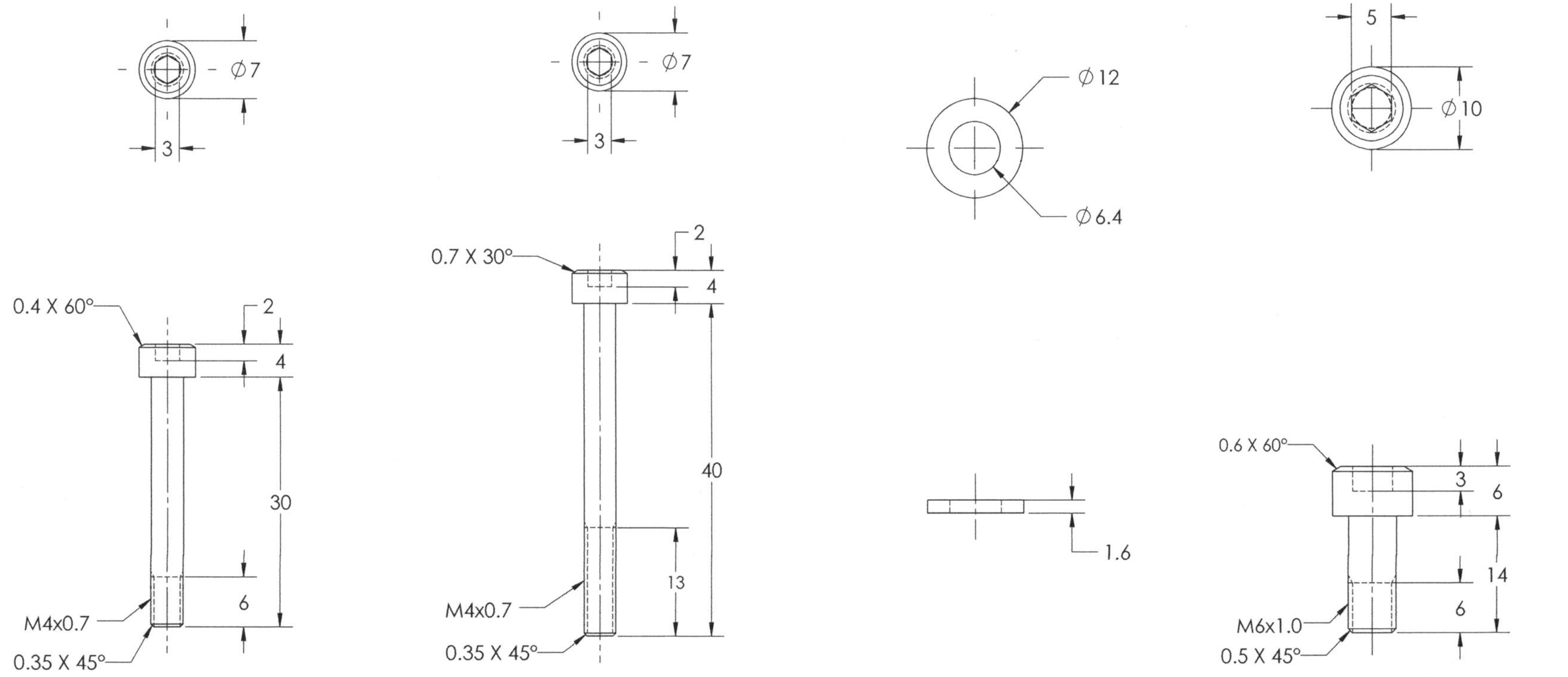

M4X0.7X30 Socket Head Cap Screw

M4X0.7X40 Socket Head Cap Screw

M6 Plain Washer

M6X1.0X14 Socket Head Cap Screw

NOTES

1- Material ASTM A36 Steel
2- Deburr sharp edges

TOLERANCES UNLESS OTHERWISE SPECIFIED

X	+/- 1
X.X	+/- 0.5
X.XX	+/- 0.2
ANGLE	+/- 0.5

ALL DIMENSIONS IN MM

FIRST ISSUED	
DRAWN BY	
CHECKED BY	
APPROVED BY	

CADCIM TECHNOLOGIES

1. M4X0.7X30 Socket Head Cap Screw- ANSI B18.3.1M
2. M4X0.7X40 Socket Head Cap Screw- ANSI B18.3.1M
3. M6 Plain Washer Grade A- ISO 7086
4. M6X1.0X14 Socket Head Cap Screw- ANSI B18.3.1M

SIZE	DRG NO.	SHEET REV
A3	14-027	A
SCALE 2:1		SHEET 33 OF 36

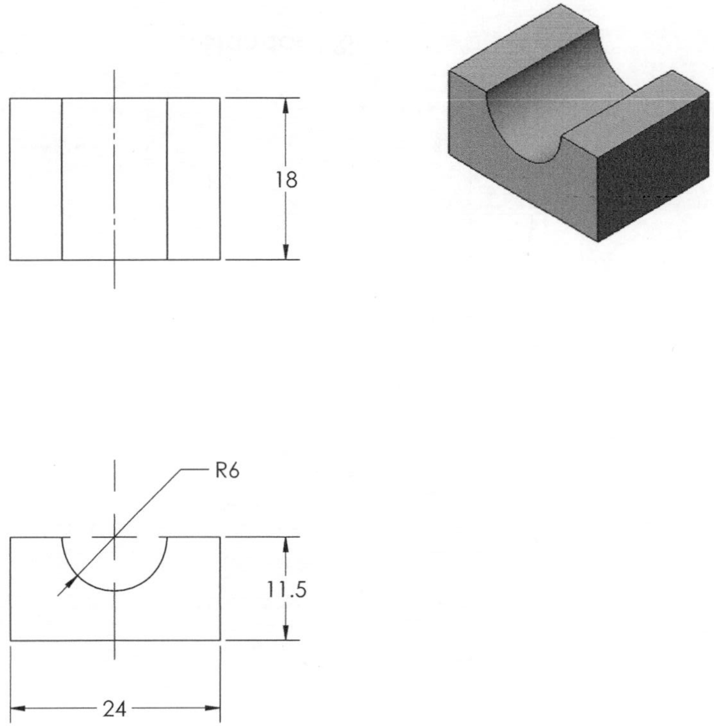

Lower Base Bearing Holder 1

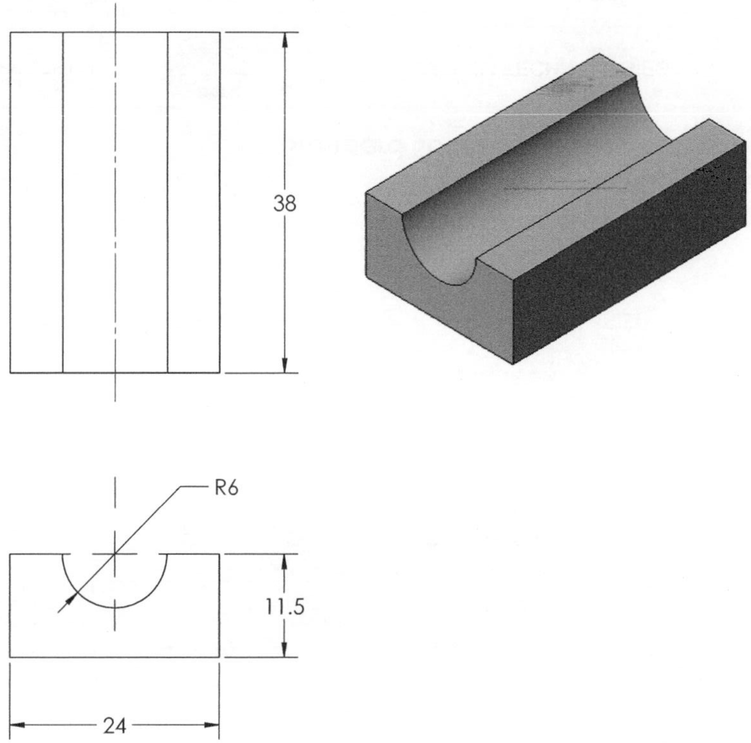

Lower Base Bearing Holder 2

NOTES

1- Material Brass
2- Deburr sharp edges

TOLERANCES UNLESS OTHERWISE SPECIFIED

X---------------------- +/- 1
X.X-------------------- +/- 0.5
X.XX------------------ +/- 0.2
ANGLE---------------- +/- 0.5

ALL DIMENSIONS IN MM

FIRST ISSUED
DRAWN BY
CHECKED BY
APPROVED BY

CADCIM TECHNOLOGIES

1. Lower Base Bearing Holder 1
2. Lower Base Bearing Holder 2

SIZE	DRG NO.	SHEET REV
A3	14-028	A
SCALE 2:1		SHEET 34 OF 36

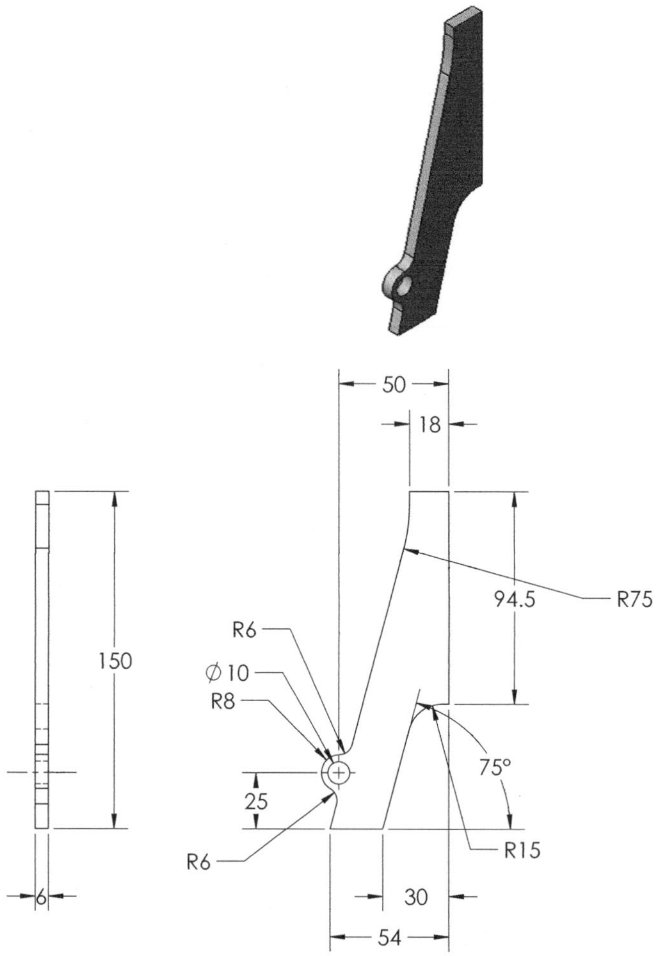

Standard Rib

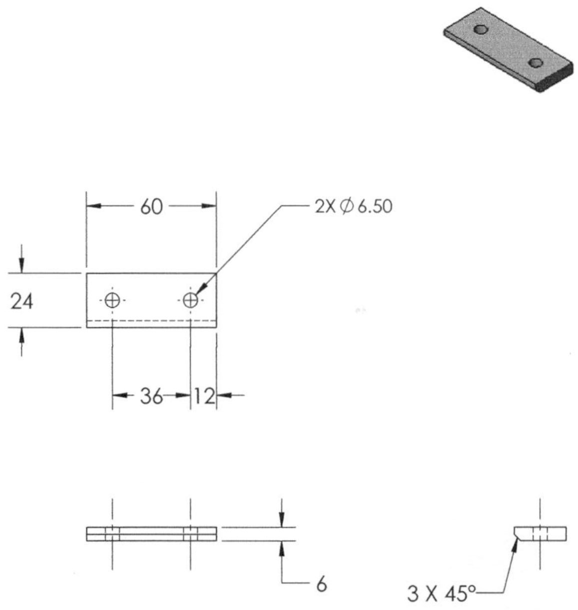

Standard Socle

NOTES

1- Material Steel
2- Deburr sharp edges

TOLERANCES UNLESS OTHERWISE SPECIFIED		CADCIM TECHNOLOGIES	
X---------- +/- 1 X.X---------- +/- 0.5 X.XX---------- +/- 0.2 ANGLE---------- +/- 0.5	FIRST ISSUED DRAWN BY CHECKED BY APPROVED BY	1. Standard Rib 2. Standard Socle	
ALL DIMENSIONS IN MM		SIZE A3 / DRG NO. 14-029	SHEET REV A
		SCALE 1:2	SHEET 35 OF 36

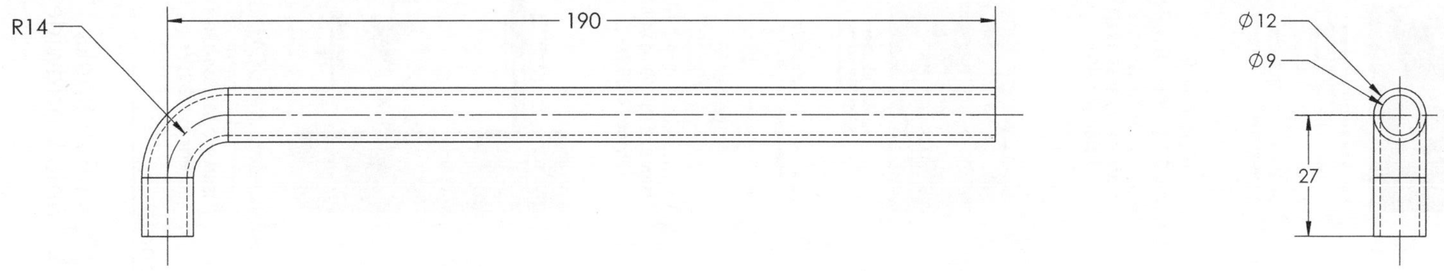

Cylinder Piping tube entry

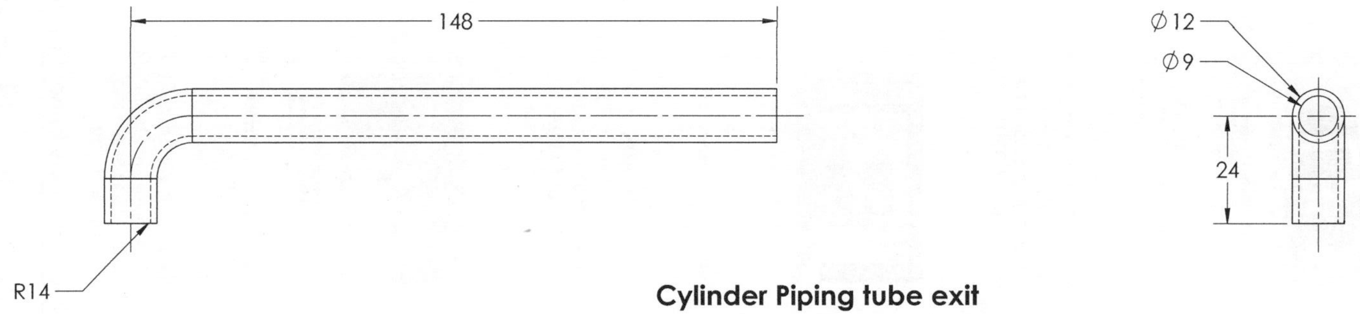

Cylinder Piping tube exit

NOTES

1- Material Copper
2- Deburr sharp edges

TOLERANCES UNLESS OTHERWISE SPECIFIED

X---------------------- +/- 1
X.X-------------------- +/- 0.5
X.XX------------------- +/- 0.2
ANGLE------------------ +/- 0.5

ALL DIMENSIONS IN MM

FIRST ISSUED	
DRAWN BY	
CHECKED BY	
APPROVED BY	

CADCIM TECHNOLOGIES

1. Cylinder piping tube entry
2. Cylinder piping tube exit

SIZE	DRG NO.	SHEET REV
A3	14-030	A
SCALE 1:1		SHEET 36 OF 36

CAD/CAM/CIM/GIS/ANIMATION/CIVIL BOOKS

by **Prof. Sham Tickoo** (Purdue University, USA and Autodesk Authorised Author)

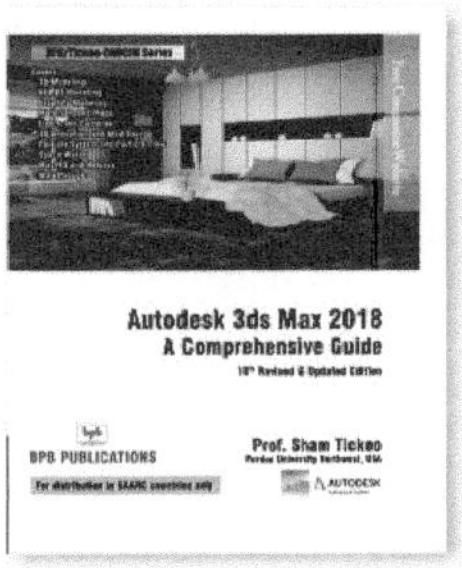

Autodesk
3ds Max 2018
A Comprehensive Guide
ISBN 978-93-8655-168-9
Price: ₹ 999/-

Autodesk
3ds Max 2018 For Beginners
A Tutorial Approach
ISBN 978-93-8655-167-2
Price: ₹ 899/-

Autodesk
3ds Max 2017
A Comprehensive Guide
ISBN 978-93-8655-113-9
Price: ₹ 999/-

Autodesk
3ds Max 2017 For Beginners
A Tutorial Approach
ISBN 978-93-8655-112-2
Price: ₹ 999/-

Autodesk
3ds Max 2019
A Comprehensive Guide
ISBN 978-93-8817-627-9
Price: ₹ 999/-

Blender
For Digital Artists
ISBN 978-93-8817-626-2
Price: ₹ 599/-

Autodesk
Maya 2018
A Comprehensive Guide
ISBN 978-93-8655-170-2
Price: ₹ 899/-

Autodesk
Maya 2017
A Comprehensive Guide
ISBN 978-93-8655-114-6
Price: ₹ 899/-

Pixologic Zbrush 4R8
A Comprehensive Guide
ISBN 978-93-8728-412-8
Price: ₹ 899/-

Pixologic Zbrush 4R7
A Comprehensive Guide
ISBN 978-93-8655-115-3
Price: ₹ 899/-

AutoCAD 2018
Basic and Intermediate
ISBN 978-93-8655-163-4
Price: ₹ 1299/-

Advanced AutoCAD 2018
3D and Advanced
ISBN 978-93-8655-160-3
Price: ₹ 899/-

Available on **www.bpbonline.com** and all leading book stores.

bpb PUBLICATIONS | #1 Publisher of Computer Books | 62 Years of Excellence | OVER 90 Million Books Sold Worldwide

CAD/CAM/CIM/GIS/ANIMATION/CIVIL BOOKS

by **Prof. Sham Tickoo** (Purdue University, USA and Autodesk Authorised Author)

Solid Works 2018
For Designers
ISBN 978-93-8728-409-8
Price: ₹ 1299/-

Solid Works
Simulation 2018
For Designers
ISBN 978-93-8728-411-1
Price: ₹ 599/-

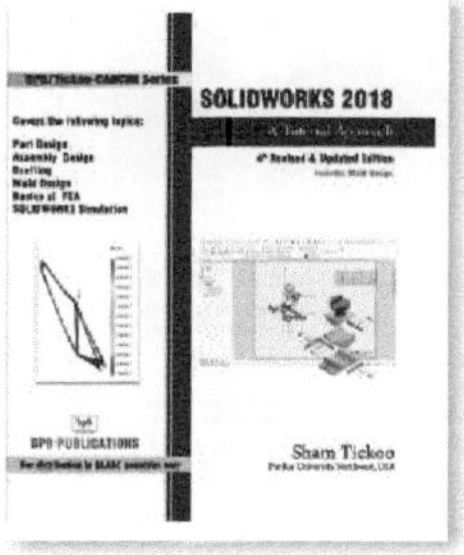

Solid Works 2018
A Tutorial Approach
ISBN 978-93-8817-631-6
Price: ₹ 799/-

Learning Solid Works 2018
A Project Based Approach
ISBN 978-93-8817-632-3
Price: ₹ 699/-

Exploring AutoCAD
Civil 3D 2017
ISBN 978-93-8655-102-3
Price: ₹ 999/-

Exploring AutoCAD
Civil 3D 2018
ISBN 978-93-8728-413-5
Price: ₹ 999/-

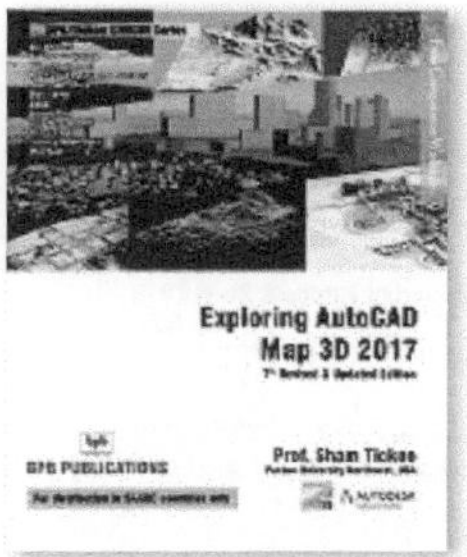

Exploring AutoCAD
Map 3D 2017
ISBN 978-93-8655-103-0
Price: ₹ 875/-

Exploring AutoCAD
Map 3D 2018
ISBN 978-93-8655-166-5
Price: ₹ 799/-

Exploring Autodesk
Navisworks 2017
ISBN 978-93-8655-104-7
Price: ₹ 699/-

Exploring Oracle
Primavera P6 R8.4
ISBN 978-93-8655-105-4
Price: ₹ 599/-

Exploring Autodesk
Revit 2017
For Architecture
ISBN 978-93-8655-106-1
Price: ₹ 999/-

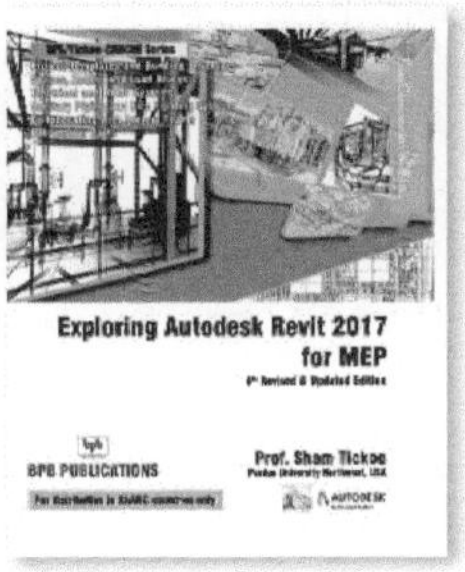

Exploring Autodesk
Revit 2017
For MEP
ISBN 978-93-8655-107-8
Price: ₹ 799/-

Available on **www.bpbonline.com** and all leading book stores.

PUBLICATIONS | #1 Publisher of Computer Books | 62 Years of Excellence | OVER 90 Million Books Sold Worldwide